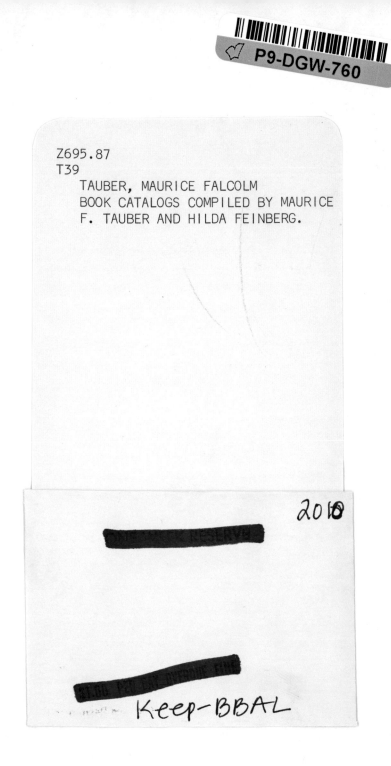

BOOK CATALOGS

by
Maurice F. Tauber
and
Hilda Feinberg

The Scarecrow Press, Inc.
Metuchen, N.J.   1971

Preface

In the intervening years since the appearance of the first collection of papers concerning book catalogs (Kingery, Robert E., and Tauber, Maurice F., <u>Book Catalogs</u>, N.Y., The Scarecrow Press, 1963), attention has been concentrated on the book catalog as a substitute for, or an auxiliary to the card catalog.

This selection of papers has identified some of the efforts to solve particular problems concerned with book catalogs. The published papers, as well as those which have been written specifically for this volume, bring additional observations concerning the place of the book catalog in library service.

Although there may be some overlap and duplication in certain papers, there is, within the papers as a whole, an effort to provide some description of what is developing in the total area of book catalogs.

The editors have tried to isolate specific problems relating to format, cost, and usefulness of book catalogs in various types of libraries. The book constitutes a record of what has been accomplished. It not only brings together journal and report literature otherwise requiring much searching, and for which it is not always easy to find citations or to locate copies; it also provides illustrative examples and information on methodology either not previously published or available only by painstaking collecting or copying of sections of published book catalogs themselves.

It is important that librarians continue to describe the essentials for making it possible to develop book catalogs as significant in themselves, or as an effective tool in the total usefulness of catalogs.

The editors are very grateful to the authors and the editors for permission to reprint papers which have appeared in journals, and to writers of original papers which are included in this volume.

Gratitude is expressed to Dr. Theodore C. Hines, for his many suggestions and contributions, and to Dr. Jessica L. Harris, for her participation. Miss Helen Blankenagel, who assisted in gathering material for the volume, is also to be thanked.

Maurice F. Tauber
Hilda Feinberg

Contents

CHAPTER I

Books Catalogs: Introduction

by

Maurice F. Tauber and Hilda Feinberg

INTRODUCTION

The emergence of new technical developments has
made it possible to reevaluate the relationship of users to
the contents of libraries, and the application of the newer
technology has demonstrated the possibility of providing
readers with information in book catalog form that has not
been available to them in the past.

A revived interest and activity in book catalog experimentation and production has been evident in recent years,
continuing a cycle of early book catalogs, then card catalogs,
and now again, book catalogs. The changing technology of
the times in each case contributed to a great extent to the
substitution of one form for the other. A history of early
printed catalogs in American libraries has been presented
by Ranz. [1]

The manuscript or printed book catalog, varying
widely in format and quality, served until the latter part of
the nineteenth century as the standard form of the library
catalog. The catalogs of this period have been described by
Hines:

> Often the listing was a single-entry one for each
> item. The base arrangement was frequently ac-
> cidental, by such aspects as size or other shelf
> arrangement not reflecting the contents of the
> works. Subarrangement in these cases was
> usually by author. Sometimes the base arrange-
> ment was by author. Early catalogs tended to be
> rudimentary, both in the provision of access
> points and in the fullness and accuracy of the in-
> formation provided for each title. Indexes were
> sometimes provided for the base listing, comple-
> menting the base access system. Broad class
> arrangement was not unusual, whether supplement-
> ed by title and author indexes or not. By the last
> quarter of the nineteenth century, all of the
> essential bibliographic techniques currently avail-
> able were developed and available to compilers of

book catalogs, whose choice of catalog elements
was limited only by economic considerations of
production. 2

During the period from the beginning of the 20th
century until the present, the card catalog has served as
the standard tool for revealing the holdings of libraries.
Among the factors which led to the emergence of the card
catalog and its substitution for the book catalog were the
continuing growth of library collections, the increasing cost
of producing book catalogs, and the introduction of the
Library of Congress printed card service in 1901.

Recent advances in machine technology and equipment,
and growing problems related to the card catalog have led
to a new interest in the book-form catalog. Among the
technological advances which influenced this revived interest
were such developments as the emergence in 1953 of a high-
speed sequential card camera; advances in relation to punch-
card equipment; the availability in 1964 of a 120-character
print chain for electronic computers, offering both upper and
lower case type with a more legible print-out; recent advances in relation to computer hardware and software;
introduction of optical scanning devices; and refinements in
offset printing methods, resulting in reduced production
costs for book catalogs.

Among other factors which have contributed to the
renewed interest in book catalogs are: (1) the increased
volume of publication; (2) the immense growth of library
collections; (3) the increased demand for information,
materials, and expanded services; (4) the growing size and
complexity of the card catalog, containing hundreds of
thousands or millions of cards in some larger libraries;
(5) the problem of maintenance and rehabilitation of the
card catalog, with varying degrees of deterioration of
present cards; (6) the time and effort required to interfile
large quantities of new cards, and to withdraw others;
(7) the alarming problem of lack of sufficient space for the
growing number of large card catalog files, and the increase
in the cost of such files; (8) the general problem of growing
backlogs of uncataloged and unclassified materials, as well
inadequately cataloged materials, and the necessity in some
cases for recataloging and reclassification; (9) the trend
toward cooperative development and use of resources of
geographically separated library units, resulting in a need
for multiple copies of the catalogs at each location; and
(10) a growing interest in specific library catalogs by

researchers, teachers, and other libraries, making commercial distribution of the book catalog economically desirable.

   The card catalog problems of the New York Public
Library, resulting from its size, its complexity, and its
physical condition, have been investigated by Matta,[3] who
explored the future prospects for the production and
maintenance of the catalog and compared the advantages and
disadvantages of card catalogs and book catalogs. It was
estimated that more than 2,000,000 of the Library's then
8,000,000 cards were in need of rehabilitation. The cost
of such a task was compared with the cost involved in
issuing book catalogs. Matta concluded that it would be
more expensive to rehabilitate, produce and maintain the
card catalog than to convert, produce and maintain book
catalogs of the holdings. It was recommended that the
catalog be supplemented by computer-produced catalogs
with cumulative monthly and annual supplements. Henderson
and Rosenthal, in a subsequent study, offered the following
major conclusions and recommendations:

> That the catalogs of the Research Libraries of
> the New York Public Library be divided
> chronologically at the earliest possible date; that
> the present (or retrospective) Public Catalog be
> reproduced photographically in book form; that the
> future (or prospective) catalogs be produced in a
> combination of card and book form from a store
> of machine-readable data...[4]

   A notable event in the production of printed book
catalogs was the issuance by the Library of Congress in
the 1940's of a depository catalog of L. C. cards in book
form, thus making it generally available to all libraries
in the United States, as well as libraries abroad. The
Catalog of Books Represented by Library of Congress
Printed Cards Issued to July 31, 1942, produced by photographing the cards and printing them in reduced size,
eighteen to a page, required 167 volumes, and reproduced
approximately 1,900,000 cards. The Library of Congress
has continued the publication of catalogs in book form. The
largest single bibliographic project in the history of the
Library of Congress has been the publication of the National
Union Catalog, Pre-1956 Imprints by Mansell Information/
Publishing Ltd. of London. It is estimated that the 16
million cards that make up the Catalog will require

approximately 610 volumes to be published over ten years,
each standard 704-page volume containing about 21,000
entries.

Book catalog trends in 1966, with emphasis on cooperative and centralized aspects, were analyzed by David C.
Weber. While he ascertained that the number of libraries
using them at that time numbered less than 50 out of over
10,000, he predicted that the impact of computers in library
applications during the next decade would increase the number of libraries producing book catalogs, and that other pioneering libraries would turn toward direct computer inquiry
in a real-time mode of operation, dispensing with the visible
catalog in card or book form. Of the continuing catalogs in
print in 1966, Weber estimated that at least fifteen used the
high-speed electronic computer, and had developed their own
programs; all but one had used a computer available within
the institution; ten used the high-speed sequential card
camera; all but one contracted the production outside; seven
used unit record equipment; and five used variations of the
Library of Congress shingling-photographic technique.[5]

In answer to queries for information on the preparation and current use of book catalogs, the American Library
Association, through the Book Catalogs Committee of its
Resources and Technical Services Division, submitted a
questionnaire in 1966 to a group of 40 libraries which were
then producing book catalogs. The Association sought to
identify trends in the use of such catalogs, the methods of
production, and the structure and format of the books. The
results of the questionnaire indicated a proliferation of book
catalog production which was not limited to any particular
type of library, but was reported in public, college, university, and special libraries.

Methods for Producing Book Catalogs

Various techniques for producting book catalogs have
been described. The Library of Congress catalogs were
made by placing the catalog cards on sheets and photographing them. The resulting book catalogs were essentially
copies of the card catalog in page form.

Many libraries have produced book catalogs using
IBM tabulating cards in conjunction with a line printer. The
information which is to appear in the book catalog is key-

punched on cards and printed by means of a conventional
print chain. The printout may be reduced photographically
for offset printing of the catalog. IBM automated equipment
was the first type used by the Los Angeles County Public
Library when it initiated its book catalog, [6] although a high-
speed special camera was subsequently employed. [7] The King
County Libraries of Seattle, Washington, also used IBM
punch cards for producing their early catalogs.

The sequential camera can be used to photograph
data that has been recorded on the space at the top of punch
cards at speeds ranging from 7, 000 to 14, 000 cards per
hour. [8] After the cards are sequenced, they enter the
camera through an automatic, precision-feeding mechanism.
Page mats are arranged by cutting the developed film into
strips. Use of this method makes it possible to obtain
varied type faces with improved legibility, and an attractively
formatted page. [9]

Recent technological advances in computer capabilities,
as well as a lowering of hardware and software costs, make
computer-aided book catalog production increasingly practical. [10] Dolby, Forsyth, and Resnikoff concluded in a recent
study that mechanizing the cataloging function is not only
necessary and desirable, but also inevitable, the primary
deterrent being the cost of converting the retrospective file
to machine-readable form. [11] The authors further noted that
present cataloging practice provides sufficient information to
obtain numerous arrangements of the catalog and subsets of
the catalog, and that in manual operations, the cost of expanding access beyond present levels increases at least
linearly with the number of access files created. Mechanization, on the other hand, provides the opportunity to create
additional access files at low cost, offering the user access
to the contents of the library from a number of points. [12]
"The computer offers the advantage not only of avoiding
repetitive keying for cumulation in the same way that the
Linotype did, but also that of deriving the entry for various
access points from the keying of a single basic record,
similar in its content to a unit card." [13]

Computer-based systems for producing book catalogs
have encountered problems in programming satisfactory rules
for filing. [14, 15] It has been necessary to modify standard
library practice in some cases in order to operate within
machine limitations, and to keep programming costs at
reasonable levels. As stated by Simonton, "a fundamental
choice must be made between revision of the form of certain

of our entries and acceptance of new filing patterns, on the
one hand, and the expenditure of considerable editing and/or
programming time in an attempt to retain the traditional
entries and patterns, on the other hand."[16] That the problem
is receiving attention is exemplified by the appearance of the
computer filing code of Hines and Harris,[17] the report by
Nugent on the Library of Congress filing rules,[18] the Dystal
Programs for library filing,[19] and various discussions of the
subject in the literature.[20] It has been suggested that the library community agree upon a set of new standards for
mechanized filing. Cartwright and Shoffner present several
advantages of a national code of rules:

> First, we feel that the advent of nationally dis-
> tributed catalog copy in machine-readable form will
> make standardization in cataloging even more
> attractive than it has been in the past, because the
> possibilities of achieving this standardization will
> be greater than have existed, and because the costs
> of applying non-standard methods will be much
> greater than they have been in the past. Secondly,
> the relationship between the form of the heading
> adopted and the filing rules is very close; therefore,
> the national agency which adopts a new set of filing
> rules should be in a position to influence cataloging
> rules as they apply to the form of headings. What
> must be sought is a heading structure which will
> both convey the information desired and be amenable
> to computer filing.[21]

A combination of more than one process may be involved in the production of book catalogs whereby random
catalog cards are arranged to form pages of a register. Indexes to the registers are provided by short catalog information, register page and entry location.[22]

Format

A lack of agreement among producers of book catalogs
has been evident in regard to the format and content of the
catalogs. The final design depends upon several factors including the purpose of the catalog, the type and quantity of information which is to be provided, the method of production,
the funds available for book catalog production, and the needs
of the users. The form and content of the entries and the
design of the printed page are important factors contributing
to user satisfaction with the catalog.

The book catalog may be produced for books and/or non-book materials. Serials, recordings, films, filmstrips, slides, etc. may be included. Depending upon its purpose, the catalog may list current and/or retrospective materials; its scope may be comprehensive or limited, and it may provide access from one or several points. The County of Los Angeles Public Library issues a separate foreign language catalog.

The amount of information included in the entries varies in different book catalogs. Some include all of the information appearing on the catalog card, others limit the entries to what may be considered as the minimum elements. The latter are intended to serve primarily as finding lists. The amount of bibliographic data appearing in each section of the catalog may be varied. The catalog may contain a full entry in the author section, and abbreviated information in the title and subject sections. Entries may be shortened by such practices as the use of abbreviations for names of publishers and other elements, by use of initials for authors, instead of the full form of the name, by limiting the title to a specified number of characters, and by limiting descriptive cataloging. The size of the total catalog may be reduced by including less bibliographic data, and by restricting the number of subject headings and added entries. Control of the quantity of material appearing in the book catalog influences the cost. Weinstein and George, considering the cost of printed book catalogs in relation to entry form and content, suggest that entries "be the shortest, physically smallest, least inclusive set of bibliographic data consistent with the needs of real use. This is not to deny the value of each bibliographic element now included on library cards, typically Library of Congress cards, but rather to question the necessity of their repetition throughout the entry set."[23]

Variations in column width and length, spacing between columns, number of columns per page, indentations, margins, size of page, size of print, type face, arrangement of elements, and method of binding may be observed. Some are perfect-bound, some are in buckram oversewn, others are wire sewn or spiral bound. Yet others are offered in looseleaf or post binder form.[24] The most popular volume size is 8-1/2 x 11 inches.

Most libraries producing computerized book catalogs have issued divided catalogs, rather than catalogs using the dictionary arrangement.

The influence of typography on the cost of printed catalogs has been investigated by Dolby and Resnikoff. They emphasized the desirability of concentrating the greatest number of characters per square inch while maintaining legibility. The more characters which can be accommodated on a page, the fewer the number of pages required, making it possible to reduce costs for paper, printing and binding. A further advantage is the saving in shelf space accomplished by densely printed catalogs. The authors conclude that "printing, binding and paper costs are primarily a function of the total amount of space taken up by the catalog material. These costs can be minimized by choosing condensed type faces in small point sizes, by restricting the use of all-caps formats, by using semibold type faces in place of bold, and by maximizing the character density per square inch."[25]

To be effective, book catalogs have to be kept current. Updating of the catalog is accomplished by issuing supplements or by producing completely new editions. Weekly, monthly, bi-monthly, and quarterly supplements may be issued. After the basic catalog is published, and between supplements, daily card records may be prepared for use until the next cumulation is scheduled. Periodically, the entire basic catalog may be reissued, incorporating all additions, withdrawals, and changes. This may be scheduled semi-annually, annually, or over longer periods of time. For some types of materials frequent updating of the catalog is not required.

Costs

The cost of publishing book catalogs includes the composition cost, printing and binding costs, and paper costs. Composition costs are relatively independent of format and type size, although this factor varies with the use of different composition devices.[26] The printing cost is influenced by the frequency of cumulation, the number of pages printed, and the number of copies printed.

The factors which are significant in evaluating the cost of producing library catalogs in book form have been analyzed in a publication investigating the economics of book catalog production. The quantitative variables were listed by Hayes, Shoffner, and Weber as: (1) the characteristics of the collections to be cataloged; (2) the characteristics of the published catalogs; and (3) the characteristics of the production method.[27] The costs of book catalogs produced by various methods were compared.

In a study of the computer-produced book catalog being used in the Baltimore County (Maryland) Public Library, 28 the basic and annual costs of the present book catalogs were compared with the cost of maintenance of the card catalogs. Considered also was the effect of the adoption of the book catalog on the costs of rendering various services, and the functions and services that have been added or eliminated. Although the costs could not be accurately estimated, it was found that the book catalog has provided significant benefits by affording the users access to the entire library collection, as was reflected by a 51 per cent increase in intra-library loan requests during the first year after the introduction of the book catalog. 29 In comparing costs of book catalogs and card catalogs, Brown has observed that "we tend to forget that we are not comparing like things. We should remember that we are not trying to obtain the same results. How do we evaluate the convenience of having a book catalog in a private office or in a district library or in another part of the state? How do we put a dollar value on the improved quality of cataloging copy?"30

An effort towards evaluation of the utility and cost of computerized library catalogs has been made in which the cost to the user, the cost of programming, cost of hardware, and cost of conversion of catalog data to machine-readable form are reviewed. 31

Advantages of Book Catalogs

1. Multiple copies of the book catalogs can be issued. It is impractical to produce multiple copies of complete card catalogs. The catalogs in book form may be widely distributed to other libraries and to individuals, extending the usefulness of the collection.

2. A number of simultaneous users can be accommodated at the same time. It is awkward for many patrons to use the card catalog at the same time, although this disadvantage is minimized to some extent by the portability of the card catalog trays. The book catalog relieves congestion at the card catalog and reduces wear on card catalogs.

3. Book catalogs are mobile. Copies are conveniently available in various areas. Users can be comfortably seated while consulting the catalog. In open stack libraries,

volumes of the book catalog may be placed in the stack area
so that patrons can have the catalogs in the same area as
the books. Book catalogs can be consulted outside of the library, and in other libraries.

4. In a card catalog only one card may be seen at a
time. The book catalog, on the other hand is easy to scan.
The layout of items on a printed page makes it possible for
the user to view numerous entries at the same time, and to
see a full sweep of the holdings on the subject at a glance.[32]
Various editions and the relationships between volumes can
be seen, and the ability to browse is enhanced. The use of
book catalogs may be easily taught to patrons. Children
have been able to use the catalogs with ease. Card catalogs
have become increasingly complex, causing difficulties for inexperienced users.

5. Book catalogs are compact, occupying less space
than is needed to house bulky card catalogs, and require no
special or expensive cabinets to house them.[33] Book catalogs
may be used on bookmobiles and small stations where there
is insufficient space for a card catalog.

6. Numerous problems relating to the maintenance of
the card catalog are avoided. The continuous cost of filing
represents a major disadvantage of the card catalog. Illegal
removal of cards, replacement of deteriorated cards, and
disarranged cards represent constant problems in a card
catalog.

7. Possible inaccuracies are more easily detected in
a book catalog than in a card catalog. The use of book
catalogs reduces the amount of clerical and professional work
required to correct errors in the catalog. When an error is
made, it may be corrected in the next issue of the catalog.

8. In situations where significant changes in cataloging are desirable, a new catalog may be produced in book
form, rather than recataloging the old one. Old catalogs
may have many inconsistencies, need to have their subject
headings updated, their author entries corrected, and may
require a general overhauling as a result of policy changes
or changes in cataloging personnel over the years.[34]

9. The book catalog encourages uniform cataloging,
classification, and subject headings.[35] Greater accuracy is

realized through standardization of methods and procedures. In library systems the quality of the catalog is uniform, and is not subject to modification by branch or departmental staff members. The control of catalog information at one point brings about uniformity through the system. Book catalogs strengthen coordinated library systems by facilitating the distribution of cataloging information to branch libraries. Duplicate branch cards are often removed as an unnecessary expense. A user in any branch has the opportunity to use any book in the collection without having to travel to the main library to consult the card catalog. Smaller libraries are not restricted by the size of their collections, and utilization of the available resources of all the libraries in the system may be increased. Member libraries of the system have the advantages of separate catalogs and central records.

10. The book catalog is of benefit to the library staff. Reference, interlibrary loan, acquisitions, cataloging and departmental librarians, as well as faculty and other personnel, have a catalog of holdings within reach of their desks for instant reference. Acquisitions policy may be under better control, as holdings are more frequently reviewed. Reference librarians find the book catalog easy to use and helpful in answering telephone requests. Much time is saved in being able to consult the catalogs at the cataloger's desk without having to walk to the central catalog.

11. Bibliographic control is increased by constant revision of holdings. The publication of periodic cumulative supplements assures the maintenance of currency of the book catalog, and the availability of accurate information about new books. In the computer-produced book catalog, new records may be inserted rapidly, facilitating frequent updating with supplements and cumulations.

12. For closed stack libraries, the book catalog can be used as an aid in browsing. The patron can photocopy any section of the book catalog which contains the desired material.

13. Other libraries may use the book catalog as a book selection and buying guide, and as a key to scholarly resources in other libraries. It may aid them in cataloging their collections and in verifying citations for interlibrary loans. The volume of interlibrary loan transactions may be increased, and interlibrary loan operations improved by the provision of book catalogs. The book catalog may be

considered as a reference and research tool.

14. Libraries may consider the possibility of selling printed copies of their catalogs or special-purpose bibliographies produced from cataloging data to scholars, other libraries, and possibly to the public.

15. Mail-order library service may be instituted by provision of book catalogs to homes, industries, businesses, schools and other institutions.

16. In a computer-based system for book catalog production, it is possible to obtain many more approaches to the holdings of the library than is feasible in a card catalog system, increasing the number of access points under which information about library items is filed. The fact that the computer can sort information rapidly into a variety of sequences makes multiple uses of the machine-readable catalog files possible. Various listings can be produced--by subject, author, title, type of material, language, chronological order, and others. The machine-readable data may be used for acquisitions, circulation, and information retrieval purposes, as well as for the preparation of special bibliographies.

The inherent restrictions of the fixed format of the printed unit catalog card are eliminated, making it possible to construct bibliographic tools in a variety of formats and arrangements.[36]

Disadvantages of Book Catalogs

The drawbacks as well as the advantages of book catalogs have been cited in the literature.[37] The following have been noted by various authors and users:

1. Book catalogs are less current than card catalogs; the book catalog may be obsolete as soon as it is produced. Since the book catalogs are not up-to-date, a supplementary listing must be available to assure access to the complete collection between printings of the catalog. Problems are created by books that are acquired after publication of the catalog, and by books withdrawn or transferred to different locations. The use of the book catalog necessitates looking into several volumes, the main catalog, and possibly many supplements.

2. The cost of production of the book catalog is higher. Cost figures for the production of various types of book catalogs are included in the text of this book. The small library may find the computerized catalog beyond its financial means. When more experience is gained in the preparation of book catalogs, when cooperative efforts in this area are realized, and when the fringe benefits resulting from the use of book catalogs are utilized, the cost may not be as excessive over a period of time as it now seems.

3. Many libraries, in an effort to reduce costs, have limited their cataloging when preparing book catalogs, making it briefer, including less bibliographic information, or limiting the number of subject headings. The practice of crowding the information on the page in order to reduce the size of the catalog has decreased legibility. Some patrons have stated that they cannot read the print as well as that on a file card.

4. The book catalog is inflexible. To make changes or deletions requires defacing the work.[38] In the card catalog, changes and deletions are relatively easy to effect and new entries can be inserted without difficulty.

5. The book catalog is susceptible to wear, mutilation and theft. Pages may be removed from the catalog. Normal wear and tear may present problems.

6. The book catalog volumes may be large and heavy, creating problems in binding and in handling.

7. When a patron carries a volume of the book catalog to the stacks, to the photocopy area, or to other areas in the library, he has removed a large part of the catalog. Using a card tray, the reader has removed only a small portion of the alphabet, and the tray is generally available to others in the vicinity of the card catalog.

8. Changes in filing rules in computer-produced book catalogs may cause problems for the user.

9. There is no general agreement on the part of librarians and users that the book catalog surpasses the card catalog for use in a single location.

The final consideration in regard to the use of book catalogs will be based upon such factors as the particular

type of library; the character and size of its collection;
its objectives; its clientele and their present and future needs;
library personnel, equipment and funds available; and the
relative advantages and fringe benefits provided to the users
in comparison to the costs involved. Such benefits include
the wide distribution of book catalogs representing the library's collections. The advantages of extending services
and cooperative uses of resources are factors to be
considered.

> There is great need for experimentation, with
> close attention to cost, both of present and pro-
> posed methods, in a wide variety of types and
> size of libraries, before the question of feasibility
> can be answered. In this period of experimenta-
> tion, the precepts, patterns, and products of the
> past must be carefully scrutinized, and only those
> of firmly established and continuing validity and
> utility permitted to influence our judgment of
> feasibility. 39

A decision facing the library which is considering the
adoption of book catalogs is whether the book catalog should
supplant or supplement the card catalog. Some regional and
public library systems have discontinued card catalogs in
branch and extension divisions but have retained the main
public card catalogs. The Science Libraries Consolidated
Short-Title Catalog of Books, issued by the University of
Rochester, is designed as a supplement to the catalog on
cards. The Free Library of Philadelphia has removed all
card catalogs of their collections from branch libraries.
Many branch libraries which have discarded card catalogs
continue to maintain a shelf list.

A description of some ongoing book catalogs is offered
in detail in following chapters. A number of different
methods of production have been used. Libraries generally
do not undertake the complete production themselves. For
computerized catalogs the production would include the steps
of cataloging, preparation of work sheets, keypunching,
programming, running of the programs, printing and binding. 40
In most cases, a part of the job, or the complete process,
is performed outside of the library. Increasingly, keypunching, data processing, printing and binding are contracted to outside firms with specialized capabilities. Keypunching is occasionally done in the library.

A prolific producer of printed library catalogs over the past few years has been the commercial firm of G. K. Hall in Boston. Its book catalogs, primarily of special collections, are made by microfilming the catalog cards, making electrostatic prints from the microfilm, arranging the prints in three columns of seven cards each, and rephotographing them at a reduction of two-thirds to make the offset plates. The process, however, produces a bulky and costly catalog with considerable loss of space. The quality of reproduction depends to some extent on the condition of the card entries.

The Center for Research Libraries has issued a catalog in book form. Five folio volumes dated 1969-1970 are devoted to monographs, and one volume covers newspapers. The newspaper volume lists by title all newspapers housed at and available through the Center. Reproduced from the Center's card catalog by Mansell, the Catalogue totals almost 3, 700 pages. As a rule, monographs are cataloged under main entry only, although cross references are included when necessary or useful. 41

Among other commercial organizations that have engaged in book catalog production are Econolist (ceased), which prepared and printed book catalogs for various libraries in California; Alanar, a subsidiary of Bro-Dart Industries; Leasco Systems and Research Corp. (formerly Documentation, Inc., Bethesda, Md.); Science Press, Fairfax, Virginia; Professional Library Service (a Xerox Co.); the ALPS System (Automated Library Processing Services) of the System Development Corporation, Santa Monica, California; Rocappi, Inc., Composition Division of the Lehigh Press Inc., Pennsauken, N.J.; Greenwood Press, Inc., Westport, Connecticut; and Compucenters, Inc., Santa Barbara, Calif., which performs the optical scanning and computer work for the book catalogs of the Los Angeles County Public Library.

A book-form catalog at the London Borough of Camden Library has been produced by ICT (International Computers & Tabulators). Each computer print-out is microfilmed and reproduced by Rank-Xerox to provide copies in the lending libraries. 42

Future of the Book Catalog

Recent technological advances in computer capabilities,

along with decreasing computer costs, increase the likelihood that libraries will venture in the future towards increased computer-aided book catalog production. The discussions in this collection clearly indicate that there has
been a turn of the circle in regard to the identification of
holdings of libraries through book catalogs as opposed to
card catalogs. It would appear that there would be a proliferation of book catalogs with the advantages clearly identified
in the preceding pages. The need for card catalogs for current records and for special listings will no doubt continue.

It is expected that interlibrary loans will increase,
the facilities for large-scale reproduction of requested materials will be expanded, and that the number of qualified
personnel must be increased to meet the growing demand
for services which can be expected to result from wider
distribution of book catalogs.

The publication of the card catalogs of many libraries
by commercial organizations and other agencies will undoubtedly result in easier identification of the holdings of libraries
of various types. Such information should help to achieve
one of the goals of librarians--to provide access to particular titles for the use of scholars wherever they may be
located.

Further studies to indicate how access to library collections is facilitated through use of book catalogs; to investigate user and staff reactions to the book catalogs; and
to observe changes in patterns of library service occurring
as the result of the introduction of book catalogs would be
most valuable for the future development of the book catalog.

References

1. Ranz, James, The Printed Book Catalogue in American
    Libraries: 1723-1900. Chicago, American Library
    Association, 1964.

2. Hines, Theodore C., "Book Catalogs," in: Kent, Allen
    and Lancour, Harold, eds., Encyclopedia of Library
    and Information Science, Vol. 2. N.Y., Marcel
    Dekker, 1969, p. 661.

3. Matta, S., The Card Catalog in a Large Research
    Library: Present Conditions and Future Possibilities

in the New York Public Library. DLS Dissertation, Columbia University School of Library Service, N.Y., 1965.

4. Henderson, James W. and Rosenthal, Joseph A., Library Catalogs: Their Preservation and Maintenance by Photographic and Automated Techniques. Cambridge, Mass., The M.I.T. Press (M.I.T. Report No. 14), 1968, p. ix.

5. Weber, David C., "Book Catalog Trends in 1966," Library Trends 16: 149-64, July, 1967.

6. Hewitson, Theodore, "The Book Catalog of the Los Angeles County Public Library; its Function and Use," Library Resources & Technical Services, 4: 228-32, Summer, 1960.

7. MacQuarrie, Catherine, "The Metamorphosis of the Book Catalog," ibid., 8: 370-8, Fall, 1964.

8. Becker, Joseph, "Automatic Preparation of Book Catalogs," ALA Bulletin, 58: 715-6, Sept., 1964.

9. Cartwright, Kelley L., "Automated Production of Book Catalogs," in: Salmon, Stephen R., ed., Library Automation; A State of the Art Review. Chicago, American Library Association, 1969, 58-60.

10. Zuckerman, Ronald A., "Computerized Book Catalogs, and Their Effects on Integrated Library Data Processing: Research and Progress at the Los Angeles Public Library," in: Proceedings of the 1967 Clinic on Library Applications of Data Processing, ed. by Dewey E. Carroll. Urbana, Ill., Univ. of Illinois, Graduate School of Library Science, p. 70-89.

11. Dolby, J. L., Forsyth, V., and Resnikoff, H. L., An Evaluation of the Utility and Cost of Computerized Library Catalogs. Washington, D.C., U.S. Dept. Health, Education and Welfare, Office of Education, Bureau of Research, 1968, 203 pp.

12. Ibid., p. 20.

13. Hines, Theodore C., op. cit., p. 664.

14. Perreault, Jean M., "The Computer and Catalog Filing Rules," Library Resources and Technical Services, 9: 325-31. 1965.

15. Popecki, Joseph T., "A Filing System for the Machine Age," Library Resources and Technical Services, 9: 333-37, 1965.

16. Simonton, Wesley, "Automation of Catloging Procedures," in: Salmon, Stephen R., ed., Library Automation; A State of the Art Review. Chicago, American Library Association, 1969, p. 47.

17. Hines, Theodore C. and Harris, Jessica L., Computer Filing of Index, Bibliographic, and Catalog Entries. Newark, N.J., Bro-Dart Foundation, 1966.

18. Nugent, William R., "The Mechanization of the Filing Rules for the Dictionary Catalogs of the Library of Congress," Library Resources & Technical Services, 11(2): 145-66, Spring, 1967.

19. Richmond, Phyllis A., and Gill, Marcia K., "Dystal Programs for Library Filing," in: Proceedings of the American Documentation Institute, Vol. 4. New York, American Documentation Institute, 1967, p. 197-201.

20. Cartwright, Kelley L. and Shoffner, Ralph M., Catalogs in Book Form: A Research Study of Their Implications for the California State Library and the California Union Catalog, with a Design for their Implementation. Berkeley, California, Institute of Library Research, University of California, 1967, p. 26.

21. Ibid.

22. Zuckerman, Ronald A., op. cit., p. 71.

23. Weinstein, Edward and George, Virginia, "Computer-produced Book Catalogs: Entry Form and Content," Library Resources & Technical Services, 11: 185, 1967.

24. Weber, David C., op. cit., p. 157.

25. Dolby, J. L., et al., op. cit., p. 81.

26. Ibid.

27. Hayes, Robert M., Shoffner, Ralph M., and Weber,
    David C., "The Economics of Book Catalog Produc-
    tion," Library Resources & Technical Services,
    10(1): 57-90, Winter, 1966.

28. Childers, Thomas, Kieffer, Paul, Leonard, Faye, and
    Susaki, Sharon, Book Catalog and Card Catalog: A
    Cost and Service Study. Towson, Md., Baltimore
    County Public Library, March, 1967, 45 pp.

29. Griffin, Hillis L., "Automation of Technical Processes
    in Libraries," in: Cuadra, Carlos A., ed.,
    Annual Review of Information Science and Technology,
    Vol. 3. Chicago, Encyclopaedia Britannica, Inc.,
    William Benton, 1968, p. 241-62.

30. Brown, Margaret C., "A Book Catalog at Work,"
    Library Resources & Technical Services, 8(4):
    356, Fall, 1964.

31. Dolby, et al., op. cit., 25-60.

32. MacQuarrie, Catherine, "Library Catalog, a Comparison,"
    Hawaii Library Association Journal, 21: 18, Aug.,
    1965.

33. Pizer, Irwin H., "Book Catalogs versus Card Catalogs,"
    Medical Library Association Bulletin, 53: 225-38,
    April, 1965.

34. MacQuarrie, Catherine, op. cit., p. 19.

35. Weber, David C., op. cit., p. 152.

36. Library Automation--Computer Produced Book Catalog.
    IBM, Data Processing Application. New York,
    International Business Machine Corp., 1969, p. 1.

37. Tauber, Maurice F. and Stephens, Irlene R.,
    Technical Services in Michigan State Library. New
    York, N.Y., 1965, p. 101-5.

38. Pizer, Irwin H., op. cit., p. 229.

39. Simonton, Wesley, "The Computerized Catalog; Possible,

Feasible, Desirable?" Library Resources & Technical
Services, 8(4): 407, Fall, 1964.

40. Library Automation--Computer Produced Book Catalog,
op. cit., p. 12.

41. Library of Congress Information Bulletin, 29(14): 166,
April 9, 1970.

42. Maidment, W. R., "The Computer Catalogue in
Camden," Library World, 67: 40, Aug., 1965.

Chapter II

Book Catalogs and Card Catalogs

Library Catalog, A Comparison

by Catherine MacQuarrie

The author is President of Catherine MacQuarrie
Associates, specialists in library book catalog
planning. This article is reprinted by permission
from Hawaii Library Association Journal, 21:
18-24, August 1965.

Three main types of library catalogs now in use are
card catalogs, book catalogs, and the possibility sometime in
the future for consoles with direct access to memory banks.
Card catalogs, either dictionary arrangement or divided by
Author-Title and Subject, have served well for the past fifty
years and will continue to serve in many types of libraries.
However, size of collection, number of outlets and cooperative library complexes can mitigate against their use.

Large libraries with departmental libraries and with
many branches are better served with book catalogs. Book
catalogs index the entire collection and can be issued in
many copies so that no matter what part of the library user
is in, he has access to the entire collection through the use
of catalogs.

Since book catalogs, except the card lay-out type,
if made properly, can be arranged any way the library
decides, the library can have sorted out all the books on
science, for example, and have a science catalog as well as
a union catalog in the science department.

From the use point of view, the book catalog for a
large collection is much better. The full sweep of the
holdings on a subject can be seen at a glance instead of
having to flip through card by card. In branches particularly, book catalogs are good because, no matter in what branch
the user is, he can have equal service and equal opportunity
to use any book in the collection without having to take the

time and expense of going downtown to consult the card catalog.

Usually an old catalog, and many that aren't so old, have many inconsistencies, need their subject headings brought up-to-date, their author entries corrected and generally need a good overhauling. During the years policies have changed, different systems of subject headings are used. With each new Head Cataloger, differences creep into the card catalog. Seldom does a catalog department have the time to overhaul the card catalog particularly when it means retyping thousands of cards. Changing to book catalog form gives a library this opportunity. The revision and up-dating of the catalog can be done as part of the process of changing to the book catalog form, particularly if there is a cataloger in charge of the conversion.

Either for cooperatives or state libraries, book catalogs are the ideal form as a union catalog of the holdings of the entire group can be made available to any user. A state library can supply copies of its book catalog to every library in the state which does interlibrary loan from the State collection, or uses the State collection to back up its services.

Book catalogs can be made much more complete than card catalogs. After a point, card catalogs become very bulky and push the reference department out of its space; whereas book catalogs can contain analytics, annotations, many more subject headings, and still be shelved in a comparatively small space. They can contain all the bibliographic information desired. They can contain many helps to reference librarians and to researchers. Instead of each reference librarian maintaining his private indexes, this information can be incorporated into the book catalog for the use of everyone.

Another advantage of book catalogs is cleanliness. Have you ever tried to use an old card catalog? Certain places are extremely dirty. It is difficult and expensive to retype cards to replace the spoiled ones.

There are several types of book catalogs. The first kind made in recent years, the Library of Congress Catalogs, are made as card layout catalogs where the catalog cards are laid out on sheets or pages and photographed. This is the simplest kind of catalog, a direct copy of the card catalog which adds nothing and cannot be up-dated except by interfiling, usually by hand, laying out the cards again and rephotographing. It is bulky as there is lots of white space, unused space, on a page, even when cards are made for this specific purpose. To overcome this bulkiness, some catalogs have the print reduced in size to such an extent that the catalog is hard to use.

The next type of catalog, produced from IBM tabulating cards or tape, and reproduced for printing with a #405 printer or a computer, sometimes with all capital letters, sometimes with the newer IBM equipment, with upper and lower case letters, also has the problem of bulkiness. Its print can be reduced in size, but only to a point. If it is reduced too much it loses its usefulness as it is too hard to use. The Los Angeles County used this type of catalog for over ten years until it became very bulky. Los Angeles County has fourteen 60-tray card cabinets which in book form reduced to 55 large volumes in the IBM print catalog. If Los Angeles County had used the usual round type that is on the computers, their catalog would have taken sixty some volumes. They had the advantage of using the print on the Registrar of Voters equipment, which was a narrower typeface. Some of the recent catalogs produced with computers use double columns and reduce the print almost to the point of illegibility.

A further disadvantage is the sameness of the print. Overprinting can be used for headings to give the effect of boldface print, but it has to be very skillfully done for if it does not hit the line exactly it gives the effect of a shadow which makes it rather illegible. Los Angeles County underlined headings but it had to be done by hand as computer equipment could not supply an underline in the proper place.

Another type of book catalog uses a combination of IBM equipment and printing, either varitype or linofilm. The internal controls, up-dating, arranging, etc., are all mechanical but the end result or print is varied. Any size or type of print, upper or lower case, diacritical marks, bold face or italic can be used, as desired by the library. This type of book catalog is much less bulky as the lines can be justified, narrow type faces can be used and spaces determined by increments so that the end result, the book catalog, takes considerably less space, even though larger type is used. For example, the Los Angeles County catalog took 55 volumes, 13 inches high, when produced with IBM print, whereas it takes 33 volumes, 11 inches high, using varitype print.

A further advantage of the catalogs using print is the variation in size of print. The author, title, and body of the card can be in one size or type of print; annotations, collation, notes, etc., can be in a smaller or different type; and heading lines, both author and subject heading, can be bold face, so that they stand out for ease in finding them.

The latest substitute for a card catalog that is being considered is a system similar to information retrieval-- the use of a console. The library user operates the console, activating the computer or memory equipment to get the information desired. This type of operation might be good in large research centers that could be directly hooked up with the LC memory bank where there would be special operators who knew how to phrase the questions to activate the equipment. In a small branch library or even in a large public library, to expect the public to know how to use a console is definitely for in the future. In the mean time, card or book catalogs will serve better.

Cost factors are a problem for which there are no flat answers. The catalog produced by card layout seems to be the cheapest; but is it really the cheapest? Printing is one of the most expensive parts of the operation and these catalogs are very bulky. They get out-of-date and cannot be up-dated or reproduced except by redoing the entire job, which means that the card catalog has to be continued. In the long run, they are far more costly than they seem.

IBM produced catalogs, either from tab cards or type, cost more for the initial job but they are less bulky than the card lay-out catalogs and thus cost far less to print. Once they are completed, the card catalog can be discontinued. When they are up-dated, the second printing is about one-third as costly as the original job as all the internal work has been done and can be reused, with new material interfiled mechanically.

The varitype or linofilm catalogs are, in the long run, the least costly as they take the least space for printing and they have hee same advantages as the computer catalog in up-dating and reuse of original data. Costwise, there is up to a 40% differential in printing costs because of the compact print and better use of space on a page.

Cost factors have another point that should be considered. Libraries need to install internal cost accounting into their operations before they can know what they should put into their catalogs. Many libraries recently, in an effort to reduce costs, have limited their cataloging, making it briefer, including less bibliographic information or limiting the number of subject headings. However, each time catalog information is reduced, reference and readers aid costs are doubled or trebled, increasing overall library costs. If libraries, before embarking upon a simplified catalog, would make surveys into catalog costs, reference costs, etc., then they would be in a better position to know what kind of information is needed in their catalog; what would help the reference librarian the most; what would help the user to help himself, thus reducing reader costs; what is needed to make the best use of the expensive collection of books that has been built up over the years.

The catalog in book form is a tool that can be readily used by the public, usually with little help from the reference staff. It should contain all types of information--extensive subject analysis, analytics, bibliographical data that will help make the contents of the books available to the user. If the catalog which is available to the library user is made into a better index to the collection, then information retrieval and other mechanical searching methods will not be needed except perhaps in very specialized libraries. The emphasis should be placed on making the catalog in whatever form the best possible index to the collection.

Librarians should investigate the ways catalogs are used. Instead of trying to learn a new field, they should be informed of ways that catalogs can open up the contents of their holdings. Answers should be determined to questions concerning the uses to be made of catalogs, the future need for card and/or book catalogs, the depth of indexing required, the part the catalog is to play in the overall use of the library.

Librarians should be knowledgeable as to costs of reference services vs. catalog services and be able to instruct the computer people or the companies who make other types of catalogs in what they need in their catalogs that they are able to finance within their budget structure.

Catalogs to library collections, no matter which type, are the index to the book collection. Each library or system of libraries should analyze its needs, then determine which type will serve it best.

Book Catalogs versus Card Catalogs

by Irwin H. Pizer

The author is Associate Director of Libraries,
State University of New York at Buffalo. This
article is reprinted by permission from Medical
Library Association Bulletin, 53:223-238, April
1965.

Book catalogs, contrary to the beliefs of many
machine salesmen, are not an innovation in library technology. Although this fact can hardly be construed as news
to librarians, it is surprising that the card catalog, for all
practical purposes, is little more than seventy years old.
In these seventy years it has proved its utility with such effectiveness that it has replaced the earlier book catalog and
almost erased it from memory.

Libraries have existed from the civilizations of
Mesopotamia and Egypt, and it is not unreasonable to suppose that these libraries had catalogs. In Mesopotamia,
where the writing material was clay, the catalog might have
been comprised of clay tablets, and, since the records
would probably have filled several of them, one can imagine
a series of tablets as the first card catalog. The techniques
of this type of catalog, however, had to be reinvented
thousands of years later, when the book catalog apparatus
succumbed to its inherent problems.

Portability was not always a feature of early catalogs,
and, although some librarians today complain of having to
lift 7-1/2 pound printed volumes, at least they are movable.
In the temple libraries which existed at Karnak, Dendera,
and Idfu, Dr. Dorothy Schullian has written that "incised
on the walls...is a full catalogue of all the hieratical works
which the library contained."[1] Surely the weight of a 7-1/2
pound volume is preferable to the immobility of a stone
wall. Even our present card catalogs are more mobile
than that, for one can easily transport a single tray

comfortably within the confines of the library.

The next type of catalog was probably the scroll. Its main disadvantage was likely to have been its tendency to re-roll itself while the user was making his bibliographic notes, a situation somewhat akin to Alice at the Queen's croquet party, attempting to play the game with a flamingo mallet.

The scroll gave way to the codex, and the book, as we are familiar with it, came into being. Large private libraries were amassed in monasteries and palaces, as well as by individuals, and these were often housed in elaborate, if not sumptuous, rooms. As libraries grew larger, and as scientific publication began to increase, the need for bibliographic control was obvious. In the library it was met by the book catalog and in scientific publishing by the index and, soon after, the abstract.

Then, as now, the production of a catalog presented various problems, not the least of which was the mode of arrangement. Fortunately, we do not have to deal with those complexities in detail. Suffice it to say that there were catalogs published which were arranged by author, such as Pinelo's catalog of the first library dealing with the literature of the Americas (see Fig. 1), and chronologically by the date of the subject matter, rather than by publication date, such as the Primordia of Bishop White Kennett, a catalog of the first library assembled of works on America written in English (see Fig. 2). The index to this volume is interesting in that it includes both subjects and authors and thereby prefigures the dictionary catalog. Book catalogs were also arranged by title, by subject, by donor, by size, by accession date, and so on.

All of these catalogs had the same basic goal: to provide the owner or user with information as to what was available and where it could be found. The form of the early catalog does not seem to have been in doubt; a manuscript catalog, with space provided for interlineation, was adequate for libraries because they were not of great size. The manuscript catalog of the Library of the Surgeon General's Office, dated 1840, (see Fig. 3) was probably as typical as any. It was small enough to be recopied, perhaps annually, to include new accessions. How different the situation had become by the 1870's, when that library was forced to undertake its first printed catalog (in three volumes), to be followed later by the monumental Index Catalogue!

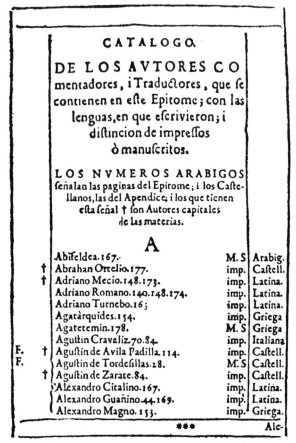

CATALOGO.

DE LOS AVTORES CO
mentadores, i Traduclores, que se
contienen en este Epitome; con las
lenguas,en que escrivieron; i
distincion de impressos
ò manuscritos.

LOS NVMEROS ARABIGOS
señalan las paginas del Epitome; i los Caste-
llanos,las del Apendice; i los que tienen
esta señal † son Autores capitales
de las materias.

A

		Abiseldea.167.	M. S	Arabig.
	†	Abrahan Ortelio.177.	imp.	Castell.
	†	Adriano Mecio.148.173.	imp.	Latina.
		Adriano Romano.140.148.174.	imp.	Latina.
		Adriano Turnebo.163	imp.	Latina.
		Agatàrquides.154.	imp.	Griega
		Agatetemin.178.	M. S	Griega
		Aguſtin Cravaliz.70.84.	imp.	Italiana
F.	†	Aguſtin de Avila Padilla.114.	imp.	Castell.
F.		Aguſtin de Tordeſillas.28.	M. S	Castell.
	†	Aguſtin de Zarate.84.	imp.	Castell.
		Alexandro Citalino.167.	imp.	Latina.
		Alexandro Guañino.44.169.	imp.	Latina.
		Alexandro Magno.153.	imp.	Griega.

✱✱✱   Ale-

Fig. 1.--A Page from El Epitome de Pinelo, Primera
Bibliografia del Nuevo Mundo.   Information about language
is given, as well as a note which indicates if the work is in
manuscript or is printed.

As libraries began to grow ever more rapidly, the
need for a better solution was imperative, and that solution
was eventually found in the card catalog.   One major factor
in its successful substitution for the book catalog was the
changing technology of the times, as represented by the invention of the typewriter and its ultimate, though grudging,
acceptance as a library tool.

AMERICAN LIBRARY.   179

A Defence against the Scots Abdicating DARIEN, including an *Anfwer* to the *Defence of the* Scots *Settlement* there. *Authore* Britanno *fed* Dunenfi. Printed in the Year 1700. 8*vo. p.* 168.

A fhort Vindication of *Phil. Scot's* Defence of the *Scots* abdicating D A-RI E N. Being in Anfwer to the Challenge of the Author of *The Defence* of that Settlement, to prove the *Spanifh* Title to *Darien*, by Inheritance, Marriage, Donation, &*c.* With a Prefatory Reply to the falfe and fcurrilous Afperfions of the new Author of *The Juft and Modeft Vindication*, &c. And fome Animadverfions on the material Part of it, relating to the Title of *Darien. London*, Printed in the Year 1701. 8*vo. p.* 48. [See more on this Subject under the Years 1697, 98, and 1701.]

A Trumpet Sounded out of the Wildernefs of *America*, which may ferve as a Warning to the Government and People of *England* to beware of QUAKERISM. Wherein is fhewed how in *PENSILVANIA*, and there away, where they have the Government in their own Hands, they hire and encourage Men to *Fight* ; and how they *Perfecute, Fine*, and *Imprifon*, and take away Good for Confcience fake. By *Daniel Leeds*. Printed by *William Bradford*, at the *Bible* in *New-York*. 1699. 8*vo. p.* 151.

A Paper to *William Penn*, at the departure of that Gentleman to his Territory for his Perufal in *PENSILVANIA*. Wherein two Points are propofed to him concerning the *Quakers* Religion, that he may receive himfelf Conviction, or render to others that are Confcientious about them, Chriftian Satisfaction ; The one is their Belief of an *Infallible Guidance* : The other is their Difufe of the two Holy and Blefled *Sacraments*. With an occafional Differtation concerning Predeftination, or God's Decree about faving Man, in reference to the Doctrine of others, and *not* the *Quakers* only. By a Friend unknown. *London*, Printed for *H. Mortlock*. 1700. 4*to. p.* 24.

The Order of the Gofpel Profefled and Practifed by the Churches of Chrift in *NEW-ENGLAND*, Juftified by the Scripture, and by the Writings of many Learned Men, both Antient and Modern Divines, in Anfwer to feveral Queftions relating to Church-Difcipline. By *Increafe Mather*, Prefident of *Harvard Colledge* in *Cambridge*, and Teacher of a Church at *Bofton* in *New-England*. Re-printed at *London*, and fold by *A. Baldwin*. 1700. 8*vo. p.*

More Wonders of the Invifible World. Or the Wonders of the Invifible World difplay'd in five Parts. Part I. An Account of the Sufferings of *Margaret*

Fig. 2.--A page from the Bibliothecae Americanae Primordia, the first English bibliography on America, compiled by Bishop White Kennett. The interesting arrangement of this work was in the main chronological. The guiding principle was not, however, publication date but rather the major time period with which a work dealt. In this example, the year 1699 ties all these works together, even though publication dates are later.

We have thus reached the point where we must analyze the good and bad features of book and card catalogs.

Among the advantages of the book catalog, the ability to
make multiple copies is an indisputable one. We mean the
printed book catalog, since making multiple copies of manuscript catalogs is an impractical task (print is, of course,
more readable than manuscript, even that wonderful creation,
library hand). Since the expense of publication lies mainly
in typesetting, etc., little additional cost is added when
printing 100 copies rather than 25. On the printed page,
furthermore, we have the ability to scan numerous entries;
consequently, we can browse easily. But there are even
more cogent points. The catalog does not need to remain
only in the library, but can be widely disseminated to other
libraries or individuals, a most attractive feature in the
areas of scholarship and research. The books which comprise the catalog occupy considerably less floor space than
the same catalog in card form and, of course, need no
special and expensive cabinets to house them. In addition,
possible inaccuracies can be spotted more easily in a book
catalog; this capability is especially advantageous when one
considers modern book catalogs produced from cards. In
this age of Xerography, it is a great help to be able to
photocopy any section of the book catalog which contains
desired material and make notes and comments. One more
advantage is that which occurs when any work is produced
for print. An author is apt to be careful and ruthless in
editing away unnecessary information in this process, but
the same restraint is not always evident in the production of
a card catalog.

There are, nevertheless, major disadvantages in book
catalogs. The cost of production is high, and, more important, the catalog is out of date before it is issued, since
the very acts of typesetting, proofreading, printing and
binding take much time. The book catalog is inflexible; to
make changes or deletions is to deface the work, an act
which goes against the grain in many of us. Additions present a larger problem, which cannot be solved simply by
interleaving with blank pages, since the rational sequence is
eventually destroyed. Book catalogs, like all books, have
the tendency to be purloined or, euphemistically, borrowed
unofficially. Pages may be removed, and normal wear and
tear may be a major problem, as we are now aware from
the appearance of volume I of the Cumulated Index Medicus.
Since the book catalog is out-of-date, a supplementary tool
must be used to find out what has happened since the book
went to the printer. We shall consider some of these book

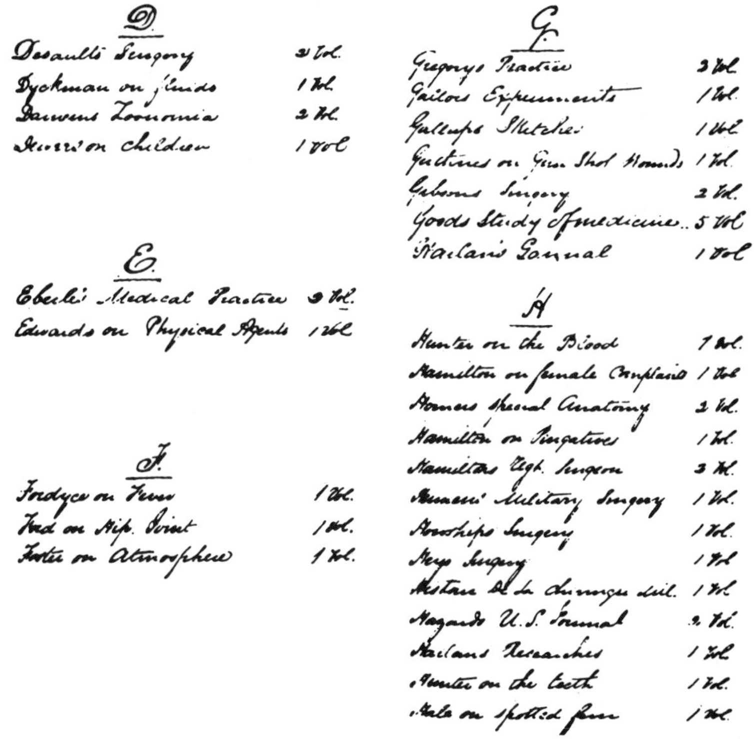

D

Desaults Surgery 2 Vol.
Dyckman on fluids 1 Vol.
Darwins Zoonomia 2 Vol.
Dewees on children 1 Vol

E

Eberle's Medical Practice 2 Vol.
Edwards on Physical Agents 1 Vol

F

Fordyce on Fever 1 Vol.
Ford on Hip Joint 1 Vol.
Foster on Atmosphere 1 Vol.

G

Gregorys Practice 3 Vol
Gallons Experiments 1 Vol
Gallups Sketches 1 Vol
Guthries on Gun Shot Wounds 1 Vol
Gibsons Surgery 2 Vol.
Goods Study of Medicine 5 Vol
Harlans Journal 1 Vol

H

Hunter on the Blood 1 Vol.
Hamilton on female Complaints 1 Vol
Horners Special Anatomy 2 Vol.
Hamilton on Purgatives 1 Vol.
Hamiltons Regt. Surgeon 3 Vol.
Hennens Military Surgery 1 Vol.
Howships Surgery 1 Vol.
Heys Surgery 1 Vol
Histoire de la Chirurgie Mil. 1 Vol.
Hazards U.S. Journal 2 Vol.
Harlans Researches 1 Vol
Hunter on the teeth 1 Vol.
Hale on spotted fever 1 Vol.

Fig. 3.--An illustration from A Catalogue of Books in the Library of the Surgeon General's Office. A more traditional arrangement (according to present standards) than in Figure 2, although "books" is slightly misleading, as journal volumes are also included.

catalog extensions or solutions shortly. In today's catalogs produced by photographic methods, an optimal size type for ease of reading and mental well-being is repeatedly ignored. That the volumes may be heavy and oversize, like the British Museum Catalogue or the Cumulated Index Medicus, tends to create problems with their binding, as well as difficulties in handling. When one volume of a book catalog is in use for a long time, the reader has effectively removed a large portion of the library's resources from the perusal of others, although with a Xerox 914 this need not be as serious a problem as it once was. Finally, it is easy to lose one's place in reading or transcribing information from a page with many entries.

On the other hand, the card catalog is constantly up-to-date, and it is extremely flexible. We can insert new entries at will, in any fashion we devise. The only limitation on the number of entries and the depth of analysis in which we may indulge is the number of card trays available. A card catalog wears well and resists mutilation. Generally speaking, the loss of a single card from the catalog is not as serious as the loss of a page from a book catalog. Changes are easy to make, and mistakes easy to correct. In using a card tray, the researcher has removed only a small portion of the catalog from the reach of others and probably for a shorter time than if he had a volume of a book catalog. When copying data from a single card, we are less liable to err than in copying from a printed page with many entries. Finally, tradition, which may or may not remain inviolable, is in favor of the card catalog. This preference is especially interesting, since the card catalog has been in existence for so short a time.

The card catalog, however, also has its disadvantages. It is impractical to make multiple copies of a card catalog, although to keep up an existing duplicate catalog is little more work than must be expended on the original. Only one title may be seen at a time, and the catalog must be consulted within a narrowly defined area; it also occupies a large amount of space in the library. It would be interesting to determine whether the space the card catalog occupies grows in relation to the size of the library on an arithmetic or a geometric basis. The catalog must be housed in expensive card cabinets, costing approximately 11 to 15 dollars a tray for ready-made ones. It is awkward for many persons to use at the same time, although the partial portability of the card catalog helps to minimize this disadvantage. Should a tray become completely disarranged, a major refiling job ensues, the librarian's nightmare, and there are intriguing hazards created when the floor above the library houses a laboratory or an electron microscope. Finally, it is difficult to locate errors in filing, although serendipity is often helpful in this case. These factors not withstanding, the card catalog has become as much a fixture of the library as the circulation desk.

One of the purposes of this paper is to compare the two techniques of making catalogs, and we must briefly examine the schemes which were tried to keep the book catalog abreast of the library's acquisitions. The methods were many, and most will be familiar and thus will not need elaboration. Supplements of some kind were obviously needed, and these could be created in book form, if the library were affluent, or in card form. Either of these methods had the same disadvantage; it forced the user to search subsidiary alphabets. The library could have the entire catalog reprinted in a cumulative edition, but this soon returned the user to the supplement problem and was a very expensive undertaking. Many libraries have taken to publishing current awareness sheets in the form of acquisition lists, and others have published catalogs of parts of the collection or of special collections. At the turn of the century the brief catalog enjoyed a short vogue among librarians who, although realizing that the card catalog solved many of their most pressing problems, still felt that some sort of printed catalog was desirable. They accordingly published brief or condensed catalogs which were author lists with locations of the books.

Charles C. Jewett's plan for producing a book catalog was far more ingenious than any of the above. Since many libraries purchased the same materials, Jewett reasoned that if duplication of work could be eliminated among libraries the book catalog might remain viable. He, therefore, proposed to prepare stereotype plates for each title. The plates would be stored at the Smithsonian Institution, where Jewett was Librarian and where all the printing would be undertaken. A library desiring a printed catalog would pay the Smithsonian for the assembly of the appropriate plates and the printing costs, thus saving all composition and correction costs, except for the unique titles which it presented. All of this proposal depended on the adoption of standardized rules for cataloging among the participating libraries. The plan was doomed to failure for a variety of reasons, the main one being technological. It is interesting to observe, however, that the idea did not die and is very much in evidence today in the Library of Congress printed card plan. The same basic principle is embodied here, that is, the nonduplication of existing work, but, instead of paying to have a book catalog printed, the library pays to buy sets of cards. Each plan in its way provides a custom-made catalog.

The sheaf catalog was predicated on the notion that the flexibility of a loose-leaf manuscript or typewritten catalog was preferable to the inflexibility of a bound printed one. Any librarian who has spent a few minutes adding the latest issues of Modern Concepts of Cardiovascular Disease to its binder or has added pages to the prior publications is familiar with its principle. A loose-leaf binder with any one

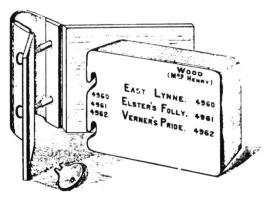

Brown's "Adjustable Catalogue-Holder."

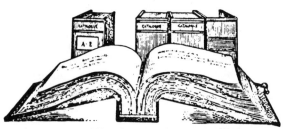

Adjustable Sheaf Catalogue. Locked.

Fig. 4.--One of the many types of adjustable or "loose leaf"
catalogs which tried to bridge the gap between the book and
card systems and take advantage of the benefits of both.

of various types of post mechanism was used to hold the
pages (see Fig. 4). These could be removed at random for
the addition of new or the correction of old entries. Since
there were not many items to a page, alphabetization did
not suffer, and new sheets could be made up to maintain the
order. In effect, it was a card catalog in a binder, but
without the idea of a unit record.

Finally, it is worth mentioning one last attempt to
wed book and card catalog principles, developed by Alexander
Rudolph. Called the Rudolph Indexer, the machine consisted
of pressboard panels chained together in a loop. The panels

passed over a hexagonal drum and appeared under a glass
window when moved by turning a crank at the side of the
machine.   Each panel contained 35 entries, and the machine
was made up of a bank of five chains, so that at each turn
175 entries came into view.   It is unclear whether the five
panels were able to be moved independently, but we may
suppose that they were not.   This scheme, which failed, had
the advantage of presenting many entries to the viewer at
once and also of being kept current to some extent by changing the cards on the panels.   It failed because it was subject
to most of the disadvantages of both the book and card catalog.

It may be seen that the greatest stumbling block in
these systems was the inadequate technology of the various
periods in which they were attempted.   But if we reach a
stage where technology is able to achieve the goals we have
set, and if the problems created by the technology are of
smaller magnitude than the ones it solves, then we may
achieve at least a workable system.   With the postwar
development of computers, we have been presented with such
technology; now let us see what it can do for us.

If we examine the advantages and disadvantages of
computerized catalogs, we find not only many problems
solved, but also some new benefits.

Let us assume that the costs of producing a computerized catalog and a card catalog are comparable.   The
computer catalog may be updated at any time, and a new
print-out is available as often as necessary or desirable.
Multiple copies can be created directly on the computer by
using carbon paper forms, or, if more than a limited number of copies is required, offset or mimeograph masters
can be printed directly, or the normal print-out can be converted to printing masters easily by Xerography or other
photographic methods.   The input costs are nonrecurring for
each item, and, once the information is recorded, it can be
manipulated in almost any fashion the librarian can contrive,
depending on the skill of the programmer.   This manipulation capability makes the production of a union list and its
correction a practical and easy task; special catalogs may be
created, or statistical surveys made; the acquisitions department in a university can easily ascertain how much is being
spent on each or any subject area, etc.   These are
wondrous boons.

HQ / 21/EL 5/961

ABARBANEL, ALBERT BRANDT. ED.

ELLIS, ALBERT. ED.

ENCYCLOPEDIA OF SEXUAL BEHAVIOR. EDITED
BY ALBERT ELLIS AND ALBERT ABARBANEL.
NEW YORK, HAWTHORN BOOKS, 1961.

2 V., ILLUS., 27CM.

QH / 312/AB 3/962

ABERCROMBIE, M.

DICTIONARY OF BIOLOGY, BY M. ABERCROMBIE
ET AL.
CHICAGO, ALDINE PUB. CO., 1962.

254 P., ILLUS., IUCM.

QZ / 206/AB 8/959

ABSTRACTS OF SOVIET MEDICINE

CANCER RESEARCH 1953-1959.
NEW YORK, EXCERPTA MEDICA FOUND., 1959.

709 P., 26CM.

A TRANS. OF SOVETSKOE MEDITSINSKOE
REFERATIVNOE OBOZRENIE ONKOLOGIYA, V.
5-9. ED. BY M. A. SISSONS.

WB / 200/AD 1/958

ADAMS, FRANK DENNETTE, 1892-

PHYSICAL DIAGNOSIS. 14TH ED.
BALTIMORE, WILLIAMS & WILKINS, 1958

926 P., ILLUS., 26CM.

WW / 100/AD 5/962

ADLER, FRANCIS H.

TEXTBOOK OF OPHTHALMOLOGY. 7TH ED
PHILADELPHIA, SAUNDERS, 1962.

560 P., ILLUS., 24CM.

WM / 460/AD 5/961

ADLER, GERHARD, 1904-

LIVING SYMBOL. A CASE STUDY IN THE
PROCESS OF INDIVIDUATION.
NEW YORK, PANTHEON BOOKS, 1961.

463 P., ILLUS., 24CM.

BOLLINGEN SERIES 63.

Fig. 5.--A page from the catalog of the University of New
Mexico Library of the Health Sciences. Produced by computer, this catalog takes advantage of the new technology to
produce the copy, but casts it in the format familiar to most
users of a card catalog.

On the other side of the coin, however, there are
some drawbacks. Unless it is a large library and can
justify a computer of its own, the library loses direct
control over its catalog. The library may have to wait

its turn in the use of computer equipment, rather than have immediate access to the machine. Then, too, magnetic tape is more susceptible to destruction than either the card catalog or the book catalog, and, since the print-out is in book form, we have some of the disadvantages from which it suffers. Since machines are most efficient when doing repetitive work or handling vast quantities of data rapidly, the small library may find that, no matter how good the technology, the computerized catalog is impractical, and it can do better, or as well, by maintaining its manual methods. Finally, we come back to the great human bug-a-boo, that tradition now favors the card catalog.

Before summing up, we can examine a few examples of computer-produced catalogs to see what is currently being done, particularly in regard to different approaches to the problem of format determination. The first example is a page from the catalog of the University of New Mexico Library of the Health Sciences (see Fig. 5). This catalog is a good one with which to start, since it maintains much similarity to those which are familiar to us. It appears that everything needed is given, and one may ask whether more is included than is necessary, since it records size in centimeters and the fact that a book is illustrated. (A recent article describes this catalog.)[2]

A second catalog is one from the Monsanto Company Technical Information Center (see Fig. 6). This is a union catalog for all branch libraries and gives location information in addition to the bibliographic data. The three traditional approaches are used: author, title, and subject. Aside from some truncated entries which may prove bothersome, the catalog is neat and easy to read, as was the previous example.

A third example is a book catalog produced by IBM (not illustrated). The main difference is that this is a KWIC, or Keyword-In-Context, index. Consequently, one finds the subject (keyword) approach presented first. In the bibliography section, the complete citation is given, and, finally, in the third portion or author index one finds the author's name and an identifying code number. This type of catalog is rapidly created by machines with minimal amount of editorial work required. The main problem is that the columns have been photoreduced and have become harder to read, though still twice as big as some columns in the Science Citation Index, where there are four to a page.

PAGE A   13

```
CONWAY HM                                    551.5      CO        C
    WEATHER HANDBOOK   CONWAY PUB 1963
COOKE NM & MARKUS J                          R621.3803  CO        O
    ELECTRONICS & NUCLEONICS DICTIONARY   MCGRAW HILL 1960
COOLIDGE JL                                  519.1 *    CO        C
    INTRODUCTION TO MATHEMATICAL PROBABILITY   DOVER PUB 1962
COOMBS WE                                    692.       CO        C
    CONSTRUCTION ACCOUNTING & FINANCIAL MANAGEMENT   FW DODGE 1958
COOPER JD                                    658.39     CO        C
    HOW TO COMMUNICATE POLICIES & INSTRUCTIONS   BNA 1960
COPPOCK JC                                   338.1      COP       C
    NORTH ATLANTIC POLICY THE AGRICULTURAL GAP   TWENT CENT FUND 1963
COPSON DA                                    664.8      CO        U
    MICROWAVE HEATING   AVI PUB 1962
COPSON HR  & LAQUE FL                         620.1122  LA        C
    CORROSION RESISTANCE OF METALS & ALLOYS   2 ED REINHOLD 1963 /ACS
    MONOGRAPH 158/
COREY ER                                     658.8      CORE      C
    INDUSTRIAL MARKETING   PRENTICE HALL 1962
COTTON FA                                    512.86     CO        C
    CHEMICAL APPLICATIONS OF GROUP THEORY   INTERSCIENCE 1963
COX EB                                       658.1145   CO        C
    TRENDS IN THE DISTRIBUTION OF STOCK OWNERSHIP   PENNSYLVANIA U 1963
CRISP RO                                     658.8      CR        C
    MARKETING RESEARCH   MCGRAW HILL 1957
CRISP RO                                     658.8      CRS       C
    SALES PLANNING & CONTROL   MCGRAW HILL 1961
CROSFIELD LTD                                R338.4766  CRC       C
    CAUSTIC SODA & CHLORINE IN THE SOVIET UNION   CROSFIELD 1959 /EAST
    EUROPEAN CHEM IND 2/
CROSFIELD LTD                                R338.4766  CRCO      C
    COST & PRODUCT DISTRIBUTION IN THE HUNGARIAN CHEMICAL INDUSTRY
    CROSFIELD 1962 /EAST EUROPEAN CHEM IND 8/
CROSFIELD LTD                                R338.4766  CRE       C
    EASTERN GERMANY   CROSFIELD 1959 /EAST EUROPEAN CHEM IND 3/
CROSFIELD LTD                                R338.4766  CR        C
    HUNGARY   CROSFIELD 1958 /EAST EUROPEAN CHEM IND 1/
CROSFIELD LTD                                R338.4766  CRP       C
    POLANDS TRADE IN CHEMICALS 1958   CROSFIELD 1963 /EAST EUROPEAN CHEM
    IND 9/
CROSFIELD LTD                                R338.4766  CRS       C
    SOVIET UNIONS CHEMICAL EXPORTS 1955- 1959   CROSFIELD 1960 /EAST
    EUROPEAN CHEM IND 4/
CROSFIELD LTD                                R338.4766  CRSO      C
    SOVIET UNIONS CHEMICAL IMPORTS 1955- 1959   CROSFIELD 1961 /EAST
    EUROPEAN CHEM IND 5/
CROSFIELD LTD                                R338.4766  CRSV      C
    SOVIET UNIONS CHEMICAL TRADE 1959- 1960 CROSFIELD 1962 /EAST EUROPEAN
    CHEM IND 7/
CROSFIELD LTD                                R338.4766  CRT       C
    TECHNICAL PROGRESS & ECONOMICS IN THE SOVIET NITROGEN INDUSTRY
    CROSFIELD 1961 /EAST EUROPEAN CHEM IND 6/
CROSS PC  & ALLEN HC                         535.842    AL        C
    MOLECULAR VIBRATORS   WILEY 1963
CROSSWELL CM                                 658.22     CR        C
    INTERNATIONAL BUSINESS TECHNIQUES LEGAL & FINANCIAL ASPECTS   OCEANA
    PUB 1963
```

Fig. 6.--A computer-produced catalog prepared by the Information Center of the Monsanto Company in St. Louis. Here the format is rearranged to take advantage of the width of the page.

These three examples are of computer-produced catalogs, but other ways exist of producing a book catalog, using a step-and-repeat camera. The Index Medicus used such methods during 1960-63, employing a Kodak Listomatic

Table I

Does Modern Technology Enable Us to Obtain the Best
Features of Both Book and Card Catalogs?

Features of Book or Card Catalogs	Computer Catalog		
	Yes	No	Maybe
Some Advantages:			
1. Constantly up-to-date	X		
2. Flexible--new entries inserted at anytime	X		
3. Limitless cross-references and entries possible	X		
4. Changes easy to make	X		
5. Mistake easy to correct	X		
6. Multiple copies practical	X		
7. Readable	X	X	X
8. Photocopyable	X		
9. Errors easy to find	X		
10. Cost within reach			X
11. Subcatalogs easy to create	X		
12. One-time cost per item for entry	X		
Some Disadvantages:			
13. Space and cabinets required		X	
14. Susceptible to mutilation and theft			X
15. Volumes unwieldy due to weight and size			X
16. Inconvenient for many users simultaneously			X
17. Reworking data for subcatalogs needed	X		

camera, which photographed IBM cards. One does not even have to use IBM cards, but can photograph existing catalog cards. An example is a divided book catalog created for the St. Louis Junior College District, using a machine called the Compos-O-List (not shown). The Compos-O-List has been set to leave off the bottom of the card, thus getting a few more entries onto a page and making a neater format. This is a good, serviceable way to make a catalog, and, if it is not especially beautiful, it has the advantages of book form and speed of production.

With both computer and camera produced catalogs, where updating is required we are back where we started, issuing supplements and eventually cumulating them.

To summarize, let us look at the main advantages of the book catalog and the card catalog and see what the computer has achieved (see Table I.)

After examining the three columns, it appears that we are in a position really to benefit from the improved technology which now is available. We have gained most of the advantages, have minimized a few of the disadvantages, and, indeed, can look forward like Dr. Pangloss to a computer produced catalog which will be the best possible one, in this best of all possible worlds.

References

1. Schullian, Dorothy M. "Libraries. I. History to 1600." In: Encyclopedia Americana. New York, Americana Corp., 1964, vol. 17, p. 358.

2. Divett, Robert T. "Mechanization in a new medical school library: I. Acquisitions and cataloging." Medical Library Assoc. Bulletin 53:15-25, Jan. 1965.

Bibliography

Kingery, Robert E., and Tauber, Maurice F. Book Catalogs. New York, Scarecrow Press, 1963.

Ranz, Jim. The Printed Book Catalog in American Libraries: 1723-1900. Chicago, American Library Association, 1964.

Chapter III

The Computerized Book Catalog

The Computer Produced Book Catalog

by I. A Warheit

The author is concerned with Information Systems Marketing in IBM'S Data Processing Division in San Jose, California. Reprinted from Special Libraries, 60 (no. 9) 573-77 (Nov. 1669).Copyright by Special Libraries Association.

Until about ten years ago, the American library patron essentially knew only the card catalog. Book catalogs were a historical curiosity that one could see at the British Museum, or they were the ponderous bibliographic tools with which catalogers panelled their offices and occasionally consulted for mysterious and esoteric reasons. Suddenly, beginning in the middle 1950's, book catalogs began to appear everywhere and to be used as finding tools not only by librarians but also by the general public. Book catalogs were to be found in public libraries, medical libraries, technical libraries in companies, undergraduate college libraries, university libraries, government research laboratory libraries and even in bookmobiles.

There are a number of reasons for the resurrection of the book catalog. The rising demands for library services are forcing librarians to provide additional services, to establish more branch libraries, provide mobile services via bookmobiles, build undergraduate and departmental libraries, provide library service at remote locations, expand interlibrary loans, transfer and rotate collections and, in many ways, increase access to the collections and spread library services over larger and larger areas. Union catalogs, library networks, centralized processing and other systems and techniques are being adopted to meet these increasing demands. It is very expensive and, in many cases, quite impossible to provide duplicate card catalogs for all these outlets. Increasingly, therefore, librarians are turning the book catalog to provide bibliographic control

54

to their expanding domains.

In addition, card catalogs are proving hard to maintain. As they age, they deteriorate. Cards are lost and destroyed. Deletions and revisions are neglected, and vandalism is always a threat.

But the most important reason for the recent popularity of the book catalog is the fact that a new technology has made it possible to update and publish book catalogs with great ease and flexibility. Business and industry were quick to grasp the potential of using data processing equipment to produce directories and parts catalogs and librarians were not far behind.

My office started receiving so many inquiries from the IBM field representatives about book catalog problems, that finally in self-defense I prepared an IBM manual on the subject. This was issued in September 1969 as IBM Manual E20-0333, Library Automation--Computer Produced Book Catalog. This manual will be available from local IBM representatives.

The manual does not discuss the utility of the book catalog nor is it concerned with the bibliographic aspects of the catalog. The manual concentrates primarily on the techniques involved in using data processing equipment to produce book catalogs. In this paper, only a few highlights are presented.

Input Devices

First, to use a data processing expression, the record has to be captured. There are a number of different devices that can be used and a number of different work forms. The best known and most used device is, of course, the keypunch. It is cheap, efficient and readily available. Its major deficiencies are that special coding is necessary to produce upper and lower case characters, proofreading the output is awkward and, since it does not produce continuous copy and a bibliographic record fills a lot more than one punch card--it usually takes eight or more cards--special controls must be exercised to keep the decklets of cards together.

It is better, therefore, to use a keyboard device, like a typewriter, that records a continuous record on paper

tape or magnetic tape and at the same time types the information on paper for proofreading.   Paper tape, though,
has several deficiencies.   It is difficult to correct errors on
paper tape and, on occasion, error is introduced by the
mechanism that punches the paper tape; because such errors
are not recorded on the typed copy, they cannot be caught
by the proofreader.

The recording on magnetic tape can be easily erased
and corrected, and since the hard copy which is proofread
is generated from the magnetic record and not directly from
the keystroke, the printout is a true copy of the record.   The
major drawback of the key-to-magnetic-tape recorder is that
it is a more expensive device.   However, its versatility and
the ease by which data input can be accomplished, as well
as the fact that it can be used for many other purposes in
the library--it can produce catalog cards, spine labels, form
letters, serials lists, offset masters for book catalogs, etc.
--are influencing a number of libraries to adopt a magnetic
tape recorder.

The bibliographic record can also be captured by
means of an optical character reader.   Using an IBM
Selectric typewriter with a special type font, the catalog
record can be typed on paper.   The paper copy is scanned
by an optical scanner, and the information is recorded in
machine readable form on punch cards, paper tape, or magnetic tape.   Because of the expense and the very large
capacity of the optical scanner, it is not feasible for a library to do its own optical scanning.   Several libraries,
however, have made arrangements with service bureaus to
have typewritten copy scanned and converted to magnetic
tape at costs that are competitive with other conversion
methods.

It must be emphasized that there are no optical
character recognition devices presently available that can be
used with printed library catalog cards.   The present character readers are limited to restricted fonts and to special
man-machine recognizable characters which have fixed spacing.   The scanners or readers cannot handle proportionally
spaced characters nor the great variety of fonts encountered
on catalog cards.   Even more important is the fact that our
present catalog cards lack such essential information necessary for computer processing as the language of bibliographic
items and field designators.

The best and certainly the most expensive means for capturing data is by a direct on-line terminal connected to the computer.

Information can be encoded directly into the computer via typewriter or visual display terminals. Such on-line preparation of inputs can take advantage of the powerful editing capabilities of the computer. On-line operation not only permits the capture of information while the actual record is being prepared, but, in an integrated or "total" library system, such capture begins with the first acquisitions record. Erroneous data can be "erased" during initial typing. Changes, additions and reorganization of text can be made simply by updating the necessary portions of the original information in storage. Manual retyping of corrected draft or final text is eliminated. Information, therefore, can be captured as it is generated, eliminating the cost and time of retranscription by a keypunch operator.

Although the greatest benefits from on-line operation are obtained as records are being created, this method is also used for the conversion of existing cataloging information into machine readable form. This seems to be especially attractive where the amount of material to be converted is very large.

The more expensive, sophisticated devices have higher throughputs and provide savings in labor costs. They are, therefore, attractive when a large amount of data must be captured. It also explains why the actual reported conversion costs using different input equipment are about the same. As a rule, the economics seem to be affected primarily by the volume of material to be processed and not by the equipment used.

Work Forms

With unit record systems and with some of the early computer systems, librarians and data processing personnel were very concerned about the accuracy of their inputs, notably the recording of data in specific columns of the punch card. As a result, the work sheets were ruled into 80 columns like the IBM card and each letter was carefully written in the proper square. This process is being abandoned in favor of a preprinted work sheet in which each data element of the bibliographic record is set out in a separate box or field. In order for the computer to detect

and identify the various data elements contained in a
bibliographic record such as author, call number, title,
publisher, date, etc., each element has to be identified by
a tag or field designator. The tag can be either numeric or
alphabetic, the latter usually in the form of a mnemonic.
Mnemonics have been used in order to help the cataloger,
reviser, and keypunch operator remember and identify the
field designators. It was soon realized, however, that the
tags were really just a computer problem and the cataloger
and reviser need not be involved at all with the tags. Nor
did the keypunch operator have to remember them if these
tags were preprinted on the work form. In other words, the
human involvement with tags should be minimized as much as
possible.

Where a library already has printed catalog cards or
proof slips, it is unnecessary to make a work sheet. In such
cases the catalog card or a reproduction of it can be super-
imposed on a work sheet outline and the fields indicated, or
the card itself marked, preferably in red or some other con-
trasting color. In some instances where the keypunch operators are part of the cataloging staff, they have been trained
to assign codes or tags, and then no editing of the catalog
card is necessary. The assignment of codes, however,
slows down the keypunch operators and reduces both output
and efficiency.

Of course, where the cataloging is done on-line and
the cataloger himself prepares the inputs and stores them
in the computer, then no work sheets are required. In such
a case, the cataloger can assign the field designators as he
enters each field or, in more advanced systems, as the
terminal calls for each field (author, title, imprint, etc.)
the stored program assigns the field designator. In such
systems, every effort is made to keep from burdening the
cataloger with any of the computer housekeeping, and to
enable him to communicate with the computer, via the
terminal, in a language as close to natural language as
possible.

Programs

Book catalogs may be produced by using the available
program modules of a "total" or integrated library system
or by using a separate book catalog program. From a set
of library programs, the normal catalog creation, selection
and extraction modules can be supplemented by standard

publishing or formatting programs.

Since "total" library systems are just getting under way, all book catalogs to date have been produced by separate catalog programs.

The special programs usually involve the normal card-to-tape and edit modules as well as the various sort and format modules to set up the individual outputs desired: shelf list, author catalog, and subject catalog--the title breakdown usually being combined with the author or subject catalog. There may be other programs such as special cross reference print, special merge modules to print cumulations, authority list prints, especially for catalogs which include report literature where corporate author, contract, and report number cross reference lists are required.

The most important program and one too often neglected is the maintenance program. Since library records are considered to be very stable, and to require few changes, most programmers have not provided special maintenance capabilities. As a rule, when part of a record has to be changed, the whole entry or major portions of it are removed and replaced by a new record. Experience has shown, however, that records are more dynamic than expected. This is especially true for catalogs of several libraries, such as union catalogs or catalogs prepared for libraries in a consortium. Also, catalogers find it a chore to prepare complete work sheets just to make a minor change in an entry. It is strongly recommended, therefore, that a good maintenance program be provided which will expedite the changing of a catalog record.

As part of the card-to-tape program there should be an editing module which checks the validity of the inputs. Some of the possible validity checks are:

Various field lengths such as the LC card numbers are checked.

Sequences of fields and date ranges are verified.

Specific fields such as call number, title and imprint must be present in every record.

If LC classification is used, then the initial character of the call number must be alphabetic and a capital.

Data which must be numeric such as number of
copies, Dewey class number, and line numbers
or tags are checked to see that they are numeric
and not alphabetic.

Termination symbols must be present.

The number of lines for an entry must not exceed
a preset limit.

Duplicate entries must be noted.

Maintenance messages are accepted only for
existing records and the code designating the action
must be present.

Codes for field designators and location symbols
as used to designate branch and departmental libraries are verified.

Filing Order

Filing order is, of course, very important for library
catalogs. Depending on the construction of the heading of
the entry a sort key or tag is created which is used by the
sort program in alphabetizing the entries. Since library
filing has special requirements and because they vary from
library to library, the librarian must take special pains to
indicate all exceptions to the normal sequence or collation
of the computer. Since word by word filing is generally
used in libraries, the presence or absence of a blank is an
important consideration especially when used with abbreviations. For example, U.S. will file differently from U. S.

Two devices are used to indicate exceptions to
machine filing:

Symbols may be placed around a word that is to
be ignored in filing--initial articles for example;
or

A non-printing sort field can be set up.

The latter is especially useful for the proper sequencing of
Roman numerals and B.C. dates as well as handling such
special cases as multipart names. Care should be taken to
select as non-printing symbols those characters which are

not required in cataloging. The greater than (>), less than (<), and @ are examples of characters seldom if ever used in a bibliographic record. Therefore, they may be used as non-printing symbols. Care must also be taken to determine how the computer files punctuation marks, special symbols, ampersands (&) and diacritical marks. In some equipment they are interpreted as a blank, in others they are ignored entirely and in a few they may change the value of a character.

For monographic materials, a primary or major sort key of 80 to 100 characters seems to be adequate. The major sort key is formed from the first 80 to 100 characters of the entry. The minor sort key is formed from the first 40 to 80 characters of the element that follows the heading, usually the title. A third minor sort key of from 5 to 10 characters for the edition statement or date may also be necessary. Public library catalogs have been produced with 40-16-4 sort keys for author and title catalogs and 70-16-5 for the subject section. College and university library catalogs, however, have found the longer sort keys necessary. A few librarians feel that a longer major sort key is necessary in order to file properly the very long corporate author and serial title entries. The total sort field, however, should not exceed 256 characters (bytes); otherwise sorting costs are increased appreciably.

Machinable Inputs

The discussion so far has been restricted to entries generated in the library. Where an entry is received in machine readable form from an outside source, as for example a MARC input, then some additional program modules are required. These programs must be able to read the input, select the records desired and reformat them to fit the format requirements of the library's catalog program. The MARC tapes, for example are in USASCII code. For those installations using EBCDIC codes, it will be necessary to use a formatting program which reads MARC tapes, converts USASCII to EBCDIC and selects records from the input tape and writes them onto an output tape. This program should also be able to select (on the basis of any MARC tag number or the bibliographic data associated with a particular tag number) and then selectively print any designated field, thus performing all selection and extraction functions. It also should punch an identifying card for all or selected records. Such a program is presently in use to match MARC and BNB (British National Bibliography) records.

Printing

The IBM manual includes some discussion of publishing schedules and formats of catalogs, including cumulations, as well as the arrangements necessary for successful coordination of library operations with the keypunch, data processing and printing departments. These are large topics that cannot be covered in this brief review. They are, however, extremely important for the success of any book catalog.

Methods of reproduction are also analyzed including:

1. Directly by the computer line printer as an original plus carbon copies.

2. Directly by the computer line printer onto offset masters with subsequent printing from these masters.

3. Photoreduction of line printer copy with subsequent printing by offset.

4. Electrostatic reproduction directly from paper copy printed by the computer printer; the reproduction is either full size or reduced.

5. Machine composition with the MT/SC (Magnetic Tape/Selectric Composer) and other Selectric machines.

6. Photocomposition with inputs taken directly from the computer or magnetic tape.

7. Microfilm copy either as roll film in a cartridge or as microfiche.

8. Electrostatic printed copy produced from microfilm input.

The various reproduction methods must be carefully considered if one is to have a successful product.

Special Catalogs

One last word is necessary. Special librarians are very often concerned with materials that are neglected because, for one reason or another, they are not amenable to standard cataloging practices. Such materials can be brought under bibliographic control by KWIC (Keyword-In-Context) or better, KWOC (Keyword-Out-of-Context) systems. These are very inexpensive yet extremely effective methods for the preparation of catalogs.

The preparation of such book catalogs requires very little or no additional effort on the part of the librarian. Practically all the work--extraction of the author and subject entries, the bibliographic identification, the sorting, formatting and printing--are all computer controlled and produced. Such catalogs are easy to use and hence, very popular.

Book catalogs, although almost as old as libraries themselves, are only now, with today's technology, becoming a very powerful bibliographic tool.

The Computerized Catalog:
Possible, Feasible, Desirable?

by Wesley Simonton

The author is Professor at the University of Min-
nesota Library School. Reprinted by permission
from Library Resources and Technical Services,
8 (4): 399-407, Fall 1964.

Developments of recent years make it increasingly
clear that we are at the beginning of a new era with respect
to the form and method of production of library catalogs--an
era in which an old product, the book catalog, has been revived as a result of new technological developments, and now
challenges the card catalog as the basic device for maintaining our bibliographic records. It is not yet apparent how
wide-spread or how rapid the change from the card to the
book catalog may be, but because of the clear superiority of
the book catalog on the points of ease of scanning and ease
of reproduction of multiple copies, and because of the hope
it offers of reducing or eliminating the clerical work involved
in catalog preparation and maintenance, it is essential that
we give careful consideration to the feasibility of a book catalog in many library situations.

Of the several possible methods for producing a book
catalog, the most revolutionary one is production by a computer. The product, being basically similar to other book
catalogs, is reasonably familiar to librarians; the production
method as yet is not. This paper represents an attempt to
relate the general parameters of computer operations to the
accepted goals and procedures of our present cataloging
operations, considering whether these goals and procedures
can, should, or must be modified to take advantage of computer techniques and capabilities. In view of the wide range
of computer capabilities and of the sizes of library catalogs,
generalizations are risky, but certain basic questions may be
identified.

In any consideration of the possibility of applying computer techniques to an existing operation, the first step must be a rigorous analysis of the present procedures in their totality. This step, usually done in flow chart form, is necessary because a computer cannot operate or make decisions on the basis of incomplete information, as a human being frequently can and does. This analysis often reveals illogical or inefficient steps in the present operation, as well as gaps in our knowledge of the total process. The second step involves a careful consideration of both present and future goals and products: What are we producing? Does it meet our needs? Do we want something different?

Having, then, analyzed present procedures and con-sidered desired products, it remains to analyze the machine's capabilities and operations, to answer the questions: Can the machine do the job as it is planned? If not, are there alternative ways of achieving the desired results? Or, should the job be re-planned? (The question of relative cost is of course of basic importance, but will not be discussed directly here.)

In considering the present goals and procedures of cataloging as they are reflected in the card catalog, we may identify three broad areas of relevance to our topic:

1. Descriptive cataloging, including entry;
2. Subject control, through subject headings;
3. Filing.

Descriptive Cataloging

With regard to descriptive cataloging, three goals may be discerned:
1. To provide a description of the physical object;
2. To provide one or more "entries" or "access points", with a full description of the work at each point;
3. To "explain" the reason for each entry, that is, to show why it has been made.

The techniques for achieving these goals are essentially identified in the American Library Association Cataloging Rules for Author and Title Entries and in the Library of Congress Rules for Descriptive Cataloging.

Looking first at our techniques for description of the

physical object, the objectives of descriptive cataloging are, in the familiar words of the LC Rules, "(1) to state the significant features of an item with the purpose of distinguishing it from other items and describing its scope, contents and bibliographic relation to other items and (2) to present these data in an entry which can be integrated with the entries for other items in the catalog and which will respond best to the interests of most users of the catalog." To accomplish these objectives, we organize the description into three major parts:

1. The "body of the entry", consisting of the title, the subtitle, if any, the author statement (in some instances), the edition statement, if any, and the imprint;
2. The "collation";
3. "Notes", used as necessary.

We employ a format utilizing sentences and paragraphs, working under basic but not unanimous agreement as to what information should be placed where, and in how much detail. Application of the rules involves examination of the title-page and other parts of the item being cataloged and organizing the derived description into the parts noted above. In passing it may be noted that the tendency to place title-page information in the body of the entry persists, although such a procedure is much less mandatory than under earlier rules.

The Rules for Entry provide guidance in determining the various entries (other than subject headings) for a work and in selecting one of these as the so-called "main entry." In most instances, an attempt is made to select a person or a corporate body as the main entry and the person or group so selected is considered to be the "author" of the work. The main entry is frequently, though not always properly, referred to as the "most important" entry for the work. Hopefully, the rules provide sufficient guidance that the same main entry will be selected by all persons cataloging the work, so that the listing in union catalogs and other single-entry bibliographic tools will be consistent, recognizing, of course, that complete unanimity for all titles cataloged is unlikely.

In applying the rules, the cataloger first considers the physical object, noting what information is given on the title-page, where it appears, and with what degree of typographic prominence. He may also take account of other information found in the work, occasionally even information found outside the work. He then applies the "logic" of the rules to determine the "main" and "added" entries to be made, seeking always to anticipate the "user's" approach and convenience as much as possible. However, the "logic" (at least the logic of "authorship" and "main entry") sometimes conflicts with the assumed, stated, or demonstrated convenience of the user. Thus, for maps, it is frequently asserted that area or subject is a more important entry than the author entry; the recent Standard for Descriptive Cataloging of Government Scientific and Technical Reports, prepared by the Committee on Scientific Information of the Federal Council for Science and Technology, calls for main entry under corporate body for all reports, even if personal authors are identified; for laws, we reject the authorship principle, making entry under an arbitrary "form" heading instead of under the legislative body responsible for them. To an extent, but not completely, the "added entries" solve the problems raised in these and other situations.

Why, then, do we establish a "main entry" for each item cataloged? What are the functions of the main entry? At least five reasons or functions may be discerned. First, in most instances we feel the necessity of assigning primary responsibility to some person or corporate group, that is, of establishing the "author" of the work, on the assumption that selection for purchase or use may be influenced by this assignment of responsibility. Second, in single-entry listings, the main entry represents the only access point. Third, hopefully, we establish an "authority" for subsequent bibliographic references to the item. The fourth and fifth functions are more practical than theoretical; the main entry provides a convenient device for sub-arrangement of items under a given added entry and for locating all the entries for a given item in the catalog.

As a part of the authorship principle, the rules also provide that all of the works of a single author, either personal or corporate, shall be assembled at one point in the catalog. This collocation is achieved by adhering to the use of a single, un-varying form of the author's name, which must differ in some respect from any other similar names in the catalog.

The third goal of descriptive cataloging, explanation of the relationship of a heading to the item described, may be explicit, as in the case of editors, translators, and second

authors, all carefully identified in the heading; it may be
implicit, as in the case of main entry, where the format of
the card identifies the entry as the author; or it may be
tacit, that is, not shown directly and determined only by a
reading of the card.

Subject Headings

In selecting the headings by which we provide subject
access to our collections, we attempt to select a single word
or phrase, usually from an "authority" or "standard" list,
which encompasses the "specific" contents of the item being
cataloged. The term or phrase, however, must be capable
of being used for more than one item in the collection. We
attempt to minimize the user's difficulties in several ways:
by following the practice of specific entry consistently, by
"pre-coordinating" terms to form concepts, e.g., "Classifica-
tion--Music," and by a straight alphabetic filing of multi-
word headings. The structure and punctuation of multi-word
headings vary considerably, again in response to supposed
user convenience, as we utilize adjectival phrases, inverted
adjectival phrases, prepositional phrases, inverted prepositional phrases, and subdivided headings. No attempt is
made to limit the length of the heading. In practice, we frequently find it necessary to use more than one heading for an
item, either because it treats of more than one subject (the
subjects not being subordinate to a single more generic term)
or because no "existing" heading (existing, that is, in our
authority list) covers the concept.

Filing

The various entries for the cataloged items are then
arranged in either a single or a divided file (the latter usually
in no more than two sections), with a growing tendency toward "straight alphabetic" filing arrangement insofar as possible. The "filing medium," that is, the part of the card
which must be considered in filing, may consist of one, two,
or three parts. In the case of main entries, the entry
itself must be filed; unless it is the title of the work or
represents the only entry for the "author" in the catalog,
sub-arrangement by title (the second part) will be necessary.
In the case of added entries, the third part may be added to
the filing medium, with necessary consideration being given
in some instances to the added entry, the main entry, and the
title. Practice varies both between libraries and within a
single library on the point of regarding the main entry in

the filing of added entries; that is, filing of added entries may
be either <u>direct to the title</u> or <u>indirect through the main entry.</u>
Subject entries are sub-arranged either by the main entry or
by the date.

Computer Techniques and Capacities

A computer has been defined as "a device capable
of accepting information, applying prescribed processes to
the information and supplying the results of these processes."[1]
For present purposes, its functions may be identified as
<u>reading</u> (that is, accepting information), <u>computing</u> and <u>sorting</u>
(that is, applying prescribed processes) and <u>printing</u> (that is,
supplying the results). As applied to the cataloging process,
we may say that the computer can:

1. reproduce information with, if desired, either the
   addition of designated new information or the
   deletion of designated parts of the original
   information;
2. sort, that is, file information at designated points;
3. print the results.

How do these abilities relate to the established goals
and procedures of cataloging? Our techniques have for the
most part worked well in our established technology of a catalog made up of cards produced by the typewriter (or some
substitute therefor), but even in the past our goals and procedures have not been accepted without question. For the
most part, the implications of these questions could not be
thoroughly explored because of the limitations of the existing
technology. At the least, the computer provides a chance for
experiments with new formats and new methods of display for
our bibliographic record, and makes it necessary to re-
examine our goals and procedures.

Questions Regarding Descriptive Cataloging

With regard to our present procedures of descriptive
cataloging, there are three basic questions. First, do we
organize the information in the most effective manner? Are
there situations in which material from the title-page, traditionally placed in the body of the entry, might more effectively be presented in "note" form? Second, do we need
the same amount of information at each entry? Third, is the
author statement as necessary as we have assumed? Further,
might it be more effectively presented in note form?

Questions Regarding Entry

With regard to present procedures relating to rules
of entry (other than subject headings), again, three basic
questions may be raised. First, is it necessary, assuming
multiple entry points for a work, to establish a single entry
as the "main entry"; may we not, instead, think in terms
simply of "entries" rather than "main and added entries" for
a work? This question relates to our conception of the basic
function of the catalog--is it primarily a finding list or does
it seek to go further and become, so to speak, an authority
list, determining the "author" for each work listed? Second,
is it necessary always to explain the reason for an entry?
Undoubtedly, we must do so in cases such as editors and
translators, so that we do not present a misleading entry,
but can we logically explain our present practice of using
the term "joint author" on only one of the two entries for a
work of joint authorship? Third, is it essential to assemble
at one point and identify as such the works of a single author?
If no attempt were made to distinguish the various Smith's
in our catalog, it would be easier to locate "Smith's
Principles of Chemistry" than it is at present. Are there
individual libraries or library situations in which the need
for assembling the works of a single individual is so slight
as to lead us to prefer the suggested alternative?

Questions Regarding Subject Headings

With regard to subject heading practice, two basic
questions may be identified. First, do we provide a sufficient number of headings for an item? (Certainly we provide far fewer on the average than are being used in indexing the technical report literature.) Second, should subject
headings describe the contents of the item, as at present, or
should they merely indicate the contents? That is, should
we continue to use our pre-coordinated phrases as necessary,
as opposed to the currently fashionable post-coordinated
"descriptors" so widely used for indexing report literature?
Although both of these questions are of fundamental importance
in our procedures of bibliographic control, they are not as
crucial to the format of the catalog as the others being discussed here and they will not be considered further.

Questions Regarding Filing

With regard to filing techniques, three questions
may be asked: First, how far can and should the practice

of straight alphabetic filing be applied? Second, in subarranging under our present added entries, is it more useful to file by the main entry or by the title of the work? Third, in subarranging under a subject heading, which pattern is more useful: sub-arrangement by main entry or by date of the item?

The Computerized Catalog

Figure 1 illustrates a possible new pattern for a computerized catalog, as compared with present practice. The entries on the left reflect our present practices, with full entries under the first author, the second author, and the subject entry, the latter two entries being duplicates of the first with the addition of the added entry heading. Assuming a printed catalog which stresses brief name entries for ease of scanning and arranges its subject entries in order of cataloging, on the assumption that subject entries are created for browsing, rather than locating a particular item, we might have a catalog with entries like those on the right. Here, instead of a main and an added entry for the two authors, we have simply two entries, each indicating only the entry, the title, the edition and the imprint. We have taken advantage of the computer's ability to rearrange, to add, to subtract data. We have given very brief information under the name entries, on the assumption that the user looking under a name is looking for a single work, or all of the works with which an individual is identified, and not for full bibliographic information concerning those items. We have given fuller information under the subject entries to aid the user in selecting from among the several works on this subject in our library.

Burnett, George Wesley
Oral microbiology and infectious disease, a textbook for students and practitioners of dentistry, by George W. Burnett and Henry W. Scherp. 2d ed. Baltimore, Williams & Wilkins, 1962.
1003 p. illus. 27 cm.

Burnett, George Wesley
Oral microbiology and infectious disease. 2d ed. Baltimore, Williams & Wilkins, 1962.

Scherp, Henry W.
Burnett, George Wesley
Oral microbiology and infectious disease, a textbook for students and practitioners of dentistry, by George W.

Scherp, Henry W.
Oral microbiology and infectious disease. 2nd ed. Baltimore Williams & Wilkins, 1962.

Burnett and Henry W.
Scherp. 2d ed. Baltimore,
Williams &Wilkins, 1962.
    1003 p. illus. 27 cm.

MOUTH-BACTERIOLOGY
Burnett, George Wesley
    Oral microbiology and
infectious disease, a textbook for students and practitioners of dentistry, by
George W. Burnett and
Henry W. Scherp. 2d ed.
Baltimore, Williams& Wilkins,
1962.
    1003 p. illus. 27 cm.

MOUTH-BACTERIOLOGY
    Oral microbiology and infec-
tious disease. 2d ed. Baltimore, Williams &Wilkins, 1962.
    1003 p. illus. 27 cm.

    A textbook for students and
practitioners of dentistry, by
George W. Burnett and Henry
W. Scherp.

Figure 1

    The filing problem remains, however, and it may
prove to be the single element of the process which will
make the application of computers to cataloging most difficult.   There are two major problems here.   First, a
computer can handle readily only straight alphabetic filing
(not to mention the difficulties introduced by punctuation).
Second, the length of the filing medium creates certain practical problems.   With regard to the first problem, the findings of the detailed study made of the feasibility of programming the ALA filing rules for computer filing in connection
with the University of Illinois, Chicago Undergraduate Division
Library project on mechanization of library processes are of
interest:

> 1. A complex coding system must be developed so that
>   the various data which constitute an entry can
>   be recognized and manipulated by a computer.
>
> 2. Codes from this system must be assigned manually
>   by a librarian and translated to a specially de-
>   signed coding form before the input data for a
>   data processing system could be created.
>
> 3. Quite large and comprehensive tables must be
>   developed and be accessible to the computer
>   during the running of the program.   Such
>   tables do not now exist. [2]

In the light of these findings, the following recommendation was made:

> It is felt that most nuances of library filing rules, no matter how worthy their original reason for existence, are largely lost not only upon most patrons, but also upon most librarians. If library cataloging is to be economically assisted by computers and automation, the filing rules should be simplified. Ideally, the arrangement should be straight alphabetical letter by letter to the end of the word, i. e., follow a typical sort routine already available for computers. [3]

The problem of length of the filing medium may also prove a very serious one. A human being can scan as many characters as necessary to file a catalog card, and we have as yet imposed no constraints on the length of our subject headings or on our other entries. If the computer is to file as efficiently as a human being, the length of the sorting area must be as great as that of the maximum entry to be filed, which will run well over one hundred characters. Sorting of this magnitude is costly, and, as a result, some of the presently operational systems utilizing computers have employed numerical codes to represent names or subject headings, to effect more economical filing.

Administrative Questions

Although the purpose of this paper has been primarily to explore the technical questions relating to a computer-produced book catalog, there are two closely related administrative considerations which should be discussed briefly. First, it is a commonplace in enlightened library theory, if not practice, at least as reflected in our literature, that work once done should not be repeated. This assertion is made most frequently with relation to bibliographic verification work in the acquisition and cataloging departments. The introduction of any sort of mechanization in the library will emphasize this position even more, since it is a basic tenet of machine operations that data be recorded only once in the total system. Strict application of this idea to bibliographic processing would call for initiating the bibliographic record of an item when it is ordered, in as close to complete form as possible, the record to be changed or supplemented as necessary later. In the last analysis, the question arises:

Can we catalog a book when we order it? Obviously not, in
many cases.   But if we are ordering from a Library of
Congress proofsheet and we ordinarily follow LC practices
in our cataloging, perhaps we can.   The advantage of such a
procedure would be that both acquisition records and catalog
records might be produced from a single typing.   In any
case, it would seem that we may soon be able to consider a
system in which we change and add to a basic record as an
item moves through the processing cycle, rather than one in
which we create separate, partially duplicative, records at
different stages in the cycle.

     The second administrative consideration relates to the
psychological problems involved in changing from an essentially manual system to an essentially mechanized system, particularly on the point of the degree of technical knowledge
necessary to be attained by the user of the machine.   The
analogy between the computer and the automobile on this point
has by now become a commonplace: just as the driver of the
automobile need know very little of what goes on under the
hood, so the cataloger in a computerized system need know
very little about why the lights are blinking.   After the basic
goals and decisions have been established (not that this is
simple) and programs written to accomplish the goals, the
original form of input to the computer may be quite similar
to that used presently.   Specifically, if the bibliographic information can be presented in a form similar to what Fasana
has called "machine-interpretable natural formal,"[4] employing
various simple devices to impose precision on the data, the
cataloger's work-sheet may look only slightly different from
that of today.

Summary

     A computer-produced book catalog is certainly possible;
its format may or may not be much different from that of
our present card and book catalogs, depending mostly on our
own preferences in the matter.   A computer-produced book
catalog is desirable to the extent that any book catalog is
desirable;   if the filing problem can be solved, eliminating
possible human errors in filing, it becomes even more
desirable. "Feasibility" remains a question, at least if we
include the question of cost.   Book catalogs are being produced by computers today, but for the most part in relatively small, technical libraries with ready access to a
computer.   There is great need for experimentation, with

close attention to cost, both of present and proposed methods, in a wide variety of types and sizes of libraries, before the question of feasibility can be answered. In this period of experimentation, the precepts, patterns, and products of the past must be carefully scrutinized, and only those of firmly established and continuing validity and utility permitted to influence our judgment of feasibility.

References

1. U. S. Bureau of the Budget. Automatic Data Processing Glossary, 1962, p. 12.

2. An Investigation into the Application of Data Processing to Library Filing Rules. A joint endeavor by the University of Illinois Library, Chicago Undergraduate Division, Navy Pier, Chicago, Illinois, and the Burroughs Corporation, 1962, p. 2.

3. Ibid., p. 3.

4. Fasana, Paul. "Automating Cataloging Functions in Conventional Libraries." Library Resources & Technical Services, 7: 352, Fall 1963.

Library Computerization in the United Kingdom

by Frederick G. Kilgour

The author is Director of Ohio College Library Center, Columbus, Ohio. His article is reprinted by permission from Journal of Library Automation, 2: 116-24, September 1969.

When the Brasenose Conference in Oxford convened in June 1966, there were represented only two operational library computerization projects from the United Kingdom: W. R. Maidment, Britain's pioneer in library computerization, had introduced his bookform catalog at the London Borough of Camden Library in April 1965[1]; and M. V. Line and his colleagues at the University Library, Newcastle-upon-Tyne, had introduced an automated acquisitions system just a year later[2]. During the three years following the summer of 1966, British librarians moved rapidly into computerization and have made novel contributions which their American colleagues would do well to adopt. In the spring of 1969 there were more than a couple of dozen major applications operating routinely with perhaps another score being actively developed. The most striking development in the United Kingdom is computerization in public libraries, whose librarians are considerably more active than their colleagues in the United States; at least nine public libraries have computerization projects that are operational or under active development, and as already mentioned, it was a public library that led the way.

The sources for this paper are published literature and an-all-too-brief visit to the United Kingdom in April 1969 to see and hear of those activities not yet reported. The principal literature source is Program: News of Computers in Libraries, now in its third volume. R. T. Kimber, of The Queen's University School of Library Studies at Belfast, edits Program, which he first published

as a gratis newsletter in March 1966.   Kimber has published
the only reviews of library computerization that have contained adequate information on activities in the United Kingdom; the first appeared in Program[3], and the second, an expansion of the first, is in his recently published book.[4]
Program became an immediate success, and beginning with
the first issue of Volume 2 in April 1968, it became available on a subscription basis.   A year later, Aslib assumed
its publication, with Kimber still as editor, and Program
will undoubtedly continue to be the major source of published
information about library computerization in the United Kingdom.   Information & Library Science Abstracts, formerly
Library Science Abstracts, is the one other major source of
published information about British library automation.   It
abstracts articles appearing in other journals and report
literature as well.

Most library computerization in the United Kingdom
has been a genuine advance of technology, in that computerization has introduced new methods of producing existing
products or products that had existed in the past, such as
bookform catalogs.   To be sure, relatively more British libraries than United States libraries have maintained catalogs
in bookform, but the pioneer project at Camden produced a
bookform catalog to take the place of card catalogs.   The
time has come, however, when it is fruitful to think of
products with new characteristics or of entirely new products
unknown to libraries heretofore.   British librarians have already begun to think in these terms. One example (and others
will be reported later in this paper) is the pioneering W. R.
Maidment, who feels that the problem of application of computers to produce existing products has been solved intellectu-
ally.   Maidment is giving serious thought to development of
management information techniques, and automatic collection
of data to be used by librarians, sociologists and others as
a data base for research.   Such research could produce many
findings, including knowledge of effectiveness of formal education programs as revealed by subsequent public library usage,
as well as better understanding of the social dynamics of
public libraries within their communities.

Catalogs

Although users searching by subject may find more
material by going directly to classified shelves than by any
other subject access[5, 6], the library catalog is nevertheless
a major and indispensible tool for making books available

to users. Taken together, descriptive cataloging, subject
indexing, and subject classification constitute the bridge
over which the user must travel to obtain books from a
library. In libraries that are user-oriented, it can be expected that the greatest gain will be achieved by computerization of the cataloging process. Moreover, acquisition activities, as well as circulation procedures, are essentially
based on, and must be interlocked with, cataloging products.

It is, therefore, of much interest that the first
routine British computerization was of the catalog at the
Camden Borough Library[1]. Impetus for this event occurred
several years earlier when the London Metropolitan Boroughs
of Hampstead, Holborn and St. Pancras were combined to
become the Borough of Camden. The problem thereby
generated was how to combine catalogs of three public library
systems so that users of the new system could take advantage
of the increased number of books available to them. Maidment decided to cope first with the future, and introduced a
bookform union catalog in 1965 listing new acquisition in all
Camden libraries and giving their locations. Of course, users
have consulted both the bookform catalog and older card catalogs, but with the passage of each year, the card catalogs
become less useful.

H. K. Gordon Bearman, who directs the West Sussex
County Library from its lovely new headquarters building in
the charming little city of Chichester, is another imaginative
pioneering public librarian. Bearman has keenly evaluated
potential contribution of computerization to public libraries,
and has amusingly assessed the opposition of some to such
advances.[7] The West Sussex County Library possesses more
than a score of branches, for which Bearman has introduced
a computerized bookform union catalog[8], In April 1969 this
computerized catalog contained nearly 23,000 entries.

The library at the University of Essex produces com-
puterized accession lists, departmental catalogs, and special
listings for its science books[9]. At least four libraries are
putting out computerized alphabetical subject indexes to their
classification schemes or to their classified catalogs: the
Library of the Atomic Weapons Research Establishment
(AWRE) at Aldermaston; The City University Library[10],
London, formerly the Northampton Technical College; the
Loughborough University of Technology[11]; and the Dorset
County Library[12], which may be the first library in the

United Kingdom to use a computer, for it issued a computerized catalog of sets of plays in 1964.

One of the most exciting cataloging computerization
projects in the United Kingdom is the British National
Bibliography MARC project under the extraordinarily skill-
ful leadership of R. E. Coward[13, 14]. The BNB MARC
record is entirely compatible with MARC II, and Coward
has introduced worthwhile improvements to it. For example,
he uses indicator positions to record the number of initial
characters to be omitted when an entry possessing an initial
article is to be sorted alphabetically.

In April 1966, the British National Bibliography was
using its MARC records in its process for production of
cards for sale to British libraries. BNB intends to use
the same records for production of the British National
Bibliography. In addition, BNB is fostering a pilot project,
quite like the MARC pilot project, among a score of British
libraries. F. H. Ayres[15] has published perceptive suggestions for use of BNB MARC tapes for selections, acquisitions,
and cataloging.

Although Coward was able to take full advantage of
work done at the Library of Congress, it is enormously to
his credit that he did take that advantage, and that he has
moved so far ahead so rapidly. Since British book production somewhat exceeds American, Coward has doubled the
size of the pool of machine readable cataloging records
available at the present time.

The Bodleian Library at Oxford will be an important
early user of BNB MARC tapes. Robert Shackleton, who
became Bodley's Librarian shortly before the Brasenose
Conference, has worked wonders at that ancient and honor-
able institution, and his principal wonder is Peter Brown,
who became Keeper of the Catalogues late in 1966. Brown
is one of the few members of classical librarianship who
has trained himself in depth in the programming and operation of computers. Oxford possesses no fewer than 129
separate libraries acquiring current imprints and has no
instrument that remotely resembles a union catalog. Hence,
each user must guess which library out of 129 is most
likely to have the book he wishes to use--a guessing game
of which Oxonians notoriously tire. Brown has developed
a system for bookform catalog production which will place
a union catalog of Oxford's holdings in each of its libraries.

Conversion

        The Bodleian is also the scene of the most ambitious
of retrospective conversion projects.   Involving 1, 250, 000
entries, it is by far the largest conversion project in either
the United States or the United Kingdom.   Entries being
converted constitute the Bodley's so-called "1920 Catalogue",
which includes the Bodley's holdings for imprints of 1920
and earlier.   For some years the manuscript bookform slip
catalog that houses these entries has been in advancing
stages of deterioration, and indeed since 1930, entries have
been revised in anticipation of printing the catalog.   To reprint the catalog would require keyboarding the entries to
prepare manuscript copy for the printer, who in turn would
keyboard the entries again in setting type.   There would be
only one product from this process, namely a printed catalog.   Bodleian officials wisely decided to do a single keyboarding that would convert the entries to machine readable
form from which a multiplicity of products could be had,
including a printed catalog.   Brown has worked out details
of schedules and procedures whereby conversion will take
place during the next five years.   A contractor employing
optical character recognition techniques performs actual
conversion, but the contractor does not edit, code, or
proofread the entries, although he is responsible for accurate conversion.   Brown has skillfully developed techniques to diminish the number of keystrokes required in
conversion, and what with labor costs being lower in the
United Kingdom than in the United States, the contractual
cost of 4.17 pence per record is certainly low enough to
attract work from outside the United Kingdom.   The most
significant part of this operation is, however, the identification by computer program of the individual elements of information in the text.   This puts into practice the concepts
of John Jolliffe of the British Museum on the conversion of
catalog data[16];   it was Jolliffe who programmed Oxford's
KDF 9 computer to convert the text coming on tapes from
the contractor to true machine records that are compatible
with the MARC II format.

        Despite the fact that these entries contain no subject
heading tracings, they will constitute the first major source
of retrospective machine readable cataloging records.

        The West Sussex County Library in Chichester and
the University Library at Newcastle-on-Tyne have already
converted their catalogs to machine readable form, the

former having done somewhat less, and the latter somewhat
more, than 200,000 entries. At Chichester, former library
employes did the job on the piece-work basis; at Newcastle
the Computer Laboratory employed a special group. [17]

The large number of records produced by these conversion projects forces urgent consideration of files designed
to house huge numbers of entries. Approaches to solutions
of this problem have begun at the level of individual records
or of file design as a whole. Nigel S. M. Cox, at Newcastle, one of Britain's most widely known library computer
people and co-author of the best-selling The Computer and
the Library (it has been translated even into Japanese), has
developed a generalized file-handling system [18] based on
individual records. Cox has demonstrated that his system is
hospitable to demographic records as well as bibliographic
records. His file handling will surely play a role in future
library computerization.

Circulation

Britain's first computerized circulation system went
into operation in October 1966[19] at the University of Southampton. Books contain eighty-column punched book cards
which are passed through a Friden Collectadata together with
a machine readable borrower's identification card. Punched
paper tape is produced that is input to the computer system.
The principal output is a nightly listing of charges having
records in abbreviated form, with a print-out of the complete
records being produced once a week. The Southampton circulation system works well, and obviously the staff finds it easy
to use. Borrowers also enjoy the system; when the Collectadata is down, as it occasionally is, circulation volume also
goes down, for borrowers avoid filling out charge cards
manually.

F. H. Ayres and his colleagues at the AWRE Library
at Aldermaston are a productive group in research and
development. Aldermaston has a partially computerized
circulation system wherein the computer segment of the
system maintains control features of the circulation record
file, but the master record is maintained manually. [20]

It is understood that the library of the Atomic Energy
Research Establishment at Harwell is developing an on-line
circulation system, but the West Sussex County Library is

the only British library to have on-line access to a circulation file [8], [21]. The circulation system in Chichester is
both experimental and operational. The punch-paper-tape
reading devices at the circulation desk and in the discharge
room were specially designed by Elliott Computers for experimental application for library purposes. However, it
appears that the experimental period is ending, and that the
production of a new model is about to be marketed by Automated Library Systems Ltd. The experimental equipment at
Chichester was to be replaced during Summer, 1969, and six
further installations introduced at the major regional branch
libraries during the next two years.

The on-line circulation records are housed on an
IBM 2321 data cell in the Computer Centre in an adjacent
County Council building. There is an IBM 2740 terminal in
the Library from which special inquiries are put to the file.
For example, overdue notices are sent out by computer using
the same records to which inquiries can be made, but there
are sometimes lag periods, particularly over weekends, so
that an overdue notice may be sent on a book already returned.
When the borrower reports that he has already returned the
book, the file is queried from the terminal. Processing of
these special and time-consuming tasks is thereby greatly
facilitated. On-line circulation files are a rarity, and the
West Sussex County Library and the County Computer Centre
are to be congratulated on their achievement.

Acquisitions

The already mentioned acquisition system at Newcastle [2], [22] has been in continuous and successful operation
for over three years. Although the system does not handle
large numbers of orders, there being only slightly more
than a thousand active orders and four thousand inactive
orders in the file at any one time, there is no reason to
think that it could not cope with a larger volume. Output
from the computer consists of purchase orders, the order
file, claim notices, a fund commitment register, and an occasional list of orders by dealers.

The City University Library has computerized its
book fund accounting[23], its general library accounts, and
its inventory of over 350 categories of furniture and equipment[24]. The last procedure is unique.

AMCOS (Aldermaston Mechanized Cataloging and Order System) appears to be the British pioneer integrated acquisitions and cataloging system[25]. The IBM 870 Document Writing System originally used for output became overburdened after it had produced the second bookform title catalog with classed subject and author indexes. A title listing is employed in the main catalog because the Aldermaston group found in a separate study[26] that users as they approached the catalog possessed less than seventy-five percent accurate author information, while their information about titles was over ninety percent correct.

Serials

The University of Liverpool Library[27] and The City University Library[28] produce periodicals holding lists by computer. At Liverpool the list is restricted to scientific serials but contains 7,600 entries of holdings in 28 libraries, not all of which are university libraries. With each entry are holding information, the name of the library or libraries possessing the title, and the call number in each library. Similarly, The City University Library list contains holdings information and frequency of appearance for each title. The computer program at City University also puts out a list of titles for which issues may be expected during the coming month as well as of all titles having irregular issues. However, this procedure for checking in issues did not prove to be wholly satisfactory and is not currently in use.

The Library of the Atomic Energy Research Establishment at Harwell also puts out a union holdings list for the several sections of the Library [29]. In addition, the Harwell programs, which run on an IBM 360/65 and are written in FORTRAN IV, produce for review annual lists of current subscriptions taken by each library; it also produces annual lists of periodicals by subscription agencies supplying the periodicals.

Dews[30, 31] has described computer production of the Union List of Periodicals in Institute of Education Libraries. This union list first appeared about 1950, was republished annually, then biennially, as magnitude of effort to revise it increased. Both the manipulation and typesetting programs employ the Newcastle file handling system.

Assessment

The most gratifying development in library computerization in the United Kingdom during the last three years has been the rapid expansion of numbers of individuals who have made themselves competent in the field. Among the British participants at the Brasenose Conference were barely a half-dozen who had had first-hand experience in library computerization. The group has increased considerably more than tenfold and has brought quality of British library computerization to a level surpassed by none. Continuing advances depend on the calibre of those advancing; the competence of the present cadre assures exciting future developments.

Perhaps the most distinguishing characteristic of library computerization in the United Kingdom as compared with that in North America is the relatively larger role played by public libraries. Indeed, it was the public libraries at Dorset and Camden that first used computers. American public librarians would do well to follow the lead of their British confreres. In general, Americans can learn from British imagination and accomplishment, can learn of exquisite refinements and major achievements.

British librarians, particularly of large British libraries, have not been a notoriously chummy group. It is, therefore, interesting to observe computerization bringing them together. The new style in solving problems made possible by the computer has suddenly made it clear that libraries heretofore deemed to have nothing in common now seem surprisingly alike. For example, bookform union catalogs at the Camden and West Sussex Public Libraries and at the Oxford libraries can now be seen to be essentially the same solution to the same problem.

Although library computerization in the United Kingdom is but half the age of that in the United States, the quality if not the quantity of British research, development, and operation has rapidly pulled abreast of, and in some areas surpassed, American activities.

References

1. Maidment, W. R. : "The Computer Catalogue in Camden, " Library World, 67 (Aug. 1965), 40.

2. Line, M. V. : "Automation of Acquisition Records and Routine in the University Library, Newcastle upon Tyne, " Program, 1 (June 1966), 1-4.

3. Kimber, R. T. : "Computer Applications in the Fields of Library Housekeeping and Information Processing, " Program, 1 (July 1967), 5-25.

4. Kimber, R. T. : Automation in Libraries (Oxford, Pergamon Press, 1968), pp. 118-133.

5. Bundy, Mary Lee: "Metropolitan Public Library Use, " Wilson Library Bulletin, (May 1967), 950-961.

6. Raisig, L. Miles; Smith, Meredith; Cuff, Renata; Kilgour, Frederick G. : "How Biomedical Investigators Use Library Books, " Bulletin of the Medical Library Association, 54 (April 1966), 104-107.

7. Bearman, H. K. Gordon: "Automation and Librarianship-- The Computer Era, " Proceedings of the Public Libraries Conference Brighton, 1968, pp. 50-54.

8. Bearman, H. K. Gordon: "Library Computerisation in West Sussex, " Program, 2 (July 1968), 53-58.

9. Sommerlad, M. J. : "Development of a Machine-Readable Catalogue at the University of Essex, " Program, 1 (Oct. 1967), 1-3.

10. Cowburn, L. M. ; Enright, B. J. : "Computerized U. D. C. Subject Index in the City University Library, " Program, 1 (Jan. 1968), 1-5.

11. Evans, A. J. ; Wall, R. A. : "Library Mechanization Projects at Loughborough University of Technology, " Program, 1 (July, 1967), 1-4.

12. Carter, Kenneth: "Dorset County Library: Computers and Cataloguing, " Program, 2 (July 1968), 59-67.

13. BNB MARC Documentation Service Publications, Nos. 1 and 2 (London, Council of the British National Bibliography, Ltd., 1968).

14. Coward, R. E.: "The United Kingdom MARC Record Service," In Cox, Nigel S. M.; Grose, Michael W.: Organization and Handling of Bibliographic Records by Computer (Hamden, Conn., Archon Books, 1967), pp. 105-115.

15. Ayres, F. H.: "Making the Most of MARC; Its Use for Selection, Acquisitions and Cataloguing," Program, 3 (April 1969), 30-37.

16. Jolliffe, J. W.: "The Tactics of Converting a Catalogue to Machine-Readable Form," Journal of Documentation, 24 (Sept. 1968), 149-158.

17. University of Newcastle upon Tyne: Catalogue Computerisation Project (September, 1968).

18. Cox, Nigel S. M.; Dews, J. D.: "The Newcastle File Handling System," In op. cit. (note 13), pp. 1-20.

19. Woods, R. G.: "Use of an ICT 1907 Computer in Southampton University Library, Report No. 3," Program, 2 (April 1968), 30-33.

20. Ayres, F. H.; Cayless, C. F.; German, Janice A.: "Some Applications of Mechanization in a Large Special Library," Journal of Documentation, 23 (March 1967), 34-44.

21. Kimber, R. T.: "An Operational Computerised Circulation System with On-Line Interrogation Capability," Program, 2 (Oct. 1968), 75-80.

22. Grose, M. W.; Jones, B.: "The Newcastle University Library Order System," in op. cit. (note 13), pp. 158-167.

23. Stevenson, C. L.; Cooper, J. A.: "A Computerised Accounts System at the City University Library," Program, 2 (April 1968), 15-29.

24. Enright, B. J.; and Cooper, J. A.: "The Housekeeping of Housekeeping; A Library Furniture and Equipment

Inventory Program, " Program, 2 (Jan. 1969), 125-34.

25. Ayres, F. H.; German, Janice; Loukes, N.; Searle,
R. H.: AMCOS (Aldermaston Mechanised Cataloguing
and Ordering System). Part 1, Planning for the IBM
870 System; Part 2, Stage One Operational. Nos.
67/11, 68/10, Aug. 1967, Nov. 1968.

26. Ayres, F. H.; German, Janice; Loukes, N.; Searle,
R. H.: "Author versus Title: A Comparative Survey
of the accuracy of the Information which the User Brings
to the Library Catalogue, " Journal of Documentation,
24 (Dec. 1968), 266-272.

27. Cheeseman, F.: "University of Liverpool Finding List
of Scientific Medical and Technical Periodicals, "
Program, 1 (April 1967), 1-4.

28. Enright, B. J.: "An Experimental Periodicals Checking
List, " Program, 1 (Oct. 1967), 4-11.

29. Bishop, S. M.: "Periodical Records on Punched Cards
at AERE Library, Harwell, " Program, 3 (April
1969), 11-18.

30. Dews, J. D.: "The Union List of Periodicals in Institute
of Education Libraries, " In op. cit. (note 13), pp.
22-29.

31. Dews, J. D.; Smethurst, J. M.: The Institute of Education Union List of Periodicals Processing System
(Newcastle upon Tyne, Oriel Press, 1969).

Chapter IV

Book Catalog Costs

The Economics of Book Catalog Production

by Robert M. Hayes, Ralph M. Shoffner

and David C. Weber

Robert M. Hayes is Director of the Institute of
Library Research at the University of California,
Los Angeles; Ralph M. Shoffner is with
Informatics, Inc., and David C. Weber is
Director, Stanford University Libraries. This
article is reprinted by permission from Library
Resources & Technical Services, 10(1): 57-90,
Winter 1966.

A study was recently undertaken for the Stanford University Libraries to evaluate the economics of various major
methods of producing book catalogs. So as to make it possible for the results to be developed in a form suitable for
wider application, the Council on Library Resources provided part of the funding. This article summarizes the
results of that study. It presents the historical background
and discusses the specific approach, including the use of
equations for each alternative step in production, the information that the user of this method must supply, and
the relationship to typographical quality. It discusses the
particular needs of Stanford University and presents the
results of the application of these equations to the Stanford
Undergraduate Library. It comments on the areas of intellectual judgment involved in designing a catalog.

A. The Rationale for a Book Form of Catalog

The development of the library catalog has paralleled
the growth of libraries. As libraries have increased in
size and complexity, the difficulties in finding books easily
and quickly--by author or title or subject or form--have
similarly increased, and have forced librarians to a continuing exploration of more efficient cataloging forms and
formats.[1] The recent problems of libraries, resulting from

the increased volume of publication and the widened interest
in world literature on the part of scholarly communities,
are not really new.   But the need to solve them is urgent,
as library systems expand rapidly and as collections increasingly are counted in hundreds of thousands or millions
of volumes.   Just as size, economics, and demands for
better service are forcing libraries into branch systems, so
they are forcing library catalogs into various combinations
of card and book listings and away from the ideal of a
single master file.   The reasons are clear:

1.   The need to have catalogs at affiliated libraries:
the growth of the "multi-versity," as well as public and
county library systems, has led to the provision of duplicate
catalogs--such as have been used for the several campuses
of the University of California or for the Los Angeles
County system--and the production of duplicate catalogs is
most feasible in book form.

2.   The size and complexity of any single library
catalog itself: the larger libraries are literally outgrowing
their space for card files, and catalogs are getting too large
to be used easily and effectively.   This has led libraries to
turn toward the book form to ease the physical pressure--
and the book form of catalog seems particularly suited to
materials selected for secondary access or auxiliary
collections.

3.   The heavy turnover of book titles within one collection: with the large effort required to interfile new cards
and withdraw older records, libraries dealing largely with
current publications (increasingly since 1951) have been
prompted to turn to the mechanically-produced catalog, and
again the book form is most convenient for automated output.

4.   The need for consolidated catalogs of holdings,
even on a single campus: since inter-disciplinary growth
complicates the formerly rather clear division among major
departmental libraries, union lists of currently-received
journals and joint catalogs of science holdings are increasingly useful when there is a dispersion of resources--and
these lists and catalogs are most practicable in book form.

5.   The need for multiple copies of the catalog for
distribution over a single campus because of the very heavy
and wide use: again, the easy reproduction of the book-form
catalog makes it attractive.

At the same time, a radically different machine technology is available to meet these requirements. Thus, despite the greatly-increased magnitude of the problems, there may well be less of a gap between them and the ability to meet them than has existed for well over a hundred years. This fact gives administrators a greater possibility than ever before to meet their service requirements. The question which must be answered is this: How should the available technology best be used?

B. Methods for Producing a Book Form of Catalog

To answer this question requires careful, detailed, comparative analysis of the various methods for producing a book catalog. The approach presented in this paper is an analytical one (as contrasted with that of a case study.) It therefore starts by defining those quantitative variables which are significant in evaluating the cost of producing a book form of library catalog and the quality of the resulting product. It analyzes each method into its component productive operations and develops equations which relate their costs to the significant variables.

Specifically, the cost of producing a book form of library catalog and the quality of the resulting product are functions of three classes of variables or constraints that must be related to each other: (1) the characteristics of the collection to be cataloged; (2) the characteristics of the published catalog; and (3) the characteristics of the production method. The important variables in each of these classes have been defined and are listed in Tables 2 and 3. Where possible, normal or typical values are presented for each, but only for the sake of illustration and particular application in the Stanford Library example presented in Sections E and F.

Regardless of the particular method chosen, the production of the book catalog requires the following component steps:

1. Provision of the bibliographical-entry citation.
2. Input of the citation and duplication for the required number of catalog entries.
3. Editing of the input to correct errors.
4. Sequencing or sorting of the new entries so as to put them into the appropriate order with respect to the existing catalog information.

5. Merging the new material with the existing catalog information.
6. Creation of the new page masters from which the catalogs will be produced.
7. Reproduction, collating, and binding to produce the requisite number of catalogs.

Table 1 is a block flow diagram illustrating the sequence of these operations with respect to the various catalog production methods. It can be seen from this figure that there are a large number of alternative procedures which can be utilized in producing a book catalog within most of the major methods. For example, virtually any card catalog can be utilized to produce a book catalog through the use of the first four methods for page-master creation: typing pages, photographing of a shingled layout, photographing of a side-by-side layout, and photographing by use of a sequential camera. Although special arrangements are needed to use the other methods for page-master creation, there are a similar number of choices that can be made.

For each of the processing stages, a number of functional equations have been developed expressing the time and cost in terms of the characteristics of the collection and the catalog to be produced. * The costs of offset reproduction have been expressed in tabular form in Table 4, rather than as an equation, to reflect the many variables involved: weight of paper, type of reproducing master, number of pages printed per run, nature of binding, etc.

C. The Allocation of Costs

In these equations, the cost per unit time for personnel is based on a normal wage per hour for people performing that category of job. For equipment, the "per hour cost" is derived from its purchase and operating costs over the life of the equipment. Indirect, or overhead, costs are for purposes of this study not considered in either case. Particular care, therefore, must be taken in this area. First, the use of "per hour costs" assumes full-time use of the people and equipment, either in direct production or in alternate useful work. Second, overhead costs have been deliberately excluded because methods of allocating burden vary so widely. As a result, the relative costs of the various production methods may be different, depending upon whether overhead is considered.

---

* Tables in which the equations are found have been omitted.

Though these restrictions in the methods of estimation may seem arbitrary, they should not create a great problem for the individual using them. Even in their present form, these equations will at least provide "order of magnitude" estimates which will help people decide whether they are interested at all. If there is interest, a small number of rates may need to be specially determined to obtain more accurate estimates.

The operations listed above as required to produce a book catalog can be grouped into three categories: maintenance of the information file to be made into the catalog; creation of the catalog page masters; and reproduction of copies of the book catalog. The maintenance activities include introducing and duplicating new citations, merging them into the master file, changing records to correct errors, and deleting records for obsolete citations.

The requirements for maintaining the catalog information file are virtually the same regardless of the final form of the catalog--card or book. The costs of the operations in this category will be incurred simply to have available the information about the collection and, therefore, one may question whether they should be considered as a cost of book-catalog production. They are included to ensure a uniform treatment of all sources of cost. However, in establishing a true picture of the cost of the book catalog, particularly in arriving at a selling price for it, these catalog maintenance costs should probably be handled separately.

Furthermore, certain costs, such as those involved in key-punching, may become absorbed by other major functions. For example, an automated acquisition process within an integrated system would also take advantage of the key-punching and could therefore be assigned some proportion of those costs.

Creation of the catalog page master is, of course, a function whose costs are wholly assignable to the production of a book catalog. These costs are dependent upon the number of pages created and, thus, upon the total size of the collection and upon the catalog-page layout chosen. Similarly, the reproduction operations are concerned solely with the production of a book catalog. Reproduction costs consist of a fixed setup charge plus a "per-page copied" charge and, thus, are a function of the number of pages in the catalog and the total number of copies produced.

Because these variable costs are directly attributable to the publication of the catalog and are almost solely a function of the number of copies, it would probably be advisable to print only that number of copies for which there is a guaranteed market. This obviously includes those used in the library itself; it may also include those distributed to other departments. Those which are anticipated for sale to students and outside the library should be estimated very conservatively--the additional spread of fixed costs over a large printing just does not compensate for the gamble with large variable costs.

Due to the large number of equations available for each stage in the production process, no attempt has been made to discuss each possible alternative set of procedures for the production of a book catalog. Instead, a limited number of selected methods have been applied to the Stanford University Undergraduate Library as an example.

As shown in Tables 6, 7, and 8, the analysis of the Stanford University Undergraduate Library demonstrates that, if only the actual utilization of the computer installation is allocated against library usage, the computer is a very efficient approach to standard library technical operations. It must be recognized, though, that the actual amount of usage of the computer is very low and certainly not sufficient to justify a computer installation by itself.

The computer approach is of additional value if consideration is given to the possibilities of special bibliographies, easy catalog revision, integration with acquisitions, and similar fringe benefits. However, costs should not be allocated to these "intangible" benefits unless they are actually included in the design from the beginning. In other words, a system must be completely justified on the basis of all economic considerations involved in its own operation and not on some larger system considerations, "possible" extensions, intangible benefits, and similar arguments. On the other hand, if a system is judged as economically competitive on its own merits, then the fringe benefits are of greater significance. The results of this study indicate that the use of a computer for production of a book catalog is competitive, and therefore, the extended possibilities which it provides should be given consideration.

D. Quality of Typography

Before discussing the Stanford example in detail,

some summary discussion of the over-all characteristics of catalog production should be presented. With respect to methods of reproduction, it was found that offset is the only useful one to be considered as a result of the relatively small printing volume. Offset reproduction can provide a quality of result which for most applications is competitive with that of hot-type printing. The only applications in which hot type would be preferable are those in which a high degree of pictorial quality is required or in which the volume of reproduction is on the order of 20, 000 or more copies. Because the cost of a copy of the book catalog is nearly linear with respect to the number of pages it contains, it is a direct function of the density of entries per page. This entry density in turn is a direct function of the number of characters or lines per entry and the character size (or reduction ratio) utilized.

Because it is desirable to get the maximum number of entries on a page, set-up for the page master by "shingling" is, in general, superior to the "side-by-side" approach. The only application in which this would not be the case would be the one in which the information was located on the card in a manner such that no reduction of white space could be obtained by shingling.

The quality of the typography and the number of fonts available for use in the production of the book catalog have an effect upon the cost. 2 In general, the greater the typographical quality required, the more expensive the creation of the page master. At the same time, the better the typography, the higher the entry density that can be provided on the page, thereby reducing the total number of page masters required and the cost per copy of the book catalog produced. However, though the higher quality typography does allow a more dense catalog, the effect is not great enough to overcome the higher costs involved in producing the page masters. The major justification for the higher-quality typography, therefore, must be greater user satisfaction or utilization. Table 5 shows the relation between the production method and the typography available....

E.   The Needs at Stanford University

In looking forward to the opening of a new Undergraduate Library in the fall of 1966, the librarians of Stanford University began discussion in 1962 of the format and desirable features of the catalog for this library which

will serve most undergraduate needs.   There was general
feeling that, because of the decentralized nature of undergraduate instruction, housing, and library services, no conventional card catalog would be quite as useful as a portable
printed book catalog.   The ideal was to be able to issue to
every incoming student a catalog of the holdings of this core
collection at the same time he received his catalog of courses
of instruction.   Although slight educational advantage might
be gained from having the author and title part of the undergraduate catalog in book form, the subject part of the catalog would on the other hand certainly be a most useful book
when issued in many copies.   "Such a tool in the hands of
each college student would become the first bibliographical
reference work with which the aspiring scholar would be expected to become thoroughly familiar.   From this bibliography of one library the junior and senior would move up to
the use of more specialized bibliographies in the area in
which he is working. "3

In a library building with some 1600 seats on three
large floors, each divided into four major areas, the collection is widely scattered.   To encourage the general education which is a major goal at Stanford, it was decided to
inter-shelve the required reading with the general collection,
marking the assigned books of limited circulation with some
visible sign to indicate their limited duration of circulation.
(Required reading where the library has too few copies to
serve all students from public shelves would, however, be
serviced from a control desk.)   This inter-shelving will
make it essential for the student to work from classified
shelves, being directed there by the catalog.   Thus a student
will use the catalog heavily, and catalogs in each major part
of each floor of the building would seem to be required in
one form or another.   Although subject directories can be
of some use, the index to the entire library should be in
each portion of the building, because a student in his undergraduate years is of necessity crossing major disciplines.
He will do at least some sampling of the literature in all
fields; an index or catalog restricted to one major subject
field would stultify the student's education.

There is not only the need for several catalogs in the
building.   Catalogs would also be useful in the offices of
departments of instruction, in several administrative offices,
at a number of service points in libraries, and, of course,
the chimeric image still permits of issuing each student his
catalog of the core collection.

The extra costs of a book catalog over the traditional card catalog are justified if the service of the library to the student body is markedly improved. When there is simplicity of organization of and access to the library collections, the library is a more efficient instrument of teaching.

F.   Applications to Stanford University Undergraduate Library

The initial holdings of the Stanford Undergraduate Library are planned to comprise some 40,000 titles (60,000 volumes). Additional titles are anticipated the first few years at the net rate of 10,000 per year, with 100,000 titles in the ultimate collection.

This represents, therefore, an ideal example on which to illustrate the application of the general approach presented in Section B. To do so requires the specification of the quantitative characteristics of this particular library. These are listed below. Other parameters, such as equipment speeds, personnel rates, error rates, etc., are taken at the estimated normal values listed in Tables 2 & 3.

The organization and physical characteristics of the book catalog have been decided, insofar as possible, on the basis of criteria external to the intellectual content. In particular, individual subsection volumes should be of a size to be carried in a typical 3-hole notebook, should cover related subject fields--referencing a shelf area in the library--so as to be useful as a study volume, and should be reasonable enough in cost to be sold to the individual student.

First Year:

V_{tf}	= 40,000 (40K citations to start with)
V_{mf}	= 0 (all new entries in the system)
V_e	= 180 (average citation length, 180 characters)
$V_a = V_s = V_t$	= 1 (1 subject code, 1 author, and 1 title per citation)
V_{cop}	= 500 (20 volumes, 1300 pages, 500 copies)
V_{pl}	= 110 (catalog 110 lines per page)
V_{pc}	= 2 (catalog columns per page)
V_{lcm}	= 60 (catalog column-line length 60 characters)

Second Year:

V_{tf}	= 10,000
V_{mf}	= 40,000

Succeeding Years:

V_{tf}	= 10,000
V_{mf}	increased by 10,000 each year

Calculations were carried out using equations in the Tables for the following methods: shingle layout of Library of Congress cards; sequential camera; tabulating record equipment; and computer utilizing upper case only, upper and lower case, and photo-composition. The particular equations represent the preferred approach within each method, based upon considerations of cost and of simplicity of operation. Within each method the appropriate values from above and from Tables 2 and 3 were substituted, and the equations solved for the time and costs required for each operation.

Tables 6-8 summarize the costs calculated for the first, second, and fifth years. It must again be emphasized that because of the choice made for costs of personnel and equipment, these figures represent direct costs before the allocation of non-productive time of overhead. The equations will, of course, permit the use of burdened rates instead.

The results of this calculation were encouraging. The next step was a cost comparison conducted at Stanford of the card catalog and the book catalog in the particular setting of Stanford's library. For the test to be fair, it was decided to compare three complete card catalogs (one on each floor of the building) with fifty copies of the book catalog (distribution is suggested in Table 9). It should be added that the size and configuration of the building seemed to urge complete card catalogs on each floor; and, in addition, it could hardly have been a fair comparison to place the costs of a single card catalog against the substantial advantages of having fifty book catalogs in strategic locations. The results of this detailed comparison are summarized in Table 10.

The book catalog, it may be noted, would be printed once each yeer, in August. During the following ten months, cumulated monthly lists would be prepared, in a few copies, recording the new books added to the collection and including notices of books being purchased but which are not yet formally added to the collection.

Consideration of these figures showed that if the cost of the special computer printing chain is eliminated, which was thought reasonable, a book catalog would initially be $13,000 less expensive than a card catalog. When the collection is mature, as in the theoretical year 7, the book catalog would cost annually approximately $9,000 more than the card catalog.

The cost differential could be reduced by printing the complete catalog only every second or third year. This seems feasible, with monthly cumulated supplements between full editions, after the large initial build-up--say after the fifth or sixth year. And it might be desirable periodically to publish a larger edition of the whole catalog, or subject parts, with consequent economies to be realized through the larger edition. Finally, it was acknowledged that, while machines have their hidden costs, personnel recruiting, training, benefits, and so forth also constitute very substantial hidden costs. While salaries for manual tasks will continue to rise, it may be hoped that improvements in computer technology and printing techniques will hold these expenses to more modest increases.

In a meeting held December 9th, 1964, Stanford University administrators regarded the costs of the book catalog as reasonable in relation to its value, and it was decided to proceed with the book catalog for the Undergraduate Library.

G.   Judgments in Designing a Library Catalog

In selecting the form of a library catalog there are various judgments to be made. First and foremost, the intellectual values must be studied. It seems clear that there have been, up to now, far too few of these studies seriously undertaken. There have been some studies of catalog use, particularly the 1958 Jackson and Mostecky study, [4] the studies of the use of the catalog at the University of California in Berkeley, [5] and a careful review by Robert D. Stevens. [6] But these studies still fall short of the total requirement.

An even greater lack exists: there has been exceedingly little effort to understand fully the human elements in the use of library catalogs. For example, almost nothing exists on the "human engineering" of the catalog as a gross instrument for assisting an intellectual effort. This needed type of study is exemplified by "Report on a Study of Behavioral Factors in Information Systems," conducted by John A. Postley and Gary Carlson of the Advanced Information Systems Department of Hughes Dynamics in 1963; and R. W. Trueswell, "User Behavioral Patterns and Requirements and Their Effect on the Possible Applications of Data Processing and Computer Techniques in a University

Library" (Ph. D. dissertation, Northwestern University, 1964.)

The human engineering of the book catalog divides into three major aspects, each of which deserves further study.   One is the design of the bibliographical entry, treatment of cross references, formatting of the secondary entries, and syndetic relationships to supplements and indexes.   The second is the formatting for ease of scanning, including matters of type face, column length, size of page, bold face use, proportion of white space in leading and margins, and running heads and other devices which help the rapid narrowing of the search range (as is accomplished by the tray labels and guide cards in the card catalog). The third aspect is the packaging for ease in handling, the first approach to this being Section C of the "Preferred Practices in the Publication of Book Catalogs" issued by the American Library Association in 1962. 7

Once the intellectual values of the content and the format design of a catalog can be determined, there is a further question of the number of copies required--the advantages of multiple location.   The need and value of this duplication can only be determined through a local study of the means of communication in a campus geography, as in any community as an ecological environment.   It requires weighing of ease of access and time-access factors with costs. 8

Finally, the content and format of the catalog having been chosen and its multiple locations determined, the next step is to select the method by which to produce the instrument.   For this procedural decision, the recent study summarized by this article provides a methodology applicable to any library system or other document retrieval agency.

References

1.   The historical development is indicated in: Weber, D. C. "The Changing Character of the Catalog in America. " Library Quarterly, 34:20-33. January 1964.

2.   Cornog, D. Y. , et al. Legibility of Alphanumeric Characters and Other Symbols, I. A Permuted Title Index and Biography.   United States Department of Commerce, December 15, 1964.

3. Freitag, W. M. "Planning for Student Interaction with
    the Library Through Bibliographical Analysis and
    Physical Organization. " California Librarian, 26:95.
    April, 1965.

4. Jackson, S. L. Catalog Use Study, ed. by Vaclav
    Mostecky.   American Library Association, 1958.

5. Amy W. Nyholm in College and Research Libraries,
    9:195-201, July 1948; and Anne Ethelyn Markley,
    in Journal of Cataloging and Classification, 6:88-95,
    Fall 1950.

6. Stevens, R. D. "Bibliographic and Cataloging Standards
    for Book Catalogs. " In Kingery, Robert E. , et al. ,
    eds. Book Catalogs.   Scarecrow Press, 1963, p.
    129-43.

7. ALA Bulletin, 56:836-37, October 1962.

8. Cf. Piternick, George. "Duplicate Catalogs in Uni-
    versity Libraries. " Library Quarterly, 34:68-76.
    January 1964.

Table 1

Flow Chart Summary of Book Catalog Production Methods

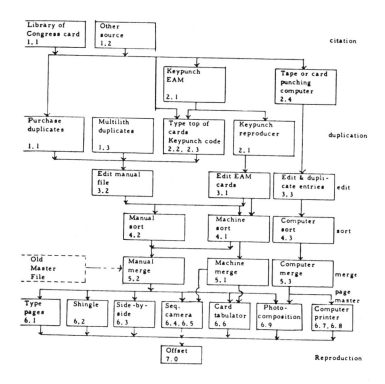

Table 2

Quantitative Parameters

Variable Quantities--Characteristics of Catalog Produced	Estimated normal values
V_{tf} = size of transaction file, number of new citations	
V_{mf} = size of total collection (master file), number of citations	
V_c = average number of characters per citation	180
V_{cop} = number of catalog copies	
V_{error} = error rate; percent of citation errors	3
V_a = average number of authors per citation	1
V_s = average number of subjects per citation	1
V_t = average number of titles per citation	1
V_{asf} = number of characters per author sort field	15
V_{ssf} = number of characters per subject sort field	20
V_{tsf} = number of characters per title sort field	15
V_{ah} = number of author headings per author entry	0
V_{sh} = number of subject headings per subject entry	.06
V_{th} = number of title headings per title entry	0
V_{ahl} = number of characters per author heading	
V_{shl} = number of characters per subject heading	30

Table 2, Quantitative Parameters (Cont'd) — Estimated normal values

			Estimated normal values
V_{thl}	=	number of characters per title heading	
V_{cfsl}	=	cards per frame for shingle layout	30
V_{cfssl}	=	cards per frame for side-by-side layout	21
V_{linofa}	=	number of fonts per author entry	2
V_{linoft}	=	number of fonts per title entry	2
V_{linofs}	=	number of fonts per subject entry	2
$V_{tab\ b}$	=	blank lines per entry (tabulator)	1
V_{lcm}	=	column line length, number of characters per line column	60
V_{cms}	=	column line spacing, number of blank column lines per column line	.25
V_{pl}	=	page spacing, number of lines per page	110
V_{cp}	=	number of columns per page	2
V_{cmcl}	=	number of computer core locations	8000
V_{ppcl}	=	number of core locations used by print program	2000
V_{tab}	=	number of columns for tabular method-- sequencing within citation and gang punching (sort and control)	20
V_{page}	=	number of pages per sheet side	2
V_{pass}	=	number of passes per copy sheet side	1
V_{td}	=	number of characters per magnetic tape designator	$\log_{10}(10V_{tf})$

Machine Speeds (K = 1000)

S_{sort}	=	card sort speed in senses per hour	60K

Table 2, Quantitative Parameters (Cont'd)   Estimated
                                                   normal values

S_{col}	=	card collator in cards per hour	14K
S_{rep}	=	card reproducer in cards per hour	6K
S_{int}	=	card interpreter in cards per hour (will not be needed unless different procedure)	
S_{tab}	=	card tabulator in cards per hour	6K
S_{tt}	=	speed of tape typewriter in characters per hour	29K
S_{kd}	=	keypunch duplication speed in characters per hour	65K
S_{phot}	=	photon speed in characters per hour	29K
S_{lino}	=	linofilm speed in characters per hour	18K
S_{list}	=	listomatic speed in cards per hour	14K
S_{cmp}	=	computer printer speed in lines per hour (1403) upper and lower case upper case	14K 36K
S_{cs}	=	card switch time for keypunch, hour per card	.003
S_{cmc}	=	computer card read time in cards per hour	48K
S_{cmt}	=	computer paper tape read time in characters per hour	1800K
S_{cpt}	=	computer paper tape punch time, characters per hour	540K
S_{linofc}	=	time per font change (linofilm), hour per change	.0003
S_{recon}	=	read speed of linofilm tape converter computer, characters per hour	420K

Table 2, Quantitative Parameters (Cont'd)   Estimated
normal values

S_{wricon} = punch speed of linofilm tape converter,
lino characters per hour   140K

Machine Constants

C_{sort} = senses per column sort   1. 7

C_{lino} = computer codes per linofilm code   3

Manual Rates

M_t = manual typing rate in characters per hour   7K

M_k = manual keypunching rate in characters
per hour   7K

M_f = fixed sort, collate time, hour per entry   . 0025

M_v = variable sort, collate time, hour per card   . 0008

M_{cs} = card switch time, hour per card   . 0015

M_{sl} = side-by-side layout time and shingle
layout time, hour per card   . 0017

M_{pl} = photo layout time, hour per frame   . 004

M_{check} = check characters per hour   18K

Prices

P_{LC1} = price for first Library of Congress library
card $. 07

P_{LCe} = price for each extra Library of Congress
library card $. 05

P_{md} = price per citation source material multilith
duplication $. 17

P_{cc} = price per card catalog card $. 0045

P_{pc} = EAM price per card $. 001

P_s = strip in cost $. 20

Table 2, Quantitative Parameters (Cont'd)

Estimated
normal values

P_{fo} = fixed price per offset master

P_{fm} = fixed price per multilith master

P_{paper} = paper price per copy sheet side

P_{run} = run price per pass

P_{ocp} = offset price per copy page

P_{mcp} = multilith price per copy page

See Table 4

P_g = gathering price per sheet side

P_{gcp} = gathering price per copy page

P_{fold} = folding price per sheet side per fold

P_{fcp} = folding price per copy page per fold

P_c = cutting price per sheet side per cut

P_{ccp} = cutting price per copy page per cut

Table 3
Equipment Costs

Equipment	Rate	Cost	Inferred Cost/Hour
IBM Card Punch 26		\$ 60/month	\$ .35
IBM Sorter 83	1000 senses /min	110/month	.70
IBM Reproducer 514	100 cards /min	110/month	.70
IBM Collator 85	240 cards /min	125/month	.75
IBM Tabulator 407 (96 col.)	100 cards /min	400/month	2.40
Tape Typewriters			
DBM Dura Machine 10	15/char sec	3,300	.40
Friden Flexowriter	8 char/sec	2,400	.30
Friden Justowriter			
Punch unit		3,160	.35
Print unit	8 char/sec	2,910	.35
Invac TMP-200	15 char/sec	4,300	.50
Smith Corona Typetronic	30 char/sec	4,295	.50
Line Composer (Varityper)	manual	3,165	.35
Photon Keyboard	manual	18,500	2.20
Linofilm Keyboard	manual	18,500	2.20
Photon Photo Unit	8 char/sec	40,000	4.75
Linofilm Photo Unit	5 char/sec	44,950	5.35
Linofilm magnetic to paper tape converter	40 Linofilm char/sec	60,000	7.15
Sequential Cameras			
Foto-list (Vari-typer)	120 cards/min	18,500	2.20
Listomatic (Kodak)	230 cards/min	20,500	2.45
Compos-o-Line (Lithoid)	120 cards/min	13,700	1.65
IBM 1401 Computer	11 milliseconds access time[1]		100.00

[1]Rates are dependent upon function performed

Table 4

Costs of Offset Printing

7.0

Paper Size	V_{copies}	P_{paper}	P_{run}	V_{pass}	V_{page}	P_{fm}	P_{fo}	P_{mcp}	P_{ocp}
8-1/2x11"	100	$.001	$.003	1	1	$2.00	$5.50	$.024	$.059
8-1/2x11"	500	.001	.003	1	1	2.00	5.50	.008	.015
8-1/2x11"	1000	.001	.003	1	1	2.00	5.50	.006	.010
11"x17"	100	.0025	.005	1	2	---	8.00	---	.044
11"x17"	500	.0025	.005	1	2	---	8.00	---	.012
11"x17"	1000	.0025	.005	1	2	---	8.00	---	.008

Paper Size	V_{page}	P_g	P_{fold}	P_c	P_{gcp}	P_{fcp}	P_{ccp}
8-1/2x11"	1	.001	.0005	.0002	.001	.0005	.0002
11"x17"	2	.0015	.0005	.0002	.0008	.0003	.0001

The prices shown are for black ink on 20 or 16# white bond.

Table 5

Typography Available

Output Method	output form				
	upper case		upper and lower case		
	1 font 1 type size	1 or 2 fonts 1 or 2 type sizes	1 font 1 type size	1 or 2 fonts 1 or 2 type sizes	multiple fonts and type sizes
hot type	1	1	1	1	1
photo-composition	1	1	1	1	1
type pages	1	3	1	3	3
shingle layout	1	3	1	3	3
side-by-side layout	1	3	1	3	3
sequential camera	1	3	1	3	3
tab card printer	1	2	5	5	5
computer printer	1	2	4	4, 2	5

Key:

1. No restrictions
2. Must strip in sections with extra font or type size[1]
3. Possible, but preparation costs increased
4. Must use special print chain
5. Not possible

---

1. The assumption is made that the extra font and/or type size would be used mainly in headings. If a different type size and/or font were desired for each citation, the 2 in the table should be replaced by a 3.

Table 6

Summary of First Year Costs Estimatss
for Stanford Undergraduate Library[1]

Operation	Manual	Sequential Camera	Unit Record	Method Computer Upper Case	Computer Upper & Lower Case	Computer Photo-Composition
1. Citation	$ 2,800	$ 2,800	$ 2,800	$ 2,800	$ 2,800	$ 2,800
2. Duplication	6,800	8,240	6,005	4,440	4,440	4,440
3. Editing	4,300	4,480	2,390	2,195	2,370	2,370
4. Sorting	1,000	1,000	725	430	430	430
5. Merging	-	-	-	-	-	-
SUBTOTAL	$14,900	$16,520	$11,930	$ 9,865	$ 10,040	$ 10,040
6. Page Creation	26,200[2]	255	880[3]	805[3]	1,315[3]	9,480
7. Reproduction	14,700	14,700	14,700	14,700	14,700	14,700
SUBTOTAL	$26,725	$14,955	$15,580	$15,505	$16,015	$ 24,180
TOTAL	$41,625	$31,475	$27,510	$25,370	$ 26,045	$ 34,220

1. These figures represent direct costs before the allocation on nonproductive time or of overhead.
2. Reproduction costs are higher than for other methods due to lower entry density on the page.
3. Cost includes $480 for stripping in 3,000 subject headings in a special font, such as bold face.

Table 7

Summary of Second Year Costs Estimated
for Stanford Undergarduate Library

			Method			
					Computer	
Operation	Manual	Sequential Camera	Unit Record	Upper Case	Upper & Lower Case	Photo-composition
1. Citation	$ 700	$ 700	$ 700	$ 700	$ 700	$ 700
2. Duplication	1,700	2,060	1,500	1,100	1,110	1,110
3. Editing	1,075	1,120	595	550	590	590
4. Sorting	250	250	185	110	110	110
5. Merging	1,000	1,000	428	40	40	40
SUBTOTAL	$ 4,095	$ 5,130	$ 3,405	$ 2,510	$ 2,550	$ 2,550
6. Page Creation	655	315	1,100	1,005	1,645	11,850
7. Reproduction	32,750	18,300	18,300	18,300	18,300	18,300
SUBTOTAL	$33,405	$18,615	$19,400	$19,305	$19,945	$30,150
TOTAL	$37,500	$23,745	$22,805	$21,815	$22,495	$32,700

Table 8

Summary of Fifth Year Costs Estimated for Stanford
Undergraduate Library

Operation		Shing-ling	Sequen-tial Camera	Tabu-lating	Computer		
					Upper Case	Upper & Lower Case	Photo compo-sition
1.	Citation	$ 700	$ 700	$ 700	$ 700	$ 700	$ 700
2.	Duplication	1,700	2,060	1,500	1,000	1,100	1,100
3.	Editing	1,075	1,120	595	550	590	590
4.	Sorting	250	250	185	110	110	110
5.	Merging	1,000	1,000	425	70	70	70
	SUBTOTAL	$ 4,095	$ 5,130	$ 3,405	$ 2,540	$ 2,580	$ 2,580
6.	Page Creation	1,050	510	1,760	1,610	2,630	18,960
7.	Reproduction	52,400	29,400	29,400	29,400	29,400	29,400
	SUBTOTAL	$53,450	$29,910	$31,160	$31,010	$32,030	$48,360
	TOTAL	$57,545	$35,040	$34,565	$33,550	$34,610	$50,940

Table 9

Tentative Distribution List of Book Catalogs
Stanford University Undergraduate Library

4-Second floor pavilions in Undergraduate Library

2-Second floor lobby, in front of staff service center

4-Third floor pavilions

2-Fourth floor central area, north and south of light well

1-Reference desk

2-Reference and Librarian's offices

1-Audio Library service desk

—

16-Total in Undergraduate Library

2-Main Library union catalog (on north and south counters)

3-Main Library service desk (Circulation, Reference, and Government Documents)

9-Departmental libraries (Engineering, Education, Music, Art, Physics, Mathematics, Biology, Earth Sciences, and Chemistry)

2-Catalog Division and Gift Department

3-Administrative offices (Dean of Undergraduate Instruction, Humanities and Sciences, and Western Civilization Office)

2-Library offices (Director and Chief of Acquisition Division)

13-Unassigned (to Overseas Campuses or campus residences?)

—

50

Table 10

Comparative Costs: 3 Card Catalogs and 50 Book Catalogs

	Year 1: Basic Collection, 40,000 Titles		Year 2: 50,000 Titles		Year 5: 80,000 Titles		Year 7: 100,000 Titles	
	card cat.	book cat.	card cat.	book cat.	card cat.	book cat.	card cat.	book cat.
A. Preparation of entries:								
1. Card Cat.:Typing of masters; adding headings to cards.	$11,200	$11,060	$ 2,800	$ 2,765	$ 2,800	$ 2,765	$ 2,800	$ 2,765
2. Book cat.: Keypunching.								
B. Sorting:								
1. Card:Filing cards.	4,800	3,050	2,400	3,312	2,400	4,272	2,400	4,939
2. Book:Machine sorting;page creation;cumulative monthly list of new books								
C. Reproduction:								
1. Card:Offset reproduction of cards.	10,800	4,324	2,700	5,405	2,700	8,649	2,700	10,811
2. Books:Offset reproduction of pages.								
D. Equipment:								
1. Card:Catalog cases	7,200	3,750	1,800	938	1,800	938	1,800	938
2. Book: Binders								
E. Services: Book:Programming	---	3,000	---	---	---	---	---	---
SUB-TOTALS	$34,000	$25,184	$ 9,700	$12,420	$ 9,700	$16,624	$ 9,700	$19,453
F. Special charges: Book: Attachment to computer for upper and lower case typeface	---	6,080	---	2,880	---	2,880	---	2,880
TOTALS	$34,000	$31,264	$9,700	$15,300	$9,700	$19,504	$9,700	$22,333

Chapter V

The National Union Catalog

History of The National Union Catalog,

Pre-1956 Imprints

by John W. Cronin

John Cronin is the former Director of the Processing Department at the Library of Congress. This
article is reprinted by permission from Prospectus
for the National Union Catalog, Pre-1956 Imprints.
London, Mansell, 1967, p. 11-18.

The National Union Catalog, maintained by the Library
of Congress since 1901, is the central record of the locations of important research titles in the major research libraries in this country and in Canada.[1] More than seven
hundred research libraries are reporting to it, mostly university libraries, large and small. Included also are
special libraries and a few libraries with basically general
collections which acquire and report such unusual materials
as products of local presses, non-American publications,
and non-trade publications. The establishment and maintenance of such a control record serve in various ways.
Many conceive of it as a general bibliography, that is, a
list of books and pamphlets published anywhere at anytime.
But, to quote Richardson, speaking at the ALA Conference
of St. Louis in 1904:

> With pure bibliography the librarian, as librarian,
> has nothing to do, although as student or book-
> lover he may be deeply interested in it.... The
> special applied bibliography in which every librari-
> an is most directly interested is the catalog of
> his own library.... But every librarian very soon
> finds the limitations of his own library at a
> thousand points, and the practical need of referring
> readers to books that one does not have in one's
> own library has led to the ... inter-library cata-
> log.... This joint catalog, or cooperative catalog,

or inter-library catalog, is the highest development of applied bibliography to-day and the proper theme of such a session as this is the possible extension of the cooperative catalog. 2

This general catalog, which makes the important book resources of the nation accessible to the scholarly community and, so to speak, makes them part of each scholar's own library, is a key to the major part of the knowledge recorded in book form in this country's large libraries. This control function, presently limited to the approach by main entry and, to a certain degree, by added entries for persons or organizations connected with the authorship of book, sometimes also by added entries for titles, is the main function of the interlibrary catalog.

Other secondary functions, or, one might say, by-products, of the National Union Catalog should not be neglected: the "pure" bibliographical or reference function, the identification or confirmation of the existence of a publication, as mentioned above; the acquisition function, not in the sense of where to acquire a specific item but whether to acquire it, perhaps better called the book-selection function, that is, the strengthening of American resources by acquiring materials not yet reported, and correspondingly by refraining from expenditures resulting from needless duplication of acquisitions; finally, and very much in the foreground today, the function of a cataloging tool.

To have the entire National Union catalog made available to all American libraries to use for location, reference, book selection, and cataloging, will be a step comparable only to the establishment of the card-distribution service by the Library of Congress at the beginning of the century. It will constitute the greatest cooperative library tool in existence. Such developments were clearly foreseen long ago.

Background of the National Union Catalog

The standardization of cataloging, which had received its greatest impetus from Charles A. Cutter's Rules for a Dictionary Catalogue in 1876, and the introduction of the standard catalog card were the two basic factors which made possible the beginning of cooperation, namely, the interchange of cards among libraries. Thus the foundations of the National Union Catalog of today were laid. As soon as the

Library of Congress had undertaken to print cards for its
own catalogs, Herbert Putnam, then Librarian of Congress,
in his Report of the Librarian of Congress for the Fiscal
Year Ending June 30, 1901, wrote:

> It is fully recognized by the Library of Congress
> that next in importance to an adequate exhibit of
> its own resources, comes the ability to supply in-
> formation as to the resources of other libraries.
> As steps in this direction may be mentioned:
>
> First. The acquisition of printed catalogues of
> libraries, both American and foreign.
>
> Second. An alphabetic author catalogue on cards
> of books in department and bureau libraries in
> Washington.
>
> Third. A similar catalogue of books in some of
> the more important libraries outside of Washington.
>
> The library of Congress expects to place in each
> great center of research in the United States a
> copy of every card which it prints for its own
> catalogues; these will form there a statement of
> what the National Library contains. It hopes to
> receive a copy of every card printed by the New
> York Public Library, the Boston Library, the
> Harvard University Library, the John Crerar Li-
> brary, and several others. These it will arrange
> and preserve in a card catalogue of great collec-
> tions outside of Washington [p. 241].

In following up this program he reported for the fiscal year ending June 20 1909 on the exchange arrangements
with a number of libraries including the Boston Public Library, Harvard, John Crerar, and the New York Public
Library, and expressed his belief that after completion of
the filing "the Union Catalogue ... will constitute the closest
approximation now available to a complete record of books
in American libraries" (p. 57). With the contribution by
these libraries and other institutions joining later, notably
the Newberry Library and the libraries of the University of
Illinois and of the University of Chicago, the National Union
Catalog became "a selective repertorium of the research
libraries of the United States. "[3]

For the first quarter of a century the Union Catalog was operated by the Card Division of the Library of Congress without a special staff for maintenance or service. No attempt was made to revise main entries or to avoid duplication, and the principal use made of the Union Catalog was by Library of Congress catalogers, although a limited location service was offered.

By 1926 the Union Catalog had grown to a file of nearly two million cards, but it was inadequate to meet the needs of American scholarship or to assist librarians in solving the problem of locating research books in other libraries. The resulting widespread demand for a comprehensive union catalog was presented by the American Library Association to John D. Rockefeller, Jr. Rockefeller gave the Library of Congress a gift of $250,000 ($50,000 a year for five years) for the purpose of extending the Union Catalog as rapidly as possible to locate at least one copy of every important reference book in American libraries. This gift was administered during the period 1927-32 as "Project B." During the operation of the project, 6,344,356 cards were added to the Union Catalog. The termination of "Project B" was followed by the establishment of the Union Catalog Division in September 1932.

From 1932 until 1943 the appropriation for the Union Catalog Division averaged about $25,000 per year as compared with the annual budget of $50,000 per year available under the Rockefeller grant. During this period of severely curtailed activity, the growth to the catalog was pushed to limit possible under the reduced budget and a total of 3,355,941 cards was added to it. Mention should be made here of the encouragement and assistance provided during a difficult period by the American Library Association's Committee on the Resources of American Libraries, which was established in 1923 under the chairmanship of James T. Gerould and reorganized in 1936 as an ALA board, with William Warner Bishop as chairman.

As early as 1912 Bishop had mentioned the need of a tool to locate books in the United States, had pointed to the cooperative cataloging on Library of Congress printed cards undertaken by the government libraries in the District of Columbia and files of cards printed by other libraries for books not represented in the Library of Congress, and had called for the expansion of the small Union Catalog. "The next step," he said, "is to go on with this union catalog

enlarging it in every way possible, and making it available
to investigators, both away from Washington and here."[4] His
membership of the ALA committee gave an especial continu-
ity to the group, since he had served on the first committee
in 1923 and continued to serve on the board as consultant for
a number of years after he ceased to be its chairman.

In 1943 the Union Catalog appropriation was increased,
making it possible during the next five years to bring into it
the contents of the regional union catalogs in Cleveland and
Philadelphia, and to add 221,000 cards from the other federal
libraries. In 1948 the Union Catalog was officially designated as the National Union Catalog. Between 1948 and 1950
the Yale University Library catalog was microfilmed and the
contents of the North Carolina Union Catalog were copied.
Later the shelf list of the University of California was microfilmed and other important collections copied. Growth since
then has been steady, and the National Union Catalog now
contains more than 16 million cards. These cards reflect
about 10 million titles and editions.

The Book Catalogs: their development from
Library of Congress Catalogs to Union Catalogs

The National Union Catalog and the other card catalogs of the Library of Congress have continued their growth,
but the first half of the 1940's brought a new development.
For many years the Library of Congress had placed in over
one hundred other large libraries "depository sets" of Library of Congress printed cards which were kept up to date
by the addition of new cards as printed. These catalogs
were available only in large centers. In 1941 a committee
of the Association of Research Libraries, under the chairmanship of William Warner Bishop, was successful in
sponsoring a project of reproducing a depository catalog of
Library of Congress cards and issuing it in book form, thereby making it generally available to all libraries in this
country and abroad. Another purpose to be served by the
project was to relieve American libraries of the considerable
expense of maintaining the depository catalogs in card form.
It was estimated that the cost even at that time of filing
alone approached $1,000 a year for each library and that at
least $200 worth of catalog equipment had to be added each
year to house additions to the depository set. Moreover,
many libraries found themselves hard pressed for space in
which to house the growing catalog. The expense to the
Library of Congress of providing the printed cards for

depository sets was not inconsiderable. The book catalog would make it possible to provide depository service to more libraries at a lower cost, in a more useful format and with the cost of the undertaking shared jointly by all subscribers, including the Library of Congress. These plans resulted in a printed catalog, produced by photographing the cards and printing them in reduced size, eighteen to a page. The project was completed in 1946, and its outcome was A Catalog of Books Represented by Library of Congress Printed Cards Issued to July 31 1942, published by Edward Brothers, Inc., of Ann Arbor, Michigan, for the Association of Research Libraries. This massive work ran to 167 volumes and reproduced approximately 1,900,000 cards. Thus, the cycle came full circle and the book catalog, abandoned by most American libraries for half a century, was reborn. A Supplement: Cards Issued August 1 1942--December 31, 1947, in 42 volumes followed in 1948.

In the meanwhile, in March 1946, the publisher Halsey William Wilson had proposed a continuation of this catalog in book form. 5 This proposal and the success of the sale of the Catalog of Books Represented by Library of Congress Printed Cards encouraged the Library of Congress to investigate the possibility of the continuing publication of a catalog in book form from the same type which was used to print the cards. Many technical and fiscal difficulties stood in the way, but after a series of experiments and inquiries the Library began to publish in January, 1947, the Cumulative Catalog of Congress Printed Cards. In 1950 it began the publication of the Library of Congress Subject Catalog, and the Cumulative Catalog was renamed the Library of Congress Author Catalog. With the publication in 1953 of separate catalogs for maps, motion pictures and filmstrips, music and phonograph records, the earlier catalogs became the Library of Congress Catalog--Books: Authors, and the Library of Congress Catalog--Books: Subjects.

These two catalogs soon established themselves as the most nearly comprehensive currently published library catalogs in book form. Despite this, the Library recognized that they fell short of listing the full annual increment of important books in the nation's research libraries. It was also aware that much of this record existed in the form of entries submitted to the National Union Catalog and that their inclusion in the book catalogs would add immeasurably to the usefulness of these catalogs. There was general agreement that the Library of Congress Catalog should aim

at the goal of becoming a national catalog of American library holdings, and the Library of Congress began to work
toward this goal.

In 1954 the American Library Association's Board on
Resources of American Libraries appointed a new Sub-committee on the National Union Catalog with Frederick H. Wagman as chairman. This committee met in the Library of
Congress in October 1954, and January 1955, to consider a
proposal that the Library of Congress Catalog--Books:
Authors be expanded to include the catalog entries of other
libraries, thus becoming a current author catalog of the significant research books acquired by the American libraries
and making available to these libraries and their users the
information contained in the National Union Catalog. Such a
catalog, it was thought, should have numerous beneficial
effects. The inclusion of information about the locations of
the publications listed would make possible regional and
national planning of acquisitions programs and should reduce
the unnecessary duplicative purchase of expensive works; it
should also lead to a more equitable distribution of the
burden of interlibrary loans. The ready availability of a
great body of current bibliographical information should
somewhat reduce costs of acquisition, cataloging, and
reference work. Finally, it should give an impetus to editing and publishing the older section of the National Union
Catalog and also to issuing a current subject catalog of
American library resources. A careful study of the economics of the proposal showed that it could be effected if a
sufficient number of libraries would support it. Accordingly, in January 1956, the Library of Congress Catalog--
Books: Authors was expanded to include titles and holdings
of books of 1956 and of later imprints that were reported by
other North American libraries, in addition to titles covered
by Library of Congress cards. The response from libraries
was enthusiastic, and the expanded publication was renamed
The National Union Catalog: A Cumulative Author List, in
recognition of its new role. This development marked a
turning point in the long history of efforts toward the
bibliographical control of library resources, and it presented
a challenge to further developments.

The National Union Catalog in book form has shown
an amazing growth since 1952. The total number of reports
made by all libraries in 1956 was 103,000; in 1957,
326,000; in 1958, 507,000; in 1959, 635,000; in 1960,
696,000; in 1961, 742,000; in 1962, 823,000; in 1963,
933,000; in 1964, 1,141,000; in 1965, 1,409,000; and in

1966, 1, 571, 000.   This growth may also be measured in
terms of the successive quinquennial cumulations.   The
1953-57 cumulation appeared in 28 volumes totaling 18, 826
pages, and it reproduced some 700, 000 cards at a subscription price of $255.   The 1958-62 quinquennial runs to
54 volumes of about 35, 000 pages and contains 780, 000 titles,
308, 000 added entries and references, and gives over
3, 200, 000 locations.   In addition, there are 239, 000 entries
for music and motion-picture film titles included.

    This break-through in the bibliographical control of
current acquisitions and cataloging was a remarkable achievement and most encouraging.   But it made even more evident
the need for further extension of these controls.   The greatest need was for the editing and publication of the pre-1956
National Union Catalog in order that an efficient bibliographical apparatus might be provided for older titles as well as
current ones.   Through the years, Ernest Cushing Richardson, James Christian Meinich Hanson, Keyes DeWitt
Metcalf, Charles W. David and Robert Bingham Downs,
among others, had stressed the need of editing and publishing the National Union Catalog.   With the advice and
assistance of the ALA's Committee on Resources of American Libraries and its Sub-committee on the National Union
Catalog, under the leadership of, among others, Verner W.
Clapp, Frederick H. Wagman, Charles W. David, Ralph E.
Ellsworth, Herman H. Fussler, Douglas W. Bryant and
Gordon R. Williams, the Library of Congress for some
time explored the possibility of publishing this catalog.   The
publication of The National Union Catalogue of 1956 and later
imprints in book form had the effect of stabilizing the growth
of the older portion of the National Union Catalog by establishing its terminal date with imprints of 1955.   Even with
this terminal date, the problem of publishing the entire
National Union Catalog presented many difficulties--editorial,
technical, and economic.   In 1952, as a step in planning for
the publication of the National Union Catalog and particularly
as a means of estimating its probable size and cost, the
Union Catalog Division began to set aside in a separate file
all cards for publications bearing 1952-55 imprints, including copies of Library of Congress printed cards.   This segment of the National Union Catalog contained approximately
376, 000 cards at the beginning of 1956.   By January 1960,
it had grown to about 560, 000 cards, representing about
215, 500 Library of Congress cards, 225, 000 different
entries from other libraries and 100, 000 added-entry cross-
references including duplicate cards.

As a result of the demonstrated value of The National Union Catalog in book form and in recognition of the fact that the 1952-55 file formed a compact, separate union catalog which would readily lend itself to efficient editing and publication, the Subcommittee on the National Union Catalog decided in 1959 to sponsor the publication of this segment in convenient printed form and succeeded in obtaining the necessary funds.   The project, with Johannes L. Dewton as supervisor and editor, was completed in 1961.   It resulted in the distribution to the subscribers of a 30-volume set, The National Union Catalog, 1952-1955 Imprints.   The 25,946 pages contain entries for all 1952-55 imprints reported to the Union Catalog Division up to 1960 by more than five hundred research libraries.   It pushed the coverage of The National Union Catalog back from January 1, 1956 to January 1, 1952, and demonstrated that, with sufficient effort, its coverage could be pushed back to the beginning.

This publication would, of course, be a massive undertaking, but the benefits to be derived would be correspondingly great.   In January, 1952, Rudolf Hirsch, in a letter to the chairman of the ALA's Subcommittee on the National Union Catalog, spelled out these potential gains in some detail:

1.   Acquisitions: (a) avoiding duplicate purchase of expensive items on a national basis; (b) filling in of gaps on a national basis; (c) verification of prospective purchases; and (d) definition of degree of scarcity in evaluating offers of second-hand books.   In other words, a published National Union Catalog would be most important as a guide to book selection and it would simplify the task of verification.

2.   Cataloging: (a) standardization of entries in accordance with forms found in the printed National Union Catalog; (b) use of the descriptive portion of the entry, as far as is acceptable; and (c) bibliographical reference to the published National Union Catalog, whenever there is a simpler description sufficient for local or institutional use.

3.   Interlibrary Loans--locating copies of older imprints on a national basis, with minimum effort.

4.   Reference and Research: (a) Library Use: (1) verification of titles; (2) direction service (telling

readers where items wanted can be found); and (3) serving as a substitute for a number of individual author bibliographies and library catalogs which are now consulted; (b) Readers' Use: bibliographical value to all concerned with information on titles by known authors (author bibliography, government documents bibliography, etc.).

5. Public Catalog--it may be possible to achieve great savings in space and filing costs by dividing present public catalogs and withdrawing from the author file entire groups to be found in the reference copies of the printed National Union Catalog.

The editing of the catalog would be essential and presented the chief problem. A limited amount of editorial work would result in a practical and highly useful tool and would be well worth the cost. It was proposed that this might proceed along the following lines:

1. Combine multiple reports for the same title and edition on one master card. The card chosen would be the Library of Congress printed card or the card with the fullest information.

2. Eliminate conflicts between main entries and added entries serving as entries for the same work and change entries conflicting with straight cross-references;

3. Adopt one form of name for authors entered under variants of the name.

4. Adjust entries obviously in conflict with the ALA Cataloging Rules, such as omission of jurisdiction in the case of subdivisions under United States, entry under place rather than name, etc.

5. A minor amount of transferring bibliographical information from other cards to the master card; that is, the preparation of some composite cards.

The correctness of choice or form of entry would not be checked in bibliographical sources or with the authority cards in the Library of Congress Official Catalog unless there were obvious conflicts with the ALA Cataloging Rules or with other entries in the catalog or unless differentiation

of authors with the same name required consultation of
bibliographical or biographical sources. In cases of doubt
regarding the identification of an edition, the two or more
entries would be retained.

Possibilities of publication of Pre-1956 entries

The Subcommittee on the National Union Catalog went
on record as believing that a way had to be found to publish
the pre-1956 catalog and as desiring to sponsor its publication. It proposed to integrate 1952-55 imprints into any
publication of the older part of the National Union Catalog
in order to provide a single control for the period through
1955. Certainly, few projects would be more useful to
libraries generally than the publication of this great catalog.
Writing in 1943, J. C. M. Hanson, a prophet too often without
honor in his adopted country, noted that an edited and published National Union Catalog "would rank with the great
catalogs of the British Museum, the Bibliothèque Nationale
and the German Gesamtkatalog as a bibliographic apparatus
of prime importance."[6]

It followed that the publication of the pre-1956 portion
of the National Union Catalog would indeed bring into existence
and completion the universal and interlibrary catalog of the
important books in the research libraries of the United States
and Canada which is so urgently required to meet the present
and future needs of American scholarship. The effectiveness
of its service as a location tool is illustrated by the Table,
which shows requests for location received during the twenty-
two-year period 1945-66. This analysis shows that requests
for location have increased on an annual basis in this period
from 9,125 in 1945 to 40,937 in the fiscal year ending June,
1966, an increase of more than 4.5 times the 1945 figure.
Titles not located in 1945 averaged 30 per cent as compared
to 19 per cent in 1966. A noteworthy trend, not revealed
in the table, has been a very insignificant number of requests
for location for post-1955 titles since publication of The
National Union Catalog was begun in 1956. It is reasonable
to assume that requests for location of needed titles would
have been at a much higher rate in 1966 if The National
Union Catalog and the 1952-55 part had not been published.
(These would probably now average more than 60,000 requests annually.) Libraries purchasing the planned publication could, therefore, expect to meet more than 80 per cent
of their location needs by using this tool.

Requests for Research in the National Union Catalog

Date	Items Requested	Items Found	Items Not Found
1945	9, 125	6, 371	2, 754
1946	9, 308	6, 670	2, 638
1947	11, 609	8, 117	3, 492
1948	11, 745	9, 243	2, 502
1949	12, 522	8, 557	3, 955
1950	15, 815	11, 084	4, 731
1951	17, 272	12, 199	5, 073
1952	17, 274	11, 874	5, 400
1953	17, 899	12, 016	5, 883
1954	15, 918	11, 261	4, 657
1955	18, 861	13, 331	5, 530
1956	19, 451	14, 382	5, 069
1957	20, 383	15, 490	4, 893
1958	24, 270	18, 066	6, 024
1959	25, 999	21, 772	4, 227
1960	27, 671	21, 793	5, 878
1961	30, 062	24, 313	5, 849
1962	32, 825	24, 451	8, 374
1963	32, 345	25, 367	6, 978
1964	32, 478	25, 557	6, 921
1965	35, 013	28, 563	6, 450
1966	40, 937	33, 283	7, 654

Planning the publication

Encouraged by its success in publishing the 1952-55 imprints, the ALA Subcommittee on the National Union Catalog decided in 1963 to make every effort toward the publication of the entire older portion of the National Union Catalog. It was agreed at a meeting in Washington in October 1963, that it would invite bids for the publication of the pre-1956 Catalog. The successful bidder would be required to pay for the editorial costs, these costs to be recouped through the sale of the catalog. If no satisfactory bids were received an attempt would be made to secure a foundation grant to cover the editorial costs. If this failed, libraries would be asked to underwrite the editorial costs.

As a necessary preliminary, a formal agreement was signed between the American Library Association and the Library of Congress in June 1964. The Association undertook to procure funds which would enable the Library to edit

the catalog for publication.   It was further agreed that the
Subcommittee would arrange for the issuance in book form
of the sequential segments of the catalog as they were edited.

At the Subcommittee meeting in Washington in December
1964, Chairman Gordon R. Williams of the Center for Research Libraries, Chicago reported that at least three publishers were definitely interested in bidding for the right to
publish the pre-1956 National Union Catalog in book form
and were prepared to advance the editorial and printing
costs.   The Subcommittee discussed the alternatives presented by three possible forms of publication: in book form,
in microform, and in form for computer processing.   The
decision was in favour of having the National Union Catalog
printed by offset methods in a readable type size but with
several stipulations looking forward to a possible later
change of plan.

Meeting again in March 1965, in Washington, the
Subcommittee gave further consideration to the problems
involved in the relationship of a machine-readable National
Union Catalog to a printed book catalog.   It was agreed that
the problems are particularly complex because of the size
of the catalog, the necessity of editing the cards for correctness and consistency, and, not least, the format and relationship of this publication to the presumably eventual automation of the current National Union Catalog.

The Subcommittee arrived at several determinations.
Most important was its conclusion that publication of the
present National Union Catalog in book form was desirable
even if it were also eventually to become available in
machine-readable form.   The Subcommittee felt that this
would be true for the many smaller libraries that will find
the Catalog essential but will not have convenient access to
computer facilities.   It believed that it would be no less
true for the larger libraries with full-scale computer
installations since, for many purposes, the convenience and
speed of access to the catalog in book form will make the
publication a valuable collateral tool.   Accordingly, the Subcommittee decided to invite publishers' proposals to com-
mence publication of the National Union Catalog in book form
as quickly as possible, with printer's copy to be provided
initially in the form of catalog cards for photo-offset reproduction.   At the same time, it asked the Library of
Congress to investigate the feasibility of producing a
machine-readable record as a simultaneous by-product of the

retyping it might have to do in preparing some of the catalog cards for reproduction. This would assure that maximum
assistance is given to a later conversion of the entire National Union Catalog, should this occur. The Subcommittee
also decided to reserve the right to provide the publisher
with printer's copy in some other form than 3x5 cards at
any time during the course of the Catalog's publication in
book form, if technological developments should make this
feasible.

After discussions of several informal proposals from
publishers in 1965, the Subcommittee drafted an invitation
to bidders and mailed it in February 1966, to eleven firms
that had expressed interest. On examining bids submitted
by several publishers in May 1966, the Subcommittee found
that all bids contained some terms or conditions not
specified in the invitation, and these points were then
clarified with each bidder. At its July 1966 meeting, however, the Subcommittee was not satisfied that every potential
bidder had had an adequate opportunity to bid. In view of
the importance of this publication to libraries and of the
Subcommittee's obligation to insure to the best of its ability
that the publication would be issued in its most useful and
least expensive form, it was the concensus that the Subcommittee should make certain that it had as many bids to consider as could be obtained. It therefore rejected the bids
before it and issued a new invitation to bid. At the dead-
line date in August 1966 three firm bids were submitted
with sample pages. The bids were based on the price at
which the publisher would make the printed volumes available
to libraries and research institutions, and the Subcommittee,
after discussing all phases of the individual bids, chose the
bid of Mansell Information/Publishing Ltd, as providing the
lowest sale price and the most satisfactory format. Under
the agreement, Mansell undertook to pay all costs and expenses of publication and to make available to the American
Library Association funds to finance the cost of the editorial
work at the Library of Congress. The Subcommittee then
asked the attorney for the American Library Association to
negotiate a contract satisfactory to both parties, and negoti-
ations were concluded in January 1967. The American Library Association announced the project in February 1967
and later that month the Library of Congress organized a
staff in its Processing Department to edit the pre-1956
entries in the National Union Catalog for publication, with
Johannes L. Dewton at the head of this editorial project and
Nathan N. Mendeloff as assistant head. The Catalog is

being published as the Library of Congress completes portions of the editorial work; and in March 1967 the American Library Association appointed Ruth Eisenhart, formerly head cataloger at the Union Theological Seminary in New York City, to serve as bibliographical adviser and editor at the London operation. That same month, the first 27,000 edited cards (through "Absyrtus") went to London for the first of the 610 projected volumes of 704 pages each. The work on what is undoubtedly the largest single bibliographic project in the 167-year history of the Library of Congress and certainly the largest book catalog in the history of printing was under way.

References

1. In the following article, the expression 'National Union Catalog' means this catalog as defined here. Where the same expression, National Union Catalog, is underlined, it means the printed book catalog as issued from the Library of Congress since 1956.

2. Ernest Cushing Richardson, "International Bibliography," Library Journal, XXIX (1904), 94.

3. Ernest Cushing Richardson, Paper XIV: Project B-Increase of the Bibliographical Apparatus: From the Report of the Librarian of Congress, December 3 1928, pp. 238-50, in General Cooperation and American Research Books (Yardley, Pa.: F. S. Cook & Son, Inc., 1930), p. 106.

4. William Warner Bishop, "Two Unsolved Problems in Library Work," Library Journal, XXXVII (1912), 9.

5. Halsey William Wilson, A Proposed Plan for Printing Library of Congress Cards in Cumulative Book Form (New York: H. W. Wilson Co., 1946).

6. J.C.M. Hanson, "What became of Jens; A study in Americanization Based on the Reminiscences of J.C.M. Hanson, 1869-1964" (from the unpublished Hanson papers at the University of Chicago Library).

Chapter VI

Applications and Techniques:
Colleges and Universities

A Book Catalog at Stanford

by Richard D. Johnson

The author is Librarian of the Honnold Library
for the Claremont Colleges, Claremont,
California. Reprinted by permission from Journal
of Library Automation, 1: 13-50, March 1968.

In November, 1966, a new library opened at Stanford
University. Designed primarily to serve undergraduates, the
J. Henry Meyer Memorial Library is a major addition to the
libraries on the University's campus. A four-story structure
with 88,000 square feet of usable space, it has shelving for
140,000 volumes and seating for 1,900 readers. The new
library has numerous distinctive features. One is the subject of this account--the catalog. There is no standard card
catalog in the building. Instead, copies of a book catalog
are situated at eighteen locations throughout the library,
easily accessible to all students and staff. In addition,
copies of the catalog have been placed at other points on the
campus: the main and departmental libraries, offices of
academic departments, and student dormitories.

The literature now contains numerous accounts on the
preparation of book catalogs in libraries[1,2]. One may
question the value of yet another narrative, but an account
of the Stanford experience is valuable for several reasons.
The genesis of the Stanford book catalog has been recorded,
and a follow-up describing what happened subsequently is the
next chapter in the story. The book catalog experience at
Stanford is now sufficiently advanced that one may recount
the undertaking both in depth and breadth--from its inception,
through design, implementation, and first full year of operation. Such an account can give Stanford's approach to some
still unsolved problems; for example, filing order, and the
innovations it has made. The particular environment within
which the book catalog was designed was conducive to innovation, because the entire University Library system was

not itself committed. Finally, the approach here employed
has been eclectic, and this report can record thanks to the
many individuals and institutions whose ideas and plans have
been examined for possible use in the Stanford undertaking.
Of particular importance to this project were the example
and experience of Florida Atlantic University, the Ontario
New Universities Library Project at the University of
Toronto, and the Columbia-Harvard-Yale Computerization
Project.

Origins

The Stanford book catalog had its origins in 1962.
During planning for an undergraduate library it was felt a
catalog in book form and available in many locations would
have immeasurable educational benefits for the students.
Particularly was it felt that the subject portion of such a
catalog would prove a valuable bibliography to students in the
University[3]. Somewhat later, when the size and proposed
layout for the new library indicated the desirability of at
least three complete card catalogs as an adequate guide to
the collection, further emphasis was given to the possibility
of a book catalog in multiple locations.

A grant in 1963 to Stanford University from the Council
on Library Resources, Inc. , permitted a study by Robert M.
Hayes and Ralph M. Shoffner on the economics of book catalog production. This investigation compared the costs of the
various ways in which a book catalog can be produced. [4]
Of the methods considered, Stanford selected the computer to
study further. The computer was chosen not only because
equipment was already available on campus but also because
of the recent introduction of an expanded print chain with the
capability of printing upper and lower case letters as well as
necessary diacritical marks.

In the fall of 1964 Stanford undertook further study,
employing the Hayes-Shoffner report as a basis but now comparing refined costs of a computer-produced book catalog
with costs for three complete card catalogs in the new library, as well as costs for two shelf lists and main entries
in the University Libraries' union catalog. This second
study was completed in December, 1964, and University
officials approved the preparation of a computer-based book
catalog for the library when it was determined that such a
catalog would prove more useful, and for a few years less
expensive, than the three card catalogs[5].

While the autumn study was in progress, cataloging of the new library's collection began. Plans were made for three card catalogs. Although the card catalogs were never prepared, the planning was of considerable value later in establishing field and record lengths for the machine record, as well as in securing general agreement on the kind of information to include and the format of the final catalog.

Systems Design

Preliminary systems design began in January, 1965. A systems engineer from IBM guided a team of University staff composed of librarians and personnel from the Administrative Data Processing Center in the Controller's Office. At the outset it was recognized that the assignment to produce a book catalog for the new library did not call for consideration of the other aspects involved in the library's operations, such as acquisitions, circulation and reference. But as work proceeded, efforts were consciously made to design a system that could be integrated into a larger system at a later date.

The basic object of the preliminary systems design was to refine further the cost estimates from the study of the preceding autumn. The system as it was being designed, however, called for increased machine time and corresponding increases in cost for processing as well as for programming.

In retrospect, the major achievement of the preliminary systems design was to establish the environment for a meaningful dialogue between the librarian and systems and computer personnel. When the study began, the librarian requested a system that would have involved use of a large configuration of equipment with direct-access capability. The systems and computer staff approached the design with knowledge of the equipment that would be used for the project (an IBM 1401 Computer, 12K storage, 4 tape drives) and thought in terms of fixed-length records and fixed-length fields. Through a program of mutual education, the librarian learned of the computer and what it could do and what it could not do; and systems and computer personnel learned of the library's requirements and desires. There evolved the basic design for a system capable of being implemented on the equipment at hand and acceptable to the library.

As preliminary systems design drew to a close,

necessary equipment was ordered. The principal element was the expanded print chain for the IBM 1403 Printer, containing 100 different characters and developed earlier by Florida Atlantic University, Yale University, and the University of Toronto. In addition, appropriate modifications were made to the central processing unit of the 1401 Computer to be used in the project. For the inputting of data the IBM 026 Card Punch was selected. It was available, and there was considerable local experience in its use. A modification made to it simplifies punching of one character, the word-separator character, used to designate an upper-case letter. Delivery time on the 026 Card Punch was four months. Although it was realized that the newly announced IBM 029 Card Punch would be superior for our project, delivery time on it was one year. Even before the 026 Card Punch was received in July, 1965, an order was placed for an 029. The 029 replaced the 026 in August, 1966. The 029 Card Punch, designed for use with System/360, was considered superior to the 026, because it is possible to punch each of the characters specified on the expanded print chain without resorting to the multi-punch key. Appropriate modifications were ordered for the 029 so that desired characters would print at the top of the punched cards.

Detailed systems design was completed by June, 1965, and the system may be described in the following manner.

Output

The design called for four basic outputs from the system:

1. An edit list to facilitate proofing of the items converted into machine readable form. This was considered essential because of print-out in upper and lower case.

2. An author & title catalog listing items under their author and title entries.

3. An alphabetical subject catalog listing items under Library of Congress subject headings.

4. A shelf list entering all items in call number order (the Library of Congress classification was adopted in May, 1965), giving all tracings for a particular entry, as well as the number of

volumes and copies and their location in the library.

A complete catalog was to be printed annually (author & title, subject, and shelf list) with cumulative monthly supplements to each. Output for the annual author & title catalog and subject catalog from the computer printer were to be photographically reduced, offset masters created, and fifty copies printed. The catalogs were then to be bound in reusable binders. Later it was decided to restrict use of the reusable binders to the shelf list, printed in four copies, and the supplements for the author & title and subject catalogs, to be printed in six copies, and to bind the basic annual catalog in standard book form. It was also decided to print ten copies of the author & title and subject supplements.

It was originally proposed to divide the catalog in a slightly different manner: names (as authors and as subjects) and titles in one section, and topical subjects in the other. Although this seemed to have considerable logical value, it proved impossible to implement during preliminary work with card files, given the time and staff available.

Provision was also made to print the catalog in one section as a dictionary catalog if so desired, or on cards if the book catalog should be abandoned at a later date.

Input

To achieve the above output, the design called for four kinds of input into the system:

1. Entries for titles cataloged. A separate record was to be made for each volume or copy of a title cataloged so as to provide holdings information for the shelf list and for integration into a circulation system at a later date.

2. Cross references to connect headings in the author & title catalog and in the subject catalog. In addition, the cross reference format would permit the introduction of information notes into any of the catalogs.

3. Changes to entries that are in the catalog.

4. Entries for items that are on order, with a view to integrating this form of input into a larger acquisitions system at a later date.

Implementation

The systems design called for the preparation of eight different computer programs to transform the input into the various documents as specified above. The basic programs were written during the six-month period of June-December, 1965. During the first part of 1966 the programs were debugged and the very important change procedure prepared that enables revision or deletion of a record. Coincident with the preparation of the programs, library staff began in July, 1965, the inputting of cataloging information. The expanded print chain was installed in June, 1965, and edit listings for proofing purposes were available in August. In order to test the programs and study the catalog's format, a first test catalog was prepared in January, 1966. A second test, incorporating the change procedure, was undertaken in April; and a third, partial, test was run in June.

The Machine Record

When Stanford first considered the costs of a book catalog in 1962, it was quickly discovered that the most expensive element was reproduction of the individual pages. This factor influenced many decisions in design: The more entries per page, the fewer pages and less overall expense. It became necessary then to consider which elements in a standard catalog entry could be omitted or abbreviated. Decisions were fairly simple to make. The collection duplicates almost entirely material in the main research library's collection, with full bibliographical information given in that library's union card catalog. In addition, browsing is encouraged among the open shelves of the new library. The books are readily available should further information be required.

Along with the factor of cost another element appeared--the desire to make a book catalog that would be something more than reproductions of unit catalog cards. As this thought evolved, it was learned that more space could be saved in the catalog through abandonment of the unit card and main entry concept. Articles by Ralph H. Parker[6] and Wesley Simonton[7] were instrumental in developing this aspect of the system.

The Library was amenable to a short entry in the catalog, but the actual length was another matter. From a sampling of items cataloged, it was learned that more than 99 per cent of the entries would be less than 500 characters in length. There was considerably less certainty on maximum lengths for the individual units, or fields, composing each entry. Computer personnel argued in favor of a fixed-length machine record in order to simplify programming, and a successful compromise was made: There was to be a fixed-length record composed of one fixed-length field and six variable-length fields. Each record is 570 characters in length. For the few catalog entries that are extremely long it is possible to use two records for one catalog entry. The maximum length for any catalog entry is thus approximately 1,000 characters. It is possible to enter even longer units by dividing them into sections and entering each as an analytical entry. To speed input-output time and to conserve space on tape, the records are placed on magnetic tape in blocks of two records each.

Each of the six variable-length fields in the record is individually tagged. It was learned during the preparation of a later program that it would be necessary to restrict the overall length of any one field, and it was agreed that the maximum length of any one of the variable-length fields would be 400 characters. Through a misunderstanding, the author did not realize that in tape storage an upper-case letter is equivalent to two characters, a factor not taken into account when record and field lengths were established. Fortunately, this minor error has occasioned no problem.

The Master Tape Record

The master tape record (Table 1) illustrates how all of the information appears on magnetic tape. (Figure 5 gives an example of the layout.)

Table 1. Map of Master Tape Record

Position	Type of Information
1-30:	Library of Congress classification
31-35:	Size and/or format of publication (e. g. , folio, Mfilm)
36-42:	Volume number
43-44:	Part number
45-46:	Copy number
47:	Type (blank: monograph, no analy.; 1: monograph, anals. made; 2: serial received in unbound form; 3: serial, unbound, anals. made; 4: serial received in bound form; 5: serial, bound, anals. made; 6: analytic; 7: author-title cross reference; 8: subject cross reference; 9: item on order)
48:	Record indicator (program supplies "1" if there is an overflow record and "2" in second record)
49:	Special location in library (code A-Z)
50:	Change indicator (code C for revision; Code D for delete)
51:	Title indicator (code T if entry desired under title)
52:	Shelf list indicator (code S if entry is to appear in shelf list only)
53-54:	Year acquired (e. g. , 67)
55-57:	Month and year reported missing (e. g. , 117 for Nov. 1967). It is assumed a book will be removed from the catalog if missing more than nine years.
58-71:	Future codings
72-77:	Address and length of main entry (Area 20) (three positions for address, three for length)
78-83:	Address and length of conventional title (Area 30)
84-89:	Address and length of title paragraph (Area 40)
90-95:	Address and length of notes (Area 50)
96-101:	Address and length of subject headings (Area 60)
102-107:	Address and length of added authors and added titles (Area 70)
108-570:	Variable length fields

The Fields

To simplify coding and keypunching, each field in the
record is called an Area and numbered 10 through 70.   As
will be shown later, these numbers are not transferred to tape.
A description of the seven fields in each record can give a
good idea of the elements included in cataloging and how the
unit card/main entry concept was abandoned.

Area 10 is the one fixed-length field in the record.
It is 71 characters long and contains positions for call number, volume number, and copy number.   In addition, it contains indicators for other elements: type of publication;
record indicator (program supplied if there is overflow to
a second record); special location in the library; change
indicator; title indicator; shelf list indicator; year of acquisition; and date missing.   Fourteen positions remain blank
for future use.

Area 20 contains the main entry, Area 30 the conventional title, Area 40 the title paragraph.   The title paragraph includes: the title; author statement; edition statement;
imprint, limited to publisher and date; and collation, limited to pagination.   Area 50 contains notes.

Subject headings are recorded in Area 60, entered one
after another and separated one from another by a record mark,
a symbol resembling a double dagger.   Added authors and
added titles are entered in Area 70, similarly separated
one from another by the record mark.   Only added titles
are entered in Area 70.   If a catalog entry is desired under
title, then the title indicator is marked in Area 10.

Personal Names

On the form of personal names in the catalog, it was
decided to anticipate the Anglo-American Cataloging Rules,
publication of which was imminent.   In general, the title-
page form of a personal author's name is used.   On the
one hand, this has meant a shorter record and greater simplicity in inputting data; on the other hand, it became necessary to maintain a name authority file when the form adopted for the book catalog differed from that established by the
Library of Congress or earlier cataloging rules.

The relator, the element that describes the relationship of a person used as an entry to the work being cataloged

(e. g. , ed. , tr. , comp. , illus.), is omitted in the heading to save space. The relationship is shown in the title paragraph. A heading in the book catalog, either author or subject, is printed once before a group of titles and repeated only if the titles associated with it are continued in another column.

In addition to not permitting use of the relator, the system does not permit in the author & title catalog "added" entries composed of an author and a title. In standard cataloging such a technique may be used instead of a separate analytical entry. In the author & title catalog, however, such a composite entry would establish a new "author" (name plus title of the work) and would file as a separate unit after all works by that author. In the subject catalog the author-title entry is permitted so that books about voluminous authors and their individual works may be better displayed.

The Conventional Title

The conventional title has been employed to assemble under an author's name editions of a work with variant titles. Collected writings of an author, or selections, are given the conventional title [Works] or [Selections]. Through a combination of coding and programming, they are entered first under an author's name before titles of individual works are listed. (See in Figure 8 the entry under Karen Horney for an example.) The conventional title has meaning only as it is related to the main entry. For that reason it prints only in the catalog when preceded by the main entry.

The Title Paragraph and the Unit Record

As summarized above, the title paragraph includes the title, author statement, edition statement, imprint and collation. With one major exception this involves the copying of, or truncation of, information present on a Library of Congress card. The exception is the author statement. As shown in a recent investigation[8], this element was present in but twenty-five per cent of the entries studied. Current cataloging rules permit in some cases the omission of the author statement when it is identical with the form used in the heading[9, 10]. These rules are based upon a cataloging system employing unit records on cards, the first element of which is the main entry. In unchanged form the author statement is used as the main entry; for added entries another heading, such as author, title, or subject, is superposed on the card.

In the Stanford system a new unit record was introduced. The first element of it is the title paragraph. All
headings, main or added, are placed directly above it; and
if entry under title is desired, a title entry is made in
hanging-indention form.

The Stanford book catalog thus does away with the
main entry concept completely. The necessity, or even
wisdom, of setting apart one field in the machine record as
main entry may be questioned. Why not group the main
entry with the other added author entries in Area 70? There
were two reasons: First, it is simpler to adapt the information from Library of Congress cataloging information if the
form can be followed relatively closely. Second, we wished
to allow for the possibility of printing standard catalog cards
if necessary, and this would allow for a reinstatement of
the standard unit card concept.

A basic requirement of the system is that the author
statement must be included in the title paragraph. If for
any reason it cannot be listed there, then it is recorded in
note position in Area 50. Although no formal study was
undertaken, it was believed that works by single personal
authors would constitute more than fifty per cent of the collection. The addition of the author statement in the title
paragraph for each such book could add considerable bulk
to the catalog. Accordingly, through the use of record
marks as coding symbols, the author statement is set off
in the title paragraph for those works by single personal
authors. Through programming, the author statement is
suppressed when the work is entered in the catalog under
the name given in the main entry; whereas it appears under
all "added" entries.

The system as it has been established calls for works
to be entered alphabetically by title under the heading in the
catalog. In the subject catalog this means, too, that works
are listed alphabetically by title under each subject heading
and not by author. It was felt that this form of arrangement
is quite satisfactory for a selective collection, such as the
Meyer Library; and it offers the possibility of scanning a
page of thirty or more entries. It has occasioned one
problem--when a subject heading expresses form and not
subject. For example, under "SYMPHONIES," works are
arranged alphabetically by title and not by composer.

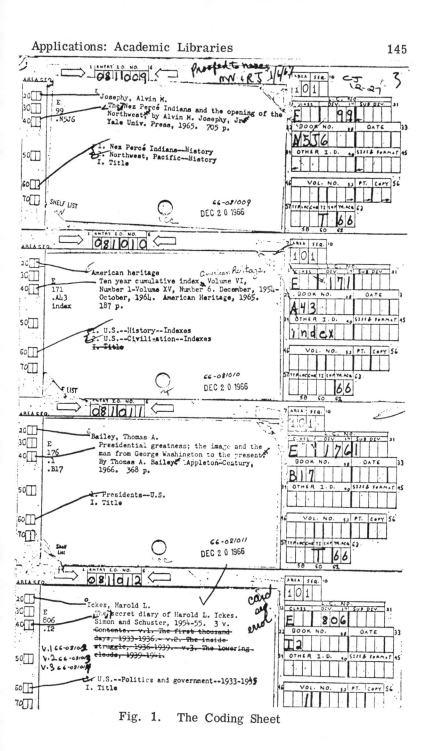

Fig. 1.   The Coding Sheet

Conversion

The basic source document used is the Library of
Congress catalog card. Although the card itself could be
used by crossing out unnecessary information and adding
other data, it was felt that a clearer document would result
if the needed information were copied onto another catalog
card. Examples of such cards are shown in Figure 1.
(Subsequent figures depict the manipulation of the entry for
the book by Thomas A. Bailey, Presidential Greatness.)
As illustrated in Figure 1, an identification number is assigned to each catalog card and four catalog cards are
placed upon a coding board and a xerographic copy made.

The original cards are filed in a manual shelf list
with the identification number as an indication that the information has been coded. The coding sheet is given to the
coder, who enters Area 10 information in the blocks at the
right and indicates to the keypuncher where other areas
begin and what special symbols should be used.

To simplify the inputting of data and the scanning of
punched cards, a special data-processing card was designed
for input (see Figure 2). Each title converted is represented by a decklet of punch cards averaging six. Each of the
seven areas or fields begins on a separate card. Although
this may be considered wasteful of cards and indicative of
"80-column mentality," it does have its benefits. A mistake
in punching in one area requires repunching of the material
in that area only, the area being the smallest unit for editing purposes.

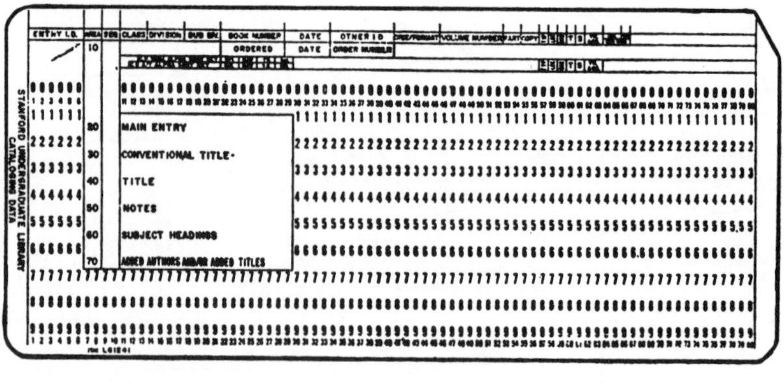

Fig. 2.   The Data Processing Card.

So that the cards are kept in correct order for processing, the first ten columns of the card are used for identification numbers. The six-digit identification number assigned to the original card is punched in the first six columns. The first digit is the month, 1-9 being January through September and zero being October-December, one "month" of 92 days; the second and third digits are the day of the month; and the fourth through sixth a consecutive number assigned each day. It is possible thus to code 999 entries each day. The year is omitted, because it was assumed data would be transferred to magnetic tape at least once a year and probably more often. The area number is punched in columns 7 and 8 and the sequence within the area in columns 9 and 10. Cataloging information begins in column 11. Figure 3 shows a decklet of cards for one title.

Information in Area 10 is formatted somewhat differently for books on order or for cross references. To enter a book on order, the word "ORDERED" is punched in columns 22 through 28, the data and order number in columns 29 through 40, and 9 in column 57, the type indicator. This information prints in the catalog as a call number, and books on order are listed first in the shelf list. To date, entering of books on order has been limited to a few sample cases only. A cross reference in the subject catalog has a "call number" composed of the first nine characters of the entry to which reference is made (punched in columns 13-21) and an eight-digit identification number (in columns 22-29). An 8 is punched in column 57, the type indicator. A cross reference in the author & title catalog has a similar "call number" composed of the first ten characters of the entry to which reference is made (punched in columns 12-21) and an eight-digit identification number (in columns 22-29). A 7 is punched in column 57, the type indicator.

Subject cross references are listed in the shelf list in "call number" order following books on order; and author & title cross references follow subject cross references. The "call numbers" for cross references do not print in the catalog proper, and serve only as addresses to retrieve the cross reference from magnetic tape when a change or deletion is necessary.

Added copies and volumes are entered by preparing Area 10 information only and punching S in column 61, the

shelf list indicator. The first copy entered is never coded
explicitly as copy 1, even though a second copy is being
simultaneously added. The program automatically identifies
the first copy entered as copy 1, and the number prints in
the shelf list when another copy is added or a volume or location is shown.

So long as cataloging information is on punch cards and
not on magnetic tape, the 10-digit identification number is the
device used to retrieve the information. When the information is transferred to magnetic tape, the identification number is lost and the call number becomes the identification
device.

As shown in Figure 3, information in Area 40 (and in
Areas 20, 30, 50, and 70 as well) continues to successive
cards. It is not actually necessary to punch through column
80 before beginning a continuation card for an area, and experience indicates that corrections are simplified if blanks
are left at the end of each card. The only requirement is

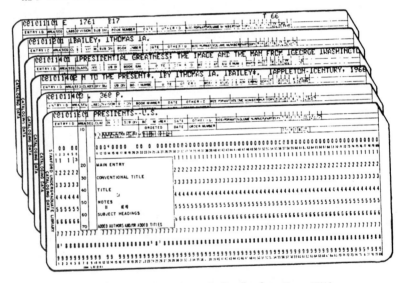

Fig. 3.   A Decklet of Cards for One Title

that if one word ends in any column on one card and a new
word starts on the next, the space separating them must be
in column 11 on the second card.

The inverted T printed on the cards in Figure 3 is the locally devised symbol to represent the word-separator character. This symbol designates the following character as a capital letter or as a special character. Through programming, subject headings are printed in upper case; and so word-separator characters are not used in Area 60.

Following keypunching and proofing, the coding sheets are filed in identification number order. The card shelf list and the file of coding sheets are the two manual back-ups to the system.

The Edit List

On a regular basis, generally once a week during activation, an edit list is run on the computer for cards punched since the last listing. An example of a page from this list is shown in Figure 4. This list is proofed against original cataloging data as represented on the coding sheets. Information still remains on punched cards, and errors detected are corrected on the cards.

As an aid to proofing, the edit program generates a number of error messages: cards out of order; absence of Area 10 information; call number incorrectly formatted; an invalid character punched; information too long to fit into two machine records; information in one field more than 400 characters in length; an incorrect use of coding symbols (for use in determining filing order and to set off author statements); and incorrect use of record marks in Areas 60 and 70.

A nagging problem encountered during proofing is the fact that it is done out of context. In the preparation of cards for a standard card catalog, a second form of proofing is possible when cards are filed and entries compared with headings already in the catalog to insure that they are compatible. With a machine performing this function, this further check is not practical with existing equipment. Similarly, the machine does not recognize human errors and will file a misspelled word as it was entered and not as the word it was meant to be. The discipline required for the accurate inputting of cataloging information intended for machine manipulation is at times frightening.

Differences between a book catalog and a card catalog became more obvious as work progressed. In a card

Edit List   1/ 5/67

```
Call   D396.F3                                              typ  loc  chg  ti. T shf  yr 66
Auth   Falls, Cyril
Titl   <A >hundred years of wars, by Cyril Falls. G. Duckworth, 1953. 419 p.
Subj   MILITARY HISTORY, MODERN--1800-1899   MILITARY HISTORY, MODERN--1900-
I.D.   081006

Call   DC195.07L4 V.1                                      typ  loc  chg  ti. T shf  yr 66
Auth   Lefebvre, Georges
Titl   Etudes orléanaises, par Georges Lefebvre.  Centre National de la Recherche Scientifique, 1962-63.
Subj   2 v.  ORLEANS, FRANCE--HISTORY   ORLEANS, FRANCE--ECONOMIC CONDITIONS   ORLEANS, FRANCE--SOCIAL CONDITIONS   FRANCE
       -HISTORY--21789 øREVOLUTION--CAUSES AND CHARACTER
I.D.   081007

Call   DC195.07L4 V.2                                      typ  loc  chg  ti.  shf S yr 66
I.D.   081008
```

(handwritten: Proofed to here MN √ eg 1-6-67)

```
Call   E99.N5J6                                            typ  loc  chg  ti. T shf  yr 66
Auth   Josephy, Alvin M.
Titl   <The >Nez Percé Indians and the opening of the Northwest, by Alvin M. Josephy, Jr.  Yale Univ. Press,
       1965. 705 p.
Subj   NEZ PERCE INDIANS--HISTORY   NORTHWEST, PACIFIC--HISTORY
I.D.   081009

Call   E171.A43 INDEX                                      typ  loc  chg  ti.  shf  yr 66
Auth   American heritage
Titl   Ten year cumulative index, American heritage. Volume VI, Number 1-Volume XV, Number 6, December, 1954
       -October, 1964. American Heritage, 1965. 187 p.
Subj   U.S.--HISTORY--INDEXES   U.S.--CIVILIZATION--INDEXES
I.D.   081010

Call   E176.1.B17                                          typ  loc  chg  ti. T shf  yr 66
Auth   Bailey, Thomas A.
Titl   Presidential greatness; the image and the man from George Washington to the present. By Thomas A. Bailey.
       Appleton-Century, 1966.  368 p.
Subj   PRESIDENTS--U.S.
I.D.   081011

Call   E806.I2 V.1                                         typ  loc  chg  ti. T shf  yr 66
Auth   Ickes, Harold L.
Titl   <The >Secret diary of Harold L. Ickes.  Simon and Schuster, 1954-55.  3 v.
       The program has encountered a card sequence error.
Subj   U.S.--POLITICS AND GOVERNMENT--1933-1945
I.D.   081012

Call   E806.I2 V.2                                         typ  loc  chg  ti.  shf S yr 66
I.D.   (16013)                                                                    081013
```

Fig. 4. The Edit List.

catalog one can see from the typography, the stains on older cards, and the kind of card stock used, that information was entered at different times. One is more willing to tolerate the differences that appear. Because it is not generally possible to compare a number of entries at the same time in a card catalog, one misses many inconsistencies. On the other hand, in a machine-produced book catalog, one scans numerous entries with one glance. Produced at the same printing, they appear of equal vintage even though they may have been entered at different times. The inconsistencies resulting from changing cataloging rules become very obvious. This is particularly annoying with respect to the matter of capitalization, and the effort to produce an internally consistent document is difficult.

Costs for Inputting

The first year's experience (1965-66) has indicated a cost of $.40 per title for inputting of cataloging information. Indications are that this cost has remained constant for the second year. Included in inputting for each title is provision for all extra records needed for added volumes and copies and cross references. The cost does not include actual cataloging, preparation of the typed catalog card, overhead, or computer charges for the edit list. The cost may be broken down as follows:

Table 2. Inputting Costs, 25,000 Titles (1965-66)

Coding: 50 titles per hour @ $2.20 per hour	$ 1,100.00
Keypunching: 12 titles per hour @ $2.20 per hour	4,583.33
Proofing: 72 titles per hour @ $7.40 per hour (2 staff members)	2,569.43
Equipment: Keypunch rental ($926.02); punch cards ($312.34); and coding sheets ($520.86)	1,759.22
Total	$10,011.98

The Stanford experience indicates that over a period of time it is possible to input 100 titles per eight-hour day on each card punch or approximately 2,000 per working month. This figure is based on a shortened catalog record as described, but includes provision for separate records for added volumes and copies and cross references. The staff employed at Stanford had no previous experience keypunching

and were instructed either in a formal school for five days
or, as is now done, on the job.   Three or four staff members are trained for keypunching at all times and have regular schedules.   With a staff of this size, punching can proceed on a steady basis in spite of vacations and illnesses.

The Programs

Systems design called for the preparation of eight
computer programs.   In addition, two package sort programs
from IBM are employed for the filing of entries in the shelf
list and in the author & title and subject catalogs.   As experience increased, it was found that the updating of entries
in the first annual catalog when merged with new data for
the second annual catalog could be simplified if three utility
programs were used; these also were prepared.   A locally
devised assembly language, SOPAT, similar to Autocoder,
was used for the programs.

The first program is the Edit Program (LB001) which
processes the cards to prepare the edit list described above.

During the first two years of operation the basic pattern has been to prepare weekly the edit list described above
using the Edit Program (LB001), and transfer data to permanent storage on magnetic tape once every three months.
(The punch cards are stored in another area on campus, as
back-up.)   The quarterly basis has coincided with the schedule for the program tests as well as the quarterly supplements and annual catalogs.   In brief, the following happens:

1. Cataloging information is transferred from punch
   cards to magnetic tape through the Card to
   Tape Program (LB010).

2. Through a Call Number Sort (IBM Sort 7) the
   above records are arranged in call number
   order for a basic shelf list.

3. Through the Format and Update Program (LB020),
   all the necessary entries for the author &
   title catalog and subject catalog are generated
   from the above records and the shelf list is
   updated.

4. Through an alphabetical Sort (IBM Sort 7 or
   IBSYS 7090 Sort depending on the magnitude)

the entries for the author & title and subject catalogs are arranged in alphabetical order. (Longer sorts have been run on an IBM 7090 Computer.)

5. Through the Author-Title and Subject Update Program (LB050), the new entries created by LB020 are merged with existing entries and existing records are deleted as specified by LB020.

6. The Author-Title and Subject Split Program (LB060) sets up the entries on magnetic tape (line length, indention) as they will appear in the catalog and establishes the two columns for each page.

7. The Author-Title and Subject Printout Program (LB070) prints the pages of the author & title and subject catalogs.

8. The Shelf List Split Program (LB030) performs the same function for the shelf list as undertaken by the Split Program for the author & title and subject catalogs (LB060).

9. The Shelf List Printout Program (LB040) prints the pages of the shelf list.

The Change Procedure

It is possible to change information in a preceding supplement by following the change procedure: To change a call number, the entire entry is deleted, employing a record consisting of Area 10 and a delete symbol in the change indicator, and a new entry inserted in a separate record. To change an area, a change record is prepared consisting of Area 10 information with the change indicator marked plus card(s) for any area(s) to be changed. For example, if there is an error in a subject heading, it is necessary to prepare only an Area 10 plus an Area 60 change record showing the subject headings desired. The smallest unit for editing purposes between supplements is the Area.

Changes in an Annual Catalog

During systems design it was realized that machine

time could be saved if a different procedure were followed
to change information in the preceding year's catalog when
merging it with fresh data to form a new annual catalog.
The procedure used is to delete through three utility programs
(LB075, LB080, and LB090) entries that are to be changed and
then enter them anew.

The first of these programs (LB075) is a card-to-
tape program. Special delete cards (essentially Area 10
information giving call number) are prepared for each volume and copy to be deleted. They are transferred to magnetic tape and sorted into order by call number.

In the second program, the Shelf List Delete Program (LB080), the last annual shelf list tape is read and
entries as specified by LB075 are deleted and a new shelf
list tape written.

Since the author-title and subject files are not in
call-number order, a table look-up technique is used in the
third program, LB090, the Author-Title and Subject Delete
Program. The table consists of call numbers (in proper
sequence) for all records to be deleted. Each entry in the
author-title and subject files is checked against the table
and deleted if the call number for the entry is listed there.
A revised author-title and subject tape is thus prepared.

Records on Tape

The basic tape record follows the format of the
master machine record described earlier. Figure 5 shows
a tape dump of the master shelf list as formatted in the
Card to Tape Program (LB010) and after having been sorted
into call-number order. As stated above, two records are
placed in a block of 1,140 characters, each record with 570
characters. Printed with a limited print chain, some characters do not appear as they will finally. The record mark
prints as a plus sign, and in the entry for the work by Kane
the symbol indicating underscoring prints as a dollar sign.
The word-separator characters and some other characters
do not print at all; spaces are left to indicate their
presence.

Once the information has been processed through the
Format and Update Program (LB020), however, the machine
record is somewhat different. New records, one for each
entry that will appear in the final catalog, are generated.

```
12      1  C  S66                                                        +E  176    D563

                                                     10       20      30      40     50 T 66  60      70      80       90      100
                                                 1                                                                          129150        27901
1  1761  10  B17  BAILEY, THOMAS A.+ PRESIDENTIAL GREATNESS THE IMAGE AND THE MAN FROM GEORGE WASHINGTON
TO THE PRESENT+. BY THOMAS A. BAILEY+. APPLETON- CENTURY, 1966. 348 P.+PRESIDENTS—U.S.+
                                                                         +E  1761   B77
                                             2   S66

                                                     10       20      30      40     50 T 66  60      70       80       90      100
                                                 1                                                                131139270055050501
1  1761  10  K3   KANE, JOSEPH NATHAN+ FACTS ABOUT THE PRESIDENTS A COMPILATION OF BIOGRAPHICAL AND HISTOR
ICAL DATA. BY JOSEPH NATHAN KANE. H. W. WILSON, 1960. 348 P.+5 SSH9ESL9VSESD ONLY IN AREA 2
30.+PRESIDENTS—U.S.+                                             +E  1762   M4
                            1  T 66        108018     124153      279C24     PEANS, MARIANNE+ THE
MCMAN IN THE WHITE HOUSE THE LIVES, TIMES AND INFLUENCE OF TWELVE NOTABLE FIRST LADIES+.  BY M
ARIANNE MEANS+. RANDOM HOUSE, 1963. 299 P.+PRESIDENTS—U.S.—WIVES+

                                                     10       20      30      40     50 KT 66  60     70       80       90      100
                                                 1                                                            1321C233C0933204
1  178  10  A24   ADAMS, JAMES TRUSLCW+ ALBUM OF AMERICAN HISTORY. JAMES TRUSLCW ADAMS, EDITOR IN CHIEF.
C. SCRIBNER, 1944-60. 6 V.+ VOL. 5 EDITED BY J. G. E. HOPKINS.+ VOL. 6 IS INDEX.+5 SSH9ESL9VS
ESD IN REFERENCE ALCOVE 340.+U.S.—HISTORY+U.S.—SOCIAL LIFE AND CUSTOMS+
                                             2   1  K  S66                +E  178    A24
```

Fig. 5. Tape Dump of Master Shelf List.

A listing of the elements in each of these records is shown
in Table 3. Figures 6 and 7 show tape dumps for author and
subject entries.

Table 3. The Author-Title and Subject Tape Record

Position	Type of Information
1:	Catalog indicator (1: Author & Title Catalog; 2: Subject Catalog)
2-81:	Major sort key
82-101:	Minor sort key
102-131:	Library of Congress classification number
132-136:	Size and format
137:	Record indicator (Program supplies "1" if there is an overflow record and "2" in second record)
138:	Delete indicator (program supplied, for use in change procedure)
139:	Address for main entry (Area 20) or added author/added title (Area 70)
142:	Address for title paragraph (Area 40)
145:	Address for conventional title (Area 30)
148:	Address for notes (Area 50)
151:	Address for subject heading (Area 60)
154-618:	Variable-length fields

The Sort Key

The Format and Update Program (LB020)
generates the sort key for each entry. The sort key
determines the characters that will be considered when the
entry is to be alphabetized. A succeeding sort program does
the actual alphabetizing. After some study, experimentation,
and conjecture a 100-character sort key was selected. It is
in two parts: a major sort key of 80 characters and a
minor sort key of 20 characters.

The major sort key is formed from the first 80
characters of the element that will serve as the entry in the
catalog--the author, the added author, the title (for entry
under title), the added title, or the subject heading.

The minor sort key is formed from the first 20 characters of the element that follows the heading--the title or

```
      1          10          20          30          40          50          60          70          80          90         100
  1   1BALCWIN  T W
101   RPR 3095    B3                                 154171            BALDWIN,  T. W.+ THE ORGANIZATICN AND PERSONNE CRGANIZATICN ANC PE
201   L OF THE  SHAKESPEAREAN COMPANY.   RUSSELL  -  RUSSELL, 1961.  463 P.+
301
401
501
601                   +

      1          10          20          30          40          50          60          70          80          90         100
  1   1BAILEY  STEPHEN KEMP
101   UJK 2265     G59                               154178            BAILEY,  STEPHEN  KEMP+ POLITICAL PARTIES    POLITICAL PARTIES
201    S. A.  ESSAYS BY  STEPHEN  KEMP  BAILEY AND OTHERS.  EDITED BY  ROBERT  A.  GCLCWIN.   RANC  MC NAL     , U.
3C1   LY, 1965.  158 P.+
401
501
601                   +

      1          10          20          30          40          50          60          70          80          90         100
  1   1BAILEY  THOMAS A
101   EE   1761   B17                                154175            BAILEY,  THOMAS  A.+ PRESICENTIAL GREATNESS  T   PRESIDENTIAL GREATN
201   HE IMAGE AND THE MAN FROM  GEORGE  WASHINGTON TO THE PRESENT.  APPLETCN- CENTURY, 1966.  368 P.+
301
4C1
501
601                   +

      1          10          20          30          40          50          60          70          80          90         100
  1   1BAILEY  THOMAS A
101   TD   643    A7828                              154175            BAILEY,  THOMAS  A.+ MCCCRCW  WILSCN AND THE G   MCCCRCW WILSON AND
201   REAT BETRAYAL.   ENCOUNTER  PAPERBACKS, 1963.  429 P.+
301
```

Fig. 6. Tape Dump of Entries in Author & Title Catalog

conventional title.   The conventional title can never be a
major sort key.   The title, on the other hand, can be either
a major sort key or a minor sort key.

During the course of the Split Program (LB060),
major sort keys are compared.   If two or more are identical,
the entry words are the second and subsequent identical headings are suppressed and do not print.   Under the heading
that does print, entries are arranged in alphabetical order
through the first twenty characters of the element generating
the minor sort key.

In a sense, there is a third sort key.   If both major
and minor sort keys are identical, items will print in call-
number order.   In no case will the element generating the
minor sort key be suppressed.

During the first test of the programs one mistake was
discovered with respect to the generation of sort keys and
the suppression of entry elements.   In a few cases the library possessed multiple copies of the same book cataloged
under different call numbers (for example, one as a separate
and one as part of a series).   The problem arose when there
was to be an entry under title, with two major sort keys
identical.   A similar situation arose for periodicals.   A
periodical might be entered itself under its title (Area 40)
and also appear in the catalog as an author (Area 20) for a
book it might issue.   To eliminate this problem, a minor
change was made in the program.   If a title generates a
major sort key, it is never suppressed if identical with a
preceding major sort key.

Filing Order

Formation of sort keys leads immediately to a discussion of the unsolved problem of alphabetization.   In the Meyer
Library catalog the aim has been to duplicate as closely as
possible the arrangement of entries found in the University
Libraries' union card catalog.   Basically, this means a word
by word alphabetization.   In addition, we have attempted to
preserve as many of the currently used typing conventions as
possible in preparing entries for the card catalog.   For
example, two or more initials separated one from another by
periods have no spaces following internal periods.   Thus, the
abbreviation for the United States is typed as U. S. and not
as U. S.   Abbreviations filed as they are spelled and Mc's
and Mac's in separate sequences are two of the major differences from standard manual library filing.

```
        10      20      30      40      50      60      70      80      90      100
  1   2PRESERVATION OF 2ZOOLOGICAL SPECIMENS
101   1 ZOOLOGICA121116616              191  154PRESERVATION OF ZOOLOGICAL SPECIMENS++ SEE Z
201   ZOOLOGICAL SPECIMENS— COLLECTION AND PRESERVATION.+                    SEE ZOOLOGICAL SPEC
301
401               +
501
601

        10      20      30      40      50      60      70      80      90      100
  1
101   2PRESIDENTS U S
201   SE 1761 K3                    171  310154PRESIDENTS—U.S.+ FACTS ABOUT THE PRESIDENTS
301   A COMPILATION OF BIOGRAPHICAL AND HISTORICAL DATA.  BY JOSEPH NATHAN KANE.  P. M. WILSON, 1960.
401   348 P.+$ S$HSE$L$V$E$C ONLY IN AREA 230.+                      FACTS ABOUT THE PRE
501                   +
601

        10      20      30      40      50      60      70      80      90      100
  1
101   2PRESIDENTS U S
201   VJK 516 R66                   171  154PRESIDENTS—U.S.+ THE LONELY QUEST  THE E
301   ON OF PRESIDENTIAL LEADERSHIP.  BY ROBERT RIENOW AND LEONA TRAIN RIENOW.  FOLLETT, 1966.  3C7
401   P.+                                                    LONELY QUEST  THE EVOLUTI
501                   +
601

        10      20      30      40      50      60      70      80      90      100
  1
101   2PRESIDENTS U S
201   EE 1761  B17                  171  154PRESIDENTS—U.S.+ PRESIDENTIAL GREATN
301   MACE AND THE MAN FROM GEORGE WASHINGTON TO THE PRESENT.  BY THOMAS A. BAILEY.  APPLETON- CENTU
      RY, 1966.  368 P.+                                     PRESIDENTIAL GREATNESS THE I
```

Fig. 7. Tape Dump of Entries in Subject Catalog

It was recognized that in generating the sort key the computer will scan the entry words character by character and space by space. Thus, it is important that each character and each space be positioned accurately. The computer checks a character and either interprets it as a blank, a letter, a numeral, a symbol, or else ignores it. In alphabetizing, this basic rule is followed: A blank files before a letter (A through Z), and a letter files before a numeral (0 through 9).

Certain marks of punctuation are interpreted as a space. They are: period, comma, colon, semicolon, hyphen, and question mark. Some marks of punctuation are ignored. They are: parentheses, brackets, dollar sign, virgule or slash (/), equal sign, number or sharp (#), per cent, asterisk, apostrophe, flat sign, and ampersand. It was believed that the presence of a space on either side of an ampersand would place entries in correct order, but in some cases this did not happen.

Some diacritical marks change the value of the character with which they are associated. For example, an umlaut over an "a", "o," or "u" changes that character to "ae," "oe," or "ue" respectively.

Non-Filing Symbols

If an alphabetical order is desired other than that explicitly given in the entry words, special symbols are employed at the time of coding. Since language of publication is not coded, it is necessary to place symbols around introductory articles for them to be ignored. The less-than (<) and greater-than (>) signs are the symbols used to set off a sequence of characters to be ignored. The placement of these symbols is important. For example, to eliminate the article from the title, The century of science, it is necessary to place the symbols in this manner: < The > century of science. In this way the sort key would be generated starting with the letter "C" in the word "century"; and a space would be left between the words "the" and "century" in the printed heading.

Use of the non-filing symbols internally in an entry is limited and must be strictly controlled through recording of decisions in authority files. So that names filed under prefixes and written as two words will be filed in the same sequence as names written as one word, the non-filing

symbols are employed internally.   For example, in order
that Van Buren and Vandenburg will file in the same sequence, Van Buren is coded as Van $<$ $>$ Buren.   In this
manner the computer is instructed to ignore the space when
forming the sort key.

The use of non-filing symbols has proved quite useful in subject headings to arrange period subdivisions in
chronological order when there is a word or words intervening between the heading and the date.   Thus, with non-
filing symbols employed as shown below, these particular
subject headings are arranged chronologically:

GT. BRIT. --HISTORY-- $<$ EDWARD, THE CONFESSOR, $>$
    1042-1066
GT. BRIT. --HISTORY-- $<$ NORMAN PERIOD, $>$ 1066-1154
GT. BRIT. --HISTORY-- $<$ MEDIEVAL PERIOD, $>$ 1066-1485
GT. BRIT. --HISTORY-- $<$ STEPHEN, $>$ 1135-1154
GT. BRIT. --HISTORY-- $<$ HENRY II, $>$ 1154-1189
GT. BRIT. --HISTORY-- $<$ ANGEVIN PERIOD, $>$ 1154-1216

The Filing Symbol

The less-than and greater-than signs are provided
on the expanded print chain purchased for the book catalog
project.   To date it has not been found necessary to use
these signs as symbols in titles, and so their use is restricted to their role in forming non-filing elements.   As
work proceeded, need was felt for another symbol--one that
would set off a field that would not print but which would be
filed upon.   For example, we wished to file the title,
1848: chapters of German history, as though it were written,
Eighteen forty-eight; chapters of German history; yet we did
not wish to violate the form of the title as given in the book.
An examination of all characters in the print chain led us to
sacrifice the symbol @ for use as a sign in its own right.
It is used solely as a filing symbol.   Thus, any characters
or spaces placed between two @'s will generate a sort key
as specified by those characters, but the information will
not print.   The title, 1848: chapters of German history, will
be coded in this manner: @ eighteen forty-eight @ $<$ 1848 $>$:
chapters of German history. It will be filed as though it were
written: Eighteen forty-eight: chapters of German history.

The use of the filing symbol has been especially useful in arranging period subdivisions in chronological order

when treating years in the pre-Christian era or before the
year 1000 A. D.   For years in the pre-Christian era, coding permits chronological arrangement of years beginning
with 9999 B. C.   The following procedure is observed: The
year in question is subtracted from 9999 and the resulting
difference, preceded by the letter Z, is entered inside the
filing symbols.   The year will thus file after all letters but
before years in the Christian era.   For years before 1000
A. D. the leading 0 is simply placed inside the filing symbol,
for example,   @ 0 @ 476.

To illustrate further, here are three subject headings
as manually filed:

ROME--HISTORY--REPUBLIC, 510-30 B. C.
ROME--HISTORY--REPUBLIC, 365-30 B. C.
ROME--HISTORY--AUGUSTUS, 30 B. C. -14 A. D.

They are coded in this manner:

ROME--HISTORY--< REPUBLIC, 510-30 B. C.>
    @Z9489-Z9969@
ROME--HISTORY-- <REPUBLIC, 365-30 B. C.>
    @Z9734-Z9969@
ROME--HISTORY-- <AUGUSTUS, 30 B. C. -14 A. D.>
    @Z9968-0014@

The following sort keys are generated:

ROME--HISTORY--Z9489-Z9969
ROME--HISTORY--Z9734-Z9969
ROME--HISTORY--Z9969-0014

The headings will file in correct chronological order and
print as originally shown above.

Observations on Filing Order

With but few exceptions, the filing order as designed
has proved a very satisfactory arrangement.   It has been
felt advisable to place notes at various points in the catalog
to link together headings which are filed separately.   For
example, the abbreviation Mr. is filed as mr, and the word
Mister is filed as mister.   Here a note refers from one to
the other.   In the subject catalog it was discovered that if
a country or local heading is abbreviated, two different
alphabets are established.   So far this has occured for the

United States (U. S.) and Great Britain (Gt. Brit.)   The
terminal period generates a space when the sort key is
established.   Thus subdivisions separated from the heading
by a dash (two hyphens equivalent to two spaces) are in fact
separated by three spaces and file before jurisdictional or
form subdivisions which do not require the dash.   For
example, U. S. --HISTORY files before U. S. DEPT. OF
STATE.   A note in the catalog gives instructions on the filing order in such a case.

Less fortunate is the situation of the author who
chooses to use a name with a first initial and a complete
middle name.   Because of the period and space separating
the first initial from the middle name, there are established
two spaces.   Thus, the following "incorrect" alphabetical
order is established.
 Smith, J. Russell
 Smith, J. A.
 Smith, J. C.

As may be expected, situations such as those
described above do not occur often.   It is hoped that through
scanning of the open page before him the reader will find the
correct heading.

It may be argued that the coding required to achieve
the alphabetical order in this catalog is too demanding for
a project based upon use of a sophisticated electronic computer.   Possibly, programming should have taken care of
all of this work.   It has been our belief that we have
achieved, in terms of the present state of the art, a good
balance between what the machine should do and what the
human should do.   In the process, we have been able to
keep the form of the information as it appears in the source.
As examples, introductory articles have not been eliminated
from titles, and Library of Congress subject headings have
been retained (11).   Most important, it has been possible to
implement these rules consistently with a relatively inexperienced staff.

Page Creation

With each entry created and alphabetized, the Author-
Title and Subject Split Program (LB060) is called upon to
generate the lines for the final catalog and create the two
columns of each page on magnetic tape.   The final program
(LB070) prints the pages of the catalog from the tape.

The computer line printer permits the use of 132 print positions in each line. The type size is the same as pica type--ten characters to the horizontal inch, six lines to the vertical inch. It was decided that the completed page size for the book catalog should be 8-1/2" x 11". With an allowance for an adequate margin on all four sides of the page, it was believed that the reduction necessary to employ the 132 characters in a line probably no longer than seven inches would be too great. Experimentation led us to accept a reduction to 68 per cent and use of 98 of the 132 print positions. This can, however, prove expensive, as the printer takes as long to print 98 characters as it does 132.

The catalog page as designed calls for two columns, each 45 characters in length, with an eight-character margin between them. The text is 80 lines, and the page is 84 lines in length because of the heading at the top and the page number centered at the bottom. Catalog entries are not split between columns, so that the bottoms of the pages are rarely even.

To simplify programming, it was decided not to attempt programmed hyphenation of words or to require right and left justification of the lines in the catalog. The first words of a catalog entry are set flush left, and all successive lines are indented two spaces. The call number is set flush right on the last line of the entry if there are three spaces separating it from the last word of the entry; otherwise, it is set flush right on the following line.

As stated earlier, entry words (authors, subject headings, added titles) are suppressed if they are the same as those found in a preceding entry and are repeated only at the head of a new column if the entries are continued there. Entry words are so clearly shown in the catalog that it was not considered necessary to use keys at the top of each page indicating which letters are included on that page.

Because an expanded print chain is employed, speed on the printer is considerably reduced, actually to 250 lines per minute. The printer requires eighteen seconds to print one page. The page image is approximately ten inches by fourteen inches. Through use of the Itek Platemaster, this image is reduced to 68 per cent and an offset master created for reproduction on offset equipment.

The foregoing account has emphasized the preparation of a page in an annual catalog. Except for the size of the page and the kind of paper used, the identical process is followed for the preparation of the supplement. Through a switch setting, a forty-line page for the supplement is printed. The supplement is printed on ten-ply paper (8-1/2" x 11"), kept in unburst form, and bound at the top in post binders.

Through similar programs the shelf list is prepared and printed in essentially the same format as the supplement, a 98-character line and a page of forty lines. A key at the top of each page indicates the first call number on that page. The shelf list is printed on four-ply paper, and copies distributed to important staff service points in the Main and Meyer Libraries.

The First Annual Catalog and Its Supplements

The first annual catalog was prepared during the summer of 1966, listing the 25,000 titles cataloged as of the end of June. The catalog was 2,804 pages long, 1,569 pages in the author & title catalog and 1,235 pages in the subject catalog.

Each page from the printer was first scanned by library staff and serious errors masked with white tape. In consequence, the user of the catalog will encounter an occasional blank on a page. The pages were then sent to the University's Photo Reproduction Service, where offset masters were created and fifty copies of each page reproduced. The Stanford University Press prepared the binding. Each set of the catalog was bound in red buckram in seven volumes, approximately 400 pages in each, four volumes for the author & title catalog, three volumes for the subject catalog. There is a title page in each volume and several pages of explanation on the use of the catalog. Letters included in each volume are imprinted on the spine. Fifty sets of the catalog were ready when the building opened in November, 1966. The shelf list, printed in four copies, contained 3,261 pages. Each set required seven binders.

In view of the fact that activation of the Library continued through the first year of opening, the collection grew at a much greater rate than is anticipated for subsequent years. Hence when the building opened, there was available besides the annual catalog a first supplement, in ten copies,

listing the 4,000 titles cataloged from July through
September, 1966.

Although it was proposed originally to prepare monthly supplements, factors of cost and staff time led to acceptance of quarterly supplements. The second supplement,
issued in January, 1967, included the 8,000 titles cataloged
from July through December 1966. A third supplement,
issued in April, 1967, included the 12,000 titles cataloged
from July, 1966, through March, 1967. The April supplement had 1,934 pages in its author & title section, 1,206
pages in the subject section, and 1,752 pages in the shelf
list.

The major drawback to an off-line, batch-process book
catalog is that it is an obsolete document when produced.
This was especially true during the first year when the library grew at the rate of 100 volumes per working day. As
a partial remedy to this situation a brief, dated catalog card
accompanies each book cataloged for the Meyer Library.
Information included consists of call number, author, and
title. This card is placed in an alphabetical file at the
reference desk and purged when a new supplement is issued.

The Meyer Library staff considered the ten copies of
the supplement inadequate for use in the building; during the
second year twenty copies of each supplement are to be
prepared by running the print program twice. Supplements
in the second and succeeding years will, of course, be considerably shorter than those issued in the first year.

The Second Annual Catalog

Preparation of the second annual catalog began in the
spring of 1967. This catalog lists the 41,000 titles cataloged as of the end of June, 1967. The first procedure was
to emend the 1966 tape by purging the entries to be changed
or deleted; corrected entries come in with new data.

In July the information for titles cataloged from April
through June was transferred to magnetic tape and merged
with the data in the April, 1967, supplement. All programs
run through the Author-Title and Subject Update Program and
at that point merged with the emended catalog from the preceding year, the Split Program was run, and the pages for a
new catalog were created.

As in the preceding year, library staff scanned the completed pages and masked noticeable errors. The Photo Reproduction Service printed 75 copies of each page during the first half of August, and the Stanford University Press bound the catalog during the following month. Completed sets of the catalog were delivered on September 20, 1967, a week before classes were to begin for the new academic year.

The 1967 catalog is 4, 612 pages in length--2, 683 pages in the author & title catalog, divided into five volumes of 530 pages each, and 1, 929 pages in the subject catalog, divided into four volumes of 480 pages each. As in 1966, there is a title page and an explanatory introduction in each volume. Floor plans of the library are on the end sheets; and imprinted in gold on the spine are the letters included in each volume, there being clean alphabetical breaks between volumes. The second annual shelf list is 5, 634 pages long, and each of the four copies requires eleven binders.

Some confusion resulted in 1966, when both author & title and subject catalogs were bound in the same color. In 1967 the author & title catalog was bound in tan bookcloth and the subject catalog in light green.

Machine Timing

As the above figures demonstrate, the 1967 edition of the book catalog is no brief document. Similarly, time required to process the information on the computer was not brief. As stated earlier, the addition of the expanded print chain considerably reduced the speed of the line printer. Instead of printing in excess of 600 lines per minute, the printer speed was reduced to 250 lines per minute. This speed was determined by timings made of the print programs. To print each page in the annual author & title and subject catalogs, eighteen seconds were required. To print each page in the supplements or in the shelf list, ten seconds were required. Thus, for example, to print the 4, 612 pages in the 1967 annual catalog, twenty-three hours were required on the computer printer.

In processing the supplements and annual catalogs, it has now become necessary to talk of time required for processing in terms of hours and not seconds or minutes. During the preparation of the 1967 annual catalog timings

were made of the various internal programs, whose output
was magnetic tape and which were not tied to the mechanical
limitations of the line printer. Sample times are shown in
Table 4.

Table 4. Program Running Times

Format and Update Program (LBO20)	6. 5 hours
Shelf List Split Program (LBO30)	11. 2 hours
Author-Title and Subject Update Program (LB050)	3. 7 hours
Author-Title and Subject Split Program (LB060)	28. 5 hours

Throughout the year time is required on the computer
for the preparation of edit lists. Timing was conducted for
this particular program as well. For each 100 records
entered, four minutes of machine time are required to prepare an edit list.

The computer employed for the project is a university facility, and the Library was billed for its use at the rate
of $32. 00 per hour. The Library receives a monthly state-
ment for various charges from the Administrative Data
Processing Center, and these have served as one basic
record to employ in calculating the actual costs of the book
catalog.

Costs

The determination of actual costs is a difficult undertaking, and a meaningful comparison with costs estimated
during the planning process is filled with problems, uncertainties, questions of definition, etc. In a sense, it is
impossible to make a meaningful comparison. An element
measured during planning is not the same as the element
actually achieved. For example, during the early planning
stages, before systems design actually began, there was no
clear plan for the shelf list nor idea of what its role would
actually be. The shelf list as finally designed and implemented is a far more sophisticated document than was then
visualized. Second, there was no clear thought given to the
inputting of separate records for each added volume or copy
of a given item in order to achieve an inventory control
document as well as a classed listing of items in the library. Third, there was no clear determination as to the

length of the sort field required and its effect on processing.
Fourth, a principal study conducted to justify the book catalog compared its projected costs with the costs of three
dictionary card catalogs in the new library.   Although the
book catalog was implemented, the three card catalogs were
not, and we have no idea as to the accuracy of our calculations of their cost, even though our experience with the
preparation of card catalogs is greater.   Fifth, cost studies
were based upon the preparation of a 40,000-title catalog as
the first product.   This was an unrealistic assumption to
make, because the library was to open with only 25,000
titles in its collection.

      Given such reservations and conditions, an effort has
been made to summarize estimated costs and so attempt an
understanding of how they compare to actual costs.   Even
the determination of actual costs is difficult.   It must be
borne in mind that the complete operation was performed
"in house." Cost statements thus omit considerations of
such necessary factors as overhead and considerable administrative supervision.   For example, during the second
year the Library was not charged for program maintenance,
a significant contribution from the Administrative Data
Processing Center.

      Initial planning was based upon preparation of a
40,000-title (60,000-volume) catalog, and it is possible to
present cost approximations in two sections, the first recording costs required to prepare 50 copies of the 25,000
title catalog issued in 1966; and, second, the additional
costs required to input the next 16,000 titles, issue three
supplements, and prepare 75 copies of the 41,000-title
(60,000-volume) catalog issued in 1967.   They are shown
in Table 5.

      If we eliminate the costs directly related to the pro-
duction of the 25,000-title catalog, we may be able to
isolate the cost of the 41,000-title catalog issued in 1967.
This calculation is subject to a certain amount of error,
because some processing done in preparation of the 1966
catalog was used again in 1967.   This may be compensated
for, however, by the time required for the utility programs
to emend and delete items from the 1966 tape.   Test
catalogs and their cost were not considered in early planning, and so their $4,000 cost is eliminated as well.

Table 5
Cost Approximations

	July 65–Aug. 66	Sept. 66 Aug. 67
Input (at $.40 per title)	$10,000	$ 6,400
Programming	5,945	--
Computer charges		
Edit lists	3,000	1,660
Test catalogs	4,000	--
Supplements	--	4,460
Annual catalog	2,500	4,950
Reproduction	4,570	5,270
Binding		
1966 (350 vols.); 1967 (675 vols.)	805	1,690
Binders for shelf list and supplements	84	300
Totals	$30,904	$24,730

In Table 6 below the actual costs for the 41,000-title catalog so derived are compared with the estimates prepared in the fall of 1964 and the estimates offered in April, 1965, at the conclusion of the preliminary systems design. Various adjustments have been made so that these figures are as comparable as possible. For example, the systems estimate did not include a cost for inputting, and this has been added. The actual figures have been adjusted to include costs only for the printing and binding of fifty sets of the catalog instead of the seventy-five which actually were prepared. Although the December, 1964, estimate included under computer charges a factor for supplements, these are not included in the systems estimate or actual charges. The format of the supplement particularly became so sophisticated in design and implementation, both in format and number of copies, that this discrepancy is minimal. These figures necessarily cannot be precise, but they give some magnitude of the work undertaken.

Although the cost figures indicate that the actual cost was more than fifty per cent greater than actually estimated in 1964, it does remain close to the estimate prepared in the systems design. The chief reasons for the discrepancy may be summarized as the underestimation of the amount of machine time needed for the various programs, the underestimation of the programming job involved, underestimating the charges for edit lists; and, most imoortant, the design

of a system that was very much more sophisticated than
that originally foreseen in 1964.

Table 6. Comparison of Estimated and Actual Costs

	Dec. 64 Estimate	April 65 Estimate	Actual Costs
Input of 40,000 titles	$11,060	$16,647	$16,400
Computer charges	1,750	8,595	9,610
Reproduction (50 copies)	4,324	4,500	5,115
Binding	3,750	2,385	1,600
Programming	3,000	6,000	5,945
Totals	$23,884	$38,127	$38,670

Even though costs were greater than expected, one
estimate did hold up, namely the time required to complete
the job.   Delivery and installation of equipment, programming, program testing, inputting of data, reproduction, and
binding--all were on schedule with only minor slippage that
did not affect the completion date of the overall job.

The Future

The publication of the second annual book catalog
coincided with the completion of the library's activation
project.   Continued work on the addition of materials to the
new library has been assigned to existing divisions within
the University Library.   Inputting of cataloging information
for the Meyer Library and preparation of supplements to
the book catalog and of new annual catalogs are now functions of the Catalog Division.   Growth of the library will
henceforth proceed at a slower rate, with from 5,000 to
8,000 titles being added each year.

The first by-product of the system has appeared--a
listing of serial publications in the library for use in ordering and claiming operations.

Even as the first annual catalog was being prepared,
the feeling was expressed that the equipment employed (the
IBM 1401 Computer) was not adequate in an economic sense
to undertake this mission for increasingly larger masses
of material.   This feeling became clearer with the preparation of the second edition.   Looking to the future, we see
at present several paths we may follow.

First, studies are under way on the conversion of the book catalog operation to larger equipment, in this case an IBM System/360, probably linking it to the overall library program of automation. Not only might this change entail use of more powerful equipment for the off-line processing necessary to prepare a book catalog, but there may be possibilities as well of instituting on-line inquiry. There could thus be eliminated the problem of supplements and time-lags.

Second, preliminary inquiries have also been made on the use of the existing tapes in computerized typesetting equipment. The hoped-for result would be the achievement of graphic arts quality on the book catalog page and less bulk to the completed catalog through the greater legibility and greater density thus realized.

Conclusion

Such success as this project has achieved may be attributed to a number of factors:

The entire operation was performed "in house;" we were able to draw upon the skills of many staff members on the Stanford campus--in the Library, the Administrative Data Processing Center, the Photo Reproduction Service, the News and Publications Office, and the Stanford University Press.

IBM representatives, and particularly the systems engineer assigned to the project, gave considerable impetus and guidance to the undertaking. Equipment was delivered on schedule and functioned well.

There was a particularly harmonious and understanding working relationship achieved among the many participants in the project, and administrative support from Library and University officials was constant.

There never was any problem in gaining access to the computer, and the staff responsible for its operation gave devoted serivce in the preparation of the catalog.

Through a happy combination of circumstances, sufficient lead time was available for the project to be completed on schedule.

When it became obvious that we should exceed the cost estimates originally prepared, Library funds were available to continue the work.

It is clear from student reactions that the book catalog is a useful tool in the new library, and it is hoped that the experience here recounted will prove valuable to the profession at large.

References

1. McCune, Lois C. and Salmon, Stephen R. "Bibliography of Library Automation," ALA Bulletin, 61 (June 1967), 674-94.

2. Weber, David C. "Book Catalog Trends in 1966," Library Trends, 16 (July 1967), 149-64.

3. Freitag, Wolfgang M. "Planning for Student Interaction with the Library," California Librarian, 26 (April 1965), 89-96.

4. Hayes, Robert M., Shoffner, Ralph M. The Economics of Book Catalog Production, a Study Prepared for Stanford University Libraries and the Council on Library Resources (Sherman Oaks, Calif.; Advanced Information Systems Division, 1964).

5. Hayes, Robert M., Shoffner, Ralph M. and Weber, David C. "The Economics of Book Catalog Production," Library Resources and Technical Services, 10 (Winter 1966), 63-65, 90.

6. Parker, Ralph H. "Book Catalogs," Library Resources and Technical Service, 8 (Fall 1964), 348.

7. Simonton, Wesley, "The Computerized Catalog: Possible, Feasible, Desirable?" Library Resources and Technical Services, 8 (Fall 1964), 403-405.

8. Avram, Henriette D., Guiles, Kay D. and Meade, Gutherie T. "Fields of Information on Library of Congress Catalog Cards: Analysis of a Random Sample, 1950-1964," The Library Quarterly, 37 (April 1967), 190-91.

9. "Rule 134, " Anglo-American Cataloging Rules.   North
    American Text (Chicago: American Library Associa-
    tion, 1967), pp. 196-97.

10. "Rule 3:6," Rules for Descriptive Cataloging in the
    Library of Congress (Washington, D. C. : U. S. Govern-
    ment Printing Office, 1949), p. 14.

11. Hines, Theodore C. and Harris, Jessica L. Computer
    Filing of Index, Bibliographic, and Catalog Entries
    (Newark: Bro-Dart Foundation, 1966), p. 18.

Harvard University's Widener Library Shelflist Conversion and Publication Program

by Richard D. Gennaro

At the time this paper was written, Dr. De Gennaro was Senior Associate University Librarian, Harvard University. He is now Director of Libraries, University of Pennsylvania. Reprinted by permission from College & Research Libraries, 31 (5): 318-31, September, 1970.

I. Introduction

In 1964, Widener Library, the central research collection of Harvard University, developed a system for converting its manuscript sheaf shelflists to machine readable form and embarked on a project to computerize the 1.6 million entries in the list. To date, more than 600,000 records from some of the most active classes in the library have been converted and used in various ways, and the project continues as an accepted and important part of the library's automation operations. The project has now come of age; its feasibility and usefulness are firmly established and it seems appropriate at this time to review briefly the essential background of the program and to report on its progress, evolution, and future outlook.

The previous papers on the Widener shelflist project were largely concerned with the strategy and the techniques of converting this large and unique file into machine readable form. This paper will stress the present and potential uses that can be made of the shelflist of a major research library after that conversion (or a large part of it) has been completed. Two main categories of uses will be discussed: 1) the production of publications of various kinds and the provision of other reader services; and 2) library management uses including the generation of statistical and other data for further automation, for managerial purposes, and for general research.

II. Review of the Project

The justification for embarking on the ambitious
project to convert the estimated 1. 6 million handwritten
entries in the old looseleaf sheaf shelflists in Widener Library can be found in an article entitled "A Computer Produced Shelflist" which appeared in 1965. [1] The project was
placed in the larger context of the Harvard Library's overall automation program in another article, "Automation in
the Harvard College Library, " which was published in
1968. [2] A technical description of the operation in its early
stages was written by Foster M. Palmer in 1966. [3] No
detailed technical descriptions of the computer systems have
been published since that time, although specific information
can be obtaindd from internal working documents. The
preparation for publication of technical descriptions of a
rapidly evolving system of a local nature is time-consuming
and difficult to justify. This article will merely sketch in
enough of the project's background to make it comprehensible
without reference to the earlier papers. No technical material will be included.

A library shelflist is a record of the books arranged
in the order in which they appear on the shelves. It is
maintained primarily as a tool for assigning new and unique
numbers to books that are added to the collection and as an
inventory record of the books in a library. Since the book
collections in most American libraries are arranged in
classified order, the shelflist is potentially useful to
scholars, particularly if it can be made available in convenient form and if classification schedules and author and
title indexes are provided. For most libraries the maintenance of a shelflist is a routine process and involves
merely filing a copy of each main-entry card into the card
shelflist in call-number order. However, the Widener shelflist, for historical reasons, is largely handwritten in loose-
leaf volumes, rather than on cards, and is, therefore, difficult to use and maintain. In 1964 it became evident that,
through the use of computer technology, the library could
modernize the shelflist maintenance procedure and at the
same time make an expanded version of the shelflist available as an additional approach to the library's holdings. Accordingly, an experimental system was designed to convert
the shelflist to machine readable form and, after a successful pilot project, a fullscale conversion and publication
program was begun in 1965.

The initial system was somewhat primitive, with input and output limited to the standard upper-case character
set that was then commonly available on computer print
chains.   In June 1966 the system was improved so that the
input could be coded with an expanded character set to produce output with both upper and lower case letters and the
required diacritical marks.   The output for the published
volumes continued to be produced by photo offset from a
computer printout until further improvements in the system
made it possible, late in 1969, to produce graphic arts
quality printer's copy in double columns by computerized
photocomposition techniques.   The evolution of the output
format is virtually complete; all further improvements will
be in the input, processing systems, and development of new
products.

To date, more than 600,000 entries of the total 1.6
million in the shelflist have been converted.   Twenty-two
volumes have been published in the Widener Library Shelflist
series and a dozen more are scheduled for publication in
1970.   An estimated twenty-five to thirty additional volumes
will be required to complete the series.   Several of the
classes that were initially keypunched in the limited upper-
case format have been converted by a combination of computer program and manual editing to the new standard expanded character set and format while the rest will be completed by the end of the year.   Thus, all the records in the
system will soon be in a single uniform and compatible machine format.   The master files are arranged in classified
or shelflist sequence on magnetic tape.   Widener call numbers are machine processible and, since the numbers are
unique, they also serve as identification numbers for the
machine records.

The entries in the old manuscript shelflists are not
bibloigraphically complete.   They were limited to call number, volume count, author, title, place, and date of publication.   Frequently the author's forenames were not
spelled out and the titles were shortened.   Notes, added
entries and subject headings were not included.   The
strategy of the conversion project is to accept the entry
essentially as it is with some few exceptions; obvious errors are corrected, authors' full names are added when
easily obtainable, abbreviations in titles are spelled out and
a language code and a code distinguishing serials from
monographs are added.   All elements present are tagged so
as to permit machine manipulation.   The average number of

characters per record is 100, while full LC records are
estimated at 350-450 characters.   This enforced limitation
on the quality and completeness of the records is unfortunate
for many reasons, but it has made the conversion and publication projects economically and technically feasible.   Had
the shelflist contained complete bibliographical records the
project would not have been attempted for various reasons.

Since clean and accurate copies of the Widener
classification schedules are a necessary prerequisite for
the preparation of the published shelflists, a major program was undertaken in 1966 to revise and edit the
schedules.   The schedules are being converted to machine
readable form, and a computer program used to facilitate
editing as well as to format them into the two distinct
forms that are required for the published lists.

All shelflist conversion and editorial work is done
in the library with regular library funds by a staff of eight
non-professionals.   It has become a routine activity of the
Data Processing Division and funds for the completion of
the project within the next several years seem assured.

The design and programming of the system has been
accomplished entirely by librarians trained as systems
analysts.   The routine computer work has been done for the
most part on an IBM 1401 which has 8,000 positions of core
storage and four tape drives and is located in the library.
In 1970 the 1401 will be phased out after the entire system
has been redesigned and reprogrammed to run on an IBM
360-65 located in the University's Computing Center.   The
system conversion will be done by the library's data processing
staff.   The occasion will be seized to convert the local
shelflist system into a more permanent and standardized
system based on the MARC II format.   When the present
system was designed the MARC II standard format for
bibliographic entries in machine readable form did not exist.
That format has now been completed and widely accepted
internationally, and programs are being written at several
centers to manipulate bibliographic data in that format in
various ways and for various purposes.

Although Harvard shelflist entries are not as complete as full LC MARC II entries, the elements that are
present can be tagged and put into the format, and those
that are not can be left blank.   When the library develops
a system to input its current cataloging in the MARC II

format those entries can be integrated into the new shelflist system since the machine format of the two kinds of entries will be compatible even though they differ in the amount of data included.

In the more distant future it is expected that the present brief shelflist entries will be superseded by standard bibliographical records in MARC II format. Given the growing interest in retrospective conversion at the national level, [4], [5] it is reasonable to foresee that a central bibliographical agency will convert and distribute these entries and that Harvard may be able to substitute them for its own incomplete entries. But this is a distant and as yet uncertain possibility. Meanwhile, Harvard will have realized a satisfactory return on its investment in converting its abbreviated shelflist entries. The nature and extent of that return is the subject of the remainder of this paper.

III. Uses of the Machine Readable Data Base

The present and potential uses of the Widener shelflist data base fall into two broad categories. The one involves creating and publishing new or special listings of the holdings of the library for the use of scholars, bibliographers, and librarians at Harvard and elsewhere. The prototype is the published shelflist series; this series and its possible future variations will be discussed first. The other involves using the machine readable data base to improve or facilitate certain library operations such as shelflist maintenance, circulation control, collection building, and the generation of statistical and other information for management and analysis purposes. This will be discussed later.

1. Publications and Reader Services

The publication of the Library's shelflist was one of the principal justifications for converting the shelflist to machine readable form. The rationale is stated succinctly in the preface to the published volumes:

> In the absence of a classified catalog, the shelflist has long been used by librarians and experienced library users as a means of systematically surveying the library's holdings in a particular subject. When perusing the shelflist one sees all

the titles that have been classified in a given area, and not merely those which happen to be on the shelves and whose spine lettering is legible.   In addition, one can take in at a glance the essential bibliographical description of a book--author, title, place and date of publication.   However, the potential usefulness to readers of the Widener sheaf shelflist in manuscript form has never been realized because it existed in only one copy.   Moreover, it was kept in a relatively inaccessible area, was awkward to read and frequently difficult to interpret.   Computer technology has made it possible to enlarge the concept and to expand the uses of the shelflist while improving the techniques of maintaining it and making it available to readers. ...   The development and publication of the shelflist in this form is an attempt to equip the serious reader with a copy of the classification scheme that has been used to organize the collection, together with lists in classified, alphabetical, and chronological order of the books and journals in each class.

After each class and its corresponding classification schedule have been converted to machine readable form, a three-part catalog of the holdings in the class is published in the Widener Library Shelflist series.   The first part contains the classification schedule and a list of the entries in the class in call number (i. e. classification) sequence with sub-class headings (derived by program from the machine readable classification schedule) interspersed throughout the list.   The second part is an alphabetical listing by author and by title and is obtained by a programmed computer sort of the original entries, and the third part lists each entry again chronologically by date of publication.   Thus, each entry is listed four times.

The first twenty volumes in the series were produced by photo-offset from photographically reduced computer printouts and averaged about seventy entries per single-column page.   Beginning with volume 21, all page copy has been set in 6-point Times Roman type in double columns by a computerized photocomposition technique, with approximately 140 entries per page.   Volumes are 8-1/2x11 inches, printed on durable paper, and cloth bound.   The library is the publisher.

The published volumes are extensively used in the Harvard libraries in a variety of ways by both readers and staff. Sets of the entire series are located in reading rooms for reference and in the stacks for circulation to readers. Copies of the volumes covering particular classes are located in special boxes attached to the end panels of the stacks in which the class is located and are used by readers as browsing guides and as convenient finding lists. The availability of the series also tends to reduce somewhat the objections to shelving in frequently used books by size in storage areas outside the library, because these titles are retained in the shelflist with a symbol showing the actual location of the book in storage. The volumes are also used by book selectors in building collections as well as by interlibrary loan staff both at Harvard and in other libraries. Since the shelflist volumes form subject catalogs of specific portions of the collection and since they can be purchased separately, unlike book catalogs of entire libraries, many individual scholars acquire personal copies of the volumes covering their field.

All costs of the shelflist conversion project, including systems development, conversion, editing and machine costs, have been borne entirely by the library from regularly budgeted funds. All costs incurred in the actual publication of the series, including final computer sorts, photocomposition, printing, binding and distribution, are met from sales recepts. Within this framework the published series has been self-supporting from its inception. The rationalization for this large expenditure of library funds is that conversion of the old manuscript shelflist is a necessary improvement of the library's record-keeping operations and that the investment in conversion (an estimated $.30 per entry) will be amply justified by long term savings in shelflist maintenance and other library management gains which will be discussed later. Other savings--impossible to measure--are in the time and effort of readers and staff who use the printed shelflist catalogs in lieu of going to the card catalogs. James L. Dolby makes this point nicely in his recent book on computerized book catalogs. 6

In particular, we claim that no careful study is necessary to show that a printed catalog on the desk of the user, or at least in the immediate vicinity of his office, is a sufficient advance over the present card catalog to provide a substantial time advantage in his use of the catalog. At the

very least, the user is saved a trip to the library
for all those searches that prove to be fruitless.
Further, in an automated catalog it is feasible to
produce many more different orderings of the catalog (and subsets thereof) than is feasible in a card
system. This in turn increases the number of access points to the library collection and the over-all
utility of the catalog of the user. It may be difficult to put a precise dollar figure on the value of
added access, but at the first level it is certainly
sufficient to offset minor cost increments in the
cataloging operation.

The selling price of the individual volumes ranges
from $10 to $45 and is based on the number of pages, the
estimated sales potential of the particular volume, the manufacturing cost, and in special cases, such as the Slavic class,
the amount and cost of extra editorial work.

Since the shelflist in this form was a new and unfamiliar kind of bibliographical tool, and since the promotion
efforts were deliberately limited, sales were initially slow
and tended to be limited to the larger American research libraries, many of which placed standing orders for the series.
Sales have increased as the series has become larger and
better known and as the format has been improved. The
market for volumes has ranged from four to eight hundred
copies, depending on the subject covered; while further improvement is possible, it is unlikely that the sales of any
volume will exceed a thousand copies. There has been a
market for these volumes because they list the holdings of
one of the world's great research libraries and as a result
are valuable tools for librarians and scholars. To date the
following volumes have been published or are in preparation:

Volumes Published:

1. Crusades. 1965. 82 pp., 1,202 titles. $3. Out
   of Print.
2. Africa. 1965. 790 pp., 13,335 titles. $25. Out
   of Print.
3. Twentieth-Century Russian Literature. 1965.
   428 pp., 9,430 titles. $20. Out of Print.
4. Russian History Since 1917. 1966. 698 pp.,
   13,722 titles. $30. Out of Print.
5-6. Latin America. 1966. 1,492 pp., 27,292 titles.
   2 vols., $65.

7. Bibliography. 1966. 1,066 pp., 19,643 titles.
    $40.

8. Reference Collections. 1966. 187 pp., 4,300
    titles. $10. Out of Print.

9-13. American History. 1967. 4,087 pp., 83,867
    titles. 5 vols., $175.

14. China, Japan and Korea. 1968. 494 pp., 11,388
    titles. $25.

15. Periodical Classes. 1968. 758 pp., 25,685 titles.
    $25.

16-17. Education. 1968. 1,610 pp., 32,722 titles. 2
    vols., $60.

18. Literature: General and Comparative. 1968.
    189 pp., 5,065 titles. $10.

19. Southern Asia: Afghanistan, Bhutan, Burma,
    Cambodia, Ceylon, India, Laos, Malaya,
    Nepal, Pakistan, Sikkim, Singapore, Thailand,
    and Vietnam. 1968. 543 pp., 10,292 titles.
    $20.

20. Canadian History and Literature. 1968. 411 pp.,
    10,212 titles. $17.50.

21. Latin American Literature. 1969. 498 pp., 16,900
    titles. $40.

22. Government. 1969. 263 pp., 7,190 titles. $20.

Volumes in Preparation:

23-24. Economics. 1970. 1,800 pp., 65,000 titles.
    2 vols., $95.

25. Celtic Literatures. 1970. 192 pp., 7,500 titles.
    $25.

26-27. American Literature. 1970. 1,600 pp., 50,000
    titles. 2 vols., $95.

28-31. Slavic History and Literatures. 1970. 2,700 pp.,
    93,000 titles. 4 vols., $190.

32-33. General European and World History. 1970.
    35,000 titles. $75.

34. Reference Collections. 1970. 160 pp., 5,000
    titles. $10.

35. African History and Literatures. 1970. 500 pp.,
    16,000 titles. $35.

36-39. English Literature. 1970. 108,000 titles. 4
    vols., $150.

Finnish and Baltic History and Literatures. 1971.
Spanish History and Literature. 1971.

Note: Another 25 to 30 volumes will be required for the remaining significant classes which are scheduled for publication. Many minor and lesser used classes will not be published in the series.

In 1968, after a thorough analysis of the cost and other factors, a decision was made to change the output system to produce printer's copy by a computerized photocomposition process and to discontinue using line-printer output for publication. The logic behind the decision was that the increased page density of photocomposed text would reduce the number of pages in a volume by approximately one-third thus reducing printing costs by a similar amount, while increasing the quality and legibility of the book. Although the cost of creating a photocomposed page is several times the cost of a line printer page, the increase would be more than offset by the reduction in printing costs. Experience proved that this was the case but the savings were not as great as anticipated because the cost of the additional computer time required to prepare the tapes for input into the photocomposition machine were underestimated. It costs slightly more to produce the photocomposed volume but this added cost is justified because it improves the quality of the finished book immeasurably. The slight increase in cost for producing printer's copy in this manner is a temporary penalty only; a significant drop in photocomposition costs can be expected in the next few years as the equipment improves, as the volume of business increases, and as the industry becomes more competitive. Even at current prices, photocomposition is a minor cost breakthrough for the production of book catalogs, particularly in large editions where the savings in printing and paper costs are important.

The relatively new COM (computer-output-microfilm) technology may well provide the solution to the problem of producing small editions of book catalogs at acceptable costs. This process produces output from a magnetic tape onto 16 or 35 mm microfilm at tape running speeds. [7] The cost of producing the film is considerably less than line printer output, and the quality of the print image is somewhat superior to that of the line printer. However, it does not compare with photocomposed copy which is significantly better but several times more costly.

The COM output can either be used in microfilm or automatically enlarged to full-sized master copy for

reproduction in small editions.   Because of the poorer quality
product and other uncertainties, the COM process is not being considered as a possible alternative to the present photocomposition process.   However, it is being considered as a
means of maintaining the official shelflist and more will be
said about this later.

In the longer range, and particularly after the entire
shelflist has been converted, COM will offer many interesting
possibilities for exploiting the shelflist data base so that a
whole variety of listings in different sequences and for different purposes can be published in small, inexpensive microform or even full-sized editions depending on the need and
use to be made of them.

The problem of issuing supplements or revised
editions of the volumes in the current Shelflist series is a
difficult one.   The publication and distribution of supplements
to the individual volumes is questionable both from the point
of view of costs as well as usability.   It has been rejected
in favor of issuing new and enlarged editions when the basic
volume has become seriously outdated, generally after five
or more years.   Thus, the contents of the first volume,
Crusades, will be included as part of the General European
and World History volume; volume 2, Africa, which was published in 1965, will be revised, enlarged and reissued in
1970 in the new photocomposed format; other early volumes in
the series will be treated in a similar manner.   In the future,
the problem of publishing subsequent editions may well be
solved by advances in technology and improvements in the
economics of publishing.   COM and reductions in the cost of
photocomposition and computing are reasonable expectations in
the near future.

As has already been suggested, these developments
may make possible the publication of special or even custom
listings of great usefulness, but of relatively limited demand.
For example, upon completion of conversion of the entire
shelflist it might be desirable and feasible to produce, by
COM at an acceptable cost, an up-to-date microform edition
of the entire file in classified, author and title, and chronological sequence.   Listings by language would also be possible
as would a listing of all serials and journals in the collection
arranged in a single alphabetical sequence.   Current accessions lists would be another useful product.

The technique of merging several related classes into

a single sequence has already been accomplished with excellent results and could be further exploited. An example of this would be to expand the Slavic History and Literature class into a comprehensive Slavic area studies catalog by adding the Slavic titles from other classes such as Education, Folklore, Philology, Sociology, Government, etc. The technique could be applied to other areas such as Africa and Latin America. New shelflist-type catalogs of Judaica and other subjects might be created by pulling together the bibliographic entries that are located in the various country and literature classes as well as in Sociology, Folklore, etc. Miscellaneous scattered titles might be located by searching the tapes for certain key words in titles. The results would have to be edited to eliminate false drops but the process might be useful as a first pass. Similar techniques could be used to search the data base and create special or custom listings for individual scholars or groups on request.

When it becomes economically feasible to store such a large data file in a direct access device and to search and manipulate it from a cathode ray tube console, the possibilities for making interesting and novel uses of the data will be expanded enormously. While mass storage and on-line direct access is an operational technology today, it will probably be several years before it will be economically feasible in the research library environment. [8] It seems idle, therefore, to speculate about these interesting but relatively remote possibilities in an article set in the context of current economic realities in libraries. However, recent experience indicates that improvements in computer and photographic technology are occurring at an ever-accelerating rate, and the possibility of dramatic advances and cost breakthroughs in the next few years should not be discounted.

A long range but still realistic idea is the possibility of turning the conventional library shelflist into a kind of classified catalog once it has been converted and is maintained in machine readable form. The basic difference between a conventional shelflist and a classified catalog is that the shelflist treats a book as a single physical object and records it only once, no matter how many subjects it covers, while a classified catalog records the book in as many places as its subject requires. With a computerized shelflist, the reason for this limitation no longer exists; a book can be given one number to record its physical location, and several other class or base numbers to indicate facets of content. Thus, a single book could appear several times and in various classes. The two types of call numbers would be distinguished by a symbol or other means, and these added entries could be printed or suppressed depending on the use to be made of the list. The introduction of this innovation in shelflisting can only be done after conversion has been completed and it has, therefore, not yet been proposed for the Widener shelflist.

2. Library Management Uses

The present system for adding entries to the official copy of the computer produced printout shelflists is identical with the system for adding to the old manuscript shelflists. The machine lists are printed with five blank lines between the entries in order to leave space for writing in new additions. Periodically, and as the pages become crowded, all new entries and changes in the list are keypunched and added to the master tape file and a new printout replaces the old one. The inefficiencies of this procedure are obvious, but they were tolerated in the early stages of the conversion project on the grounds that it was preferable to have a single shelflisting procedure for both manuscript and machine-produced shelflists until such time as the proportion of machine lists increased to a point where a second system would yield significant savings.

Now that more than a third of the shelflist, including many of the most active classes, is in machine form, the conceptual design of a machine based system for maintaining official copy has been developed and is being considered. It can be briefly described as follows: all classes in machine format would be updated and produced in an efficient single-spaced format on microfilm or microfiche using a COM (computer-output-microfilm) technique. This film would serve as the official shelflist copy along with a temporary card supplement. Book numbers for new books would be assigned by consulting both the film and the card supplement. The number would be pre-empted by making a temporary slip for it in the supplement and this slip would be replaced by a unit card after it had been produced. Periodically the contents of the card supplement would be converted to machine form, merged with the master tape, a new cumulated official film or fiche version would be produced by COM, and a new card supplement would be started. This procedure could be further simplified after developing and implementing a system to input current cataloging into machine readable form, but even in the interim the savings would be substantial. Assuming a cost of five cents per frame of microfilm containing 80 entries, the entire shelflist of 1. 6 million entries would require 20, 000 frames and could be produced for about $1, 000 on approximately 12 reels of film.   A microfiche version would require only 250 4" x 6" fiche.

Computer printing and other costs would be substantially less than in the present system.   Shelflisting now requires a staff of four persons and an area of 600 square feet.   It could probably be reduced to a single work station located in the cataloging room where it logically belongs, while reference copies could be maintained in other locations.

The completed shelflist file can be made to serve many of the purposes of a central bibliographical record in machine form.   By running call numbers against this file a variety of products could be produced such as machine readable book cards for an automated circulation system, lists of overdue books, missing books, and books to be replaced or purchased in duplicate.   In short, any list of call numbers could be expanded into full shelflist type entries by simply key-punching them and matching them with the data file by the aid of a program.

The records of the one and one quarter million circulation transactions made in Widener since 1965, when the machine system was installed, have been preserved on five reels of magnetic tape and constitute an invaluable and unique data base from which statistical analyses of the use of the collection have been made. [9]   One of the chief limitations of this file comes from the fact that the bibliographic data in the charge records is limited to call numbers.   This limitation can be overcome by using the call numbers to extract the complete entries from the shelflist file.   Thus, for example, listings of the most frequently used titles could be obtained by sorting the changes in order of frequency of use and using the resulting call numbers to obtain a listing of the bibliographical entries from the master shelflist file. Decisions about where to locate material in the library and which material to send to deposit collections can be made on the basis of these statistics.   Such potentially useful management information has never before been available to library administrators.

Another whole area of statistical analysis that is opened by the existence of the master shelflist file is the analysis of the collections themselves, their make-up, their rate of growth over the years and in various subject areas.

Detailed and accurate counts can be obtained of the individual classes and of the collection as a whole, e. g. counts by class, by language, by place of publication, by date, as well as counts of serials, monographs, and volumes. Many of these statistics have already been obtained from the converted classes and used for management purposes.

The general research value of the bibliographical data contained in large research library catalogs has already been recognized and exploited to some extent by Dolby, Forsyth, and Resnikoff. [10] They have used data from one of the published volumes of the Widener shelflist[11] and are currently working with the computer tapes of other classes. Their views on the statistical uses of catalogs in machine readable form have been summarized as follows:[12]

> Library catalogs contain a wealth of information about the historic development of the many fields of human endeavor and the interrelations that bind these activities. Mechanization of the catalog permits exploitation of this information by workers in many fields of research. Analysis of the same information can greatly assist librarians in studying their own collections and in managing the acquisition of materials for the library. Many studies of this type can be conducted on random samples of the catalog, though more detailed work requires access to the entire collection in machine-readable form.

IV. Conclusion

In 1968 this author concluded a description of the shelflist conversion project with this statement:[13]

> As it now stands, the Widener shelflist program, like many other present library computer systems, is regarded as an interim system designed to extract the maximum return from a simple existing bibliographical record of the contents of the Library. It is expected that in time the system will become obsolete and the imperfect shelflist entries will be superseded by standard bibliographical records in the emerging Library of Congress MARC II format. . . . The expectation is that a central bibliographical agency will convert and distribute these entries. It seems reasonable to suppose, however, that this conversion effort is still some years in

the future and that, in the meantime, Harvard will
have realized a satisfactory return on its investment in converting an abbreviated bibliographical
record.

Developments during the two years that have passed since that
statement was made only serve to confirm this brief assess-
ment of the program.

References

1.   De Gennaro, Richard. "A Computer Produced Shelf-
      list, " College and Research Libraries, XXVI (July
      1965), 311-315, 353.

2.   _____. "Automation in the Harvard College Library. "
      Harvard Library Bulletin, XVI (July 1968), 217-236.

3.   Palmer, Foster M. "Conversion of existing records in
      large libraries, with special reference to the Widener
      Shelflist, " pp. 57-80 in The Brasenose Conference on
      the Automation of Libraries, Proceedings of the
      Anglo-American Conference on the Mechanization of
      Libraries held at Oxford . . . 30 June-3 July 1966.
      London & Chicago, Mansell, 1967.

4.   Conversion of Retrospective Catalog Records to Machine
      Readable Form, A Study of a National Bibliographical
      Service, Prepared by the RECON Working Task Force,
      Henriette D. Avram, Chairman. Washington,
      Library of Congress, 1969.

5.   De Gennaro, Richard. "A National bibliographical data
      base in machine readable form: progress and
      prospects, " Library Trends. April 1970.

6.   Dolby, James L., V. J. Forsyth and H. L. Resnikoff.
      Computerized Library Catalogs: Their Growth Cost
      and Utility. Cambridge, Mass., M. I. T. Press,
      1969. p. 25.

7.   Avedon, Don M. Computer Output Microfilm (NMA
      Monograph No. 4). Annapolis, Md., National
      Microfilm Association, 1969.

8. The Institute of Library Research at the University of
    California, Berkeley, is operating such a system in
    a research environment as are several other groups.

9. Palmer, Foster M. Widener Library Circulation Sta-
    tistics 1965-1969: Book Use and Stack Space.
    Unpublished working paper. March 1970. 18 p.

10. Dolby, Op. cit. Chapter 6: "On Economic Growth of
    Nations and Archival Collections, " p. 115-133.

11. Ibid. Chapter 1, p. 1-19.

12. Ibid. p. 17.

13. De Gennaro, Op. cit. "Automation in the Harvard
    College Library, " p. 229.

Proposal for a Computer Produced Printed Catalog[1]

by Joel L. Samuels

The author is Assistant to the Director (for Planning), the Newberry Library, Chicago, Illinois.

Introduction

Trinity Evangelical Divinity School in Deerfield, Illinois began in 1961 as a result of the reorganization of Trinity Seminary and Bible College, Chicago. During 1961-65, some of the library materials were classified according to the Decimal Classification, but most of the new acquisitions were shelved in alphabetic order, according to author's surname. From June, 1966 to March, 1968, the present writer was responsible for supervising the developing of a card catalog with the materials shelved according to the Bibliographic Classification of H. E. Bliss. This decision was made by his predecessor.

Reclassification, using the classification scheme of the Library of Congress, was recommended by this writer and the actual work began on July 2, 1968. In an effort to relieve many of the difficulties associated with any reclassification project, the entire collection of 19,200 physical volumes was classified in fourteen months in a strategy of "temporary cataloging." The permanent shelf number was assigned and the books were physically processed, but only an author card was made for the public catalog. This card contained only the shelf number, main entry and short title.

One advantage of this strategy was that ample time would be given for the design of a permanent library catalog.

During this period of time, the Administration engaged the services of a data processing consultant to study the feasibility of using data processing for handling the information

192

needs on campus. The consultant and the librarian had a number of conferences in the fall of 1968 and, in late November, 1968, the consultant submitted the results of his study. He concluded that it would be feasible to develop a library catalog with the aid of a computer.

Further conferences followed and on April 4, 1969, the librarian presented a report to the Data Processing Steering Committee of the Administration. In this report, he discussed the function, requirements, and structure of a bibliographic system and pointed to the advantages of a computer produced printed catalog. His presentation was an oral summary of a fourteen-page report, copies of which are available to interested persons. He did not present a detailed cost analysis of the proposal. The Director of Data Processing Services, acting upon information received from the consultant, cited $2500.00 as a tentative budget for programming costs between April 4 and August 1.

The installation of such a catalog was approved by unanimous vote of the committee and the tentative budget was approved. Further, in the priorities of installation on campus, the Divinity School Library was assigned the second level of priority among four different departments.

Unfortunately there were numerous management difficulties which developed since that meeting which obscured the issues involved in making decisions concerning such an important project. Indeed, the character of these difficulties was such that the feasibility study could not be completed in a manner required by good standards of management even though action was taken to approve installation of the system.

The purpose of this report is not to give an account of management difficulties, but to outline the proposal for a computer produced printed catalog. However, this minimal amount of information is essential to understanding the conclusions of this report.

I.   The Requirements of the Library Catalog

The library catalog is used to determine if the library holds a specific work known to the user. In order to enable the user to have access to the library resources if he has a work in mind, it is essential to record authors, titles, series, and different categories of added entries in an alphabetic sequence. Whether or not there are separate sequences

for authors and related entries and titles and related entries
is not crucial to defining this purpose of the library catalog.

If a user is searching for materials on a specific subject, but has no authors or titles in mind, there must be a
means of access to the library resources to satisfy the needs
of this user. The most common means of subject access to
library resources is the subject heading with all entries on a
given subject appearing under that heading and the different
headings in alphabetic sequence.

There are a number of research and/or academic libraries in the United States who have rejected this principle
of subject cataloging. These libraries have elected to arrange
all the entries on a given subject according to a code drawn
from a classification scheme.

The codes are arranged in the order of the classification scheme in a manner similar to books being arranged by
shelf number. The advantage of this form of subject access
to library resources is that the contents of the books are arranged in the catalog in the same classified order as books
are arranged on the shelves.

A notable example of this approach, called the
"classified catalog" or more precisely, the "classified subject
catalog" is the Library of Boston University. The library
began this project as recently as 1947. During late 1968 and
early 1969, the librarian recommended that this institution
develop such a library catalog and this recommendation was
approved by the Divinity School Administration. Since this
is such an important component of the proposed library catalog,
we will summarize briefly its advantages: (1) it brings
similar subjects together and dissociates dissimilar subjects;
(2) It aids the user in developing subject bibliographies;
(3) It is more convenient to make multiple subject entries;
(4) It makes the revision of subject headings and/or addition of cross references in the subject catalog unnecessary;
and   (5) Although most librarians tend to believe that the
development of a classified subject catalog is costly, those
who have had experience with it have observed a number of
economies being introduced into the process of cataloging.

The classified subject catalog requires an alphabetic
index to serve as the key to it. Such an index actually ful-
fills many functions: (1) An index to the subject catalog;

(2) An index to the shelf list; and (3) A subject authority
file.   This latter is an administrative tool required to preserve the uniformity of entries in a subject catalog.

One of the most important requirements of an effective
library catalog is that each shelf number must be unique.
This requirement is met by the development of a shelf list.
Traditionally, the shelf list was used primarily in technical
processes.   More recently, librarians and users have begun
to use the shelf list in the same manner as one would use a
classified subject catalog. Thus, it has both an administrative
and bibliographic function.

II.   The Design of the Library Catalog

These requirements, given in broad outline, can be
met by a card catalog and a very useful bibliographic tool
could thereby be produced.   This writer had the opportunity
to examine the classified subject catalog at Boston University
in August, 1969.   It is very similar to that planned by this
writer.   If one examines the printed subject index of Boston
University and the computer produced subject index as part
of the test catalog of the Divinity School Library, he might
conclude that the latter is a better tool.   Although such a
card catalog would be serviceable, the apparent advantages
of a computer produced printed catalog were of such a character that a feasibility study seemed warranted.   This study
led to the production of a test catalog.   The design of this
test catalog will be discussed in the following order: (1) Input, (2) Processing, (3) Production, and (4) Output.

Input

The decision to include a given amount of information
in a catalog rests upon the requirements previously stated.
Enough information must be given concerning each work so
as to distinguish between similar but different items.   This
requires more detail than simply author and title.   However,
this does not require as much information as is often provided on printed cards of the Library of Congress or MARC
II tapes.   If the user desires detailed bibliographical information, he may consult the work itself or one of the many
bibliographical tools available in academic libraries.   The
primary question is: Can the user determine from the catalog if he wishes to consult a work and, then, can he identify
it?

Further, enough information must be given so as to

provide as many access points in the library catalog as the
user would reasonably expect.   The attached Input Document
illustrates the type and amount of information which would be
available for a given entry.   It must be emphasized that this
is the information which would be stored on magnetic tape--
the precise amount of information appearing on the output
(the catalog) will vary with the various components of the
catalog.

Processing

The information to be displayed in the catalog is recorded by the library staff on the Input Documents.   The
actual work is done by student assistants following the coded
directives of professional staff in consultation with "pre-cataloging information, " viz., some form of LC copy.   The
shelf and subject classification is also prepared by student
assistants with a professional librarian giving more time to
subject classification.   These cataloging rules and guides for
classification are almost identical to those standards used
for developing a card catalog.   Certain differences must
arise because the computer must follow rigid filing rules
whereas traditional filing rules are characterized by numerous exceptions to which the human mind can adjust, but
which often confuse trained librarians.

The approved input documents are routed to Data
Processing Services (on campus) where punched cards are
prepared.   At stated intervals (for example, each week),
the punched cards are used to produce an "Edit List"
which is returned to the library for proofreading.   The
approved and/or corrected Edit List is returned to Data
Processing Services and a monthly Maintenance List (or
"transactions record") is produced from magnetic tape.

Production

Complete documentation, with supporting flow charts,
is available for a more detailed picture than is given in
this volume.   The magnetic tapes developed from the
punched cards are used to update the Master Library Tape
which is sorted by shelf number.   This tape is used to produce a shelf list and to build the tapes for the alphabetic
catalog and subject catalog.   Then, the alphabetic catalog
is printed.   The tapes for the subject catalog and subject
index are then used to produce the classified subject catalog
which contains an alphabetic description of the classified

notation. The subject index is produced in a process
separate from that used to produce the subject catalog.   The
entire catalog is revised as frequently as serviceability requires and the budget permits.

Summarizing: The Library Staff prepares the input
documents, Data Processing Services prepares the punched
cards and produces the preliminary lists, the Library Staff
proofreads the preliminary lists,   and then, Data Processing Services produces the catalog. It is important to maintain constant liaison between the two different departments
and it is imperative to practice sound management.

Output

The computer imposes certain difficulties upon the
librarian because it introduces him to a different way of
thinking about bibliographical problems.   Perhaps the most
difficult is that the major output of the computer is actually
the magnetic tape on which information is stored.   The magnetic tape can be used as a source of information for pro-
ducing--on paper--the following: (1) Card catalog, (2) Book
catalog, (3) Segments of a book catalog for special purposes,
(4) Special lists consisting of an arrangement of information
not even identifiable with segments of the catalog, (5) Searching the tape for the retrieval of data, or (6) all or a combination of these uses.

Our proposal is to use the magnetic tape to produce a book catalog rather than a card catalog. The
tape is also available for other special purposes. One may
refer to the test catalog as illustrating the following discussion. The test catalog consists of three major components: (1) Alphabetic Catalog, (2) Classified Subject Catalog, and (3) Shelf List.

The alphabetic catalog contains all the information
for a given entry except the "tracings" which are not required by the user but which are essential in a library
catalog. The single alphabetic sequence contains: (1) main
entry, (2) variant forms of a main entry (eliminating cross
references), (3) added entries including series, and (4)
titles. If there is more than one title under a given sorting entry, these are sub-filed by title.

The classified subject catalog is arranged by classification notation and sub-filed by year following the notation, and further sub-filed by title. The format makes clear that only the main entry, title, and shelf number is associated with the sorting key in this catalog. When a given classification notation appears initially, the alphabetic description is drawn from the subject index tape to form a subject heading on the output for the benefit of the user. This same alphabetic description also appears at the top of each page.

The shelf list is arranged by the shelf number and since this must be unique, no sub-filing is required. It contains the same amount of information as the alphabetic catalog.

There is a Name Authority List, Index to the Subject Catalog, and Index to Subject Notations planned as part of the proposed system. However, these have not been produced in the form desired as part of the test catalog. Sample sheets are available for examination.

Critique

It appears that the proper information has been included that is required of a good library catalog. The test catalog shows that sufficient space was allocated for each part of the bibliographical information. Data Processing Services was pleased with the arrangement of the Input Document. The keypunch operator had no difficulty using input documents and batch control sheets provided by the library. The test catalog shows clearly that the computer programming was valid. Original estimates of cost by the consultant were slightly higher than the cost of actual computer time (see below). A number of persons who have examined the catalog have responded favorably to it as an adequate bibliographical tool. The library staff has found even the segments of the proposed indexes useful in cataloging. For example, when the form of the main entry was already established and recorded on the Name Authority List, the same cataloger prepared 100 percent more input documents per hour.

Although this is a favorable picture, there were problems during the design phase and during the production of the catalog. All of the technical problems in programming were resolved. However, a number of unresolved problems in the test catalog remain: (1) Even the second carbon of a printed catalog smudged; (2) Only a few usable copies can be produced by direct printing from the computer; (3) It seems an inefficient arrangement of information to print only six to eight entries per page. All of these problems can be resolved by using different techniques of producing the paper form of the catalog.

It would appear that there should be an annual revision of the computer produced printed catalog. The exact character and frequency of the supplements to the annual catalog are contingent upon the techniques used to produce a paper catalog from the magnetic tape.

III. The Economics of the Book Catalog

On December 10, 1969, a test catalog was produced at Cooperative Computer Centers in Chicago. We will cite the time required to produce each component and then calculate the project time and cost from this time. The equipment provided was an IBM 360, Model 30, two discs and four tape drives. The size of the memory used was a core of 65K. An upper and lower-case print chain permitted the use of certain non-alphabetic and non-numeric characters.

LIB05 Edit List: This represented 1332 cards or 172 books, printed on 33 pages of output in 2. 35'. Fifty edit lists per year containing information for 250 books on each list would require 4 hours of computer time. This will be estimated as 6 hours owing to starting time required.

LIB10 Sorting on Tape by Shelf Number for an identical amount of information required 2. 59' or 4 hours for fifty different sortings. Again, this will be estimated as 6 hours.

LIB15 Maintenance List: The sorting and printing of a similar amount of information required 3. 35'. Twelve such listings for one year would require 5 hours or can be estimated at 6 hours.

The production of these preliminary lists for processing 12, 000 titles on an annual basis will require 18 hours of computer time. Depending upon rental charge of a computer, the annual cost would range between $540-900.

LIB20 Print shelf list and build the alphabetic and subject tapes. 171 books with 123 title entries, or 138 added entries, and 339 subject entries required 2. 06'. The processing of 12,000 per run would thus require 2.3 hours.

LIB25 Sort on tape for alphabetic catalog.   171 books with 123 title entries and 138 added entries were sorted in 1.04'.   The annual processing time for 10,000 titles would be 1 hour.

LIB30 Print alphabetic catalog.   The total of 435 entries, cited individually under LIB20 and LIB25, required 3.54' for printing.   The estimate would thus be 4 hours for 12,000 titles.

LIB35 Sorting for subject catalog.   339 subject entries were sorted on tape in 0.53' or a sorting of 4 subject entries per title for 12,000 titles per year would require 1.25 hours.

LIB40 Printing Subject Catalog.   Precise statistics are not available, but observation of related statistics would leave one to estimate at 5 hours for the amount of information cited under LIB35.

The total of 13.8 hours should be estimated at 20 hours to allow for starting time.   Depending upon the rental charge, the annual cost would be $600-$1000.

The subject index can be compiled, sorted, and printed independent of the major components.   The size of this file will tend to stabilize within the initial years of the installation of the system.   The test list consisting of 1200 entries required 3.0'.   It is estimated that a stable list will consist of 5000 entries.   A revision of this list would thus require 15 minutes or a cost of revision of $8-$12.   Thus, it might be fair to estimate a cost of $10 per revision. Since there are two different lists, the cost of each revision would be $20.

Summarizing, the annual cost for computer rental for processing 12,000 titles and producing an annual catalog with the supporting subject indexes will cost $1160-$1920.   The rental is assumed to range from $30-$50 per hour.   The test catalog was produced at a cost of $30 per hour.

The following chart illustrates the cost of producing such a catalog during the present decade.   It is assumed that 10,000 titles will be processed per year.   As indicated in the previous paragraph, there is a deliberate over-estimating of the time required so as to allow for certain contingencies.

Cumulative Volume[1]	Computer Cost[2]	Input Forms[3]	Keypunch Charge[4]	Catalog Paper[5]
10,000	$1650	$220	$1000	$200
20,000	2450	220	1000	400
30,000	3250	220	1000	600
40,000	4050	220	1000	800
50,000	4850	220	1000	1000
60,000	5660	220	1000	1200
70,000	6450	220	1000	1400
80,000	7250	220	1000	1600
90,000	8050	220	1000	1800
100,000	8850	220	1000	2000

1. Processing 10,000 new titles annually. Lists cost $750 and this is a constant factor.
2. Cost estimated at $50 per hour.
3. Cost of forms at .02 per page plus 10%.
4. Cost of .01 per card.
5. This is highly variable, depending upon number of copies produced. The cost of one copy is cited-- multiply by as many copies as the reader might think advisable for a library.

        In evaluating this data, it must be observed that there is a maximum cost per year (excepting for the supplements, to be discussed below). There are three important factors to observe: (1) An exact calculation of time required for the project could total 27 hours for processing 12,000 titles whereas we have estimated 38 hours. (2) The rental charge for the computer time was calculated on the basis of $50.00 per hour whereas it is actually available for $30.00. (3) There are techniques different from those used for producing the test catalog which could involve substantial reduction in amount of computer running time.

        Taking only the first factor into consideration, the annual cost of the catalog during the first year of installation could have been estimated at $1150.00, the fifty year at $3500.00, and the tenth year at $6200.00.

        Taking the first two factors into consideration the costs could have been estimated at $600.00 for the first year of installation, $2100.00 the fifth year, and $3900.00 for the tenth year. These widely varying figures demonstrate that: (1) It is possible to set forth figures consistent

with a point of view.   (2) It is important to engage in
careful cost analysis prior to making a decision concerning
a given project.   For purposes of comparing the cost of
producing such a catalog, we will arbitrarily choose a middle figure of $40. 00 per hour of computer time with the
catalog requiring 32 hours of computer time.   The projected
cost of input forms, keypunch charge and paper remains
identical, but the computer cost is revised as follows:

Cumulative Volume[2]	Computer Cost	Total of Computer and Related Costs[3]
10, 000	$1150	$2570
20, 000	1750	3370
30, 000	2350	4170
40, 000	2950	4970
50, 000	3550	5770
60, 000	4150	6570
70, 000	4750	7370
80, 000	5350	8170
90, 000	5950	9970
100, 000	6550	10770

One might recall at this point that the fundamental
weakness of the test catalog was that it contained only six to
eight entries per page.   A careful observation could lead
one to believe that the cost of the amount of paper required
should be reduced.

In comparing the cost of producing a book catalog
with the cost of producing a card catalog, we are using
facts and figures derived from: Catalog Card Reproduction
(Chicago: American Library Association, 1965).   A summary
of the results of this study can be found on pages 74-75 of
the book.

Before setting forth the relative costs of these approaches to the production of a library catalog, it is necessary to emphasize that this initial comparison is between
the total of computer related costs and the total of producing
and filing catalog cards.   That is, the comparison is between
the cost of processing cataloging information from the time
that the cataloging copy is available to the time that the
product is ready for the library user.   This comparison is
reasonable because these represent parallel operations.   The
costs of developing cataloging copy must be separated for

that is <u>not</u> a data processing cost.

In 1965, the cost of purchasing and processing printed cards from the Library of Congress was $5520. 00 for 10, 000 titles.   Assuming the constant factor of $2. 00 for wages, this figure must be increased, owing to the increased costs of printed cards.   The cost of the initial card has been increased from . 07 to . 11.   Thus, this figure must be adjusted to $5920. 00.   One must account for the fact that secretaries are paid more than $2. 00 per hour, but this figure will not be changed accordingly.   The cost of filing cards for 10, 000 titles will vary with the exact number of cards filed.   An average figure for one academic library will often be eight.   Statistics recorded in January-April of 1969 indicate that it required one hour to file 64 cards, as an average.   The filing of 80, 000 cards per year thus requires 1250 hours.   If the filer if paid $2. 00 per hour, it will cost $2500. 00 for personnel to file cards.   The difficulty with this estimate is that a professional librarian must sometimes be consulted for problems concerning filing order.

To this point, the cost of producing a card catalog using printed cards is $7500. 00 on an annual basis.   There are miscellaneous operations in the development of a card catalog which parallel operations used in producing a book catalog by computer.   Such operations include the making up of guide cards for the catalog, cross reference cards for the author catalog, and cross reference cards for the subject catalog.   Although these are <u>real</u> costs, it is difficult to define the cost.

The cost of developing these two different catalogs during the present decade may be projected.   On the operations which are clearly parallel, the cost of developing a card catalog using printed cards may be estimated at $75, 000. 00 and the cost of a book catalog using the computer, $63, 770. 00.   One must add to the cost of the book catalog the annual cost of a supplement.

For present purposes, we will assume that a cumulative supplement will be issued three times on a quarterly basis with the annual revision being issued the fourth time. This will mean a total processing of 15, 000 titles (2500 plus 5000 plus 7500).   The cost, on a basis of the middle figure used for purposes of comparison, would be approximately $1500. The supplements required for the present decade

would then cost $15,000 or the total cost of the book catalog
would be $78,700 compared to $75,000 for the card catalog.

Before proceeding with a discussion of other cost
factors, one can refer again to Catalog Card Reproduction.
This study summarizes the cost of producing catalog cards
for 3000 titles by five different methods: (1) Library of
Congress cards, ($1596.00), (2) Stencil - small equipment
($991.00), (3) Stencil - large equipment ($900.00), (4) Offset ($1,537.00), and (5) Ektalith and Offset ($1,794.00).
The present librarian used this study in early 1966 when it
was necessary for him to make the decision on what method
of card reproduction to employ. After considerable investigation, he chose the small duplicator which was the second
most economical of the five methods.

There are cost factors subsequent to the completion of
a library catalog which should be considered, but these are
less tangible as far as stating cost figures. One thinks of
the floor space required by different types of catalogs with
building costs at $30.00 per square foot. The different types
of equipment required to "house" the different catalogs must
be considered. Catalog cards can become worn or lost
and thus, must be replaced. As a library grows, catalog
cards must be shifted on occasions. These cost factors
would tend to favor the adoption of the book catalog.

There are also cost factors prior to the beginning
of data processing or the beginning of card production. First,
one must compare the cost of obtaining printed cards from
the Library of Congress with the cost of preparing input
documents. I can give no exact figures in this report since
I know of no studies on the question and generalizations
can be misleading. It is undoubtedly true that the
preparation of input documents requires more time than the
ordering and receiving of printed cards from the Library of
Congress, but one cannot dismiss this latter cost factor as
trivial. One ought to reflect upon the inefficiency of waiting
for these cards and that time is required for matching the
received cards with the books being held.

Second, there will be a certain percent of books which
require original cataloging. We can give no figures for this
library, but the library of Moody Bible Institute currently
does about 40 percent of its materials by original cataloging.
Original cataloging must be done for microfilm, many older
and rare books, and some periodicals. The reason for

pointing out these factors is that there is no difference
between preparing cataloging copy for a card catalog or a
book catalog for a significant part of the materials.

When viewed in this perspective, the question to be
answered is: Is the time used for preparing cataloging copy
for library materials for which printed cards are available
worth the advantages of the book catalog? Stated differently,
does the value of the book catalog justify the preparation of
cataloging copy even though printed cards already exist?

IV.   The Advantages of the Book Catalog

When one raises the question of the advantages of the
book catalog, he ought to immediately recognize that there
are actually two separate questions: What are the advantages
of using magnetic tape as a medium of storing cataloging information? What are the advantages of developing a book
catalog? The recognition that these are separate questions
will lead to the recognition of the fundamental strength of
the system proposed in this report and the basic limitation
of the card catalog.

When a card catalog is implemented, it becomes un-
changeable in its form, it has few access points, and is
placed in only one location. The system herein proposed
can be reproduced into a wide variety of forms, it has as
many access points as a combination of the fixed access
points permits, and can be reproduced in such a manner as
to be placed in several locations.

The specific advantages may now be enumerated
since they arise from this basic recognition: (1) The computer sorts and files entries consistently whereas there will
be inconsistencies in a manually produced card catalog; (2)
Multiple copies of the catalog can be produced and placed
in different locations in the library or on campus; (3)
Special bibliographies can be produced by simply making
copies of segments of the catalog; (4) It is more convenient
for the user to examine a book format with many entries
per page than it is to use a card catalog; (5) Subsequent to
the initial installation of the system, changes in the system
or in the format of the book catalog can be made without
changing the information stored on magnetic tape; (6) While
this factor might not be crucial, the destruction of the public or even of an official catalog will not be the destruction
of the system; (7) It is not necessary to develop an official

catalog and it is not necessary for the staff to consult the
public catalog.   The staff use of the library catalog is
important for proper development and organization of the
book collections.   Indeed, staff use of a book catalog speeds
the work or reduces the personnel costs; (8) It would appear
that there are economic savings in the production of a book
catalog even though the figures cited in this report indicate
the cost is nearly equivalent.   The rising level of technology
will undoubtedly increase the value of the computer dollar
and personnel costs will rise.   These generalizations can be
documented in both the literature and through consultants;
(9)   While we have emphasized the value of the book catalog,
the fact that cataloging information is stored on magnetic
tape means that there is laid a good foundation for developing an information retrieval system.   It is possible to search
the magnetic tape for information stored according to the
familiar access points (author, title, subject, etc.), other
access points whenever a "fixed field" occurs (publisher,
date, added entry code, etc.), and most importantly, any
combination of these access points desired by the researcher.
The potential of the book catalog can thus be exploited because the bibliographical information is in machine readable
form.

        There are a number of disadvantages, but the most
significant one is that the book catalog--even with a supplement every three months--will not be as up-to-date as a
card catalog.   We believe that is not sufficiently serious to
argue against the book catalog.   A "List of Recent Acquisitions" can be printed from the same tape which is used to
print the Maintenance List.   The cost of such a list should
not be added to the system, but should be compared to the
cost of a manually typed and mimeographed list.

        This minor but important project leads to a final
observation concerning the advantages of the system herein
proposed.   Once the system is installed, various other
systems for acquisitions, periodical records, circulation
records can be easily tied into the catalog which we conceive as the core of any "total systems approach."   The
truth is that effective systems of library automation can be
installed prior to the millenial dream of a "total system."

Conclusion

        It would seem to be a sound principle of management
to install only one system, ·but permitting it to be flexible

so that other systems can be related to it. We recommend
that the Divinity School begin with the library catalog. It
would be easier to begin with an acquisition system since
such a system is available to us without cost. It would be
safer to recommend that an acquisition system be installed
first because we know that thoroughly de-bugged system is
operational and it would be good public relations to show such
a product. However, the development of a library catalog is
one of the most urgent tasks of the Divinity School Library.

It is our conclusion that the installation of a system
similar to that outlined in this report and illustrated by the
test catalog will enable the Divinity School Library to respond
to the urgent task of developing a library catalog quickly.
Our critique of the test catalog leads to the conclusion that
it is essentially sound in the information provided and in
the manner in which it is structured. However, the
problem of only six to eight entries per page with the cost of
paper must be tackled. There is a solution to this problem
available--computer produced microfilm from which paper
copies are printed. The immediate advantage is that as
many copies as desired can be printed and each copy is of
equal quality. An advantage which may not be recognized
is that it may be more economical to employ this method
than the one illustrated by our test catalog with almost no
alteration in computer programming. The procedures and
cost of this technique were not investigated. Another institution in the Chicago area is considering the development of
a book catalog almost identical to the one contained in this
proposal and its librarian is investigating such a technique.

Notes

1. This was a preliminary proposal designed to demon-
    strate the technological and economic feasibility of
    a book catalog, as well as its bibliographic
    superiority. A series of management difficulties
    prevented the further development of the pilot
    project.

2.   Constant factor is $550.00 for preliminary lists.

3.   Computer time, input forms, keypunching, paper for one copy since there will follow a comparison with the cost of developing <u>one</u> copy of a card catalog.

TRINITY EVANGELICAL DIVINITY SCHOOL

COMPUTER PRODUCED PRINTED CATALOG

INPUT DOCUMENT

ATTACH PRE-CATALOGING INFORMATION

By Whom   Date

Cataloging Approval

Cards Punched

Input Document Filed

- New
- Correction
- Deletion

24 25 LOCATION CODE

1 2 SHELF NUMBER (-----------:-----------)

1 26 MAIN ENTRY (-----------:-----------)

1 26 IMPRINT (-----------:Publ. List)

1 26 COLLATION 41 42 EDITION 49 50 BLANK

1 26 27 TITLE

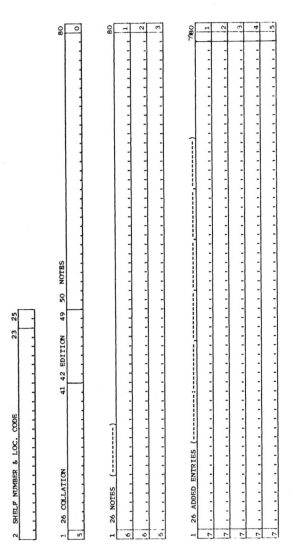

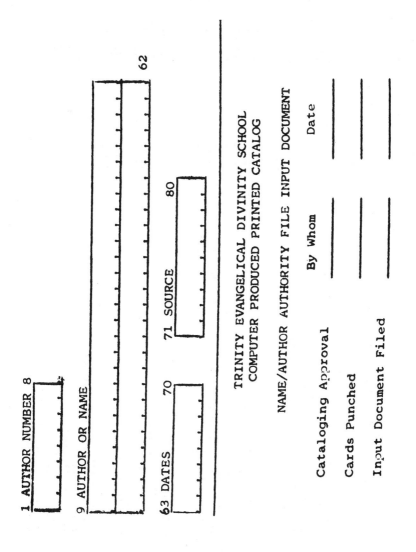

1 AUTHOR NUMBER 8

9 AUTHOR OR NAME

62

63 DATES   70   71 SOURCE   80

TRINITY EVANGELICAL DIVINITY SCHOOL
COMPUTER PRODUCED PRINTED CATALOG

NAME/AUTHOR AUTHORITY FILE INPUT DOCUMENT

                    By Whom   Date

Cataloging Approval

Cards Punched

Input Document Filed

TRINITY EVANGELICAL DIVINITY SCHOOL   NAME AUTHORITY LIST   NOV 19, 1969   P. 23

NUMBER	NAME	DATES	SOURCE
.IN3	INFELD, LEOPOLD	1898-	LCC 42
.IN4	INGE, WILLIAM RALPH	1860-1954	NUC 62
.IN7	INSIGHT, JAMES	-	NUC 67
.IN7	INTERNATIONAL CONFERENCE ON STUDENT MENTAL HEALTH	-	NUC 62
.IN8	INTERNATIONAL INSTITUTE OF PHILOSOPHY	-	LCC 52
.IN8	INTERNATIONAL SYMPOSIUM ON ANTHROPOLOGY	-	NUC 57
.IN8	IRONSIDE, HENRY ALLAN	1876-1951	BPR 68
.IR6	IRVING, ROY G.	-	NUC 62
.IR8	IRWIN, WILLIAM ANDREW	1884-	NUC 57
.IR9	ISHERWOOD, MARGARET	1839-1922	LCC 42
.IS3	IVERACH, JAMES	1860-	LCC 42
.IV3	JACKS, LAWRENCE PEARSALL	-	NUC 67
.J131	JACKSON, EDGAR NEWMAN		
.J133	JACKSON, FREDERICK JOHN FOAKES ✗SEE FOAKES-JACKSON◻	1851-1912	LCC 42
	JACKSON, SAMUEL MACAULEY	-	UTS
.J138	JACOB, GEORGE ANDREW	-	UTS
.J15	JACOBS, JOSEPH	-	NUC 67
.J153	JAI SINGH, HERBERT ✗X SINGH◻	-	LCC 42
.J199	JAMES, THOMAS, 1573-1629	1573-1629	LCC 42
.J236	JAMES, WILLIAM	1842-1910	NUC 67
.J237	JANSEN, JOHN FREDERICK	-	NUC 62 CB
.J266	JASPERS, KARL	1883-	LCC 42
.J312	JEFFERSON, CHARLES EDWARD	1860-1937	NUC 62
.J356	JEFFERY, ARTHUR	-	LCC 42
.J36	JENKS, WILLIAM, 1778-1866	1778-1866	LCC 42
.J428	JENNINGS, FREDERICK CHARLES	1847-	LCC 42
.J443	JENSEN, DE LAMAR	1925-	NUC 62
.J453	JEROME, SAINT ✗SEE HIERONYMUS◻		
	JESSNER, LUCIE	-	UTS,ME
.J497	JEWETT, EDWARD HURTT	1930-1907	LCC 42
.J552	JEWETT, PAUL KING	-	NUC 62
.J554	JOANNES OF DAMASCUS ✗X JOHN OF DAMASCUS◻	-	LCC 42
.J572	JOHN OF DAMASCUS ✗SEE JOANNES OF DAMASCUS◻		
.J631	JOHNSON, FREDERICK ERNEST	1884-	NUC 62

SUBJECT CLASS.	VERBAL DESCRIPTION
449	ABOLITIONIST
BF335	ADAPTABILITY ⟨PSYCHOLOGY⟩
BH221.F8	AESTHETICS, FRENCH
BR1460	AFRICA, WEST-CHURCH HISTORY
RC565	ALCOHOLISM
RV3785.A4	ALEXANDER, CHARLES M.
BL467	ANCESTOR-WORSHIP
DS131	ANGLO-ISRAELISM
BT1095	APOLOGETICS-COLLECTIONS
PJ3259	ASSYRO-BABYLONIAN LANGUAGE-CHRESTOMATHIES AND READERS
PJ3453	ASSYRO-BABLONIAN LANGUAGE-DICTIONARIES
BT88	AUTHORITY ⟨RELIGION⟩
BS475	BIBLE-INTRODUCTIONS
BS2302	BIBLE. N. T.-CONCORDANCES, GREEK
BS2795	BIBLE. N. T. EPISTLES OF PETER-CRITICISM, INTERPRETATION, ETC
BS2385	BIBLE. N. T.-WORD STUDIES
Z 7772.A1	BIBLE. O. T.-BIBLIOGRAPHY
BS650	BIBLE AND SCIENCE
Z 1035	BIBLIOGRAPHY-BEST BOOKS
Z 1215	BIBLIOGRAPHY-BIBLIOGRAPHY-UNITED STATES
BL1410	BUDDHA AND BUDDHISM-SACRED BOOKS
DS235	CALIPHS
BT1030	CATECHISMS
BX1749	CATHOLIC CHURCH-DOCTRINAL AND CONTROVERSIAL WORKS
Z 7204.C46	CHARACTER-BIBLIOGRAPHY
RJ499	CHILD PSYCHIATRY
HV741	CHILD WELFARE-UNITED STATES
DS721	CHINA-CIVILIZATION

Trinity Evangelical Divinity School
Index to Subject Catalog

Book Catalogs as Supplements

to Card Catalogs

by Phillis A. Richmond

The author is on the faculty of the School of
Library Science, Case Western Reserve University, Cleveland, Ohio. This article is reprinted
by permission from Library Resources & Technical
Services, 8 (4): 359-65, Fall 1964.

During the past three years, the University of
Rochester Library has been engaged in a long-term project
to make one-line, short-title, printed catalogs for each of
its science libraries. The catalog for the Engineering Library was issued in 1962, that for the Geology-Geography
Library in 1963. A third catalog, for the Physics-Mathematics-Optics-Astronomy Library is with the printer; and a
fourth, for the Life Sciences Library, is now three-quarters
punched.

The catalogs are made with the standard IBM electronic accounting machinery in the University's Data Processing Center. Keypunching has been carried on at the rate of
two hours a week since 1961, but this is much too slow, so
that in September, the Library will get its own keypunch.
The rest of the machines, sorter, reproducer, interpreter,
and 407 printer, are used on a rental basis. The annual
budget allotment for preparing and printing these catalogs,
exclusive of keypunching labor, began at $970 and is now
$1200.

The primary purpose of the catalogs is to put an
accurate list of all books and journals in the science libraries on the desk of each member of the faculty and research
staff in the departments served by each library. These catalogs save valuable faculty time and energy by making it
possible to ascertain what is in the library without actually

going there.   The professor can consult the catalog before ordering books, thus eliminating the expensive nuisance of discovering a duplicate order halfway through the ordering procedure.   He can also determine whether the library owns a book before assigning it for reserve.   Required reading assignments from books not held are distressing to student and librarian alike.

The second purpose of the short-title printed catalogs is to make it possible for every science librarian to know what is in every other science library without calling the Circulation Department at Rush Rhees Library and asking them to look in the main (union) catalog.   The Inter-Library Loan Department also makes use of the catalogs as a short cut to determining who has what.

The third purpose of the catalogs is to enable the other libraries in the Rochester area, especially the company libraries, to find out what books are in the University science libraries without telephoning for this information before they send their Inter-Library Loan requests.   This is a convenience to us as well as to them.

The printed catalog is a supplement to the regular card catalog in each library; it does not replace it.   The one-line entry does not give anywhere near the amount of information necessary to make the best use of a book.   It would be extremely abbreviated for a large collection. There are no cross-references in the printed catalogs, so that if the reader does not have a pretty good idea of what he is looking for, that is, if he does not know his author or the accurate title of his book, the catalog is useless.   It is strictly a finding tool, not a browsing one.

The one-line entry[1] necessitates extensive use of abbreviations, since only 80 columns can be used in punching information.   A reader who knows what he is looking for will have little trouble with these abbreviations, but a full listing is issued with each catalog in case of ambiguity. The short form allows entry of the Library of Congress classification number for each book, but not the book number.   This will get the reader to the shelf he wants where he can find books in the desired class arranged alphabetical-ly.   The twenty-one columns alloted to the author entry are adequate for personal names, but the names of corporate bodies have to be abbreviated.   Some of these are easily recognized, while others, particularly symposia, conferences,

congresses and the like, require interpretation. A list of
these special abbreviations is also included in each catalog.
The abbreviations are kept uniform for all science libraries;
we do not separate them by library or subject.

The forty-six column allotment for title is usually
adequate except for highly-specialized works such as disser-
tations, theses, and some conference reports. The final
two columns are used for date, beginning with 00 for 1900
and ending in 99 for 1999. Special codes are used as
blanket coverage for certain types of materials, such as
MS^2 for things published before 1900, MC for monographic
continuations which are still being issued, and ND for no
date. Periodicals are distinguished by having volumes and
dates follow the title so that the final two columns are always blank, making it easy to sort a deck for periodicals.

It turned out that the final column in the section
allowed for the classification number was unneeded except in
very rare instances because the Library of Congress
classification numbers, including the decimal, rarely take
more than ten places. This column has been used for control with the 407 printer.

Until the Library gets its keypunch, our entries continue to be recorded on graph paper each week from the
catalog cards which come through for filing in the science
library card catalogs. When we get the keypunch, we shall
punch from the cards directly and eliminate this middle
step. In beginning a new catalog, we punch directly from
the shelf list, drawer by drawer.

After the cards for a library are punched, they are
sorted by class number and author, printed on the 407
printer, and the result proofread against the shelf list.
Corrections are made, and then four decks are reproduced
and interpreted with a special plugboard that gives us initial
listings by author, title, and classification number, as well
as a deck of periodical listings.

The first printed catalog did not include a section
arranged by subject because it would have cost twice as much
to publish. We did, however, run off two copies on the 407
printer, which we placed in the Engineering Library, after
notifying the faculty and staff that they were available. To
the best of my knowledge, there has not been a single request for listing by subject since the catalog was published

in January 1962. We have not received any requests for subject listing in the Geology-Geography Library catalog, either.

We also omitted the periodical listing in the first catalog. This turned out to be a bad mistake. The second catalog contained such a list. The demand for information on periodical holdings has been so great that this spring we brought out a special catalog, again made with data processing equipment, giving a list of all scientific journals on current subscription, including those in Rush Rhees Library, and in the Chemistry Library, which is in the process of joining the group of science libraries. The demand for this list has been heavy, not only on our own campus, but from the special libraries in our area. It has also sparked a movement locally to make a cooperatively punched union list for all of the scientific and technical libraries in the city. The entries in this catalog are not as full as those in the short-title catalogs, and eventually it will be replcaed by a collected periodical list compiled from all the catalogs.

Updating the printed catalogs may be done in two ways: by periodically issuing cumulative supplements comprising the cards punched since the main work was published, or by putting out completely new editions. When the initial catalogs for all science libraries have been made, the updating program will begin. Since book budgets are increasing and the number of titles added each year is running into the thousands, and also because a single volume is much easier to use than supplements, a new edition annually seems the most likely procedure, provided costs are not exorbitant.

We have, as yet unpunched, the wherewithal to make a classified catalog for the Engineering Library. To do this, we first listed the subject headings for every title. Then we converted these to suitable Library of Congress classification numbers. I do not know whether it is worthwhile to make a classified catalog, but I think we shall try it as an experiment and see what reaction we get from the College of Engineering.

Three of our science libraries have already reached a size where their catalogs are too large to make alphabetizing an easy operation. For example, the author file for the Physics-Math Library is at least twenty-four inches, which is hard to keep in order on a sorter, since hopper and pockets only hold about ten and six inches respectively.

For this reason, we have been experimenting with use of a
computer to mechanize the full <u>ALA Filing Rules.</u>   Through
the cooperation of Dr. Philip Baumeister, Department of
Optics, we have a FORTRAN II program for filing by author,
with a subroutine in Autocoder for interfiling names beginning with MC and MAC.   The subroutine was first done in
FORTRAN II as a term paper and is shown in Figure 1. [3]

The main program has been run twice on the IBM 7074
(for sample of its print-out see Figure 2).   Currently new
items can be merged into the master tape in batches of not
more than 300 cards.   With two additions, we expect to use
the program for updating, sorting, and printing the author
and periodical listings.   The first addition is a sub-routine
for converting St. to SAINT for filing purposes.   This has
been written in FORTRAN II, but not converted to Autocoder.
The second addition, for the main program, is a routine to
interfile title entries with an editing process that will move
the first word of the title to the author position for sorting
and back again after sorting.   (All initial articles have been
omitted in keypunching titles.)   Listing by title and for abbreviations will be the next additions.   We plan to add other
sub-routines during the next year as computer funds become
available, even things we do not need immediately, because
we expect eventually to be recording via an optical scanner
rather than by keypunching.   Needless to say, to mechanize
<u>all</u> of the filing rules is a long-term project, some parts of
which will require different input routines than those used at
present.   We do NOT anticipate changing the <u>rules</u> to fit the
machine, but rather wish to devise machine techniques to fit
the rules.

Developing the beginning computer program has necessitated some changes in our keypunching procedure.   We
would like, for example, to merge all of our printed catalogs into one for all science libraries.   Because we have
used all of our columns on the IBM card for data, we had
no way of indicating which title was in which library or
where there are multiple copies.   Now we are indicating
location by putting a code number into the rarely-used
column 11 of the classification number area of the punched
card.   When the machine finds column 11 already occupied,
it looks for an 11# punch, which we use in such instances
to indicate that a trailer card with information on it follows.
We have also cleared the top of column 79 in our date area
for 11 and 12 punches by changing the code for a pre-1900
publication from HS to MS.   Both this alternative and similar

Figure 1.   University of Rochester Science
Libraries. Program for Interfiling Names
Beginning with MAC and MC, in Fortran II, for IBM 7074 Computer.

```
        RØUTINE TØ INTERFILE MC AND MAC NAMES
        TYPE 5
        PAUSE
        M=1HM
        MC=1HC
        DIMENSIØN KA(3), KB(22), KC(10)
     10 READ 60, (KA(J),J=1,3),(KB(J),J=1,21),(KC(J),J=1,10)
        KB(22)=0
        IF(KA(1))11,28,11
     11 CØNTINUE
     60 FØRMAT (2A5,A1,21A1,10A5)
        WRITE ØUTPUT TAPE 5, 61,(KA(J),J=1,3),(KB(J),J=1,21),
        (KC(J),J=1,10),TØG
     61 FØRMAT (2A5,A1,21A1,10A5,F3.0)
        IF(KB(1)-M) 20, 21, 20
C       FIRST LETTER IS M
     21 IF(KB(2)-MC) 20,22,20
C       SECØND LETTER IS C
     22 TØG=1.
        KQ=KB(2)
C       KB(2) IN KQ
        DØ 69 K=3,22
        KR=KB(K)
C       SAVES 3
        KB(K)=KQ
C       PUTS 2 INTØ 3
     69 KQ=KR
C       KQ CØNTAINS 3
        KB(2)=1HA
C       PUTS A INTØ KB(2)
        GØ TØ 25
     20 TØG=0.
     25 WRITE ØUTPUT TAPE 5,62,(KA(J),J=1,3),(KB(J),J=1,22),
        (KC(J),J=1,10),TØG
     62 FØRMAT (2A5,A1,22A1,10A5,F3.0/)
        GØ TØ 10
     28 STØP
      5 FØRMAT (50H PLEASE SET CARD READER TØ BB, THEN PRESS START    )
        END

C       SØRT RØUTINE
C       MERGE RØUTINE

C       RØUTINE TØ TAKE A ØUT OF MC ENTRIES
     64 READ INPUT TAPE 5,63,(KA(J),J=1,3),(KB(J),J=1,22),
        (KC(J),J=1,10),TØG
     63 FØRMAT (2A5,A1,21A1,10A5,F3.0)
        IF (KA(1)) 65,201,65
     65 CØNTINUE
        IF (TØG) 100,109,100
    100 DØ 108 K=2,21
    108 KB(K)=KB(K+1)
C       DELETES A IN MC NAMES
    109 CØNTINUE
        WRITE ØUTPUT TAPE 5,200,(KA(J),J=1,3),(KB(J),J=1,21),
        (KC(J),J=1,10)
    200 FØRMAT (30H AUTHØR LIST FILED BY CØMPUTER/ 22A1,3X3A5,
        3X10A5,3XI5)
        GØ TØ 64
    201 STØP
        END
```

AUTHOR INDEX

Author	Title			
LANE CECIL TAVERNER	SUPERFLUID PHYSICS	62	QC0286	2
LANG SERGE	DIOPHANTINE GEOMETRY	62	QA0564	2
LARSON DEWEY B	CASE AGAINST THE NUCLEAR ATOM	63	QC0173	2
LEFSCHETZ SOLOMON	ALGEBRAIC GEOMETRY	53	QA0564	2
LEFSCHETZ SOLOMON	ALGEBRAIC TOPOLOGY	42	QA0611	2
LEFSCHETZ SOLOMON	LECTURES ON ALGEBRAIC GEOMETRY	37	QA0564	2
LIUSTERNIK LAZAR A	METHODES TOPOLOGIQUES	MC	QA0611	2
LLOWARCH W	RIPPLE TANK STUDIES OF WAVE MOTION	61	QC0157	2
LOCHER-ERNST LOUIS	EINFUEHRUNG FREIE GEOM EBENER KURVEN	52	QA0483	2
LONGHURST RICHARD S	GEOMETRICAL + PHYSICAL OPTICS	57	QC0355	2
LOPSHITS A M	COMPUTATION AREAS OF ORIENTED FIGURES	63	QA0482	2
LUCKIESH MATTHEW	LIGHT	44	QC0241	2
LUNEBERG RUDOLF KARL	MATHEMATICAL THEORY OF OPTICS	44	QC0355	2
MACDONALD DAVID K C	NOISE + FLUCTUATIONS	62	QC0175	2
MACH ERNST	PRINCIPLES OF PHYSICAL OPTICS	25	QC0355	2
MCLACHLAN EUGENE K	EXTREMAL ELEMENTS CERTAIN CONVEX CONES	55	QA0649	2
MCLACHLAN NORMAN W	COMPLEX VARIABLE THEORY ED.2	55	QA0432	2
MACLANE SAUNDERS	HOMOLOGY	63	QA0611	2
MACLANE SAUNDERS	SIMPLICIAL TOPOLOGY	59	QA0611	2
MCLEOD EDWARD B	INTRODUCTION TO FLUID DYNAMICS	63	QA0911	2
MCVITTIE GEORGE C	FACT + THEORY IN COSMOLOGY	61	QB0500	2
MANSFIELD MAYNARD J	INTRODUCTION TO TOPOLOGY	63	QA0611	2
MARIOT L	GROUP THEORY + SOLID STATE PHYSICS	62	QC0174.5	2
MASSEY HARRIE S W	ELECTRONIC + IONIC IMPACT PHENOMENA	52	QC0721	2
MAYER WALTHER	LECTURES	38	QA0611	2
MAYRHOFER KARL	INHALT + MASS	52	QA0611	2
MEIJER PAUL H E	GROUP THEORY	62	QC0174.5	2
MENDELSON BERT	INTRODUCTION TO TOPOLOGY	63	QA0611	2

Figure 2. Computer Filed Author Listing. University of Rochester Physics-Mathematics-Optics-Astronomy Library. Program by Professor Philip Baumeister, Dept. of Optics. Code in right column is to indicate which library has book.

use of column 11 offer opportunities for shifting into special routines as we need them.

We plan ultimately to transfer our data from magnetic tape to disc, and develop a computer routine for adding new material similar to the following:

1. Read and edit
2. Sort
3. Merge to master
4. Store updated master

For output we would perform the following steps:

1. Read and de-edit master
2. Print de-edited master

Realization of this procedure is some time off, though the sorting problem is forcing it on us sooner than expected. A single, unified, up-to-date printed catalog for all of our science libraries is our next goal.

Supplementary book catalogs should be regarded as a method of selecting part of the union catalog on a subject basis. By the time a catalog gets to the multiple million card mark, necessary for indexing the collection of a large library, filing and entry rules make it difficult for non-librarians to use it easily. Our printed catalogs are subject-oriented, author-title finding lists. The subject-orientation is based on physical location of books in departmental libraries, but it could, if demand arose, conceivably be made entirely independent of this factor. One could, by selecting related categories in the classification system, produce supplementary book catalogs, from the shelf list, in any subject or area study orientation desired.

Notes

1. A detailed account of the mechanics of making short-title catalogs may be found in Phyllis A. Richmond, "A Short-title Catalog Made with IBM Tabulating Equipment," Library Resources and Technical Services, v. 7, no. 1, winter 1963, pp. 81-90.

2. HS was formerly used, but the current computer sorting program requires free 11 and 12 punches in column 79.

3.   Both the program, SHORTTITLE, by Dr. Baumeister
      and the subprogram in FORTRAN by the author are
      debugged and operational.

Notes on Updating and Searching
Computerized Catalogs

by Phyllis A. Richmond

Reprinted by permission from Library Resources & Technical Services, 10(2): 155-60, Spring 1966.

The short-title catalogs described in earlier issues of Library Resources & Technical Services[1] have been put on magnetic tape and merged by means of an IBM 1401 computer (4K capacity). Thus the title-a-line catalogs of four science libraries, comprising some 13,000 entries, are now available in a single book catalog.

In the merging procedure, the computer sorted all 80 columns of input, using an interchange sort procedure. At the end of the sorting, entries were in machine-style alphanumeric order. Early publication schedules precluded attempts to program more ALA filing rules at this time.

As part of the program, those entries which were exact duplicates were filed as a single entry with number codes to indicate which libraries possessed the book (see Fig. 1). Also a correction routine was developed which made it possible to substitute corrected entries on the tape for entries containing errors. Neither of these procedures, nor that for interfiling titles without authors in dictionary style, caused any serious problems.

However, the program for updating the tape turned up a snag which seems worth describing for the sake of librarians who may be attracted to computer routines which use column-by-column matching for interfiling or searching. The update included some 2,400 new entries. The program put the update in alphabetical order. It found the entry on tape after which each update entry would file. It then matched the update entry against the following tape entry.

Exact duplicates were rejected; entries which differed only
in library code number were merged; and update entries
which did not match or merge were added as new titles.

In the final proofreading, it was discovered that if
any single column of the update were different from the tape
entry in any way (other than library code number), the update was entered as a completely new title instead of being
rejected as a duplicate or merged as a new copy in a different library. For example, assuming that all other aspects
of an entry are identical from card to card and that there
are no keypunching errors, a title keypunched with the following single column variations would machine-file as 40 different entries:

```
THE  CHINESE   THEIR HISTORY & CULTURE
THE  CHINESE   THEIR HISTORY & CULTURE.
THE  CHINESE   THEIR HISTORY AND CULTURE
THE  CHINESE   THEIR HISTORY AND CULTURE.
THE  CHINESE  THEIR HISTORY & CULTURE
THE  CHINESE  THEIR HISTORY & CULTURE.
THE  CHINESE  THEIR HISTORY AND CULTURE
THE  CHINESE  THEIR HISTORY AND CULTURE.
THE  CHINESE.   THEIR HISTORY & CULTURE
THE  CHINESE.   THEIR HISTORY & CULTURE.
THE  CHINESE.   THEIR HISTORY AND CULTURE
THE  CHINESE.   THEIR HISTORY AND CULTURE.
THE  CHINESE.  THEIR HISTORY & CULTURE
THE  CHINESE.  THEIR HISTORY & CULTURE.
THE  CHINESE.  THEIR HISTORY AND CULTURE
THE  CHINESE.  THEIR HISTORY AND CULTURE.
THE  CHINESE;   THEIR HISTORY & CULTURE
THE  CHINESE;   THEIR HISTORY & CULTURE.
THE  CHINESE;   THEIR HISTORY AND CULTURE
THE  CHINESE;   THEIR HISTORY AND CULTURE.
THE  CHINESE;  THEIR HISTORY & CULTURE
THE  CHINESE;  THEIR HISTORY & CULTURE.
THE  CHINESE;  THEIR HISTORY AND CULTURE
THE  CHINESE;  THEIR HISTORY AND CULTURE.
THE  CHINESE,   THEIR HISTORY & CULTURE
THE  CHINESE,   THEIR HISTORY & CULTURE.
THE  CHINESE,   THEIR HISTORY AND CULTURE
THE  CHINESE,   THEIR HISTORY AND CULTURE.
THE  CHINESE,  THEIR HISTORY & CULTURE
THE  CHINESE,  THEIR HISTORY & CULTURE.
THE  CHINESE,  THEIR HISTORY AND CULTURE
THE  CHINESE,  THEIR HISTORY AND CULTURE.
```

THE CHINESE: THEIR HISTORY & CULTURE
THE CHINESE: THEIR HISTORY & CULTURE.
THE CHINESE: THEIR HISTORY AND CULTURE
THE CHINESE: THEIR HISTORY AND CULTURE.
THE CHINESE: THEIR HISTORY & CULTURE
THE CHINESE: THEIR HISTORY & CULTURE.
THE CHINESE: THEIR HISTORY AND CULTURE
THE CHINESE: THEIR HISTORY AND CULTURE.

In an ordinary card catalog, these would file as one entry, not 40.   For the actual example of this phenomenon, see Fig. 2.

This type of filing is to be expected in machine sorting, since the machine does not make allowances or recognize similarities as a human does.   It was slightly devastating to encounter it, however, when multiple eye checks by several proofreaders had been made on the update list.   One hundred percent accuracy in proofreading is much harder for humans than for machines.

Since differences of one or two columns were all that separated editions in many cases, the computer could not be directed to disregard a one- or two-column variation.   A possible antidote might be to have an "attention" routine which would tag for inspection all entries which varied from the tape by one to ten columns.   It would be necessary to counter the inaccuracies of eye-checking without at the same time sacrificing high keypunching standards.

The fact that minor errors in keypunching cause a duplicate entry to file as two titles in a list is annoying but not particularly damaging.   However, such deviation from perfection could be much more serious in computer searching operations depending on column by column matching.   In book ordering, for example, a single error could result in purchase of an unwanted duplicate.   In cataloging, a title could be cataloged twice.   In periodical reception, recording, and updating, an issue could have all kinds of adventures.   If a patron inquiring at a console made an error in keying, he could be informed that the library lacked a title which was available on a shelf in the stacks.   The longer the entry, the greater the possibilities for error in matching procedures.   In any of these cases, would one dare accept a negative report?

The reason that such a trivial matter is important is that in advanced systems thinking with regard to libraries of the future,[2] it is proposed to query the information in computer storage directly by means of the consoles mentioned above. A description of the console-computer interactions runs as follows:

> The user sits at his typewriter or teletypewriter and types messages to the system, which sends messages back to him, sometimes full, long or short, in natural language or in mathematical notation, all depending upon the nature of the program that is running in the computer for the user at the time.[3]

This description, and others like it, does not emphasize just how exact the message must be, partly because this is "old stuff" to those who use computers and partly because many systems designers wistfully hope that intellectual access to information can be made much simpler than it is now. Unfortunately, since the public has difficulty now in using the catalog, it is more reasonable to expect this difficulty to be compounded when extreme accuracy of punctuation, spacing, and terminology are added to other criteria for successful retrieval.

Here again, one might say that this is only a clerical matter and of little import. However, it is further proposed that output be, not in regular computer printout, but in the form of answers "printed" on the surface of a cathode ray tube, or as immediate hard copy (by xerography or similar processes).[4] If the Library of Congress, for economic reasons, did not publish its catalog at all, then how the console was keyed by the user would be vital in getting or not getting answers from computer storage. The possibilities of purely clerical error assume an importance out of all proportion to their significance. So far, there does not appear to be any way out of the dilemma. Somehow, without prohibitively expensive programming, there has to be a margin for error.

Experience with matching procedures suggests that a book or serial code might be more suitable for machine updating or searching entries on tape. The code could be an alphanumeric one, a classification notation, or plain letters as in a subject heading or index term. But in any case, to get the correct code, humans would always have to consult some prior source for checking. The question still remains: if a printed source is not used for checking by eye, how can humans query a tape accurately except by producing a perfect entry?

Author	Title	Call No.	Code
VON HIPPEL ARTHUR R	DIELECTRICS + WAVES	54 QC585	1
VON HIPPEL ARTHUR R	MOLECULAR SCIENCE + MOLECULAR ENGINEERING	59 QC173	1
VON KARMAN THEODORE	AERODYNAMICS	54 QA593	2
VON KARMAN THEODORE	FROM LOW-SPEED AERODYNAMICS TO ASTRONAUTICS	63 TL573	1
VON KARMAN THEODORE	MATHEMATICAL METHODS IN ENGINEERING	40 QA0C37	1
VON LOESECKE HARRY W	DRYING + DEHYDRATION OF FOODS ED.2	55 TX06C9	12
VON NEUMANN JOHN	COLLECTED WORKS	61 QAC0C4	2
VON NEUMANN JOHN	COMPUTER + THE BRAIN	58 QA0076	2
VON NEUMANN JOHN	CONTINUOUS GEOMETRY	36 QA0471	2
VON NEUMANN JOHN	CONTINUOUS GEOMETRY	60 QA0611	2
VON NEUMANN JOHN	FUNCTIONAL OPERATORS	MC QA0320	MC
VON NEUMANN JOHN	MATHEMATICAL FOUNDATIONS OF QUANTUM MECHANICS	55 QC0174.3	12
VON NEUMANN JOHN	THEORY OF GAMES + ECONOMIC BEHAVIOR ED.3	53 HB0199	12
VON TERSCH LAWRENCE W	RECURRENT ELECTRICAL TRANSIENTS	53 TK3226	2
VOORHOEVE NICOLAAS A	LOW-FREQUENCY AMPLIFICATION	53 TK6565	4
VOOUS KAREL HENDRICK	ATLAS OF EUROPEAN BIRDS	60 QL0690	2
VOROBEV IURII V	MOMENTENMETHODE IN DER ANGEWANDTEN MATHEMATIK	61 QAC432	2
VOROBEV N N	FIBONACCI NUMBERS	61 QA0241	2
VORONTSOV-VELIAMINOV	GASNEBEL + NEUE STERNE	53 Q00851	2
VORONTSOVA MARIIA A	ASEXUAL PROPAGATION + REGENERATION	60 CHC499	4
VOSKOBOINIK D I	ANGLO-RUSSKII IADERNYI SLOVAR	60 QC0C0?	2
VOSKOBOINIK DAVID I	SEMIIAZYCHNYI IADERNYI SLOVAR	61 QC0772	2
VRANCEANU GHEORGHE	VORLESUNGEN UEBER DIFFERENTIALGEOMETRIE	MC QAC641	2
VRIES HUGO DE	MUTATION THEORY	09 QH0366	4
VRIES HUGO DE	SPECIES + VARIETIES	05 QH0366	
VSESOIUZNAIA AKAD	SITUATION IN BIOLOGICAL SCIENCE	49 QH043?	
VSESOIUZNAIA KONF	ULTRASOUND IN INDUSTRIAL PROCESSING + CONTROL	64 TA0367	1
VSESOIUZNOE	STRUCTURE OF GLASS	60 TP0848	1
VSESOIUZNYI SOVET	INTERCRYSTALLINE CORROSION	62 TA0467	1
VULIKH BORIS Z	INTRODUCTION TO FUNCT ANAL SCIENTISTS + TECHN	63 QAC32?	
VULIS LEV A	THERMAL REGIMES OF COMBUSTION	61 QD0516	1
VUYLSTEKE ARTHUR A	ELEMENTS OF MASER THEORY	60 QCC483	12
VZOROVA A I	TABLES SOLVING LAPLACE EQUA INSIDE ELLIPSE	58 QA04C5	1
WACKS NORMAN	RECOVERY OF ALPHA-METHYL STYRENE	47 AS0038.495	1
WADDAMS AUSTEN L	CHEMICALS FROM PETROLEUM	62 TP0690	1
WADDINGTON CONRAD HAL	BIOLOGICAL ORGANISATION	59 QH0573	4
WADDINGTON CONRAD HAL	EPIGENETICS OF BIRDS	52 QL0959	4

Fig. 1. Sample print-out of merged catalogs. Code in right column: 1=Engineering Library, 2=Physics Library, 4=Life Sciences Library, 12=book in both Engineering and Physics.

Book Catalogs

Title	Author		Call No.	Lib.
WYOMING OIL + GAS FIELDS SYM	WYOMING GEOL ASSN	57	TN0872.89	5
WYOMING STRATIGRAPHY	WYOMING GEOL ASSN	MC	QE 181	5
X-RAY ABSORPTION + EMISSION ANALYTICAL CHEM	LIEBHAFSKY H A	60	QD0095	1
X-RAY ANALYSIS OF ORGANIC STRUCTURES	NYBURG S C	57	QD0945	4
X-RAY CRYSTAL STRUCTURE	MCLACHLAN DAN	60	QD 945	2
X-RAY DIFFRACTION BY POLYCRYSTALLINE MAT	PEISER H S	54	QC0482	5
X-RAY DIFFRACTION PROCEDURES	KLUG HAROLD PHILIP	64	AS0038.495	2
X-RAY MEAS + CORRELATION RETAINED AUSTENITE	HOCHREIN AMBROSE A	63	AS0038.49	1
X-RAY MEASUREMENT RESIDUAL STRESS DISTRIBUTION	KIMMEL EDWARD ROGER	61	TN0690	1
X-RAY METALLOGRAPHY	TAYLOR ABRAHAM	57	QC0373	1
X-RAY MICROSCOPY + MICRORADIOGRAPHY	INT UNION PHYSICS	60	QC0373	4
X-RAY MICROSCOPY + X-RAY MICROANALYSIS	INT SYM X-RAY MICROS	49	QD0945	2
X-RAY OPTICS	WILSON A J C	62	QE 369	5
X-RAY POWDER DATA FOR ORE MINERALS	BERRY LEONARD G	59	QD0095	1
X-RAY SPECTROCHEMICAL ANALYSIS	BIRKS L S	30	QC0481	2
X-RAYS	WORSNOP BERNARD L	46	QC0481	1
X-RAYS IN PRACTICE	SPROULL WAYNE T	46	QC0481	2
X-RAYS IN PRACTICE	SPROULL WAYNE TREBER	43	QC0481	2
X-RAYS IN RESEARCH + INDUSTRY	HIRST HENRY	35	QC0481	2
X-RAYS IN THEORY + EXPERIMENT	COMPTON ARTHUR HOLLY	60	QD0095	5
XRAY ABSORPTION + EMISSION IN ANALYTICAL CHEM	LIEBHAFSKY H A	51	QD0945	5
XRAY ANALYSIS OF CRYSTALS	BIJVOET JOHANNES M	54	QC0482	5
XRAY DIFFRACTION PROCEDURES	KLUG HAROLD P		AS0032	2
YEARBOOK V.55-60 1955/56-1960/61	CARNEGIE INST WASH	49	QR0151	4
YEAST CELL, ITS GENETICS + CYTOLOGY	LINDEGREN CARL C	43	QL0949	4
YEUX + VISION VERTEBRES	ROCHON-DUVIGNEAUD A		QA0001	2
YOKOHAMA MATHEMATICAL JOURNAL V.1- 1953-			QA0001	1
YOUNGS MODULUS OF GLASS AT ELEVATED TEMP	BOASE ELMER EDWARD	56	AS0038.49	4
YOUR A-Z GUIDE TO COLOUR PHOTOGRAPHY	BOMBACK EDWARD S	61	TR0510	2
ZADACHI PO URAVNENIAM MATEMATICHESKOI FIZIKI	SMIRNOV MODEST M	53	QC0020	2
ZAHLENTHEORIE	HASSE HELMUT	49	QA0241	2
ZAHLENWERTE + FUNKTIONEN AUS PHYSIK ED.6	LANDOLT HANS HEINRICH	MC	QD0065	2
ZEHNSTELLIGE LOGARITHMENTAFEL REV. ED.	PETERS JEAN	57	QA0055	1
ZEITSCHRIFT ANGE MATH + MECH V.38- 1958- INC			TA0001	1
ZEITSCHRIFT ANGEWANDTE MATH + PHYS V.1- 1950-			QA0001	2
ZEITSCHRIFT ANGEWANDTE MATH + PHYS V.12- 1961-			QA0001	1
ZEITSCHRIFT F NATURFORSCHUNG V.1A- 1946-			Q 0003	2

Fig. 2. Keypunching errors resulting in unwanted duplicate entries. Code 5 in right column=Geology Library.

References

1. Richmond, Phyllis A. "A Short-Title Catalog Made with IBM Tabulating Equipment. " Library Resources & Technical Services, 7:81-90. Winter 1963. "Book Catalogs as Supplements to Card Catalogs. " Ibid., 8:359-365. Fall 1964.

2. King, Gilbert W. , and others. Automation and the Library of Congress. Washington, Library of Congress, 1963. Swanson, Don R. "Design Requirements for a Future Library. " Conference on Libraries and Automation held at Airlie Foundation, Warrenton, Va., May 26-30, 1963. In Libraries and Automation. Washington, Library of Congress, 1964. pp. 11-21. Licklider, J. C. R. Libraries of the Future. Cambridge, Mass. , MIT Press, 1965. Overhage, Carl F. J. and R. Joyce Harmon, eds. INTREX; Report of a Planning Conference on Information Transfer Experiments, September 3, 1965. Cambridge, Mass., MIT Press, 1965.

3. Overhage & Harmon, INTREX, p. 28 (Italics mine.)

4. Ibid., passim.

Chapter VII

Applications and Techniques:

Medical Libraries

Mechanization of Library Procedures

in the Medium-Sized Medical Library:

Alphabetization of the Book Catalog

by Justine Roberts

The author is Cataloger, University of California
Medical Center Library, San Francisco. This
article was based on work supported in part by
funds from U. S. Public Health Service Grant No.
1TO1 LM 00106-01 for training in computer
librarianship. It is reprinted by permission from
Medical Library Association Bulletin, 56:71-79,
January 1968.

Introduction

Sorting characteristics of catalog records in Washington University School of Medicine Library's (WUSML) magnetic tape files were examined as part of the Library's current work on adaption of its Acquisitions-Cataloging system to greater machine capacity. Computer programs were written to obtain specific and quantitative description of alphabetization problems noted by the system's original designers,[1] both to assist in solution of the problems and to ensure optimum use of computer storage and sorting capabilities.

The three "edited" tapes examined were those which are used to produce the sections of a complete printed book catalog[3]: Names, Subjects and Titles. Although the Titles section has not actually been produced in any form since 1965, both the Names and Subjects sections have been issued and cumulated at regular intervals for internal library use, and have been published twice since the system began operation in January 1965.[3,4] The book catalog editing programs "rewrite" the Master Catalog file by duplicating and sorting the "added entries" for each record on additional tapes.[5] The sorting itself is done through use of fixed-length fields in which the heading elements of the record are repeated, character by character, to the limit of the sorting fields.

For each catalog section, examination included a basic tally which counted the number of character positions in the headings of adjacent, sorted entries which had to be scanned before an entry could be differentiated from its predecessor and given its final position on the tape. (Although the sorting programs actually sort by a right-to-left scan, the tally scan was naturally made in the reverse direction.) Secondary computer tallies, and visual inspection, were then made to examine all "sort failure" entries, i.e., those cases where adjacent entries were necessarily in random order because their sorting field(s) contained identical characters, spaces, and punctuation, and thus did not actually provide any distinguishing character for the sort procedure.

Names Catalog

Sorting characteristics were examined for 5,792 records on the edited Names Catalog tape as of May 15, 1967. These records included both main entries, whether title or author, and added author references to main entry. These entries are currently sorted by a forty-nine-character sort field for "author" name and a one-character sort field for subarrangement by title, as needed.

No effort was made to distinguish between main entry, added entry, and author cross references for the purposes of this sorting statistics program. However, statistics taken from the preceding month's master tape indicate that the 5,792 records are comprised of 4,029 main entries cataloged prior to May 1, 1967; 1,644 added author entries from these records, 49 author cross-references, and 70 records entered since April 1, 1967. The latter group could include all three types of records.

Separate tallies were taken for "single-title" authors and "multiple title" authors, but the quotation marks are necessary because the sort field limit of 49 characters leaves a certain number of names registering as identical by the 49th character, which may, nevertheless, be different names that could only be sorted by a longer sort field. Since it was not practical to make comparisons on the full name, a count was kept of these potentially "false" multiple-title authors, but they were otherwise tallied as belonging to groups of authors represented by two or more titles in the Catalog.

The first tally, Table 1, shows that a total of 4,637 sorts[6] was made to alphabetize entries that could be ordered

Table 1

Names Catalog

Tally 1: Authors Sorted by Name at Character
Positions 1-49

Character Position	Number of Entries	Cumulative Number	Character Position	Number of Entries	Cumulative Number
1....	26	26	26....	20	4377
2....	202	228	27....	28	4405 95%
3....	968	1196	28....	35	4440
4....	1020	2216 50%	29....	49	4489
5....	465	2681	30....	13	4502
6....	198	2879	31....	8	4510
7....	174	3053	32....	18	4528
8....	161	3214	33....	13	4541
9....	210	3424	34....	13	4554
10....	179	3603	35....	8	4562
11....	123	3726	36....	10	4572
12....	64	3790	37....	4	4576
13....	54	3844	38....	8	4584
14....	64	3908	39....	4	4588
15....	111	4019	40....	4	4592 99%
16....	98	4117	41....	7	4599
17....	46	4163	42....	15	4614
18....	52	4215	43....	6	4620
19....	36	4251	44....	2	4622
20....	14	4265	45....	5	4627
21....	21	4286	46....	1	4628
22....	18	4304	47....	4	4632
23....	17	4321	48....	2	4634
24....	13	4334	49....	3	4637
25....	23	4357			

by name. This total includes a duplication factor for 500 "multiple-title" authors, all but one of whom was tallied twice, once in the first tally as it was sorted from preceding entries for other authors, and again in the separate tally of "multiple-title" authors, for determination of other sorting characteristics.

Of the 4,637 name sorts, more than half were

completed by the 5th character position, 90 percent was complete by the 17th character position and 99 percent (4, 592) was complete at the 40th character position. Distribution of the sorts is shown in Figure 1.

Table 2 shows the group of 500 "multiple-title" authors who required further sorting by title. This group includes 435 "certain" multiple authors (i. e., authors with names shorter than 49 characters) and 65 names for whom multiple-title authorship was not certain, i. e., the names were at least 49 characters long, and were still identical at the 49th character. The total group was responsible for 1, 654 entries in the catalog, distributed as shown in the table.

The title sort field ("Character 50") is automatically filled by the Cataloging program when the call number for an entry includes a conventional title mark, i. e., a single letter representing the first significant word of the title which is appended to the Cutter Number representing author name. For pamphlets, government documents, or any other entry not including a title mark in the call number, a fixed field sorting code indicator can be used by the cataloger to supply this one-character title letter.

As expected by the project's original designers, this single position sort field for the subordering of authors by title was not sufficient. Of the 1, 654 titles which required title sorting, 912, or 55 percent, were successfully ordered by title, and 742, or 45 percent, were not. The sort failure group included 622 titles in which the title sort position was used (i. e., filled), but where the title characters for two or more works by the same author were identical. For the remaining 120 titles, 7. 5 percent of the total group, the title sort field was blank, i. e., the call number for these titles did not include a title mark, and the sorting code indicator had not been used.

The three authors responsible for more than 20 titles apiece (141 entries in all) had the largest proportion of unordered titles, with more than twice as many unsorted as sorted. Authors represented by 5 titles and by 7 titles respectively also had more unsorted than sorted titles, while the remaining groups showed the majority of titles successfully sorted.

Statistics from the Titles Catalog examination will undoubtedly help in determining the optimum number of title

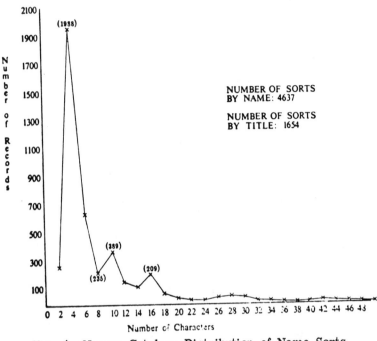

Fig. 1--Names Catalog--Distribution of Name Sorts

sort positions which might be used by the Names Catalog
program to reduce the percentage of unordered titles for prolific authors.   The effect of a longer author sort field in reducing the number of unsorted author names appears less
crucial, since only 1 percent of the records in the Names
Catalog remained "unsorted" at the 49th character when the
sort field was full.

Subjects Catalog

        The Subjects Catalog editing program provides arrange-
ment of entries by subject and, under subject, by year and
then by author.   Space is provided in the sorting fields to
secure complete alphabetic arrangement of subject headings
(i. e., up to 70 characters), complete chronological arrangement by the four digits of publication year, and then, further
alphabetic sorting, as needed, by the first 50 characters of
author (or title, for title main entry).

Table 2

Names Catalog

Tally 2: "Multiple-title Authors" Sorted by Title Field (Character 50)

	Number of Titles per Author												
	2	3	4	5	6	7	8	9	10	11-15	16-20	Over 20	Total
Author sort field is full...	39	10	4	2	3	1	1	0	1	3	1	0	65
Author sort field is not full...	314	57	22	5	3	4	6	3	4	10	4	3	435
Total authors...	353	67	26	7	6	5	7	3	5	13	5	3	500
Titles are sorted by character 50...	400	114	72	13	26	16	36	18	35	91	48	43	912
Titles are not sorted by character 50...	252	62	26	19	8	19	18	9	10	62	41	96	622
Titles are blank at character 50 (not sorted)	54	25	6	3	2	0	2	0	5	21	0	2	120
Total titles ...	706	201	104	35	36	35	56	27	50	174	89	141	1654

As of May 1, 1967, the machine record Subjects Catalog contained 4,374 entries representing approximately 3,300
different titles.   Fifty percent (2,175) of these entries was
checked for the alphabetization of its subject headings, since

Table 3

Subjects Catalog

Tally 1: Subject Headings Sorted at Character
Positions 1-70

Character Position	Number of Headings	Cumulative Number	Character Position	Number of Headings	Cumulative Number
1....	26	26	22....	25	2062 95%
2....	147	173	23....	31	2093
3....	358	531	24....	15	2108
4....	174	705	25....	13	2121
5....	109	814	26....	11	2132
6....	118	932	27....	19	2151 99%
7....	115	1047	28....	3	2154
8....	86	1133 52%	29....	5	2159
9....	89	1222	30....	2	2161
10....	106	1328	31....	5	2166
11....	100	1428	32....	1	2167
12....	101	1529	33....	0	2167
13....	104	1633	34....	2	2169
14....	94	1727	35....	3	2172
15....	53	1780	36....	1	2173
16....	68	1848	37....	0	2173
17....	45	1893	38....	1	2174
18....	43	1936	39....	1	2175
19....	38	1974 91%	40....	0	2175
20....	27	2001	70....	0	2175
21....	36	2037			

it represented either the first, or the only, title under each
new subject (Table 3 and Figure 2).   An additional 22 percent was tallied as year-ordered entries, and not further
examined; this was either the first, or the only title listed
under a given publication year when the subject heading had
more than one entry assigned to it.   The remaining 28 percent (1,247) of the entries required further sorting by author
(Table 4 and Figure 3).   Of these, 1,115 (25 percent of the
total entries) were completely alphabetized by the 50-

character author sort and 132 (3 percent of the total entries) were not.

Complete alphabetization by subject used a maximum of 38 of the 70 available sorting positions. Of all entries initially alphabetized by either subject or author, 99 percent was alphabetized by the 28th sorting position of its respective sort fields, compared to the 70 subject and 50 author positions provided. More than 90 percent of the authors was alphabetized before or at the second character position.

A printout was obtained of the sorting fields for the 1 percent of subject sorts not completed by the 27th character position, and for the 2 percent of completed author sorts which occurred between the 10th and 50th character positions. Of the 24 subject and 26 author sorts thus listed, five subject and three author sorts were due to keypunch error, i. e., either misspelling or irregular punctuation had incorrectly distinguished identical authors or subjects. The 21 valid subject sorts were made on subdivided subject headings, all but one of which was completed at the first letter of the subdivision, or at the hyphen itself. The one exception involved headings using both subject and chronological subdivision.

The 23 valid author sorts included 12 government agencies and four other corporate authors, three congresses, and two titles. A maximum of 38 character positions was required to distinguish all but one of these entries. The single exception sorted at the 49th character position. Two author sorts were also made on identical personal names, each of the sets differing by the addition of "ed. " to the name. These sorts were completed by the 14th and 15th character positions.

The relative absence of personal name sorts from the listing, and the fact that all but one of the corporate authors listed was effectively sorted by 38 character positions suggests that a major source of the 132 sort failure entries may be personal and/or corporate name main entries which could be ordered only by adding a title sort field, or by filling out any blank positions in the author sorting field with the initial characters of the entry's title.

Titles Catalog

Sort field requirements for the Book Catalog's Titles section were determined by inspection of an edited titles tape

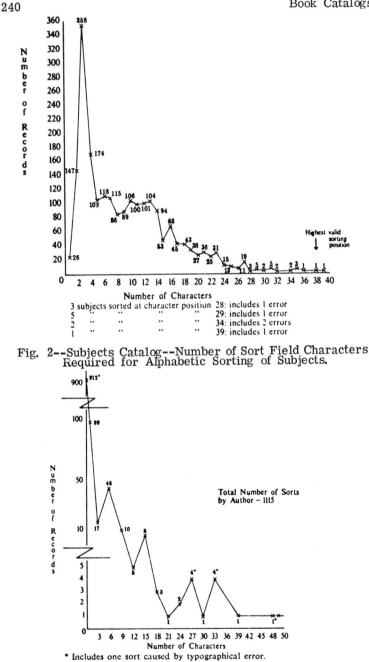

Fig. 2--Subjects Catalog--Number of Sort Field Characters Required for Alphabetic Sorting of Subjects.

Fig. 3--Subjects Catalog--Number of Sort Field Characters Required for Alphabetic Sorting of Authors Under Subject and Year.

which included 5,421 full title, short title, and series added entries as of May 1, 1967. The edited tape excluded records for all titles which had been coded "N" (Not to appear in public catalog) but did include any series or short title added entries which had been made for such works.

Table 4

Subjects Catalog

Talley 2: Authors Sorted at Character Positions 1-50

Character Position	Number of Authors	Cumulative Number	Character Position	Number of Authors	Cumulative Number
1....	912	912	22....	0	1101
2....	99	1011 91%	23....	1	1102
3....	17	1028	24....	1	1103
4....	4	1032	25....	0	1103
5....	0	1032	26....	0	1103 99%
6....	42	1074 96%	27....	4	1107
7....	7	1081	28....	1	1108
8....	2	1083	29....	0	1108
9....	1	1084	30....	0	1108
10....	5	1089	31....	1	1109
11....	0	1089	32....	2	1111
12....	0	1089	33....	1	1112
13....	0	1089	34....	0	1112
14....	3	1092	37....	0	1112
15....	5	1097	38....	1	1113
16....	0	1097	39....	0	1113
17....	1	1098	46....	0	1113
18....	2	1100	47....	1	1114
19....	0	1100	48....	0	1114
20....	0	1100	49....	1	1115
21....	1	1101	50....	0	1115

Table 5

Titles Catalog

Tally: Titles, Short Titles, Series Sorted at
Character Positions 1-50

Charac-ter Position	Number of Entries	Cumulative Number	Charac-ter Position	Number of Entries	Cumulative Number
1....	30	30	26....	37	4769
2....	214	244	27....	32	4801 95. 0%
3....	579	823	28....	32	4833
4....	423	1246 25. 0%	29....	18	4851
5....	274	1520	30....	12	4863
6....	245	1765	31....	24	4887
7....	272	2037	32....	23	4910
8....	227	2264	33....	16	4926
9....	241	2505 50. 0%	34....	13	4939
10....	292	2797	35....	2	4941
11....	255	3052	36....	12	4953
12....	239	3291	37....	5	4958
13....	214	3505	38....	9	4967
14....	208	3713	39....	8	4975
15....	187	3900 77. 0%	40....	10	4985
16....	116	4016	41....	7	4992
17....	109	4125	42....	8	5000
18....	93	4218	43....	16	5016 99. 0%
19....	56	4274	44....	2	5018
20....	48	4322	45....	4	5022
21....	55	4377	46....	6	5028
22....	63	4440	47....	17	5045
23....	91	4531	48....	11	5056
24....	170	4701	49....	1	5057
25....	31	4732	50....	2	5059

Entries were arranged in the alphabetic order provided by one
50-character sort field for the title element.

For this count, no distinction was made between different types of entry, nor was this group of records further checked to exclude keypunch or cataloging error. The tally total of 5,059 included 1 tally for each title or series entry[7] in correct alphabetical order and 1 tally for each group of sort failure entries, i. e. , 1 tally for the character position at which the group was alphabetically sorted from preceding entries. A listing was obtained of the full title, or the first 80 characters of the full title, for the second and succeeding entries of each group of two or more sort failures. The 361 listings obtained repeated any one title as many times as its title or series added entries were found to duplicate those of an adjacent entry. This listing was manually inspected and tallied to determine the nature of the sort failure and the actual frequency of titles in each unsorted group and category. These secondary tallies excluded 63 listings (representing 126 Title Catalog entries) where the actual fact or cause of duplication could not be quickly verified by a check of the Library's official catalog printouts or of the card catalog.

Table 5 shows the number of Titles Catalog records sorted at character positions 1 to 50. One half of the 5,059 sorts had been completed by the 9th character position and 99 percent of the successfully ordered entries was alphabetized between the 1st and 43d character positions. A graph showing distribution of these sorts is given in Figure 4. Its shape is markedly similar to that displayed by the Names Catalog sort distribution but reflects the more "drawn-out" use of the sort field for title entries. In addition to the 26 alphabetic sorts which would be expected at the first character position, the tally for this position also reflects the fact that titles do not always begin with alphabetic characters by indicating that four (or more) titles in the file began with a digit or other non-alpha character. These entries would appear at the end of a printed Titles Catalog.

Table 6 shows the count of sort failure entries, by type of entry. More than half of the sort failure groups consisted of two titles each, with the remaining sets ranging from 3 to 40 titles. The single 40-title group was for the Excerpta Medica International Congress series where the "sortable" publication number fell at the 56th character position, and thus was unavailable to the computer sort procedure. The total of 392 entries in the unordered entry groups comprises 7. 2 percent of the total entries, but this percentage excludes the unverified listings which represent an additional 126 entries.

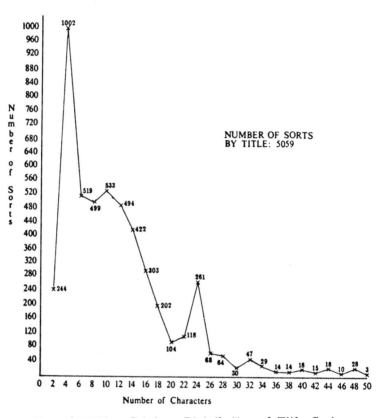

Fig. 4--Titles Catalog--Distribution of Title Sorts

Table 7, indicating sources of sort failure, shows that 58. 8 percent of the (verified) failures was caused when different works bearing the same title or short title, or the Library's holdings of more than one title in an unnumbered series, could not be subarranged (by main entry or date) because of the lack of a secondary sort field. A sort field which was too short to distinguish the different titles of two or more works caused sort failure for 26. 6 percent of the unordered entries. A small number of these failures involved full title entries; the largest single group of this type had a title beginning and ending in the sort field as: Standards for the breeding, care and management of .... These National Research Council publications, which included works on laboratory cats, guinea pigs, dogs, primates, etc., would

Table 6

Titles Catalog

Number and Distribution of Sort Failure Groups[1]

	Number of Unordered Entries per Title											Total Groups
	2	3	4	5	6	7	8	9	10	11	40	
Full Titles.........	57	6	1	--	1	--	1	--	--	--	--	66
Short Titles.......	30	6	5	--	--	--	--	--	--	--	--	41
Series.............	14	3	5	1	1	--	2	1	--	1	1	29
Total Groups......	101	15	11	1	2	--	3	1	--	1	1	136
												Total Un-ordered Entries
Total number un-ordered entries	202	45	44	5	12	--	24	9	--	11	40	392

1. Excluding unverified listings and errors; see discussion in text.

Table 7

Titles Catalog

Cause of "Sort Failure"

	Full Title		Short Title		Series		Totals		Percent
	Number of Groups	Number of Entries	Number of Groups	Number of Entries	Number of Groups	Number of Entries	Number of Groups	Number of Entries	
Sort field too short[1]	7	22	--	--	17	100	24	122	26.6
2d sort field needed[2]	59	128	41	98	12	44	112	270	58.8
"Error" entries[3]	5	27	18	36	2	4	25	67	14.6
Total	71	177	59	134	31	148	161	459	100.0

1. Includes titles that required an alphabetic sort field of more than 50 characters and numbered series when the sort field was too short to include the series number.

2. Includes unnumbered series and titles which represent works by different authors or different editions of the same author.

3. See discussion in text.

have required a sort field of 70 characters to alphabetize correctly.

The greatest number of failures produced by a "too-short" sort field were for the entries of numbered series such as the Excerpta Medica series noted above.   Sort fields long enough to include all of the series numbers now in the file would need room for 124 characters.   If this particular sorting problem were controlled (e. g. , by the provision of a secondary sorting field for series publication numbers) the percentage of entries too long to be sorted by a 50-character sort field would be reduced to less than 1 percent of the total entries. [8]

The "Error entries" shown in Table 7 were excluded from the count for Table 6 since, in each case, the apparent "sort failure" was caused by factors unconnected with the Title Catalog's programmed sorting provisions.   These are entries which should probably not be in the Titles Catalog at all, but would, in fact, be included if the catalog were printed at this time.   For full title entries, the "error" group included 27 "N" titles such as Abstracts and Proceedings, i. e. , titles that would normally be coded "N, " but were not so coded.   The two "series errors" were for records where the identity of their duplicated series titles indicated a possible failure to exclude the full record for a second WUSML copy from the public catalog rather than a true failure in sorting.   The group of 36 "short title" entry errors reflects a temporary misunderstanding of the computer procedures for entering titles in the Titles Catalog; this produced duplicate title entries for a single work, but such sets were not, of course, "out-of-order. "

Conclusions

1.   Examination of the entire body of machine catalog records at WUSML indicated some similarities in length and frequency of elements between its records and the sampled records of other biomedical libraries, but considerable differences in certain elements and in the lengths of notes and tracings.

2.   All WUSML entry components required less latitude in length than is now provided, and 99 percent of the records could be contained in less than three-fourths of the total area allowed.   Relative frequency of components indicated that compression may also be possible in the mapping area of the record.

3.   Acquisition records were found to be little more than half the length of cataloged records and to comprise a small part of the total file.

4.   Alphabetization could be accomplished for 99 percent of the entries by shorter sorting fields than now provided, but the Title Catalog requires addition of subsorting fields, and a longer subsorting field is needed for the Names Catalog.   Visual inspection of draft printouts for final alphabetization would allow considerable space-saving in the machine record.

Notes

1.   Washington University. School of Medicine. Library. Book Catalog, 1965.   St. Louis, 1965, p. vi.

2.   Moore, Evelyn A., Brodman, Estelle, and Cohen, Geraldine S. "Mechanization of library procedures in the medium-sized medical library: II. Acquisitions and cataloging." Medical Library Association Bulletin, 53:305-328, July 1965.

3.   Washington University. Op. cit., v. p.

4.   Washington University. School of Medicine. Library. Catalog of Books. St. Louis, 1967. 336 p.

5.   Moore, Evelyn A., Brodman, Estelle, and Cohen, Geraldine S. Op. cit., p. 313-314.

6.   Since all entries were already in the alphabetic order provided by the editing programs, these figures reflect the final, rather than the total, number of machine manipulations required for sorting.

7.   Excluding the first entry on the tape.

8.   This figure involves the assumption that less than 25 percent of the 126 unverified sort failures would prove to be instances of "excess length" titles.

Acknowledgment:

Mr. Donald Franz, senior programmer at the Washington University Computing Facilities, originated the general structure and programming logic for the study of alphabetization characteristics. However, his inability to participate in later stages of the project prevented him from anticipating or correcting any errors that were present in its execution.

Printed Catalogs: Retrospect and Prospect

by Estelle Brodman and Doris Bolef

Dr. Brodman is librarian and Professor of Medical
History at the School of Medicine, Washington Uni-
versity, St. Louis, Missouri. Mrs. Bolef is
Deputy Librarian of the School of Medicine. This
article is reprinted by permission from Special
Libraries, 59: (no. 10) 783-88 (Dec. 1968).
Copyright by Special Libraries Association.

The late 19th and early 20th centuries saw the flower-
ing of printed catalogs and also their decline. The mid-
twentieth century, on the other hand, has seen their re-
surgence--a resurgence brought about under the belief that
the reasons for the decline of the printed catalog had somehow been overcome by the computer. Today, however, there
are voices crying aloud that the computer has not solved the
fundamental reasons for the decline of the printed catalog;
that, indeed, the true causes for the decline were not those
emphasized by present-day computer enthusiasts, but were
an entirely different set, having nothing whatever to do with
the technical capabilities of computers or the limitations of
printing devices. In the view of these people, we may be
attacking the wrong problem at the wrong time. According
to them, the present emphasis on printed catalogs by computers could be a begging of the question and might lead to
serious disappointments and frustrations. It is this dichotomy
of feeling which we propose to discuss in this paper.

History of Printed Catalogs

We should start, perhaps, by asking what were the
purposes of printed catalogs? They are well set forth in the
prefaces of many such catalogs printed in the United States
between the Civil and the Spanish-American Wars, and occasionally in other places as well. Since this was the era
of the extension of public libraries, we may expect that our

greatest font of information would be the printed catalogs of
such institutions, and this is indeed true. But as medical
librarians, we may be forgiven for calling your attention to
John Shaw Billings, first librarian of what is now the
National Library of Medicine and first editor of the Index
Catalogue, who discussed this problem, among others, in his
many writings.

Printed catalogs were produced originally in the 16th
and 17th centuries (hand-written ones had served up to that
period) primarily in monasteries, which were required to
present inventories of all their possessions to Rome at intervals, sometimes annually, but more often at lengthier intervals. Thus the first reason for printed catalogs was to
satisfy a legal or fiscal responsibility. Inventories of libraries of estates for inheritance and tax purposes are
another example of such productions.

Secondly, printed lists were produced for sales purposes, as anyone will testify who has struggled through catalogs titled "The collection of the late so-and-so, to be sold
at the such-and-such auction house on this date," as will the
antiquarians among us who have studied the early Messkataloge
of the German Book Fairs.

Sometimes, too, catalogs of personal and institutional
libraries were produced for vanity purposes--a sign of con-
spicuous consumption--to show how rich the owner was, to
have been able to gather together such treasures. The
catalog of the King's Library at the British Museum is such
a list.

Very often, moreover, a library catalog was the
culminating proof of the scholarship of the sinecure-librarian
entrusted with the care of some ducal or princely collection--
and sometimes today, looking at certain complicated catalogs,
a question arises whether or not we are still at that stage
now!

And finally, the printed catalog was produced to show
those at a distance what was available to them in a particular
library. Mudies, the famous lending library of Victorian and
Edwardian England, which lent books by post throughout the
country--and for which so many 3-volume romantic novels
were written--needed some means of informing its country
subscribers of what was available for borrowing. So Mudies
produced a printed catalog--as did the early subscription

libraries in the United States.   Like the Sears Roebuck
catalogs, these library lists became favorite reading for all
members of the family.

As mentioned earlier, fundamental changes were taking place in libraries during the 19th Century, due to the
rising tide of literacy resulting from the Industrial Revolution.   This brought in its train the establishment of the
Mechanics Institutes at the beginning of the century, and the
Carnegie Public Libraries, land-grant college libraries,
specialized collections, and a slowly-gathering increase in
numbers of books produced by the end of the century.   All
this seriously affected the purposes both of libraries and of
their printed catalogs.   No longer were libraries the domain
of the royal and leisure classes, who could be flattered into
maintaining or contributing to a library collection by beautiful-
ly produced printed catalogs that recorded their munificence
for posterity.   No longer were librarians in a position to
devote years to the production of exquisitely turned-out
catalogs, secure in the knowledge that changes in the collection would be so few that such a catalog would reflect that
collection for years to come.

A Book Catalog in Every Home?

The librarians of the latter half of the 19th century,
quite sensibly, adapted the printed catalog to the changing
library scene.   They attempted not to put a chicken in every
pot, but a library catalog in every home.   They reasoned that
with the democratization and spread of books and learning
from the smaller upper classes to the emerging larger middle classes, with their deep concern for improving their lot
in life, the printed catalog, available as it was to all com-
ers, would be a welcome helpmate.   For that reason,
Victorian libraries accepted the burden of finding the necessary time and expense to produce printed catalogs.   This
was one more element in their recurrent drives to popularize
and increase the usage of their libraries.   In 1876, for
example, Justin Winsor, librarian of the Boston Public Library, wrote "the printing of a catalogue is a great expense
to a library, but it is a necessary one for a popular library."[1]   To all, it seemed obvious that the printed catalog
would affirm the democratic character of the libraries producing and distributing them, and that once the technological
problems and obstacles were overcome, readers would welcome them wholeheartedly.   Experience was just the op-
posite.   The popularity of the printed catalog declined

steadily. It is ironical that the printed catalog, which would
seem to be a logical element of this new mainstream of public education, attracted only a small portion of the public,
and librarian after librarian tried to modify the printed catalog to make it more attractive to readers. Ranz[2] has summarized this trend very well.

What, after all, are the advantages of the printed
catalog over a card catalog? Firstly, a book catalog is
portable and reproducible in many exact copies. Numerous
copies can be placed at many locations and distributed to
branches and individuals. Secondly, many people can use it
simultaneously.

Thirdly, gifts to the library can be solicited by the
use of attractive book catalogs mentioning the donors by name.
The printed catalog also eliminates the need for peripatetic
catalogers and filers in large library systems. Finally, it
is easier to use. The eye can far more quickly scan a page
of entries and compare them than the hand can riffle through
and the eye can comprehend a file of cards.

On the other hand, what are the disadvantages of the
printed catalog as compared with the card catalog? For one
thing, it can never be completely up-to-date. The card catalog can reflect the day-to-day additions, changes and deletions
of a particular library collection, thanks to its infinite inter-
calation feature. Further, as libraries increase in size,
the cost of producing larger printed cumulations becomes prohibitive, so that supplements rather than cumulations must be
offered. As a result, as the libraries continue to increase
in size, the user has to look through more than one printed
catalog instead of searching at one point in a card catalog.

Despite the valiant efforts of Winsor and his con-
temporaries, the printed catalog movement lost its momentum
because the masses of people who were just beginning to use
libraries did not want them. They were willing neither to
purchase such printed catalogs, even at a fraction of their
actual cost, nor to accept them free of charge. Obviously
such catalogs did not satisfy the needs of this new class of
library users; the printed catalogs did not give them whatever
it was they wanted.

What are some of the possible reasons for this rather
surprising lack of popularity and rejection of printed catalogs?
Probably no single reason can be adduced; rather a number of

reasons produced a synergetic effect. For one thing most library patrons were members of one library, and they had, therefore, one printed catalog available for use. They could not choose between the "wares" of two libraries. Not only were they limited to the use of one collection but these collections were usually not mail order houses. With certain exceptions, such as libraries for the blind, very few lending libraries in this country mailed books to their patrons. Instead, the library patron had to present himself physically at the library in order to borrow his books. Whether or not he possessed a book catalog at home was therefore of little moment. Usually he did not want a specific book anyway but a class of books, and if one were not immediately available, another one would do equally well. Even if the books he wished to borrow were listed in the printed catalog, moreover, there was always the possibility that someone else had borrowed them just prior to his visit. (Remember this was before the era of the telephone.) He would then have to arrange to borrow the books on his next visit. Besides, even if he had only a cursory acquaintance with his library, he knew what kinds of books, on what subjects, and from which point of view, he would be likely to find there. A printed catalog would not prove useful for the largest group of books that the user would expect to find in the library; it would prove useful only for the books in the borderline areas, about which he was not certain.

Lastly, if the patron wished to use the printed catalog for bibliographic purposes, he would find it not up-to-date and incomplete both in content and in bibliographic detail. Most 19th century book catalogs used abbreviated bibliographic entries to save printing costs. Besides, most public libraries were quite small and incomplete, and there was a danger in relying on it for bibliographic completeness. In the preface to the first volume of the Index Catalogue of the Library of the Surgeon-General's Office, Dr. John Shaw Billings made this quite clear. He wrote, "In conclusion, permit me to call attention to the fact that this is not a complete medical bibliography, and that anyone who relies upon it as such will commit a serious error. It is a catalogue of what is to be found in a single collection, a collection so large and of such a character, that there are few subjects in medicine with regard to which something may not be found in it, but which is by no means complete." This was written in 1880 about a library that was already one of the largest and most important in its field in the world. If this could have been written of the Surgeon-General's Library (now the National

Library of Medicine) how much truer would this have been of other, lesser libraries?

The Situation Today

Now that we have set the historical stage, let us turn to the present. The recent resurgence in interest in printed catalogs did not come about because of any sudden need that manifested itself. Rather, it came about because the computer, which has captured the imagination of the library community, can easily be adapted to produce printed catalogs, and librarians assumed--as did our 19th century predecessors--that users needed and wanted them. As a result, libraries across the nation have experimented with and produced many excellent computer produced catalogs. For example, we in St. Louis have proved (along with many others) that it is feasible, that it can be done. Just because we can do it, however, does not mean we should. Now we must ask ourselves if we should continue. Our experience with users is painfully like that of Winsor and Cutter and Poole. Readers do not seem to want the catalogs, even when they are free. To produce these catalogs is expensive and time-consuming. We must, therefore, make certain that they serve a useful purpose, that they do indeed facilitate the use of our libraries. As we say in our library, "Good Lord, keep us from doing efficiently what doesn't need to be done at all." The previous experience that libraries have had with printed catalogs is not encouraging, and it behooves us to see if conditions have changed sufficiently to warrant a return to the old system.

The immediate reason (as opposed to the proximate cause) for the abandonment of printed catalogs was the prohibitive cost, especially as increases in cataloging entries required larger cumulations. Is the cost for producing computer printed catalogs today any more or less than the cost of traditionally printed catalogs yesterday? Our brief foray into the world of computer-produced printed catalogs, and a comparison of our experience with other libraries, lead us to believe that the costs, although they may be for different things, are just as great, on the whole. Whereas formerly the costs were for time required to write out the entries, for the typesetting, for the checking of the galleys, and then for the printing, gathering and binding, now the costs are for preparing the original input, programming (including debugging), loading the data into the computer, sorting it, printing it out in one copy, and then finding a suitable method to reproduce it in many copies. In the end, it comes to the same thing. Since the cost of producing the original data is the same under each system--for, as is obvious, the same human being must do this today as did it before computers--we must compare the two methods from that point onward. If we do this, we find that what we have done in computer catalogs is to use a modern speedy, powerful, and comparatively cheap machine to prepare a result which must then be further manipulated by a technique developed in Renaissance times and not changed appreciably since then. The reference, of course, is to printing and binding, although it is conceded that printing by photo-offset is faster and cheaper than printing by hot type.

All this may be worthwhile, however, if the results justify the costs. But do they? Our own experience leads us to think that in certain circumstances, at any rate, they may not. It is pertinent now to examine the question of why readers do not wish to use printed catalogs, and this will be divided into use within the library and use at a distance.

Who Will Use them?

Like Bergson, we do not believe there is only one explanation; there are only explanations, and one of them is the cultural lag. People today are not used to getting information from a printed catalog, and it is natural for them to prefer a system they are familiar with to one they must learn. Second, the advantage of portability and use at a distance--as opposed to the static quality of the card catalog--is less important now than it was in earlier years, since the telephone makes it possible for a user somewhere else to obtain the information quickly and easily when he is not physically present. Third, the copying revolution, which has probably transformed libraries today more completely and more subtly than any other single device in the last 200 years, this copying revolution makes it possible for a reader to obtain what he wishes to use without even coming to the library. A telephone call will tell him whether the library has something and will also bring a copy of it to his desk without further ado. The general public library user, on the other hand, as we mentioned before, is usually not interested in a particular item so much as in a general class of items--novels, biographies, histories of a war, for example--and for him any one of a group of items is equally useful. Such a person in an open stack library hardly needs a catalog of any kind or description to satisfy him. Besides, as all the evidence seems to indicate, the use of public libraries as a general educational device has been going down precipitously in all parts of the country. People are not using any public library catalogs, card or printed, because they are not using libraries.

Together with the disadvantages of printed catalogs, which were mentioned before, the factors just enumerated, have

resulted in a general tendency for many printed catalogs to be
produced and not used.

Education or Re-education

It may well be that we should devote more time and attention to educate our library users in the ways of printed catalogs and all of the other newer library services that are being
introduced. It may well be that we should also educate ourselves as to what our library users really want. As one example, a group of career and heart specialists in Chicago were
recently provided with a new, and probably very expensive, information service connecting The John Crerar Library with six
Chicago hospitals by direct wire facsimile machines. According to the announcement which appeared in Library Journal,[3]
only one-third of the specialists used this service more than
once. What the significance of these findings for the future may
be is still unclear.

We have been talking up to now of printed catalogs used
outside the library quarters. What about the use of printed
catalogs within the walls of the library itself? The results reported in the literature are equivocal; some tell of enthusiastic
reception and others of dislike. In order to collect some data
in at least one situaion, we are going to make a trial (only hesi-
tatingly could it be called an experiment) to see what will happen if readers are given no alternative to the printed catalog.

Beginning in September 1968 and for four months, the
Washington University School of Medicine Library will hide its
card catalog for the period covered by the contents of its printed catalog. (We will put it in a locked room in the stacks, and
we will continue to maintain it, so we can use it again if our
trial shows the desirability of returning to a card catalog.) We
will scatter around the library copies of the printed catalogs,
which will be supplemented by a small card file of those titles
received since the appearance of the last monthly cumulated
printed catalog. We will try to keep tabs on the comments, difficulties, and surprises encountered by staff and readers in using the new set-up, and in six months or so we will try to determine the actual worth of printed versus card catalogs in our
setting. It is impossible even to guess what the results will
show, but we are willing to accept whatever they do reveal and
to act on it one way or the other.

Nor are we the only ones examining this subject anew.
The Yale University Library recently announced the start of a
two-year study to investigate the feasibility of replacing its card
catalog with computers. It will be of interest to us to see

whether the conclusions recommend the replacement of the card
catalog with printed or other catalogs, with other substitutes
made possible by computers, or not to replace the card catalog
at all.

The other thing we have not discussed here is the printed
catalog as a union catalog. Again, the picture is unclear. Would
a TWX query or other long-line query of either a card catalog or
an unprinted computer store of bibliographic data be preferable
to a printed catalog? Hopefully, someone will do some work on
this question and help us come to some conclusion about what we
should do in the near future.

Facts on Format

As the great Baltimore psychiatrist, Adolph Meyer, once
said, "The difficulty is not that people don't know anything, but
that so many people know things which are not so. " We have been
working too long on a priori knowledge, and now we need to
gather the real facts. When we have the facts and have pon-
dered their significance, perhaps we can determine what forms
of catalogs are suited to our changing and increasingly disparate
array of libraries. Our studies may lead us to consider other
forms--neither card nor printed--of which we are as yet quite
unaware. The more sophisticated computers and computer networks and the newer photo-reproduction methods will certainly
encourage additional experimentation in catalog making. They
may show us which methods of presenting this material are best
suited for these newer purposes. What are the paths that we
should take? How do we adapt the existing methods to our present needs? In all of this we need always to be certain that our
commitment to a particular format is tempered by real evidence
that these forms do indeed serve a useful function in the communities served by our libraries.

References

1.   Proceedings [of the Philadelphia Conference of the Ameri-
          can Library Association, 1876], Sixth Session. Library
          Journal, v. 1: p. 31 (Nov. 1876).

2.   Ranz, Jim. The Printed Book Catalogue in American Li-
          braries: 1723-1900. Chicago, American Library Asso-
          ciation, 1964. Chapter 5.

3.   Medical Information Service Spurned by Doctors,
          Library Journal, v. 93: p. 1846 (May 1, 1968).

Mechanization of Library Procedures in the

Medium-Sized Medical Library:

Suspension of Computer Catalog

by Doris Bolef, Lynda van Wagoner & Estelle Brodman

Two of the authors are identified in the previous article. Lynda van Wagoner is Assistant Librarian for Technical Services at Washington University School of Medicine Library. Reprinted by permission from Medical Library Association Bulletin, 57(3): 1969. July 1969.

Introduction

The literature of librarianship is replete with articles about newly installed computer systems which are hailed by their makers as the answer to all the problems the flesh of librarianship is heir to. Not so often is the demise of the vaunted system described in the literature, complete with the reasons why it failed. This is to be expected. After all, how many times does one read an article titled, "How I Treated Forty Consecutive Cases of Appendicitis Incorrectly"? Nevertheless, it is incumbent upon those who report purported new advances also to report when the new advance turns out to be neither new nor an advance. The Washington University School of Medicine Library has just put the computer-based acquisitions/cataloging system it reported as in operation in 1963[1] to a new and more severe test than it had ever had before, and under these conditions of strain, the system broke down. Together with serious doubts about the desirability of the results obtained, [2] this breakdown has caused the Library to decide to abandon the present system entirely and to design an entirely new one. The reasons for the breakdown are explained in this article, and the plans for the future now being considered are described, in the hope that such a description will be as helpful to those working in the field as was the original discussion.

Experience

The original acquisitions/cataloging system at the
Washington University School of Medicine Library was designed for the following purposes:[1, 3]

1. To produce, from a single keyboarded card source,
   multiple printouts: of both acquisitions and fiscal
   records and author, title, and subject catalogs.

2. To provide Washington University Medical Center
   personnel and interested persons from other institutions with copies of a printed Catalog of Books.

Until recently the Catalog of Books has been used
merely as a supplement to the traditional card catalog, but
it is obviously useless to have a computer catalog and a manual catalog side by side. In September 1968, therefore, a
four-month experiment was begun[2] to determine what would
happen if that portion of the card catalog whose contents were
also in the computer store and computer-produced catalogs
(i. e. , items acquired since January 1, 1965) were made inaccessible and readers had to rely on the printouts alone.

One printed catalog covered the years 1965-67, and
another 1967. An additional printout covered the period
January-June, 1968, and thereafter cumulated monthly printouts were produced. There were in all cases main entry and
subject lists, and since 1967, title lists as well. In addition
to the computer printouts, because of the time lag between the
cataloging of a book and its appearance in the monthly print-
out, a card catalog of these items was also maintained, and
weeded each month as the new printout was received.

Discussion

For the most part, readers accepted the new system
with resignation, except for a few who objected to the necessity for searching multiple alphabets when the dates for an
item were not known. One reader remarked that it made no
difference to him how the cataloging information was presented, so long as it was all there. The staff, on the other
hand, found the five alphabets a serious difficulty.

The acquisitions/cataloging/system was originally designed around a single-input multiple-output concept, as
noted above. A record could be initiated by the Acquisitions

Section and added to or changed by the Cataloging Section.
In actual practice, however, there were many differences
between these records. For example, the Acquisitions Section might order a series under a series title, leaving to the
Cataloging Section the expansion of the single record into the
necessary number of individual ones. On the other hand, the
Acquisitions Section might separate records for volumes
normally considered by the Cataloging Section to be part of a
set--say a twenty-four volume encyclopedia which appeared
over a period of years, for which twenty-four separate entries would be made by the Acquisitions Section as each volume was received and payment for it approved. It was
thought that provision had been made for this in the original
systems design, but this proved not to be so.

Another serious difficulty was in the inflexibility of
any printed record--once a record is printed, it is there to
stay. Thus deletions cannot be made retrospectively. For
example, the Nursing School Library was being disbanded,
but the records for it in the printed Catalog of Books could
not be expunged, and it became necessary to paste a general
statement on the cover of each copy in the Library. Copies
already distributed could not even have that updating.

It was soon obvious, also, that serious limitations
were present on the number of records which could be
handled at any one time. For example, the Dental Library
holdings were to be added to the computer store, and 600
records were made ready at one fell swoop. Grave difficulties were encountered; the computer refused over and over
again to accept them. Finally the input was broken down
into smaller chunks and added gradually. The explanation
here was that the internal storage capacity of the IBM 1401
was limited. In the particular design and with the particular
programming language used (SPS), a considerable fraction of
the 8, 000 byte storage capacity had to be taken up with instructions to the computer. To make the most efficient use
of the core storage remaining for manipulation, there was
considerable moving about internally of the data fed into the
machine. Unfortunately, it appears that data do not move
about and out of specific addresses quickly, but keep building
up so that the computer becomes overloaded beyond its storage capacity. It was felt that a larger computer might have
obviated this problem. This is a problem also encountered
at the SUNY Biomedical Communication Network. [4]

The poor quality of the program arose in part because

of the high systems analyst and programmer turnover, which
brought a series of persons, each with a different background,
to work on it.   Not one of them was able to see it through to
conclusion, or (in spite of reams of manual sheets) to provide sufficient documentation so that the person following
could understand fully what had gone before.   Even debugging
had been sketchy.   The result was a patchwork so difficult
to understand that necessary changes, not anticipated when
the program was first put into operation, could not now be
made.

The system worked comparatively well for some time:
after all, several annual volumes of the Catalog of Books
were produced.   However, using the printed catalog as a
supplement to the card catalog requires one level of accuracy
and speed; using the printed catalog to replace the card
catalog requires a higher level of accuracy and speed.   The
system provided the first but not the second level of
accuracy.

In retrospect, given the requirements originally set
forth--single acquisitions/cataloging input and multiple out-
puts--and the constraints of the capabilities of the IBM 1401
8K computer available when the program was being written,
it is not surprising that serious flaws became apparent.

If anything has been learned from this experience, it
is the old cliché that much more serious thought and preparation must go into the design of a system and its documentation than is generally realized.   It cannot be stressed too
often that what are problems for the computer are not at all
problems for the human, and vice versa.

It is also obvious that designing a cataloging computer
system requires catalogers to reverse their normal patterns
of thought.   Accustomed as they are to the application of a
generalized rule to a specific item to be cataloged, the catalogers designing the system must instead generalize from
each specific case to the longest, largest, most numerous,
most complex situation possible.   Provision must be made
for all the rules that do not follow logical patterns.   All
the possible variations to which publishers are prone must
thus be considered in advance.

Present Situation

Despite the inconveniences and problems encountered
during the four-month test, it has been concluded that a good

computer-produced catalog is desirable. The Library is
therefore now engaged in rethinking the entire acquisitions/
cataloging system, expecting to base it on the IBM 360/50
now available. Other changes include breaking the record
into an acquisitions record and a cataloging one. The possibility of optical scanning, rather than keypunching, is being
investigated. It is hoped to produce catalog cards as well as
a printed record, both by way of the computer. Finally, it
is expected that in the new system the printouts will be cumulated each month, to do away with the multiple alphabets, and
that the printouts will be produced in only a small number of
copies for internal use in the Library, with printed cumulated
catalogs at rarer intervals. The reason for the latter is given
in another article. [2]

Surprisingly enough, in spite of this bruising first experience, the plans for the second attempt to provide a viable
computerized acquisitions/cataloging system are being undertaken in a spirit of renewed hope. The Library will, of
course, report its results promptly.

References

1. Moore, Evelyn A.; Brodman, Estelle; and Cohen,
   Geraldine S. "Mechanization of library procedures in
   the medium-sized medical library: III. Acquisitions
   and Cataloging." Bull. Med. Libr. Ass. 53: 305-328,
   July 1965.

2. Brodman, Estelle, and Bolef, Doris. "Printed catalogs:
   retrospect and prospect." Spec. Libr. 68: 783-788,
   Dec. 1968.

3. Brodman, Estelle, and Cohen, Geraldine S. "Changes
   in acquisitions-cataloging methods at Washington
   University School of Medicine Library." Bull. Med.
   Libr. Ass. 54: 259-260, July 1966.

4. Library Bulletin, SUNY Upstate Medical Center Library
   8: 130-131, Dec. 1968.

Chapter VIII

Applications and Techniques:
County Libraries

The Metamorphosis of the Book Catalogs

by Catherine MacQuarrie

Reprinted by permission from Library Resources &
Technical Services, 8(4): 370-78, Fall 1964.

The book catalogs prepared with IBM equipment have
now been in use in the Los Angeles County Public Library
for ten years. During this time, we have had some unsolv-
able problems in connection with their preparation. These
problems are the IBM print, the lack of punctuation and diacritical marks, and the increasing bulkiness and unwieldiness
of the catalogs. Scheduling also was becoming a problem
since we farmed out various parts of the preparation of the
catalog: preparing of stencils to the Registrar of Voters,
multilithing, binding.

Our branch librarians and the library patrons have
used these catalogs and like the way they are prepared, the
cumulative supplements, and the arrangement into separate
catalogs for both adult and juvenile, author, titles and subjects, and particularly the brief annotations. The librarians
were beginning to worry, however, about the space needed
for the housing of the volumes. The catalogs take less
space than a card catalog, but they are growing by 5 to 6
volumes a year since we add approximately 9, 000 titles.
The size of each volume is 9" x 13" and about 3/4 inch
thick, so they are heavy and awkward to handle. They now
are in 52 volumes with next year's set projected for 57
volumes.

The other point that bothered the branch librarians
particularly was the sameness of the print. We used a #407
tabulator for print-out, and our tab cards were punched on
a #026 print punch; consequently, the print-out is in all
caps. This is monotonous to look at and presents difficulties
to the users in that it is hard to distinguish where an author
entry ends and the title begins or where the title ends and

264

the annotation begins.   As a result, when people copy from
the catalog preparing request slips, they often mis-copy an
entry.

There are other difficulties.   For example, the filing
word does not stand out.   In the Author Catalog the print
is all the same so the author's name does not catch the
eye.   In the subject Catalog the subject headings do not
stand out even though we centered them and allowed space
above and below.   To make them more distinctive, we underlined each subject heading.   However, there is no underline
key on IBM equipment; therefore we had to underline on the
multilith masters by hand, a very time-consuming job.

Punctuation, or the lack of it, also has caused difficulties.   We adapted and changed to fit the few punctuation
marks that are on the #407 tabulator, but there are times
when a question mark, for example, is essential.   These
again had to be added to the stencils.   Our foreign language
catalog lacks diacritical marks which in some cases changes
the meaning of the words.

The appearance of the catalogs was becoming a
problem.   We used good paper for maximum legibility but
were using the cheapest bindings made from marble board
with a cloth strip down the back.   They were designed to
last just the life of the edition--from 12 to 18 months.   Toward the end of the period the volumes became quite ragged
and dog-eared and did not enhance the appearance of the
branches.   We liked to know that the library patrons were
finding the catalogs so usable and consulted them so much
that they became worn out; but the catalogs were far from
pleasing to look at or handle after the covers became dirty
and cracked.   However, we did not want to add to the cost
by using more expensive covers.

When IBM introduced upper and lower case letters in
some of its advanced machines, we considered whether there
would be sufficient improvement to warrant changing our
basic records for the catalogs.   We rejected this for several
reasons.   In the first place only part of our problems would
be solved.   In the second place, we were using the machines
of the Registrar of Voters who did not have the new machines.
We could not justify purchasing a machine for our own use
as the catalogs did not take more than 1 day a week machine
time to prepare.   It was also suggested that we change to
tape or drums, but again the print-out was not significantly

better to warrant the change, and more problems would be encountered. We tried photography and reduction in size of
print. In order to get two columns it was necessary to reduce 4:1 which made the print too small for use by the
general public in a library. We ran one issue of the supplement with the reduced print. It took considerably more work,
but when we sent out the supplements, everyone complained.

In the fall of 1962 we learned of the possibility of using different print faces through the use of Composo-list
machines and high speed cameras. We investigated procedures and methods of adapting these machines to our requirements. After obtaining permission to experiment with
the preparation of a couple of our supplements by these
methods, the November 1962 Supplement was our first issue.
It had many mistakes; entries did not come out as we
planned and many problems developed that we had to solve.
However, basically, it answered our needs and both our library users and branch librarians liked the appearance of
the new supplements and found them much easier to use. The
Technical Services staff and the Company who had suggested
this method worked together to produce six cumulative issues--
to see if the work could be done mechanically, if the various
problems of cataloging, such as holdings changes, corrections,
last copy discards, could be handled mechanically. The Los
Angeles County Chief Administrator's staff made a feasibility
study and a budget or cost study and decided that we should
go ahead. Towards the end of the period we formulized our
catalog requirements, prepared a description and submitted
it for bid to the County Purchasing Agent. Several bids
were received. That of Econolist Company was the lowest
bid for the five-year period, so they were awarded the
contract.

Among the reasons for the change, besides the obvious
one of improved appearance from the varied typefaces, were
(1) the reduction in size--two column pages--a projected 30+
volumes instead of 57 as projected for the 1964 IBM edition
and 8-1/2"x11" instead of 9"x13" pages; (2) entries easier
to read with distinction between the body of the card, the annotations and the entry words (bold face for subject headings
and for the author entry in the Author Catalog); and (3)
schedules easier to maintain since we would be dealing with
one agency rather than several, all of which were subject to
delays. Another important point in making the change was
that during the years that we had been preparing the IBM
Catalogs we had been making changes, increasing usefulness

of the catalogs by adding analytics, series, publishers, collation, further notes, as requested by the branch librarians; but we never had had time to go back and re-do the older entries.   When making this new conversion we would have the opportunity to improve the whole catalog.   We were particularly interested in improving our method of handling classics--both fiction and nonfiction--and the basic authorities in the subject fields.   Otherwise, the new catalogs will contain essentially the same information as the old, using as many lines as needed to describe each title.

Cost was one of the most important reasons for seriously considering making the change to the new format, for a change of this magnitude is not undertaken lightly.   We reviewed the costs of producing the catalogs and the end product that we were getting as against the proposed new format. The estimated cost was slightly less than our current costs for maintenance and up-dating the catalogs on an annual basis. Several elements were of importance in our estimates. We had been using the same tabulating cards over and over again to produce the new editions of the catalogs, the main bulk of the cards for over ten years.   We were told that the life expectancy of the cards was from five to eight years, therefore it was past time to reproduce our basic decks of cards,   a considerable expense.   Since the catalogs were becoming so bulky, we were beginning to need more furniture for housing them, another added expense which would not be needed with the new format of 30+ volumes.   We were running out of multilith time to produce the catalogs so would have to get another machine and operator if we continued on the same schedule.   Actually, we already had been forced to go to an 18-month schedule, and it was probable that we would have to go to a 20-month schedule for the 1964 edition or get another multilith machine.   The new format would get us back on a 12-month schedule.   Supplements become too large when the master editions are on a 18-month or longer schedule, and the master editions become too ragged before replacement.

The conversion of the master tab decks to the format is quite expensive, but the annual maintenance costs after conversion were sufficiently less to absorb the conversion costs.   To quote from the letter of authorization from the Los Angeles County Administrative Officer: In terms of cost, although the annual processing expense will, under the Econolist system, be less, the initial conversion cost will probably not be absorbed for many years.   Using the next

five years as a basis, we estimate that the present system
would cost $524,498. This represents salaries, supplies,
and equipment for the portion of the catalog processing
which will be done under contractual agreement. This is
compared to $562,500 for the same 5-year period if the
work would be done under contract as presented by Econolist.
The difference of $38,002 represents the initial conversion
cost of $82,500 less than the total annual savings for the
next five years of $44,498. Spread out over the five year
period, this produces an average yearly increase of about
$7,600, or 1.4% increase. We do agree that the catalogs
prepared by the proposed process would be superior to the
present ones. Not only will the catalogs be more attractive,
but they can more easily be read by the patron. Also, under
the new system, a complete catalog revision of 52 volumes
can be prepared annually rather than every 19 months under
the present system. This will significantly reduce the time
span by patrons of the library and by your staff in research-
ing through supplements to find the desired title. Finally,
the new catalogs will be about 40% smaller which will save
space and reduce the number of tables needed in your branch
libraries. In light of these advances and since County
Counsel (Edward Gaylord) advises us that such a contract is
legal, we believe you should proceed in firming up the contractual agreements.

Cost Analysis for Branch Catalog Processing

1963-64	1964-65	1965-66	1966-67	1967-68	5-year Total
Total Library Cost to be Deleted					
$ 92,649	$ 98,111	$103,550	$114,263	$115,925	$524,498
Cost of Catalog Processing by Econolist					
$172,500	$ 90,000	$ 95,000	$100,000	$105,000	$562,500
Savings (Loss)					
$(-79,851)	$ 8,111	$ 8,550	$ 14,263	$ 14,925	$(-38,002)

The new format used in our current supplements was
very well received by the branch librarians and the library
users. We even received fan letters from library users con-
gratulating us for making the change to a more pleasing
print. Placing a page from each type of print side by side
is the best comparison. (See end of article for examples of
the old and new pages).

One of the questions to decide for these new catalogs
is whether to produce them in the old dictionary catalog arrangement or as divided catalogs.   The dictionary arrangement has the advantage of familiarity;   however, most indexes and catalogs, from the telephone book to some of the
Wilson publications, divide subject from author.   When we
started in 1952, we had no choice as divided catalogs were
most feasible with the IBM equipment.   Now we could change
to dictionary arrangement, using code numbers to control
the arrangement.   We have questioned our branches at various times since, and they far prefer the divided catalogs.
They say it is much easier to go directly to the title or to
the subject and not to have to explain to library users the
complicated filing of a dictionary catalog.   We have found
that the title catalogs are used most, subject next, and
author least, judging from the wear and tear of the volumes
in the branches.

A second concern is the type of catalog.   There are
three types of book catalogs being developed: the finding
list or index type used mostly by companies and usually
employing just one line per entry with many abbreviations;
the type prepared for use by librarians such as the LC
catalogs and the University of California catalogs which are
simply a photographic reproduction of card catalogs in page
form; and the completely remade catalogs such as those of
the Los Angeles County which are prepared primarily for
the users in a public library.   When we have shown the
first two styles of catalogs to our librarians, they immediately exclaim that it would be most difficult to train the
public to use them.

Since we have been producing the supplements with
the new format, many of the other libraries in the State
have become interested in our procedures.   The State Librarian called a workshop meeting in Sacramento, February
13-14, 1963.   This Workshop, made up of the county librarians and other librarians who were members of the union
catalog maintained by the State Library, discussed the possibility of converting the State Union Catalog (an author catalog in card form which shows the location of the various
titles) to the new format and providing copies for all members.   We also discussed the conversion of individual or
groups of catalogs to this same format.   A summary of the
proceedings of the Workshop is included as Appendix A of
Book Catalogs, edited by Robert Kingery and Maurice Tauber
(Scarecrow Press, 1963, pp. 279-305).

The new format used in our supplements has been so
attractive that it has also caused a revival of interest in
book catalogs for both individual libraries and groups of
libraries working together on a cooperative basis.   Many
of the district meetings of the California Library Association centered their programs on discussions of the various
methods of preparing book catalogs.   During the meeting
of the California Library Association in San Francisco,
December, 1963, the Cataloger's Round Table meeting was
devoted to the subject.   Paul Miles, of the University of
California at Los Angeles, discussed the book catalogs of
the University of California at Los Angeles Library prepared by the G. K. Hall Corporation.   Frances Alexander
of the Los Angeles County Public Library staff explained
the new methods of preparing our catalogs, and I discussed
various meetings that were held on the subject of union or
book catalogs.   Amazingly, we had over 500 librarians
attending the meeting, an unheard of number at a catalog
meeting.   It showed the great interest in the subject both
by catalogers and library administrators.   Many stimulating
questions were asked, and during the rest of the convention
it was surprising how often little groups of librarians talked
about book catalogs.   I was hailed frequently to explain a
point or describe something in fuller detail.   Cooperative
or centralized cataloging in connection with union catalogs
for groups of libraries was part of most of these discussions.

The Library Development Act passed by the California Legislature last summer (A. B. 590) promoted
cooperation between libraries and the development of
library systems.   Several groups of/libraries are discussing forming systems and cooperating to produce book catalogs, using the same format as presently used by Los
Angeles County.   These union catalogs would give location
and would be used in place of their card catalogs.   In order
to produce these catalogs economically, the system must
have centralized cataloging.   The book catalogs would be
used in all outlets of the libraries in the system.   The development and use of union catalogs for a system of independent libraries will encourage closer cooperation in loan-
ing books, in book selection, in the formation of a last
copy depository, and particularly in communication between
libraries in the system.   Reference and processing centers
will become part of each system, or possibly systems can
band together to maintain large resource centers as cooperation becomes a reality.   A union book catalog prepared by

these newer methods, with copies in all the libraries that are members of the system, would be the most effective way to make the centers truly functional.

AUTHOR CATALOG

HUNTER, DONALD
613.61   Diseases of occupations. 3d ed. Little, 1962. 1180 p. Illus.

HUNTER, EDWARD
131.33   Brainwashing, from Pavlov to Powers. Enl. ed. of Brainwashing: the story of
           men who defied it. Bookmailer, 1960. 329 p.

HUNTER, JAMES ALSTON HOPE
793.74   Mathematical diversions. Van Nostrand, 1963. 178 p. Illus.

HUNTER, LLOYD PHILIP
621.3815   Handbook of semiconductor electronics; a practical manual covering the physics,
           technology, and circuit applications of transistors, diodes, and photocells.
           2d ed. McGraw, 1962. Bibliographies.

HUNTER, NORMAN
793.8   Successful conjuring. Rev. ed. Arco Pub. Co., 1964. 256 p. Illus.
           First edition published in 1951 under title "Successful conjuring for
           amateurs".
           Earlier edition has title "Successful magic for amateurs".

HUNTER, RICHARD ALFRED
616.89   Three hundred years of psychiatry, 1535-1860; a history presented in
           selected English texts. Oxford Univ. Pr., 1963. 1107 p. Illus.,
           ports., facsims.

HUXLEY, ELSPETH JOSCELIN GRANT
           Incident at the Merry Hippo. Morrow, 1963.

HUYGHE, RENE
759.4   Cezanne. Translated from the French by K. ?
C425   87 p. Col. illus. Bibliography.
759.4 D332 Delacroix. 56 colour plates, 405 black and ??
           Abrams, 1963. 564 p. Illus., ports., facs ?
709.02   Larousse encyclopedia of Byzantine and medie?
           416 p. Illus., col. plates, ports., maps,
           Translation from v. 2 of the French work "?

HYAMS, EDWARD SOLOMON
985   Last of the Incas; the rise and fall of an Amer
           G. Ordish. Simon, 1963. 294 p. Illus
052   New statesman; the history of the first fifty ye
           by J. Freeman. Longmans,1963. 326 p.
808.8   New Statesmanship; an anthology. Longmans,

HYDE, DOUGLAS ARNOLD
#335.43   Peaceful assault; the pattern of subversion.

HYDE, HARFORD MONTGOMERY
92 W672   Oscar Wilde, the aftermath. Farrar, 1963. 22
343.1   Oscar Wilde. New and enl. ed. Penguin B??
           First published in 1948 under title "The tr

SUBJECT CATALOG

ADAMS, LOISELLE
636.8   Harris, Eleanor. Career cat. Doubleday, 1962. 64 p.
           Illus.
           The success story of a real-life cat named Nicodemus - and his
           "mother", Loiselle Adams.

ADAPTATION, BIOLOGICAL
           SEE ALSO
           Animals, Influence of environment on. Man - Influ-
           ence of environment. Origin of species. Stress,
           Physiological.

632.9   Carson, Rachel Louise. Silent spring. Houghton, 1962.
           What man is doing to destroy the balance of nature with chemicals and
           create a science of death. Drawings by Lois and Louis Darling, with
           a list of references.

ADDRESSES.   SEE
           SPEECHES, ADDRESSES, ETC.

ADOLESCENCE (Cont'd)
301.431   Parkhurst, Helen. Growing pains.
           Based on the radio series of the same
           in 1955-57. Records the opinions of
301.431   Smith, Ernest Allyn. American you
           1962.
           Group life in teenage society, descrip
           on relevant literature.

ADONIS
291   Frazer, Sir James George. Adonis
3d ed.   the history of Oriental religion.
           Re-issue, with new illustrations, of
           constitute Part 4 of the unabridged "?

ADULTHOOD
#136.7   Doniger, Simon. Becoming the co?
           Pr., 1962. 222 p.

CHILDREN'S CATALOG

SEUBERLICH, HERTHA GRIT
J   Annuzza, a girl of Romania. Rand, 1962.

SEVERN, WILLIAM
J793.9   Magic with paper. McKay, 1962. 149 p. Illus.
J920   State makers, by B. and S. Severn. Putnam, 1963.
           255 p.

SHACKELFORD, NINA
J598.2   Bird nests. Golden Pr., 1962. 32 p. Illus.

SHAKESPEARE, WILLIAM
J822   Seeds of time; selections. Compiled by B. Grohskopf.
           Drawings by K. Oechsli. Atheneum, 1963. 59 p.
           Illus.

SHEPPARD-JONES, ELISABETH
J398   Scottish legendary tales. With
           P. Hogarth. Nelson, 1962
           (part col.)

SHERMAN, THERESA, ILLUS.
           SEE
J   Goven, Christine Noble. [

SHIRER, WILLIAM LAWRENCE
J940.545   Sinking of the Bismarck. Worl:
           Random House, 1962. 178

SHORTALL, LEONARD
EB   Sam's first fish. Morrow, 196

Los Angeles County book catalogs (new format)

AUTHOR CATALOG

663.1	MASSEE, WILLIAM EDMAN. WINES AND SPIRITS. MCGRAW, 1961. REGIONS - 1, 2, 3, 4, 5, 6, 7, 8, CENTRAL
663.1	MASSEE, WILLIAM EDMAN SEE ALSO LICHINE, ALEXIS. WINES OF FRANCE.
	MASSELINK, BEN. CRACKERJACK MARINES. LITTLE, 1959. REGIONS - 1, 2, 3, 4, 5, 6, 7, 8,
M782	MASSENET, JULES. MANON. 1895.
	MASSENET, JULES. MANON SEE ALSO
782	MEILHAC, HENRI. MANON.
M782	MASSENET, JULES. THAIS. 1922.
	MASSENET, PIERRE BESSAND- SEE BESSAND-MASSENET, PIERRE.
150.72	MASSERMAN, JULES HYMEN. BEHAVIOR AND NEUROSIS. 1943.
92 M415	MASSETT, STEPHEN C. FIRST CALIFORNIA TROUBADOUR. 1954.
812	MASSEY, EDWARD. PLOTS AND PLAYWRIGHTS. 1917.
C917.94	MASSEY, ERNEST DE. FRENCHMAN IN THE GOLD RUSH. CALIFORNIA HISTORICAL SOCIETY. SPECIAL PUBLICATIONS SERIES, NO. 2. 1927.
530.9	MASSEY, SIR HARRIE STEWART WILSON. NEW AGE IN PHYSICS. HARPER, 1960. REGIONS - 1, 2, 3, 4, 5, 7, 8, CENTRAL
659.1	MASSEY, MARIA. PRINCIPLES OF MEN'S WEAR DISPLAY. 1948.
973.71	MASSEY, MARY ELIZABETH. ERSATZ IN THE CONFEDERACY. 1952.
917.1	MASSEY, VINCENT. ON BEING CANADIAN. 1948.
971	MASSEY, VINCENT. SPEAKING OF CANADA. MACMILLAN, 1959.

SUBJECT CATALOG

GAME PROTECTION

799.24	EVERETT, FRED. PRESENTING, FUN WITH GAME BIRDS. 1954. HOW TO HAVE YEAR-ROUND FUN WITH GAME BIRDS.
799	HORNADAY, WILLIAM TEMPLE. OUR VANISHING WILD LIFE. 1913.
799	HORNADAY, WILLIAM TEMPLE. THIRTY YEARS WAR FOR WILD LIFE. 1931.
799	HORNADAY, WILLIAM TEMPLE. WILD LIFE CONSERVATION IN THEORY AND PRACTICE. 1914.
92 J823	JORGENSEN, FREDERICK E. TWENTY-FIVE YEARS A GAME WARDEN. 1937.
799	LEOPOLD, ALDO. GAME MANAGEMENT. 1933.
352.9	LOS ANGELES CO., CALIF. BUREAU OF EFFICIENCY. SURVEY OF THE DEPARTMENT OF FORESTER, FIRE, AND GAME WARDEN OF THE COUNTY OF LOS ANGELES, CALIFORNIA. 1931.
DOC.	LOS ANGELES CO., CALIF. DEPT. OF FORESTER AND FIRE WARDEN. ANNUAL REPORT.
916.89	MOORE, AUDREY. SERENGETI. 1939. AN ACCOUNT OF THE WILD LIFE AND SAFARI IN THE AFRICAN GAME SANCTUARY, SERENGETI.

SEE ALSO BIRDS, PROTECTION OF.
GAME-LAWS. WILD-LIFE,
CONSERVATION OF.

GAME PROTECTION - CALIFORNIA

C799	GORDON, SETH E. CALIFORNIA'S FISH AND GAME PROGRAM. 1950. REPORT TO THE WILDLIFE CONSERVATION BOARD.
R333.78	U. S. FOREST SERVICE. WILDLIFE MANAGEMENT HANDBOOK FOR FOREST OFFICERS, REGION 5. 1947.

GAME ROOMS   SEE   RECREATION ROOMS.

GAME WARDENS   SEE   GAME PROTECTION.

Los Angeles County book catalogs (old format)

Automatic Preparation of Book Catalogs

by Joseph Becker

The author is Vice-President, Becker and Hayes, Inc.

Reprinted by permission from ALA Bulletin, 58: 714-18, September 1964.

What does automating the catalog mean to you? Some librarians view the idea in its broadest sense--the conversion of catalog data into machine-readable code for input to a computer, an automatic printing device, or communications equipment. Others think of it merely as the use of machines to facilitate the automatic preparation of a printed book catalog. In either case the objective is the same--to find an improved substitute for the card catalog that is prepared and maintained manually. In the first instance, the card catalog would be replaced by a very large capacity electronic computer memory, and, in the second, by recurring cumulative editions of a catalog in book form.

The recently published survey, Automation and the Library of Congress, deals extensively with the wider view. It suggests that the Library of Congress should provide a magnetic tape equivalent to the centralized card distribution service. Thus, bibliographical data would be available in machine-readable code for acquisition, cataloging, or reference purposes in local libraries. The survey team predicted that cooperating libraries would gain numerous advantages if they were able to communicate directly with an electronic computer memory which held the contents of the National Union Catalog. This access would be achieved, the report says, through a national library network "incorporating the telecommunications necessary to accommodate the flow of information to all its branches."

Today's rather elementary library network is exemplified by the public library and its relationship to its branches.

Although this network is not yet connected by high speed data transmission links, its closely knit system of telephone lines proves the efficacy of swift and direct communications. At the local level there is an urgent, continuing need to find improved methods for rapidly communicating catalog information of libraries comprising a regional system. The aim is to facilitate the public's use of the book collection by making certain that the catalog at all locations in the network is up to date and accurate.

Were machine-readable codes available at the national level, it is quite possible that local libraries would learn to adopt them advantageously. However, in their absence, libraries have turned to more limited approaches, such as the machine-produced printed book catalogs.

The Los Angeles County Public Library system has 117 branches and a book collection of 223,000 titles. It was one of the first libraries to use machines for producing a printed book catalog. It is an excellent model to study because it has numerous branches, its catalog is extensive, its user population has been on a steady upswing, and it has been operating for twelve years.

The library started out with the traditional manual card catalog. It purchased LC cards for most of its books, and its own cataloging staff prepared the remaining cards. Catalog cards were duplicated in sufficient quantities to satisfy branch requirements. In order to keep branch catalogs current, main library staff personnel paid scheduled visits to the branches to interfile new cards. But as the number of branches mushroomed, multiple card catalogs could not be kept up to date. After receiving the findings and recommendations of the library committee appointed to study the problem, the county librarian decided in 1952 to replace the card catalog with a printed book catalog prepared by punched card equipment.

A printed book catalog can be machine produced in one of three ways: 1) by punched cards and a line printer, 2) by card-actuated cameras and photocomposition, and 3) by computer.

Punched cards and a line printer

The Los Angeles County Public Library first tried punched cards and a line printer, employing the following techniques.

Makeready. A form was designed for recording the basic cataloging data. Unfortunately, not all of the data normally found on a catalog card could be included exactly the same way in the machine record. The punched card prints only capital letters and is severely restricted in the number of special symbols it can accommodate (e. g. , certain punctuation marks and diacritical marks are not included). Nevertheless, the final copy consisted of author, title, subject, edition, publisher's abbreviated name, copyright date, and a brief annotation.

Next, the punched card was divided into fixed fields of information. Key punch operators then were able to copy the cataloger's data and convert them into punched holes in an IBM card. Because one punched card can record a maximum of only 80 alphanumeric characters, additional detail cards were required in order to represent all of the data in one set of cards. After all the cards were punched, they were verified--verification consisted of rekeying the same information on a second key punch machine. The latter automatically compared its results with the contents of the first punched card and detected any discrepancies.

When an accurate set of cards had been prepared, the key punch operator duplicated additional sets of cards automatically on the key punch machine. A separate set was produced for each author, title, and subject heading entry. Thus, the library was able to build up punched card files to support each of the three book catalogs it intended to print.

Production. The punched card files were passed through IBM sorter and collator machines which arranged them into the desired sequences for printing editions of the book catalogs. Then, files of author, title, and subject cards were fed into an IBM tabulating machine which printed the cards a line at a time on offset duplicating masters. The masters were run off on multilith machines, and hundreds of copies of legal-size sheets were printed, collated, and quarter bound into book form for distribution. From then on, each file was maintained as an entity. New cards were interfiled by hand or deleted as titles were withdrawn from the collection. Finally, the files were rerun annually to produce the new editions of the catalog.

Current cumulative supplements were prepared monthly in the same form as the printed catalogs and bound with construction paper covers. These supplements were

cumulative so that the catalog users would have only two
places to look, the annual editions and the current cumulative
supplements.

It took the library several years to finish the onerous
task of converting the old catalog into the new punched card
format.   Once completed, however, all branch catalogs were
displaced by a shelf or two of printed book catalogs.   At
first, the staff resisted working with book catalogs.   But
later, through education and experience, their attitude changed.
The public used the catalogs so extensively that before a new
edition was issued, the old edition was in tatters.

Poor readability turned out to be the principal com-
plaint levied against the book catalog.   The line printer
produced a monotonous-looking page containing a single column of capital letters, hand-inserted editorial symbols, and
large type.   The books were very bulky, awkward to handle,
and difficult to bind.   The public disliked the physical form
and size of the books, and the staff, particularly the reference librarians and the catalogers, insisted that more cataloging information needed to be included in the system. (See
Figure 1.)

Card-actuated cameras and photocomposition

The library therefore explored ways of improving the
style and structure of the book catalog.   It also sought new
means for incorporating additional cataloging data into the
basic record.   This eventually led to a decision to employ
card-actuated cameras in place of the punched card method.

These cameras are capable of automatically photographing one, two, or three lines of data that is typed, written, or
imprinted on the white space at the top of a punched card.
The cards enter the camera through an automatic, precision-
feeding device.   One by one they are photographed at high
speeds ranging from 7000 to 14, 000 cards per hour.   The
camera automatically adjusts to mixtures of cards with one
or more lines of imprint.   A sheet of film is exposed, the
negative is developed, and then column lengths are "stripped
up" into page formats.   Photo-offset plates are prepared
from the film negatives, and listings are duplicated and assembled in finished form.

Makeready. Instead of punching cards, the library prepared source-data cards containing all information needed for

```
                        KERGUELEN ISLAND
999            MIGOT, ANDRE.  THIN EDGE OF THE WORLD.  1956.
                    REFLECTIVE ADVENTURES OF A FRENCH PHYSICIAN ON
                    KERGUELEN ISLAND AND IN THE ANTARCTIC.
                    PUBLISHED IN ENGLAND UNDER TITLE, "THE LONELY
                    SOUTH".

                        KERN, EDWARD M.
C92 K393       HEFFERNAN, WILLIAM JOSEPH.  EDWARD M. KERN.
                    KERN COUNTY HISTORICAL SOCIETY.  PUBLICATION,
                    NO. 15.  1953.
979.488        SPINDT, HERMAN A.  NOTES ON THE LIFE OF EDWARD
                    M. KERN.  KERN COUNTY HISTORICAL SOCIETY.
                    PUBLICATION, NO. 5.  1939.

                        KERN, JEROME
780.8 K39      EWEN, DAVID.  STORY OF JEROME KERN.  1953.
780.8 K39      EWEN, DAVID.  WORLD OF JEROME KERN.  HOLT, 1960.
                    A BIOGRAPHY, INCLUDES LISTS OF HIS BROADWAY
                    SHOWS, MOTION PICTURE SCORES, INSTRUMENTAL
                    MUSIC, SONGS, AND PHONOGRAPH RECORDS.
```

Figure 1: Print-out using punched cards and an IBM line printer. Courtesy of the Los Angeles County Public Library

the new form of the catalog. The library selected a preferred type font, style, and size, and then contracted with a local company to type the cataloging information across the white space at the top of IBM cards, using as many cards as were needed for each entry.   This typing was done on a Varityper rather than a typewriter.   Codes for author, title, and subject headings were key-punched into the cards.   All subsequent sorting and collating was controlled by these codes.

Cataloging data is not captured in machine-readable form when this method is used.

Production. Several special cameras are capable of taking a high-speed picture of printed information that has been typed on the top of a card.   These include Varityper's Fotolist, Recordak's Listomatic, and Friden's Composoline. Although filming occurs a line or more at a time, the end product is a two-column list of consecutive frames on an exposed film negative which is then developed and used to prepare an offset plate for printing.   Figure 2 shows the appearance of citations on a page of a recent Los Angeles County book catalog.   After the card sets are photographed in one arrangement, say by author, they can be sorted into another sequence, such as by subject, and rephotographed. Similarly, the punches in the cards make it possible to merge new cards into an established file for cumulation.

In this way the Los Angeles County Public Library is able to publish an annual cumulation and monthly supplements for three catalogs--author, title, and subject.

As a result of these innovations the book catalogs currently issued by the Los Angeles County Public Library system are of higher printing quality, smaller in size, and easier to read and handle. Because the process is photographic, the original data can be reduced or enlarged before printing, a feature which contributes immeasurably to the appearance and readability of the final page. For example, juvenile catalogs in the Los Angeles County Public Library are prepared in an enlarged edition to facilitate reading.

INTERPLANETARY ADVENTURE

Norton, Andre, pseud. Key out of time. World Pub. Co., 1963.
Aided by a Polynesian girl and two telepathic dolphins, Time Agents probe the past on the deserted planet Hawaika and are catapulted back ten thousand years among the battles of prehistoric races.

Walters, Hugh. Expedition Venus. Criterion, 1963.
English edition, with same title, has different version of the story.
A deadly mould brought to earth by an unmanned "space-probe" means a dangerous mission to Venus for a brilliant young scientist and his fellow teammates.

IRELAND

Laverty, Maura. Never no more. Templegate, 1942.
The life of an Irish village on the edge of the great Bog of Allen, in the 1920s, as seen through the eyes of a candid and sensitive girl who lives with her kindly grandmother.

ITALY

Ginzburg, Natalia. Voices in the evening. Dutton, 1963.
Also available in Italian as "Le voci della sera".
The rise and fall of a middle-class Italian family as the result of a secret love affair.

ITALY - VENICE

MacInnes, Helen. Venetian affair. Harcourt, 1963.
When an American newspaperman picks up the wrong raincoat at Orley airport, he is drawn into a Communist plot to assassinate De Gaulle.

Figure 2: Print-out using card-actuated camera and photo-composition, two columns to a page. Courtesy of the Los Angeles County Public Library.

These improvements were expensive. They required dual processing of the union card catalog of more than 2,000,000 cards, once in 1952 for the punched card method and again in 1962-63 for the Varityper operation.

It is very likely that in the near future the library at

central headquarters will abandon the manual union card
catalog. The latest version of the book catalog is so acceptable to both the professional staff and the public that maintaining a duplicate manual catalog for use by subject specialists may prove too costly.

To help keep present method costs down, the library
has contracted with a local company to produce the book
catalogs. The library continues to exercise professional
control over cataloging data and format specifications, but
the contractor assumes responsibility for the makeready and
production work-load.

Computer

A third way to print a book catalog automatically is
to use a computer. With clever programming, computer
tape can be prepared to drive one of several printing devices,
such as a line printer, an automatic linotype machine, or an
electronic photocomposition machine.

Computer processing is possible when cataloging data
is in machine-readable form. Machines like the Flexowriter
and the key punch can produce perforated paper tape or
punched cards, two basic machine-language media. Both
machines require the services of a human operator who performs the equivalent of typing. As a general rule, the key
punch machine records upper case letters only. The Flexowriter, on the other hand, is more versatile; it can produce
machine-readable codes for both upper and lower case letters.

Armed with the specifications of the printing device to
be used and with machine-readable codes for his data, the
computer programmer is able to plan his print-out to be
compatible. As appropriate, he takes into account page size,
page layout, type size, line spacing, margin justification,
column width, etc. His computer program also includes the
control codes needed to make a piece of automatic printing
equipment function as directed.

The computer's end product is a magnetic tape or a
set of punched cards to operate the automatic printing equipment. For example, IBM has a special line printer that
prints alphabetic characters in upper and lower case. While
the type quality and style are somewhat restricted, the appearance of the final line is good. (See Figure 3.) With this
printer, emphasis also can be given to subject headings by

having the computer program direct the overprinting of
selected characters for extra boldness.

Another machine which can be driven automatically with
output from a computer is the linotype.   This is the best
known of the typesetting machines and is widely used for the
preparation of newspapers, books, LC catalog cards, etc.
More flexible than the line printer, the linotype can operate
in several type fonts and sizes.   If the proper control codes
are in the computer's output tape, the machine will faithfully
execute those functions normally performed manually by an
operator.

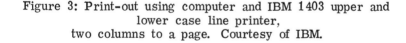

```
        MORRISON, ALEXANDER JAMES WILLIAM, ED.
    PN     SCHLEGEL, August Wilhelm von.
    1664 Lectures on dramatic art and literat
    .j43 2d ed. London, Bell, 1914. 535 p.


    PN     NATHAN, George Jean.
    1655 The critic and the drama. N.Y.,
    .N25 Knopf, 1922. 152 p.


    PN     NELSON, Robert James.
    1692 Play within a play. New Haven,
    .N43 Yale U.P., 1958. 182 p.


    PN     NORWOOD, Gilbert.
    1721 Euripides and Shaw with other essc,s.
    .N88 London, Methuen (1921) 226 p.


       OF IRONY, ESPECIALLY IN DRAMA.
    PN     SEDGEWICK, Garnett. Gladwin.
    1680 Of irony, especially in drama. 2d ed.
    .S45 Toronto, U. of T. Pr., 1948. 127 p.
```

Figure 3: Print-out using computer and IBM 1403 upper and
lower case line printer,
two columns to a page. Courtesy of IBM.

The Photon, manufactured by Photon, Inc. , is typical
of the third class of machines designed to accept instructions
from a computer-produced tape.   This equipment offers great
composing flexibility.   It has capabilities for handling multiple
type fonts, styles, and sizes and for mixing them in the same
line.   Electronic photocomposing machines are also manufactured by the Harris-Intertype Company and the Mergenthaler
Company.   Future issues of the Index Medicus will be produced by a Photon machine.

The relative cost of the various methods of production will vary with the local situation. Book catalogs, for the most part, are representative of small machine jobs. Therefore it is unlikely that a library will be able to justify outright purchase of machines for this purpose alone. Sharing or renting time on a service basis is apt to be the preferred route. The question of cost, however, is very complex and those interested in the financial considerations are referred to a recent comprehensive report prepared for the Stanford University Libraries and the Council on Library Resources by R. M. Hayes and R. M. Shoffner, The Economics of Book Catalog Production.

Until a fundamental innovation is introduced at the national level for capturing cataloging data in machine-readable form, the library profession can expect to witness independent efforts to mechanize certain cataloging functions at the local level. A range of workable techniques and equipment is now available to librarians who wish to consider changing from a card catalog to a book catalog. As usual, however, the final decision must be determined by the library's goals and its pocketbook.

The Baltimore County Public Library Book Catalog

by Paula Kieffer

The author is Coordinator, Technical Services, Baltimore County Public Library, Towson, Maryland. Reprinted by permission from Library Resources & Technical Services, 10:133-41, Spring 1966.

On July 15, 1965, the Baltimore County Public Library issued its completely-computerized book catalog to the fourteen branches comprising the Library system. Part of the story, such as the administrative decision to choose the computer process, has appeared in print,[1] but the Editors of LRTS thought its readers would be interested in more of the details of adapting conventional cataloging to the machine-produced book catalog.

The catalog was produced under contract by a commercial firm which had had experience in indexing, information retrieval, and publication, but no experience with book catalogs. While the contractor had librarians on his staff, none was assigned to this project. The Library personnel had had no experience with computers, and knew nothing about programming.

The contract called for a basic book catalog of approximately 55,000 titles, monthly cumulative supplements for 1965, and a second basic (i.e. complete) catalog incorporating the additions. The contract was later renegotiated, and the monthly supplements were changed to bi-monthly supplements cumulated for one year, with new cumulations for the second year and a second basic list incorporating the cumulated supplements and the first basic at the end of two years instead of one year.

The information is stored on magnetic tape from punched cards generated from the source documents, and the

organization of the input is by computer.   The eventual
print-out is by an IBM printer using the 120-character print
chain with upper- and lower-case letters.

The cost per year for from eight to ten thousand
titles entered will be $25,000 to $40,000 depending upon
whether there are supplements only or a basic list with
supplements.   This cost is based on a fixed charge for each
title entered on the magnetic tape plus a charge of between
$5.50 and $6.00 per page, depending on the number of copies
run.

General Procedures

In order to supply the contractor with material for
input--or the source document--we decided to use the central
shelf list, which had been developed since 1959 by running
off an extra card for every title added to the system.   In the
period from 1960 to 1965 four new branches had been opened,
so that the titles in these branches, as well as any titles
added to the older branches, were all represented in the shelf
list.   There remained about forty thousand titles of older
works which did not appear in the central shelf list. Branch
holdings were not shown in the shelf list but in a separate
alphabetical holdings file.   In some cases the shelf list did
not reflect in the tracings a number of changes which had
been made in the subject headings, notably changes of policy
as to abbreviations.

In July 1964 the Library's Processing Department
stopped all other work and arranged the shelf list alphabetically by author, then checked it against the central holdings file
to add the symbols for the holdings of the branches.   The
first decision was to include the holdings in the book catalog;
but they were later omitted from the supplements and subsequent basic catalogs, because the time and expense of updating them was found to be out of all proportion to their
anticipated use.   The process of alphabetizing the cards and
transferring the holdings took twenty people two weeks.

After the holdings had been transferred, one cataloger
spent six weeks editing the cards to add titles where necessary and, in some cases, to shorten the body of the entry.
No effort was made at this time to standardize the abbreviations used in the tracings, because at that time we thought
that abbreviations could be filed as if written out.   This
editing should have been much more extensive in the light of

future decisions, but we did not know this at the time.

Also at this time a set of six hundred cards was developed for a systems checkout. This set had examples for all the filing rules and for various kinds of entries: title, catch title, series, subject, editor and added author. However, the contractor could not run this checkout and meet his schedule, so that a great many errors appeared in the first basic catalog which might not have occurred had the systems checkout been run.

Simultaneously, conferences were held between the Processing Department staff and appropriate representatives of the contractor to try to establish a mutual understanding of terminology and procedures. Since our mutual ignorance was so vast, not much progress was made, semantically speaking. This failure did not become wholly apparent until the book catalog was finally completed. The contractor assigned no one as project coordinator, which meant that the diverse departments of the contractor were not always aware of changes, new agreements, etc. , made by the sales representative. This increased the confusion and was the source of many errors.

Early in November, 1964, the contractor began supplying the Processing Department of the Library with linear proof. Since linear proof is not page proof but is in the form of coding for the computer, the staff had to be trained and retrained several times to understand and interpret the coding and relate it to the material on the original shelf list cards and to incorporate changes due to misunderstandings. The whole proof-reading operation took seven weeks with about twenty-five people participating, not all on a full 40-hour schedule. As the proof-reading progressed, the corrected proof was returned to the contractor. There the corrections were coded in by a staff of twelve who had been hired for this particular job, and who understood very little of what was involved.

Since a new branch was scheduled to open on March 15, 1965, it was hoped that the book catalog would be ready so that it would not be necessary to provide a card catalog there. By the end of February, it was clear that the book catalog would not be ready in time for the opening. Fortunately, we had continued to make catalog cards for the branch, and 87, 500 were on hand, unalphabetized. The Processing Department again stopped all other operations for

two weeks and arranged the cards.   Card cabinets were
borrowed, and the branch opened with a card catalog.

In April, after an advance copy of the book catalog
had been received by the Library, a check was made to see
how accurately the catalog located a book.   Ten percent of
the cards in the shelf list of an area branch were searched,
and four tallies were recorded: "Found" (i. e. the book could
have been found from the information in the book catalog);
"Not Found" in three categories: "Not in Catalog, " "Wrong
Call Number, " and "Out of Alphabetical Order. "   Errors in
spelling, capitalization, etc. , which would not affect the
"findability" of the book, were ignored.   The catalog was
found to be slightly less than 90 percent accurate.   Later,
supplements 1 and 2 were similarly checked and found to be
about 99 percent accurate.

Filing

The Baltimore County Public Library uses the filing
rules listed in Appendix V of the A. L. A. Rules for Filing
Catalog Cards, with some local modifications.   In the preliminary discussions with the representatives of the contractor
it was thought that the only concession the Library would have
to make to the machine was to accept the filing of Mc after
the Ma's.   This turned out to be an erroneous conclusion.
Since the book catalog is divided, many of the rules in
Appendix V do not apply.   Some rules presented no problem;
comments on the others (by number) follow:

2.   Modified letters. The computer print chain has no
diacritical marks.

3.   Signs and symbols. The computer cannot recognize an ampersand as "and. "   It was necessary to key punch
it thus: &[and].   Now when an ampersand appears in the title
of a book, it is being written out as "and. "   The print chain
has no ampersand, and a plus sign was being used.

4.   Initials and acronyms. Initials and acronyms can
be filed before a word beginning with the same initial letter
only if they are written with spaces between the initials.   It
is also necessary to have periods either always or never.
We chose to omit the periods with one exception (see below
under #5).

5. <u>Abbreviations.</u> Abbreviations cannot be arranged as if written out. All abbreviations in titles are now being written in full. We will continue to abbreviate United States as "U. S. " (Prior to 1962 we had not abbreviated United States. This created a problem since some of the tracings were abbreviated and some not. The program was changed to take care of this in the subject catalog but not in the author catalog.)

7. <u>Initial article.</u> The Baltimore County Public Library has never used the initial article (although a few crept in by mistake). For those libraries which do use the initial article, a special symbol would have to be used to indicate non-filing. One disadvantage of this is that a symbol thus used can never be used for anything else.

9. <u>Numerals.</u> (a) In order to file numerals as if spelled out in the language of the rest of the title, it is necessary to key punch them thus: 100 [one hundred]. We are now writing out all numerals in titles. The computer cannot recognize Roman numerals as numbers and files them as letters. This causes some peculiar filing under kings, popes, etc. (b) We are now inverting titles so that the date follows "Annual report, " etc.

11. <u>Hyphenated and compound words.</u> (c) Words with hyphenated prefixes are filed as two words.

13. <u>Names with a prefix.</u> (a) Names with prefixes are filed as two words. To avoid this, we are now typing them without spaces, e. g. DeLaRoche. (b) Mc is filed as written, not as Mac.

18. <u>Forename entries.</u> Arrangement 2 (After surname). This has not been done. The result is as follows:
>Charles County, Md.
>Charles d'Orleans
>Charles family
>Charles, John

19. <u>Surname entries.</u> (f) The computer cannot disregard titles of honor. We are now omitting them.

25. <u>Arrangement under author.</u> (a) 1. The computer cannot disregard such designations as ed. , comp. , in filing. We are now omitting such designations.

4. There are no analytics in the book catalog.
There is no way in the present program of taking care of
them.

6. Editions have to be arranged with the earliest
date first. Our former practice was to file the latest date
first.

35. Subject arrangement. It was our practice to file
form subdivisions of history before period subdivisions. Since
some subdivisions under United States had no dates, we supplied them. These were to have been keyed for sorting but
not printing out. However, in the final product the filing
under United States history was so inconsistent that it was
necessary for the Library to retype these entries and have
them issued (by the contractor) as a supplement to the subject catalog.

Under Great Britain, France, and Germany, even
though the headings had dates, they were interfiled with the
form subdivisions with the headings with dates alone filing
last. Since we have relatively few entries under these and
other countries, we have decided to accept this arrangement.

A peculiar error that the contractor cannot explain occurred in the title catalog. Titles which consist of a phrase
are filed before the initial word alone, e. g. Art for everyone
                                                Art of the theatre
                                                Art
This has been corrected in the supplements.

Except for the changes mentioned above to control
the filing, it has been decided to accept the computer filing
as long as it is consistent.

Cataloging Details

The Baltimore County Public Library has always done
simplified cataloging. As work on the project progressed, we
came to the conclusion that what we wanted was a finding list
rather than a bibliographic tool. This thinking was not entirely reflected in the basic catalog but is quite apparent in
the supplements.

The call number consists of the classification number,
the author's initial, and, in the case of different editions,
the copyright date. Provision was made in the program for
Cutter numbers, should we ever decide to Cutter. In the

book catalog the call number appears in the lower right hand corner of the entry. In the lower left hand corner is the access number which is assigned to each entry by the contractor.

Author's dates are used only to distinguish authors with the same name. The Wilson publications and/or the Library of Congress catalogs are used as authorities for personal and corporate authors.

Added entries are made for all distinctive titles, including those which are identical with subject headings-- this is done because the catalog is a divided one. An added title entry is also indicated when the main entry is a title, so that it will appear in both the title and author catalogs.

No added entries are made for joint authors. Entries for added author, editor, translator, etc. , are used only when there might be difficulty in finding a book without them. In some cases, if no added entry for author is deemed necessary for the book catalog, a cross reference is made for the central-holdings file as an aid in searching by the Processing Department.

Series added entries are used for relatively few series.

There is no limit to the number of subject headings used.

The "by" phrase (or "author preceedor, " in computerese) is now used only when an added entry is made for compiler, editor, etc. It was formerly used for joint author statements and when the author's name selected for use differed from the name on the title page. This "by" phrase was the cause of many errors in the basic catalog, particularly in the title catalog where, instead of showing the first author only for joint authors, the whole phrase appeared.

Subtitles are transcribed mainly to distinguish otherwise identical titles. Subtitles are always preceded by a semicolon. Since only the short title was to be used in the title and subject catalogs, some definition had to be evolved. The short title was defined as being that part of the title up to the first stopping punctuation mark, stopping punctuation marks being semicolon, period, exclamation mark, and question mark.

Edition statements are always used.

The imprint consists of the copyright date (not preceded by a small "c") or the imprint date if there is no copyright date.

The only collation item used is the number of volumes in a multi-volume work.

Contents notes are used sparingly, annotations not at all. Series notes are used only when a series added entry is needed; these appear in the title catalog. Our former practice was to use more series notes than series added entries. Bibliographic notes are used mainly for changed titles and are written within curves as are the series notes. We changed our practice for series notes, because all notes, whether bibliographic or series, appear in the title catalog as titles, e. g. "Formerly published under title--" etc.

A note has been added to the usual list: "Consult Librarian. " This is used for annuals and frequently-revised books. The imprint date and the date in the call number are omitted for these titles.

Cross references are used in the author catalog to refer from one form of the author's name to the one established for use and from real names to pseudonyms and vice versa.

No cross references are used in the subject catalog as each branch has a copy of Sears List of Subject Headings kept near the book catalog for reference.

As soon as the book catalog was put into the branches, the Processing Department stopped making sets of catalog cards for them. The branches now receive a shelf list card and one author card, the latter showing the number of the supplement which will contain the title. These author cards are filed in an "orders received" file and kept there until the appropriate supplement has been received, at which time the file is weeded. These have come to be known as "s" cards.

Changes

An additional routine concerns changes, corrections, and withdrawals. The contractor is now designing a form to be used to record all of these transactions. At the present

writing the changes are being made on the original input
cards, if we have them, in red pencil. If the cards for a
supplement are with the contractor, a note is sent asking
that the change be made. For withdrawals, the word "kill"
is written at the top of the card in red. The top edge of the
card is coated with green so that it will be possible to re-
move all the cards easily, if necessary.

There are three sources of errors in the book catalog:
our errors (mainly misspelling and two different forms for
one subject heading), the key-punch errors, and the errors
in programming. Most of the errors in key-punching and
programming affect corporate authors, particularly those
with subdivisions. A number of headings appear in the wrong
catalogs--subjects in the title catalog, authors in the subject
catalog, etc.

The original program was for information retrieval
and has been revised for one of publication only.

Since there were so many errors in the first basic
catalog, the contractor has agreed to correct the Library's
errors along with his own and to make changes and withdrawals without charge if the Processing Department does the
proof-reading. This work was scheduled to begin in November 1965. In the meantime, the Department is sub-
dividing many overloaded subject headings.

With the book catalog, it is quite simple to make
changes in subject headings by correcting the input cards in
red, since the branches do not have to receive new cards.
Changes in classification are more complicated. It would
not be advisable to change classification numbers on books
too far in advance of the second basic catalog since the first
basic catalog shows the present number. Changes will be
made on the source document for the second basic catalog,
and the branches will be notified of the changes three weeks
in advance of the publication of the second basic catalog so
that the books can then be changed.

It is a little difficult at this time to determine how
much, if any, staff time has been saved by the book catalog.
The only time saved for the catalogers has been by being
able to consult the catalogs at their desks. Some of the
clerical time has been cut down by not having to assemble
sets of cards and type on headings for branches. A new
routine has been added: that of filing input cards and keeping

track of the number of cards for each supplement.   The
Multilith operation for running catalog cards has been cut to
50 percent.   In the branches varying amounts of time are
saved by not filing catalog cards.

Pre-1960 Records

The ten original branches of the Baltimore County
Public Library all have in their shelf lists titles which have
not been added to any branch since 1960.   It may be that in
some cases the books themselves no longer exist, or if they
do, would be candidates for withdrawal.

In order to "clean up" these shelf lists and at the
same time weed the collections, the branches are reading
their shelf lists for titles not in the book catalog.   Any title
published before 1960 which does not have a recent identification number or is not in the book catalog is being searched
for.   If it is not found after six weeks, it will be withdrawn.
If it is found, a decision is made either to keep it or withdraw it.   A list of the titles to be retained will be sent to
the Processing Department for adding to the second basic
catalog or a supplement.   Records for the remaining titles
will be withdrawn.

Reception of the Book Catalog

The reaction to the book catalog by the public, the
public service librarians, and, to a certain extent the catalogers, has been overwhelmingly favorable.

The card catalogs have been removed from all four of
the branches opened since 1960 and from the public service
areas of the other ten.   After the initial shock of looking for
the card catalog and not finding it and not seeing the sign
telling about the book catalog or the book catalog itself, the
public in most cases accepts it with little or no comment.
A few patrons show some curiosity about the reason for it.
One person to date has objected to it violently.

The reference librarians find it easy to use and find
it very helpful in answering telephone requests.   The catalogers each have a copy and use the subject catalog constantly
in their work.   Much time is saved in being able to consult
the catalogs at the cataloger's desk without having to walk to
the central catalog.

The book catalog has been put into all the county public

schools. Many of the children are using it merely out of interest to see if they can use it. It is also being taught as an instructional aid and for personal use. One month after the opening of the schools, the inter-library loan requests within the system had increased by 63 percent over the previous September. The patrons are now able, by means of the book catalog, to see the resources of the entire system instead of the holdings of one branch only, as was the case with the individual card catalogs.

In spite of the hard work and frustrations of the last year and a half, it is possible to answer the question, "If you had it to do over again, would you?" by saying, "Yes, we would."

Reference

1. Robinson, Charles W. "The Book Catalog: Diving In." Wilson Library Bulletin, 40:262-268. November 1965.

Sample Entries from the Author Catalog

HERBERMANN, CHARLES GEORGE
  Sulpicians in the United States. c1916
    0165-12484   271.75 H
HERBERT, ALAN PATRICK
  Bardot M. P. 1964   340.9 H
    0165-15261
HERBERT, SIR HENRY
  Dramatic records of Sir Henry Herbert. 1917
    0165-12318   792 G
HERLING, JOHN
  Labor unions in America. 1964
    0265-15262   331.88 H
HERNTON, CALVIN C.
  Sex and racism in America. 1965
    0265-15263   136.1 H
HERR, DAN
  Bodies and spirits. 1964
    0265-15264   M
HERRICK, CHARLES JUDSON
  Brains of rats and men. c1963
    0165-12485   596 H
HERRICK, KENNETH W.
  Total disability provisions in life insurance
    contracts. c1956
    0165-12486   368.3 H
HERSEY, JOHN RICHARD
  Campana per Adano. 1948
    0265-15265   It
  White lotus. 1964
    0265-15266   It
HERTZ, LOUIS HEILBRONER
  Complete book of model raceways and roadways.
    1964   629.2 H
    0265-15267
HERZOG, ARTHUR
  War-peace establishment. 1965
    0265-15268   355 H
HESSELTINE, WILLIAM BEST
  Lincoln's plan of reconstruction. c1960
    0165-12488   973.7 H
HEURGON, JACQUES
  Daily life of the Etruscans. c1964
    0165-12489   913.37 H

HILL, WILLIAM H.
  Antonio Stradivari, his life and work (1644-
    1737). c1963
    0165-12499   787.12 H
HILLARY, EDMUND
  Schoolhouse in the clouds. 1964
    0265-15272   915.496 H
HILLARY, LOUISE
  Keep calm if you can. c1964
    0165-12500   796.54 H
HILLCOURT, WILLIAM
  Baden-Powell; the two lives of a hero. c1964
    0165-12501   B B
HILLWAY, TYRUS
  Education in American society; an introduction
    to the study of education. c1961
    0165-12502   370.1 H
HINDE, THOMAS (PSEUD.)
  See Chitty, Thomas
HINMAN, CHARLTON
  Printing and proof-reading of the first folio of
    Shakespeare. c1963 2v.
    0165-12503   822.3 H
HIRSCHMAN, ALBERT O.
  Journeys toward progress; studies of economic
    policy-making in Latin America. c1963
    0165-12504   338.98 H
HISTORY OF CIVILIZATION
  History of civilization; ed. by C. H. King.
    2nd ed. c1964 2v.
    0165-12505   901.5 H
HISTORY OF ROME AND THE ROMANS, FROM
ROMULUS TO JOHN XXIII.
  History of Rome and the Romans, from Romulus
    to John XXIII. General director, Robert
    Laffont. c1960
    0165-12506   945.632 H
HITLER, ADOLF
  Blitzkrieg to defeat. 1964
    0265-15273   940.54 H
HJORTSVANG, CARL
  Amateur choir director. c1941
    0165-12507   784 H

Producing a Book Catalog:

The Chester County Library Experience

Gertrude B. Seybold

   The author is Assistant Reference Librarian,
   Cherry Hill Public Library, Cherry Hill,
   New Jersey.

Introduction

In June, 1967, the Chester County, Pennsylvania
library system issued its first book catalog.   This 1100-page
volume, covering some 26, 700 titles, serves as a union catalog for the nine libraries of the system.   It was computer-
created and photo-composed.   Two hundred copies were reproduced by offset printing.   A supplement was subsequently
produced and a cumulative supplement is about to appear.

Those who have been involved in this effort--Chester
County Library personnel, the staff of the computer typesetting firm, and the writer as liaison between the two
groups, believe that this effort represents a landmark in at
least two ways.   First, it is visually a more attractive catalog than others produced so far.   Second, the catalog demonstrates the advantages computers offer in this field.   With
one keyboarding of a complete entry the material can be
sorted, re-arranged, and portions can be extracted and re-
sequenced by the computer.   In addition, format and typefaces can be varied as desired.   New material can be
merged with old, old can be deleted, and corrections can be
made.

The job took about ten months from the time the library made its decision to proceed until delivery of finished
books.   Fortunately, the library and the supplier were only
twenty miles apart, which made close cooperation possible.
Since both organizations happened to be small they were able

to benefit from the necessary learning-by-doing experiences.
Those directly involved learned a great deal while , at the
same time, they successfully achieved their objectives.
Others have expressed a strong interest in a description of
the processes and an analysis of the results.

Chester County is an area of towns and farms roughly
35 miles from Philadelphia.   As far back as 1928 the county
commissioners sought to encourage cooperation among the
small libraries of the region and between the libraries and
the schools.   It was not until 1962, however, that any marked
development occurred in the growth of county-wide cooperation.   At that time a $75,000 grant became available from
LSA funds, providing book credits for libraries joining in a
county system.   Books purchased in this way were ordered
and catalogued centrally, through the main library in the West
Chester county seat.   The working catalog in the West Chester
Library, which is known as the "Chester County" Library,
thusbecame   a union catalog for all collaborating libraries.

Although a referendum for the creation of a county-
wide library system was defeated in the fall of 1962, the
county commissioners gradually became convinced that the
development of a better library system was a proper and
legitimate concern of local government.   The Chester County
Library, which had existed primarily to service the schools,
was made increasingly available for use by the general public.   It was then that a program of library development was
adopted and this made it possible for the county to obtain
state funds to match a local 50¢ per capita appropriation.

By the fall of 1965 a number of local libraries had
associated themselves with the main library, now located in
the new county building in West Chester.   Mrs. Miriam G.
Hearne, the librarian, played a leading role in encouraging
interlibrary cooperation.   Responding to her initiative the
directors of the county system and the representatives of the
associated libraries began to explore ways in which group
resources could be used more effectively. It became apparent
that one essential was to make available to each of the associated libraries a catalog of all the books to be acquired
by the participating members.   The usual way to do this
would be a duplication of the existing main library union card
file and the placement of such a duplicate file in appropriate
cabinets in each library building.   This seemed formidable
enough, but the problem was compounded by the fact that the
union list was a main entry list only.   There are no centrally-

held cards for added entries, titles, or subjects.

Thus the decision was reached that the production of a printed catalog to list substantially all of the acquisitions of the county system was indispensable. and that it should indicate which of the various libraries held which titles. With such a catalog, access to the whole system collection would be provided, associated libraries could save most of the burden for the maintenance of their own individual catalogs and schools and other interested users would have their own copies on their own premises. Inter-library book transfers would obviously be enhanced and a more efficient use of the entire collection would be achieved.

Methods of Producing a Printed Catalog

Three different methods of creating this printed catalog were considered and bids were obtained from potential suppliers in the spring of 1966. The analysis of the implications of these proposals proved to be quite complex. Initial costs were relevant but so, too, would be the upkeep of the system once the commitment was made, for its value would cease if it were not continually updated.

The three approaches which were studied were:[1]

1. The use of a sequential card system.

2. A computerized system which produced a print-out in upper and lower case.

3. A computerized system which produced camera copy by means of photo-composition.

1. The Sequential Card System

This proposal contemplated that the entry would be typed onto a machine-sortable card using IBM Registry for body composition and Varitype for bold-face subject headings. Two cards would be necessary for each fiction title; three or more for non-fiction. The author listing would be the most complete; an abbreviated version by title and an equally brief version by subject would also be created. All of these would be prepared from the main entry listing, which would have to be marked in some way to enable the typist to select from that entry the desired information.

After the cards were typed they would be keypunched so that they could be sorted into the proper sequence by mechanical sorting equipment.   However, card sorting is time-consuming and hence costly and it was suggested by the supplier that savings could be realized if the finer sorting were to be done by hand.   Specifically, all sorting beyond the first three characters would best be done this way in order to obtain correct library filing results.

Under the sequential card system the cards, once sequenced, would be mounted onto a holder attached to a sequential card camera, from one to three lines of "cold composition" in the form of impact typing would be photographed in columns and a full-page photographic negative would thus be created for offset plate making.   A new set of cards would be required for each type of listing--author, title, and subject.   (Each set has to be sorted prior to photographing.)   Cumulations would be handled in all probability by manual insertions; corrections, by the substitution of one card for another.

2.   The Computerized Line-Printer Method

The second potential supplier proposed the use of an upper and lower case line printer for final output.   These printouts would be stripped into columns and photographed to produce negatives for offset platemaking at the same time that an appropriate reduction in line-length and character image size was achieved.   While this method of output promised to be substantially cheaper than photocomposition the product would of course be visually less attractive.   Bold italics and other typographic niceties could not of course be achieved.   More pages would have been necessary because the line printer does not produce proportionally-spaced type characters.

However, despite the cost savings implied by the use of the line printer, input and computer processing costs from this supplier were high in relation to the proposals received from the third possible supplier.   Whether the computer equipment of the latter involved less overhead, whether the programmatic solutions were more efficient, or whether there was merely a difference in pricing policy cannot of course be determined.   The second supplier visualized the possibility of using for many books entries which had already been keyboarded onto punched cards for other applications.   This supplier visualized the development of a permanent file of such

such entries which could be made available to any user.
However, the price proposed to pick up these pre-sorted
listings was substantially greater than that suggested by the
third supplier to create entirely new input.   The second supplier also visualized a much more limited entry, in terms of
content.

The point must be stressed that actual differences in
quoted prices do not necessarily prove the superiority of one
system or approach as compared to another.   At this stage
in the development of the photo-mechanical arts lineprinter
output should be cheaper, all other things being equal.
Whether this will continue to be the case will depend upon
the cost and relative speeds of high-quality high-speed photocomposing devices now entering the market for the first time.

3.   Computer-Generated Photo-Composition

In the third method, information would be recorded on
punched paper tape, again using the existing main entry cards
as copy.   This file, stored on magnetic tape, would be
manipulated by the computer in a variety of ways to produce
a completely sorted full main entry listing, and a completely
filed title and subject index.   Various computer printouts
would be produced for use in proofreading and verification.
As in the other systems, entries could be input initially in
random sequence.   The final listings would be output in the
form of paper tape containing the codes necessary to produce
justified, hyphenated and paginated material from a photo-
typesetting machine.   Supplements would be produced in the
same manner, and merged for cumulation with the earlier
information already stored on magnetic tape.

The third method of production was chosen, since
prices were at least comparable and since this approach
seemed to offer the most flexibility and the best readability.
Rocappi, a small but experienced pioneer in computer applications for the printing and publishing industry, was awarded
the assignment.   This decision was made in August of 1966.
The first step in its implementation was the planning of the
format desired in the new catalog.

Catalog Contents and Format

The catalog is intended to serve a wide area, to be
used in libraries and schools and to be useful to the varied
clientele of a good public library.   A divided catalog with

full entry under author and abbreviated listings under both
title and subject seemed the most satisfactory approach. The
imprint and collation were somewhat abbreviated since, in
the interest of price and space-saving, it was felt that the
public would not be inconvenienced.   Where the publication
and copyright dates varied widely both were used.   Where
the content, especially in fiction, was identical in various
editions and there were no significant elements to differentiate
the books, such as noted illustrators, space was saved by
using the note: "editions vary. "   "Consult librarian" is the
note used for frequently revised titles, to avoid the necessity
of treating each new edition separately, and to indicate that
the same editions will probably not be found in all of the
cooperating libraries.   Since the cards used were either LC
or cards of similar content the subject heading tracings were
used rather than annotations.   This had another advantage.
Once the subject headings were keyboarded they were in the
system for extraction for the subject index.   No more than
three subject headings per title were to be included although
more could have been coped with under the program.   This
limitation has apparently caused no problem.   A maximum of
two added entries was found to be sufficient for most titles.
It should be noted that there was no arbitrary limit on the
length of an entry such as is often the case when a fixed-
field format is used.   The proposals for the other methods
studied required, too, that entries be kept to two or three
lines.

        Eight point type was chosen.   This proved to be easy
to read and still small enough to give about 50 main entries
on an 8-1/2 by 12 inch page.   The several type faces selected are shown in the Exhibit.   The results are generally successful.   As Victor Strauss points out in his definitive description of printing processes, [2] "legibility is a consideration
of type design, whereas readability refers to the arrangement
of types. "   Since, as Mr. Strauss goes on to say, most
type faces now in use are well-designed and therefore legible,
the concern here was with readability.   Caledonia (Photon's
"Highland") in roman, italic, bold and bold italic, and Univers,
in bold and bold italic, were the faces chosen but other faces
could easily be substituted in later editions of the catalog.
The samples in Figure 1 show how entry format was changed
when material was extracted from the author list for use in
the title and subject lists.

Main entry (author) as
keyboarded

LONG, Edward V, 1908-
 The intruders; the invasion of privacy by
government and industry. Praeger, 1967. 230p
il.
 Privacy, Right of; Eavesdropping—United
States; Wire-tapping—United States
323.44 L   CC T D O

Title entry, as extracted

Intruders, LONG, E. (CC T D O) . 323.44 L

Subject listings, as extracted

Privacy, Right of
 LONG, E., *Intruders* (CC T D O)
                                     323.44 L

Eavesdropping—United States
 LONG, E., *Intruders* (CC T D O)
                                     323.44 L

Wire-tapping—United States
 LONG,   E.,   *Intruders* (CC   T   D   O)
                                     323.44 L

Figure 1

Preparation of Input

Once the format was decided upon everyone was most
anxious to start.   The editing of cards for entry into the new
system began in September, 1966.   Since the actual working
main entry catalog of the Chester County Library was the
only union list in existence these cards were used as "copy. "
The catalog department did the editing of these almost 27, 000
cards over the next seven months.   As a batch of cards
was finished, they were sent to Rocappi for keyboarding.
Thus the Chester County Library staff was working throughout this entire period with one part or another of its basic
tool missing.   The staff contributed immensely to the success of the project.   Without their cooperation and good
humor the project could never have been done.

The aim of editing was to give Rocappi's keyboard
operators--excellent at their jobs but not library trained--
material in such consistent and correct form that they would
not have to slow down to make decisions or to ask questions.
The editing involved two processes.   First, accuracy and
consistency of heading and classification were checked. It
was soon found that an active card catalog being added to
and used daily by several different people is bound to contain
errors of transcription and filing.   Also, the library had
recently embarked on changes of classification which it
wished to complete.   Biographies, listed together under "B"

were being changed to subject classification, preceded by a
"B". Some numbers were being changed to conform to the
new edition of Dewey (17th). Some headings were also being
altered to conform to the new Anglo-American code. These
changes, as well as the necessity to check headings (titles,
subjects, author's names, etc.) which appeared in more
than one form, and all the little things familiar to any librarian, took a great deal of painstaking work. Taking advantage of the Library's practice of using identifying letters
before Dewey numbers, it will be possible at any time in the
future with a minimum of additional programming to pull out
such things as a list of all the biographies in the file. The
computer can be instructed to search out all entries beginning with B (biographies), BC (biography collections), F
(fiction), J (juvenile), R (reference), or SC (story collection).

After the necessary revisions had been made, material not to appear in the book catalog was marked with a yellow hi-liter. This allowed it to remain visible on the card,
but made it easy for the operators to skip. Redundant author
statements, some of the imprint, and other nonessential information was thus marked. As mentioned earlier, where
content was the same, as in novels and classics, various
editions were consolidated to save space. In this case the
note "editions vary" was used instead of imprint. This particular exercise comes hard to a librarian and it was clear
as soon as the pages were in type that not enough consolida-
tion was done. In some cases, therefore, entries were
eliminated manually, by stripping, after pages were set, and
art work was inserted.

As work progressed with respect to the perforation of
the initial input unanticipated problems came to light, sometimes necessitating a hasty back-tracking. One example was
the discovery that, in order to be extracted and filed as
titles, alternate titles had to be identified as such for the
computer. So there was a flurry of searching these multiple
titles out and marking them for the perforator operators.
Material which had already been input had to be corrected
on the magnetic tape file.

Keyboarding

As the cards were edited they were sent in convenient
batches of trays, representing A-C, D-F, and so on, to
Rocappi. Here the perforator operators' knowledge of the

requirements of their computer system came into play. Using relevant flags for codes, and other techniques, the operators reproduced the card information on punched paper tape, including at the same time information indicating to the computer the information to be extracted for sorting and manipulation and that required for typesetting.

In general the entry consisted of the following elements:

> Author's last name and first initial.
> The balance of the author's name.
> Other information relevant to the author which would appear in the main entry but would not ordinarily be extracted for title and subject listings, such as dates of birth and death.
> That portion of the title of the book which would be used for filing and which would appear in the title index.
> The balance of the title of the book.
> Other information about the book which will appear only in the main listing, such as number of pages, publisher, whether illustrated, whether translated, abridged, etc.
> The subject tracings.
> Joint author tracings.
> The Dewey number.
> The locator line--that is, the initials of the libraries in the system who hold this title.

A distinction was drawn between fields of information which needed to be marked off for typesetting purposes and those to be marked off for sorting or processing purposes. For example, an abbreviated version of the author's name appears in the Title-Author index and yet the sorting is done for this index by means of the use of the author's full name. A typical card is shown in Figure 2.

301.42 CC T c A D

Bach, George Robert, 1914–
　　The intimate enemy; how to fight fair in love and mar-
　　riage, by George R. Bach and Peter Wyden. New York,
　　Morrow, 1969.

　　　xiii, 405 p.   25 cm.   7.50
　　　Bibliography : p. 389–394.

　　　1. Marriage. 2. Fighting (Psychology)   I. Wyden, Peter, joint
　　author.   II. Title.

　　HQ728.B33   301.42′6   69—14232

　　Library of Congress   ₁69h15₁

Figure 2

(Underlined material not used in catalog.)

In effect, then, the sequence of the initial entry was
as follows:

(a)(b)(c)BACH, G(c)eorge Robert(b), 1914-
　　(d) The (d)(e)intimate enemy(e); how to fight fair in
　　love and marriage. Morrow, 1969. 405 p.
　　(f)Marriage(f) (g)Fighting (Psychology)(g)
　　(i)Wyden, Peter, jt. auth. (i)
　　(k)301. 42(k) T (a)

Here:
a----a surrounds the complete entry.
b----b surrounds the author's name.
c----c surrounds the abbreviated portion of the
　　　　author's name.
d----d surrounds that portion of the title of the
　　　　book which is to be typeset in the main listing
　　　　but not included in the title sort field or the
　　　　title-author listing--i. e. , the article.
e----e surrounds that portion of the title which is
　　　　to be used for extraction and sorting.
f----f surrounds the first subject tracing.
g----g surrounds the second subject tracing.
h----h would surround the third subject tracing.
i----i surrounds the first jt. author tracing.
j----j would surround a second tracing for jt. author
　　　　or illustrator, or editor.
k----k surrounds the Dewey number.

The input of such an entry may well appear complicated but the Rocappi system makes extensive use of shorthand keyboard techniques so that a few codes can do double and triple duty and can be used on one occasion for flagging and sorting and on still another for extractions. Then later these codes can be interpreted as typesetting instructions such as for bold type or for indent codes. Here such an entry would be perforated (or otherwise input) in such a way that the following hard copy would be produced:

$aBACH, G$beorge Robert$c, 1914-- $dThe $eintimate enemy$f; how to fight fair in love and marriage. Morrow, 1969.   405 p. $gMarriage hiFighting (Psychology) jmWyden, Peter, jt. auth. nq301. 42rTs

In view of the absence of a third subject tracing and a second joint author tracing, $k-$1 and $o-$p are not required in this particular entry.

The computer proofing runs will be explained subsequently.   At this point it may be observed that the sorting or sequencing runs consisted of runs which first created sort fields and trailers and then used these sort fields to place the trailers in proper order.   The sort field for the author index would consist of the author's complete name followed by the complete title of the book (less any beginning article, such as The or An).   The trailer would consist of the entire entry.   Merged with these complete entries in the sort would be sort fields made up of joint author listing, illustrators, editors, etc., with a trailer which contained the words "see" or "see also" and then the author and title under which the book normally appears.   Multiple titles would be input as separate entries containing their own sort field and trailer.

The sort field for the title-author listing would consist of the title followed by the author's name.   The trailer would consist of title, author, Dewey number and locator information.

The sort field for the subject listing would consist of each of the subjects followed by the same sort of trailer described above.   However, cross reference headings were input for filing along with subjects extracted from the main entries themselves.

It is evident that the entries themselves consisted of

variable fields of data but that the sort fields were formatted
as fixed fields. Since specific symbols identify each field it
is easy to ignore those not called for in a specific sort or
extraction. This is a simpler solution, from an input point
of view, than representing all sort fields whether or not they
are called for in a particular entry.

Filing Considerations

The computer can, of course, be programmed to file
in any desired manner. But every special instruction requires special attention at several levels. Sometimes solutions can best be achieved by input instructions and sometimes by programmatic ones. Rocappi has developed a very
flexible set of sort rules so that it is possible to achieve
virtually any sequencing one may desire, either word by
word or letter by letter, or combinations of the two. For
example, it is possible to achieve either of these results:

Defoe	De Gaulle
de Gaulle	de la Croix
de la Croix	Defoe
Del Ray	Del Ray

by the use of spaces of more than one type, with different
sorting values.

It is also possible to include non-typesetting information, between suppressed-setting codes to produce a "file-as-
if" result, so that St. Augustine would file as if it were
written out as "Saint Augustine." In some instances it is
easier to write out the abbreviation, as in the case of Saint.
But in the case of "Mr.", as, for example, "Mr. Bell invents the telephone," it is perhaps better to input the title
as (Mister Bell) Mr. Bell invents the telephone where the information between parentheses is to be disregarded for setting but not for sorting. There are, however, inconsistencies
in the Chester County input since both methods (i. e., spelling out or filing as if) have been used on occasion.

In Bible entries the "file as if" solution was used to
cause Bible, O. T. to sort ahead of Bible, N. T. Author's
names were occasionally re-arranged so that Churchill, Sir
Winston Leonard Spencer, 1874-1965 became Churchill,
Winston Leonard Spencer, Sir, 1874-1965.

In the case of titles such as "1984" and "1066," the

Numerals were rewritten as they are pronounced, and filed accordingly. However, names beginning with M', Mac, and Mc were left to file as spelled instead of being coded to file together as if spelled Mac.

Subject headings presented some unique filing problems. There were many inconsistencies in form, especially in the use of abbreviations. And, since the subject headings were extracted from the main entries, they were not available in list form until quite far along in the processing. Historic subdivisions caused problems, which can be largely overcome by the practice of inserting date before other information as, for example, in United States History--History--1861-1865-- Civil War. The fact that this is a divided catalog makes for fewer overall filing problems than are encountered in a dictionary catalog. So it is logical, for subject headings, to use a simple system as illustrated below:

> Art
> Art, abstract
> Art -- addresses, essays, lectures
> Art -- Africa
> Art, African

rather than a more complex system such as that suggested by Theodore Hines, [3] in which dashed entries file before those with a comma, as

> Art -- Africa
> Art -- Berlin
> Art -- Bibliography
> Art -- France
> Art -- History
> and so on to
> Art, a commodity
> Art, African

Computer Processing

The flow chart (pages 308-9) sets forth in a somewhat simplified fashion the major steps in the production sequence and illustrates the interrelationships between the Library, the perforator operators, and the computer processing. After the editing process which has been described above, the cards were turned over to the perforator operators. It was important not to disturb the order of the cards, both for the Library's sake, and because later proof-reading depended on having them in the order in which they were used. Multiple

titles were perforated as they occurred, with special identifying codes. But the subject cross references were put in as
a separate list at the end for later interfiling, since they did
not appear in the main entry file.

The paper tape produced by the perforator operators
was read into the computer and stored on magnetic tape. At
the same time an 'in-house' print-out was produced. This
was proof read, and corrections were perforated and fed into
the computer for the purpose of updating the magnetic tape
file. A new print-out of the updated file with the corrections
marked for easy checking was then produced. And at this
stage a special print-out was provided for the customer to
read. This was a much simplified version, designed to call
attention to the fact that the dollar sign codes must be read
as 'sets' of codes. If one code of a "sets" is present, the
rest of the set must be also. For example, in the tracings, if
$g is present, $h must be also. But if there is no subject
heading in that particular entry, neither code will appear.
Corrections and any "author's alterations" (changes the Library
wished to make) were marked on this print-out, perforated by
the Rocappi operators, and used to again update the magnetic
tape file.

After this proofing the cards were returned to their
places in the library. Rods on each finished drawer were
taped on the outside to remind the catalog department not to
disturb them, and new cards were filed above the rods. The
nearly 7,000 cards added during the months while this editing
and input operation was going on were then put into the system
at the end of the alphabet. This piece-meal procedure resulted, of course, in the creation of several tapes which together
comprised the master file. At this point, the middle of
April, 1967, the input operation was complete. Computer
processing of the entire body of information could then begin.

From the master file the computer now produced
another tape version, substituting for the dollar sign codes
their equivalent codes for sorting, and extraction. The file
was next divided into three parts by the computer. The first
contained all the main entries, including joint authors and
other added entries pulled from the body of those entries. The
second file contained all titles and multiple titles, again extracted from the main entries. And the third list was composed of subject headings, each with its "trailer" of author
and title, as well as the subject cross references which had
been added separately. Each of these parts was then sorted

alphabetically by the computer, and then was put through another pass which hyphenated and justified[4] the material to conform to the required measure. At this stage a final print-out was generated, in order that each section could be checked. Since title and subject material were extracted from the main entries, this was, of course, the first time it had appeared in alphabetical form. This was the stage, therefore, at which glaring inconsistencies of input were corrected. At this juncture corrections can be made most economically to the tapes of the individual sections, but they must be incorporated into the master file before it is used again.

The next computer process divided the material into column lengths and another produced a page format of three columns. This consisted of arranging the first line of each of three consecutive columns, then the second, and so on, so that the typesetting machine could set one line across the three columns of the page. The last pass through the computer produced a final set of paper tapes, this time to activate the Photon 713. Properly prepared--that is, provided with film strips of the desired typographic fonts and programmed with the corresponding character width information-- the machine reads the paper tape and produces film or paper which is ready for plate-making. The Rocappi system can, incidentally, reprocess input material for use with other typesetting equipment such as Linofilm, Photon 513, or some of the high-speed photo-composing machines now in development.

About 200 hours of Photon time were required to produce the 1100 pages of the catalog. This was at the rate of about six of the 8-1/2 by 12 pages per hour, with some reruns. After the main entry section--about 850 pages--had been typeset, one of the more exciting episodes in the production story occurred. The first pages of the title section to come from the Photon were sent, as a matter of course, to the Library for approval. At this point, seeing the abbreviated entries in type, the staff decided they would prefer to have the classification numbers and location symbols included. This meant going back to the computer again, of course, and entailed additional expense. But the important thing was that it could be done, and it was done very quickly.

Final Touches

As pages came from the Photon, they went to the stripping department for final checking and correcting. In

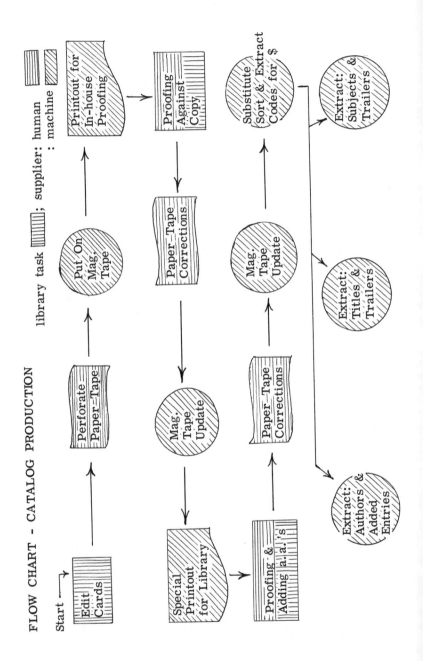

FLOW CHART - CATALOG PRODUCTION

library task ▓▓▓; supplier: human | : machine

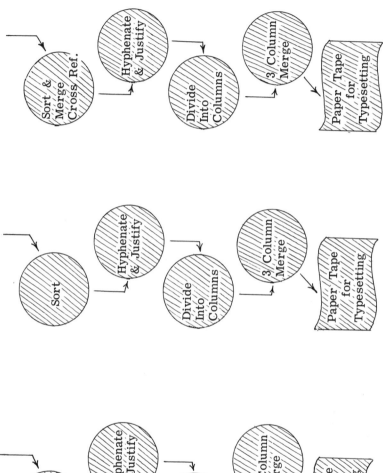

this case the photographic output was paper, so corrections
were made by cutting out and pasting in. There were, inevitably, some remaining keyboard errors, some misfiling
due to input errors described earlier, and some mechanical
errors made by the Photon. And also, as mentioned earlier,
there were still cases of redundant entries. These were particularly obvious in print. Consolidating these naturally left
blank spaces in the completely formatted pages. They were
filled with small illustrations, which turned out to be easy to
find and reproduce. An artist on the staff of the Chester
County Library generously provided many delightful small
drawings. The work of several Chester County illustrators
was also contributed. The total effect is very attractive,
breaking up some of the large expanses of print, and adding
a touch of personality.

Early in June all 1100 pages, plus the front matter,
some special illustrations, and the section dividers, were at
the printer's. There were finished signatures off the press
in time for the ALA convention in San Francisco early in July,
and the finished books were delivered a few weeks later.

It turned out that the catalog was really too big for
the perfect bound paper cover treatment which had been ad-
vised to keep costs down. So there were some delays for rebinding, and for the hard cover binding of 20 copies. Based
on this experience, it is clear that hard binding is essential
for a book of this size. It adds to the cost, but in the case,
as here, of a total of 200 copies, this is not a major factor.

The Supplements

Before the editing of the basic card collection was
finished, the Library staff had worked out a procedure for
the future which would eliminate any further disruption of the
card catalog. Titles are currently being added to the system
at the rate of 1,000 a month. As before, main entry cards
are made for each title, including the initials of the holding
libraries. The book catalog is kept in mind as these cards
are being prepared. Where feasible, obvious changes such as
the writing out of subject headings in full, the insertion of
dates in historical subdivisions, and so on, are made. In the
case of actual LC cards, however, it is usually left to the
perforator operators to accomplish these things. Before these
cards are filed each week, copies are made on the Library's
new Bruning copier. Using a large sheet of paper, 14 or 15
cards can be accommodated on each. These sheets are then
edited and sent to Rocappi in batches. The sheets are easier

to deal with all along the line, and the original cards need
never be touched for book catalog production purposes. Also,
as copies of titles already in the system are ordered for
other libraries, one part of the order form is filed in a
separate place to provide "copy" for updating the catalog.
Weekly acquisition lists are typed from the sheets of catalog
card copies, providing interim information for the patrons.
When the sheets reach Rocappi they are numbered serially, so
they can be used for proofreading without problems if they
should get out of order in some way. Thus, initial input into
the system of current acquisitions is chronological rather
than alphabetical.

The first supplement, containing about 4500 titles, has
been produced. The second, with about as many more titles
added, is in production. A great deal has been learned in the
production process which is now being put to good use as the
supplements are prepared. Many of the problems were associated with filing. It was reassuring to note that, in
general, the solutions decided upon agreed in general with
those suggested by Hines and Harris[5] in their book on computer filing, and by Cartwright and Shoffner in their study
for the California State Library.[6] This is certainly not a
closed subject. There will be adjustments made for some
time to come, since filing always has been an extremely
complex process. In the Chester County catalog, it was
evident that insufficient attention had been paid to detail in
the body of the entries. A spectacular example occurs in the
main entry section, where several names, such as De Angeli,
De Camp, and De Valois, precede Dead Sea Scrolls. The
explanation is that the names were all added entries, extracted from the body of entry information by the computer.
These items must, of course, be input in the required form
for the computer. In this case, although the perforator
operators keyboarded these names to file as one word as
main entries, they forgot to do the same thing when the names
appeared as joint authors.

A possible way to cut down total size would be to use
a slightly different approach--that of making both the title
and subject lists into simple indexes. Rocappi has done this
with another series of catalogs. It requires a different programming approach, since the page number on which a main
entry appears must be associated with the entry as part of
its trailer when a title or subject is extracted. This means
these extractions cannot be done until the main entry material

is completely sorted and arranged in page format. This
would not, of course, cut down on the number of entries in
the file.

Reception of the catalog has been excellent. The main
library personnel, since they were involved in the planning
and preparation from the very beginning, have found it easy
to adjust to. Inter-library loan requests in all of the associated libraries are said to have increased tremendously, as
was expected. Most of the schools in the area have purchased
copies of the catalog and are making good use of them. Of
course, an undertaking of this sort can only be evaluated in
terms of the individual situation. It is certainly not applicable
in toto to every library organization. But in the dynamic,
rapidly-growing context of the Chester County Library system
the book catalog is a great asset.

The Problem of Maintenance

The most serious problem remaining in the printed
catalog area is that of the cost of maintenance. As the file
of titles grow, so does the cost of updating and manipulating it,
by any method at all. A printed book catalog, whether produced by sequential card camera, an on-line computer printer,
or by means of computer typesetting, is not inexpensive. It
is far cheaper for a single library to stay with its card catalog, especially if its major objective does not include the
promotion of bibliographic research. But if a union listing
is desired in several locations, when one considers the cost
of sets of cards themselves, the labor involved in filing them
and the space they require, a printed book catalog--with all
of its other advantages--begins to make economic sense.
This has been illustrated by the studies made by Hayes,
Shoffner and Weber. [7] On the basis of an examination of
actual price quotations made to the Chester County Library,
the present writer believes that the cost elements selected in
that study are far from realistic, but they do afford an interesting comparison between card catalog and book catalog.

The major drawback to the present book catalog is, as
mentioned, the cost of keeping it current. While supplements
can be issued inexpensively a point of time is reached when a
new total cumulation is absolutely essential. How frequent
such a cumulation must be will depend upon the library
system's acquisition rate.

At Chester County the acquisition rate for the system

seems to run at approximately 1,000 books per month--a surprising figure for a system of its size. The first supplement, of approximately 5,600 titles, came out in early January, 1968, but it included books acquired only through July, 1967. However, a new cumulative supplement, comprising the same 5600 titles and 4400 more is promised for printing and delivery before the end of February, and this will include all acquisitions through November, 1967.

The issuance of a cumulative catalog does not require new cost of input because the vast majority of the entries will have already been stored. But the extraction and re-sorting computer runs are necessary, as well as the passes which reformat the file for printout or for typesetting, and the actual composition cost itself (as well as printing and binding) must be met for a larger and ever larger collection of books.

One approach, which minimizes this cost somewhat, is that offered by a major book distributor. Here library cards are photographed in what can well be or what will soon become random sequencing, but consecutively numbered pages. Only the very brief title and subject indexes are computer-produced, and they refer back to the page number on which the reproduction of the catalog card can be found. But such a catalog in some ways defeats the major purpose of collecting in one place all of the basic information needed for a bibliographic search.

If book catalogs of the quality of that of Chester County are to be maintained the community must come to value this unique service and find a way to pay for it. It is an incomparable tool. It will promote the purposes of a library system perhaps more effectively than any other single strategy. But the cost of keeping it up to date must somehow be met. In the case of Chester County, just as special funds were obtained for the production of the initial book catalog, while supplements may be paid for out of budget, the publication of a complete new catalog--which will most certainly become a necessity within a year or so at most--will probably require assistance either from the community or from sources external to the community. The cost of producing a new comprehensive catalog will run perhaps 70% of the cost of initial production, on a per entry basis.

Cost Elements in the Production of a Catalog and Supplements.

(While permission has not been obtained to cite actual
figures, Rocappi has permitted the following illustration
of relative costs to be used.   Costs are based upon the
printing and binding of 200 copies.   The figure 100%
represents the cost of a complete entry, which will be
extracted and sorted in its various forms, and will be
incorporated in the typeset, printed and bound catalog.
For example, if 100% were $1.00, the cost of produc-
ing the initial book catalog, exclusive of editorial costs
or alterations, would have been approximately $26,000
for a catalog of 26,000 books.)

Initial perforation of input.................   35%***

Computer manipulation for extracting, sorting,
    formatting for typesetting and related
    processing.............................   45%*

Printing and Binding......................   20%

*However, some small portion of this figure represents
the cost of computer processing associated with initial
input only.

***Rocappi states that the actual input cost to Chester
County was somewhat less than this, but that this
input cost was "smaller than it should have been."

However, the statistical summary disregards the editorial
costs which were major, although more or less hidden, in
the initial undertaking, but are inconsequential thereafter.

Notes

1.   While outside costs of these various methods were
        scrutinized quite carefully, relatively little attention
        was paid to the internal editorial costs, or, more
        specifically, no estimate was attempted of differences
        in these costs depending upon the method selected.
        It should be evident that the editorial work required
        to make possible the input of three or more
        separate entries from one card would have been

extensive. It would thus appear that the two computerized methods, in this respect at least, offered an advantage over the sequential camera.

2. Strauss, Victor. The Printing Industry. Washington, D.C., Printing Industries of America, 1967, p. 723.

3. Hines, Theodore C., and Harris, Jessica L. Computer Filing of Index, Bibliographic, and Catalog Entries. Newark, N.J., Bro-Dart Foundation, 1967, p. 77 & 78.

4. For reasons of appearance, since the column measure was rather short, tracings were not justified but were set with ragged right hand margins.

5. Hines, Theodore C., and Harris, Jessica L., Op. cit.

6. Cartwright, Kelly L. and Shoffner, Ralph M. Catalogs in Book Form. Institute of Library Research, University of California, 1967, pp. 21-29.

7. Hayes, Robert M., Shoffner, Ralph M., Weber, David C., and "The Economics of Book Catalog Production," Library Resources and Technical Services, Winter, 10(1): 57-90, Winter, 1966.

Chapter IX

Applications and Techniques:

Public Libraries

A Book Catalog at Work

by Margaret C. Brown

The author is Chief of the Processing Division,
Free Library of Philadelphia. Reprinted by
permission from Library Resources & Technical
Services, 8(4): 349-358, Fall 1964.

Almost anyone describing his experience in making
and using the type of catalogs we shall discuss is necessarily
presenting something in the nature of a progress report. We
at the Free Library of Philadelphia certainly have not
achieved our goals, but we have taken that all important
"first step. "

In an effort to be as helpful as possible in very practical directions, we have elected to develop our remarks
around the answers to five questions, the five questions
selected being those which have been most frequently asked
of us during the last two years while we have been developing
our own book catalog program.

The questions are: (1) Why do you do it?   (2) How
do you do it?   (3) How much does it cost?   (4) Has con-
formity to the requirements of the machine changed the kind
of cataloging you do?   (5) How do readers like it, and has
your staff accepted it?

Why do you do it?

The development of the book catalog idea in Philadelphia was closely related to the development of another
idea--the Regional Plan for Philadelphia.

It was recognized some years ago that a library
system composed of a single strong central library plus
neighborhood branches (25, 000 to 40, 000 volumes) did not
meet the library needs of Philadelphia and would be even less

adequate in the future.   Consequently, five so-called regional
libraries were planned for the five major areas of the city.
Each would be comparable in collections and service to a
main library serving a city of 400,000 and each would co-
ordinate all library activities in the region which it served.

The first regional library erected under this plan
opened its doors to the public in the fall of 1963.   Long before that time, it was apparent that, since all books composing
the initial collection of this regional library (approximately
100,000 volumes) were to be new books, there was an excellent opportunity here to explore the book catalog idea.   It was
an idea that had been successfully used in other communities,
notably Los Angeles County in California and King County in
the state of Washington, and it seemed altogether likely that
the book catalog would be appropriate for Philadelphia as well.

Buying for the Northeast Regional Library collection
began in January 1961, and at that same time card catalogs
for the library were begun.   However, by 1963 we had concluded that it was a book, not a card, catalog that would best
serve our readers.   In the preparation of the first basic book
catalog, the records originally prepared for the Northeast
Regional Library card catalog were used as the master file,
and the publication of this basic catalog coincided with the
opening of the first regional library in Philadelphia.

Today the book catalog includes current additions to all
collections in our extension agencies.   The Extension Division
of the Free Library of Philadelphia consists of 39 branches,
1 regional library, 3 bookmobiles, and 232 deposit stations.
The catalog is issued in two parts, one for the children's
collections and the other for the adult and young adult collections.   Cumulative supplements to the basic catalog are issued
monthly for the adult and young adult catalog and bimonthly
for the children's catalog.

Our goal is a catalog which records all holdings of the
agencies in the Extension Division; our achievement to date is
a catalog which describes all volumes added in the past 3-1/2
years. Since we have been building two entirely new collections
during this period, our present book catalog is by no means
restricted to books published during this period.   Many older
titles considered basic to a general collection for an extension
agency are also included in the catalog.

Since no title may be purchased for agencies of the

Extension Division that has not previously been acquired for
the Central Library, the book catalog includes some items,
probably the most frequently used items, in the Central Library collection.

Given an organization such as ours, what advantages
does the book catalog have over the card catalog? For one
thing, the Catalog Department is maintaining two catalogs--
one for the children's collection and one for the adult and
young adult collection--instead of the eighty previously maintained. Editing eighty catalogs in a city the size of Philadelphia and for collections the size of the Free Library of
Philadelphia was outrageously wasteful of time and money in
terms of the results obtained. We emphasize the words "in
terms of the results obtained." Perhaps if results had been
better, we would not have considered alternatives to the card
catalog at the time we did, but we are convinced it would have
come sooner or later.

What were some of our problems with the card catalog?
In spite of our best efforts, there were cards without books
and books without cards. The turnover of clerical staff and
professional staff in the branches presented in-service training
problems with which we never adequately coped. Hours of
time were given to answering queries from branches as to
why they didn't receive cards, why they didn't receive more
cards, or why they didn't receive different cards. There
was extensive correspondence regarding the addition of volume
to contents notes, revisions of subject headings, and requests
to return cards for correction.

Cards, when they were delivered to the branches, were
sometimes not filed promptly or were filed incorrectly; notes
from the Catalog Department were ignored, or were not correctly interpreted; cards were lost in the mail; and cards
were stolen. There was the usual problem of determining
what cards were missing when we knew some were. All this
added up to administrative headaches of large proportions.
The only conclusion that could be drawn was that long distance
editing was not satisfactory. With only two catalogs to be
edited and maintained, and those two catalogs directly under
the control of the Catalog Department, we feel that some of
these problems will be reduced to a minimum and others will
be eliminated entirely. While it is hoped that the errors will
be fewer, the ones there are will, of course, be distributed
more widely!

Moreover, because we have only two catalogs to maintain for the entire Extension Division, we feel that the quality of the cataloging will improve.   Many arguments have been advanced for the use of book catalogs, but insufficient emphasis has been placed on this particular advantage.   At least in our case, the cataloging itself is of better quality than we could hope to obtain from card catalogs.   For example, subjects can be modernized.   "Interplanetary voyages" can become "Space flight" without undertaking a six-months project of revision or preparing a bewildering number of references about books cataloged before and books cataloged after such-and-such a date.   Corrections today do not involve lengthy correspondence and explanations but only the retyping of a few cards.   The results: better cataloging and better catalogs.

In addition to having better catalogs, the catalogs we have are more accessible.   The book catalog is easily available in areas where we could never have placed card catalogs. In a given building, the catalog is now available in many different locations rather than the usual one.   The Northeast Regional Library is constructed on several levels.   This building is much admired from the point of view of architectural design and good library service, but it would have been impossible to locate a single card catalog convenient to all or even a majority of the departments.   As it is, copies of the book catalog for the adult and young adult collection are in twelve different locations in this building, including the Children's department.

Copies are also available in areas which never had access to a card catalog, such as work areas and private offices.   Even though our present book catalog is incomplete, its use in the offices of those responsible for book selection, for example, has already been considerable.

The book catalogs are not only available in many places in Philadelphia, but are also available outside of Philadelphia within our state service area.   In the present Pennsylvania State plan, Philadelphia is one of twenty-nine District libraries.   Within the Philadelphia District, there are approximately fifty libraries which it is anticipated will make considerable use of our collections.   The librarians in these libraries report that they are using the catalog as a book selection and buying guide in spending their State appropriations, as an assist in cataloging their collections, and as a means of verifying citations for interlibrary loan requests.   We have already benefited noticeably from the last use.

There are two other important reasons why we have a
book catalog in the Free Library of Philadelphia. The book
catalog makes available to the reader a union catalog of resources in all extension agencies--not just one. This fact
will become more important with the further development of
the Regional Plan in Philadelphia. However, even today,
since readers may return books to any agency of the Free
Library, and do, they are conscious of resources outside
those of a single library. The book catalog says what those
resources are.

The book catalog also facilitates the transfer of material when this seems advisable. This is an important consideration in a large library system. Capital programs with
large budgets for new agencies have sometimes resulted in
uneven distribution of resources. The transfer of books from
one agency to another has been discouraged in the past because of the multiplicity of records involved. With the book
catalog, the problem is considerably reduced, and transfers
can be accomplished quite painlessly.

<u>Why do you produce your book catalog in the manner in which
you do</u>?

Perhaps it would not be irrelevant to make the distinction at this time between the <u>idea</u> of a book catalog and
its <u>format</u>. For us the idea is <u>sound</u>. On the other hand,
there is no format or technique for making a book catalog
which is entirely satisfactory. We suggest that, if the idea
is a useful one for your institution, you do not wait until the
perfect format is available before initiating your program.

What are the possible ways of making a book catalog
today? There are not many alternatives, but any librarian
considering the adoption of a book catalog should be familiar
with all the methods available, so the advantages and disadvantages of each can be weighed. Only then can he determine
which one is best suited to his needs.

The Library of Congress catalogs and those of G. K.
Hall & Co. are today the best known book catalogs in this
country. G. K. Hall has combined microphotography with
modern methods of printing to produce over 1000 volumes of
some 100 research collections. The cards, prior to
photographing, are arranged by hand. Most of you are
familiar with the results.

Automated equipment manufactured by IBM was used

in early experiments in making book catalogs and was the method first used by the Los Angeles County Public Library. It is presently in use in a number of special libraries and public libraries. In my opinion, the typeface is not attractive enough to encourage readers in public libraries to use the catalogs alone and unassisted, but it is entirely likely that a wider choice of typefaces will soon be available. There are other built-in difficulties with abbreviations and punctuation; there are complications in coding subject heading lists, etc. The IBM printer is one of the most widely used machines to print book catalogs today and could continue to be the pre-ferred system under some circumstances. The circumstances must usually include access to keypunch and printer at no cost or at minimum cost to the library.

This leaves the sequential card cameras of which there are three: (1) VariTyper Corporation's Foto-List, presently used to produce the Los Angeles County Public Library's book catalog and the British National Bibliography; (2) Kodak's List O-Matic camera, the camera used to photograph information VariTyped on punched cards in the preparation of the new magazine and book selection aid Choice, (after issuing one issue, Choice changed to the Photon process); and (3) Lithoid's Compos-O-Line camera, used to produce the Free Library of Philadelphia's book catalog.

What are the advantages and disadvantages of the vari-ous methods using a sequential card camera? There are significant differences in cost largely because, in some in-stances, records must be retyped before being photographed. Foto-List and List-O-Matic cameras do not accept 3x5 cards. Therefore, catalog records must be retyped, usually by means of a VariTyper or IBM typewriter. Foto-List photo-graphs one line at a time; the List-O-Matic camera takes 1, 2 or 3 lines at a time.

Regarding typeface, legibility, and attractive format, honors go to Foto-List and List-O-Matic in the examples seen to date. Compos-O-Line can accept 3x5 cards and will photograph the top 2-1/8 inches of the card, but the resulting copy is only as good as the original record.

The Compos-O-Line camera was our choice for several reasons. Because the camera does accept 3x5 cards, we could use cards we were currently preparing. We are con-tinuing to make card catalogs for the Central Library collec-tion. The cards which make up our so-called master file for the preparation of the book catalog are duplicates of cards multilithed for our Central catalog. To a degree we look upon the master catalog as a kind of by-product of our total operation.

Our basic procedure can be described in three steps. (1) The camera photographs the material on the top 2-1/8 inches of the catalog card; (2) From the resulting film the lithographic plate is produced; (3) From that plate, the requisite number of copies are multilithed.

Clearly, by using the Compos-O-Line camera the printing of a book catalog could be undertaken with a minimum of retooling in the Catalog Department. Also, this may well be an interim method for us, as there are many improvements with each passing year. We recognize there could be better methods and cheaper ones available in the near future--we hope there will be. We were reluctant to punch a sea of IBM cards until we were assured that the benefits of a book catalog, as we saw them on paper, existed in actuality.

Compos-O-Line is also the cheapest of the sequential card cameras--at least in the short run. If, as in the case of Montgomery County, Maryland, a library can share equipment owned by the institution or municipality of which it is a part, costs can thereby be reduced greatly. However, we were not in a position to share the cost of equipment or the cost of operating the equipment with another department of the City of Philadelphia.

Our present method also eliminates proofreading and page composition, built-in components of systems using punched cards. Proofreading demands some library staff time, and page composition increases printing costs very markedly.

The last advantage we should mention is that our master file can be easily consulted and easily revised by the individual cataloger or typist who knows nothing about punched cards.

As with any system, there are some disadvantages to using the Compos-O-Line camera in the manner in which we do. Because the camera, in our case, photographs cards prepared in a variety of ways by a number of different typists over a period of several years and with a variety of grades of supplies--low bidder may change annually--copy is inevitably of uneven quality. The results are also of uneven

quality.   Individual pages of the Free Library of Philadelphia's
catalog sometimes show unevenness that is the result of
camera malfunctioning or faulty plates, but frequently the unevenness which can be observed is the result of poor card
copy.

The second disadvantage of our present procedure is
that cards are manually filed.   Admittedly, this is time consuming.   However, at present, there is no way in which the
filing of a dictionary catalog can be completely automated,
and punching cards for the purpose of filing when there is no
need for retrieval by the same means seems to be questionable economics.

Our catalog does not have the variety of typefaces
which are available when records are recopied, but this is
not a disadvantage of the system per se.   We could use an
IBM typewriter of a VariTyper to produce the original card
copy and thereby gain a variation in typefaces.

We are sometimes asked to supply a list of book catalog publishers.   This request reveals a misconception about
the means used to produce book catalogs.   While we can
mention concerns which have successfully printed book catalogs (G.K. Hall & Co., Boston, Mass.; Science Press,
Ephrata, Penna.; and Johnson & Prince, Philadelphia), any
printer can print a book catalog if he has the necessary equipment, even if he has never printed a book catalog before.
However, before signing a constract, it is essential to establish that the firm is a reputable one, is capable of doing the
job, and has bid with all the facts in hand regarding an individual library's requirements.

How much does it cost?

One question which must ultimately interest any librarian considering the publication of a book catalog is "How
much does it cost?   It costs a great deal.   Like most attempts at cost analysis, however, this is tricky territory.
Before giving specific figures, it might be well to mention a
few of the variables which affect cost no matter what system
is used to produce the book catalog.   Some of these are
(1) the extent to which present catalog records being transferred into the book catalog can be used without retyping or
recopying, (2) the number of cumulations required in any
twelve-month period (the cumulative supplements may well
cost more than a single annual issue), (3) the number of

copies printed and the kind of binding used, (4) the buying
pattern of an individual library, and, of course, its book budget, (5) the number of catalogers, since arrearages do not appear in a book catalog any faster than they do in a card catalog, and (6) technological improvements which may soon make
it possible to automate some procedures, such as the stripping
of film, that is presently done by hand.

It is inevitable that attempts will be made to compare
the cost of producing a book catalog with those of producing
the traditional card catalog. The comparisons are practically
impossible to make with any degree of accuracy since few libraries have reliable cost figures on preparing and maintaining a card catalog. In fact, at this moment we could not
estimate the cost of the planning and developing that has gone
into the production of our book catalog.

Someone has suggested that a book catalog could reduce
the number of catalogers a given library might require. In
fact, one librarian asked if arrearages could be eliminated if
he introduced book catalogs in his library. If catalogers are
not performing clerical duties and are spending their time
strictly on cataloging and classification, there is little about
the book catalog which is going to lighten their work. A library preparing book catalogs for its own collection will not
gain any cataloging time simply because the catalog, as we
know it, is being produced in a different form.

Although the library producing the book catalog will
not need any fewer catalogers, the libraries using the catalog
may find their cataloging can be done faster and more accurately. The libraries in the Philadelphia District are consulting the Free Library of Philadelphia's book catalog in the
process of cataloging their own collections, just as most of
us have consulted The National Union Catalog. The smaller
libraries of Pennsylvania cannot afford the Library of Congress catalogs, but our catalog is furnished them as part of
our service to the District.

Savings in personnel costs are possible in the system
publishing the catalog, but when achieved, they will occur in
clerical positions. A library may require fewer typists,
filers, or multilith operators, for example. While these
savings could be substantial, they would not be sufficient to
enable anyone to conclude that the book catalog was cheaper
to prepare and to maintain than the card catalog.

The case for the book catalog, however, does not rise
or fall on the question of costs; it is doubtful if anyone ever
published a book catalog for current acquisitions because he
was convinced it was cheaper to produce than a card catalog,
and it is unlikely anyone will very soon.   Is a book catalog
worth what it costs?   Its reference service worth what it
costs?   How much should these services cost?

In comparing costs, a book catalog versus a card catalog, we tend to forget that we are not comparing like things.
We should remember that we are not trying to obtain the
same results.   How do we evaluate the convenience of having
a book catalog in a private office or in a District library or in
another part of the state?   How do we put a dollar value on
the improved quality of cataloging copy?

Even if you are convinced of the soundness of the
above arguments--and you probably aren't--you still have the
finance officers to face.   Therefore, we would like to mention
the financial experience of two large metropolitan library systems with book catalogs, even though we recognize that, without detailed knowledge of an operation, the gross figures are
not very meaningful.

In the first year of operation with the book catalog, the
Free Library of Philadelphia spent approximately $45,000.
The first year was not a typical year for several reasons.
However, the sum of $45,000 obtained one basic volume of
the children's catalog in Grade A binding and six supplements,
perfect bound, together with a five-volume basic cumulative
issue of the adult and young adult catalog, in Grade A binding,
and ten supplements, perfect bound.   The five-volume basic
edition of the Catalog of Books for Adults and Young Adults
contains a total of 102,000 entries and 3,092 pages, 175
copies of this particular issue cost $14,685, or $84 a five-
volume set, or $16.80 per volume.   The cost of 175 copies
of the cumulative supplements ranged from $500 to $4,000
per issue.   For the current year, because of a revised publication plan and the need for additional copies, $70,000 has
been budgeted.

The Los Angeles County Public Library, whose experience with book catalogs goes back 10 years, estimates that
they will spend in the neighborhood of $600,000 over the next
five years.   Approximately $190,000 of this sum will be used
to cover the cost of converting from their old system to the
present one, and $154,000 is estimated to be the cost of

cumulating 8,000 titles per year for five years into author,
title, subject, fiction, and children's supplements. They
further estimate that the cost of cumulating supplements into
the basic catalog and reproducing annual issues will be about
$256,000 over this period.

Have the requirements of the camera brought about any changes in your cataloging policy?

The next question requires a very short and uncompli-
cated answer, but since we are asked it rather frequently, it
is included here. The question is, "Have the requirements of
the camera brought about any changes in your cataloging
policy?" The answer is "No." We do eye each note a little
more critically than we did in the past, but if we consider
bibliographical notes or lengthy contents notes important, we
always include them. We make fewer titles when subjects and
titles file next to or very near one another. This has been
our expressed policy in the past, but it has not always been
observed. The need to adhere to such policy is more evident
when 33 entries are displayed on a single page. Some dis-
satisfaction has been expressed with the book catalog because
tracings are omitted. Undoubtedly, some of this criticism
comes from those who are using the book catalog as a cataloging aid, but, of course, librarians have long known that
tracings are used as a help in finding other material on a
subject and for various related purposes by both reference
librarians and readers.

What has been the readers' reaction and how has the staff adjusted to the book catalog?

This leads to the last question. "What has been the
readers' reaction and how has the staff adjusted to the book
catalog?" The public's reaction will come as less of a sur-
prise to catalogers than to reference librarians. Prior to the
opening of the Northeast Regional Library, the staff there
was very apprehensive about the catalog's reception. They
felt unsure of the public's reaction to the new situation and
believed it might create some awkward problems which would
be troublesome to handle. The Children's Department opened
first, and, as might be expected, the children found no difficulty whatever adjusting to the new form of their catalog.
The staff was agreeably surprised but attributed this happy
state of affairs to the adaptability of the young.

A month later the adult and young adult collections

were opened to the public. The readers' delight and pleasure
in having a book catalog was matched only by their delight and
pleasure in not having a card catalog. When the staff realized that the book catalog was going to be equally popular with
adult readers, they themselves relaxed, took stock of the advantages, and found they were numerous. One staff member,
who was far from enthusiastic at the prospect of using a book
catalog, says that now he would not want to work where there
wasn't a book catalog.

When the book catalog was first proposed, some staff
members were understandably apprehensive about problems
of mutilation, theft, and misshelving. As for mutilation and
theft, we had the argument that at least we would know what
was taken, and that was more than we could tell when the
cards were stolen. It did seem likely, however, that there
would be times when five copies of Volume IV would be together on one shelf. Actually none of these predictions has
come about. The first case of mutilation has yet to be reported, and the volumes are not carried around the building,
principally because the readers seem aware that copies are
available in strategic locations throughout the building.

To the observation "But a reader is using such a large portion of the alphabet when he consults one bound volume," we would
answer, first, that the average reader manages to block access to more drawers of the card catalog than he is consulting, and secondly, some drawers of the card catalog regularly
get heavier use than others. With the book catalog, there
are multiple copies of these drawers, so to speak. A popular
drawer in Philadelphia, not surprisingly, is the drawer containing the cards on Philadelphia, and now the Northeast
Regional Library has twelve copies of this drawer!

One of the advantages readers usually mention is comfort in using the book instead of the catalog drawers and the
convenience of being able to scan a page when unsure of the
appropriate subject heading or the spelling of an entry. The
staff also appreciates these points and the fact that the book
can be carried to the workroom for checking book orders, indexes, etc.

Habit is very strong, however, and no librarian con-
templating a book catalog should overlook this point. A book
catalog is not likely to be used by staff or public while a
card catalog is available. On the other hand, public library
users in Western Australia and Northeast Philadelphia, where

the catalog in book form is the only catalog, encounter no problems. Habits of the staff are of longer standing and are more deeply ingrained than habits of readers. However, the staff of our Northeast Regional Library has been very enthusiastic ever since the readers' acceptance of the catalog became apparent. In our opinion, for readers and staff alike, the book catalog is a proven success.

Book Catalogs in the Austin Public Library

by Faye Bock

> The author is Head of Technical Services at the
> Austin Public Library, Austin, Texas.

The Austin Public Library was founded in March 1933
and its first branch library was opened the same year. By
1965 it included five branch libraries, three stations, and
three bookmobiles which were served by the Extension
Division's rotating collection of approximately 120, 000 volumes, including some 25, 000 titles. Each of these units
had on its shelves or circulating in its service area a segment of the total collection. Books not circulating well at
one location were returned to headquarters to be transferred
to another outlet. Books not currently in demand at any location were held at headquarters for occasional calls. Books
were exchanged monthly or more often, if desired, by branch
or station librarians. Such movement of books is not possible if catalog cards are involved, therefore the Extension
agencies had no catalogs. The first book catalogs were designed in 1965 specifically to index the book collection of
the Extension Division. With the advent of the book catalogs,
all titles in the Extension collection could be brought to the
attention of readers at any library agency, and any title
desired could be requested if it was not available on the
agency's shelves. Daily deliveries from headquarters to
each agency expedited this service.

Although the idea of book catalogs was certainly not
new in the library profession, the decision to use them in
the Extension Division of the Austin Public Library was not
arrived at hurriedly. Other possibilities were examined,
particularly the possibility of duplicate card catalogs in all
branches. At least six catalogs would have been required,
approximately 100, 000 cards to each catalog. The cost of
production alone of 600, 000 cards was estimated at over
$20, 000. Card catalog cabinets would have been an additional

expense. The cost of card catalogs in all outlets was found
to be prohibitive even if there had been physical space in the
branches and on the bookmobiles to accommodate them and
personnel to maintain them. Card production is slow. Card
filing and withdrawing in a growing collection puts an increasing burden on the Technical Services Division. Studies[1] have
shown the card catalog in even the most reputable of libraries
to be about 30 percent in error at any given time because of the
constant need of revision, particularly in the subject heading
area, if holdings are not to become obsolete.

Library literature was searched and correspondence
was inaugurated with other public libraries in an effort to
determine the best possible solution to the problem. Book
catalogs seemed to provide the best answer because they cost
less than duplicate card catalogs, because they could be used
on the bookmobiles and in smaller stations where there was
lack of space for card catalogs, and because of the desirability of maintaining fluid, rotating collections.

Even after the decision was made to use book catalogs,
there was much doubt as to the best way to produce one. The
Los Angeles County Library, the Montgomery County Library
in Maryland, and the Tulsa (Oklahoma) City-County Library
System were among those already using book catalogs, or in
the process of producing some, which were consulted. The
Director of Technical Services in the Austin Public Library
found that all used, totally or in part, the services of commercial firms to produce their catalogs. Some of these firms
were also consulted; however, a minimum of $25,000 was
quoted for producing book catalogs under contract with a commercial firm. Supplements would have been an additional expense. This would have been the easiest solution and the
catalogs produced by these firms had already proven their
usefulness. However, since the cost was high, alternatives
were explored. The Austin Public Library is a city department, and the City of Austin already had in use in the finance
department an IBM 1401 computer and a Data Processing
Center staff who were cooperative in making their services
available to other city departments. Over a period of several
months library personnel met frequently with the Data Processing staff in an attempt to work out a feasible method of locally producing a book catalog.

The chief difficulty encountered by the two groups
working together was found to be lack of communication. No
person on the library staff had had any experience with the

tools of automation, and the Data Processing staff was quite
unfamiliar with library practices and problems. Even the
two terminologies were different. It took many hours to
learn to talk to each other, but after the problem was understood by both sides, the actual working out of the basic program was fairly simple. Briefly, the plan was this: information was to be punched on IBM cards by library personnel;
the program for the computer was to be prepared by the Data
Processing Center; the punched cards were to be stored on
magnetic tape; the stored information was to be sorted and
printed on multilith mats by the computer; the mats were to
go to the City Print Shop where the catalogs were to be
printed, assembled, and bound. The cost was estimated to
be around $7,000, less than one third the estimated cost by
a commercial firm.

Once the decision was made to produce the book catalogs locally, plans were worked out for the format of the
catalogs and the coding and sorting (filing) of the cards.
Other catalogs were studied and a great variety was found in
format: some closely resembled printed catalog cards; some
were merely indexes; in some, the computer-produced page,
printed in double columns, was photographed and reduced in
size to fit on 8-1/2" x 11" page; some were printed straight
across the page. Since the Austin Public Library staff was
inexperienced, it was determined to seek the simplest possible approach. In addition, only upper case letter and few
punctuation marks were available, and it was felt that brief
entries under these circumstances would be easier to comprehend. Since the catalogs were to be used in a public library where the approach is general rather than specialized,
it was felt that the complete bibliographical information needed in research or special libraries was not required. For
all these reasons, it was decided that the catalogs would be
a finding list rather than a complete bibliographic tool.
Since an Official Catalog is maintained in the Technical Services Division of the Central Library, it was felt that any
additional information could be obtained quickly by telephone
if the necessity arose. In the meantime, the catalogs as
planned would offer adequate service to the great majority of
the library's patrons and to the library staff.

A six-volume set of book catalogs was planned: three
for children's books, three for adult books. Each set of
three was to consist of an author, title, and subject catalog.

It was also decided to use a very simple format with

the information printed straight across the page.

The programming for these catalogs was done by the Data Processing Center and called for four programs and three tape sort routines:

1. Program 1 was to build the master book file from the punched cards. Card codes were used to determine where on the tape record the data in the punched card was to be placed. For each book the following data created the master catalog record: serial number, author's name, title, by-line, call number, publisher and date of publication, subject or subjects.

2. Program 2 was to print on multilith mats the adult and juvenile book catalogs by title, author, and by subject.

3. Program 3 was to add records (titles), delete titles, and/or change any part of an existing record.

4. Program 4 was to print serial numbers or title control list or lists for reference and maintenance purposes.

The sorts involved were by author, by title, and by subject and were programmed as follows: (1) in the author catalog, sort first by the author card, dropping duplicates disregarding serial number; sort second by the title card, leaving in all duplicates which carried different serial numbers. (2) In the title catalog, sort by title card, leaving in all duplicates which carried different serial numbers. (3) In the subject catalog, sort first by subject cards, dropping all duplicates disregarding serial numbers; sort second by title card, leaving in duplicates when serial numbers differed; provide for subject reference cards to sort ahead of the title cards.

To produce the format described, one IBM punched card was required for each line appearing in the book catalog. For each title, a set of punched cards was required. Each title was assigned a serial number which holds together the cards for this title as they are sorted by the computer. Each card of a set has the same serial number. A set for a single title includes the following cards:

1. An author card with full name, except that this
name must fit on one IBM card with 70 columns
allowed for it.

2. A title card with 14 columns in the call number
field, 56 columns in the field for title together with
the by-line.

3. A publisher card giving publication date and publisher's name in brief form, the length being
tailored to fit on a single line with the title when
the by-line is dropped.

4. One to four subject cards, 70 columns being allowed for each subject.   No more than four subjects
were used with any title.

Other sets of cards are made for subject cross references, title cross references, and author and title analytics.
Subject cross reference sets include the subject card and
from one to three reference cards depending on the length
of the cross reference.   Title cross references and author
and title analytics were added in later programming.   Title
cross reference sets include author card, title card (including title, by-line, and word "see") and reference card (including call number, title, and by-line).   Author and title
analytics differ only from title cross references in that the
word "in" is substituted for the word "see" on the title card.
The card coding is the same.

Each type of card was assigned a code number as
means of identification: author's name - 01; author cross
reference - 01; title - 21; title reference or analytic - 22,
23; publisher and date - 41; subject 1 - 61; subject reference
- 11, 12, 13; subject 2 - 71; subject 3 - 81; subject 4 - 91.

By using this code, instructions were given to the computer to print out the information for each catalog using this
sequence of cards:

Author Catalog

1. All 01 cards (author's names and references) -
sorted alphabetically.   Each author's name appears
only once in the catalog, duplicates not being
printed out.

2. All 21 cards (title cards)--excluding those for titles

which have no author entry, sorted alphabetically
and listed under the author's name.

3. All 22 and 23 cards (title reference cards or title
analytics)--these to follow the title card immediately.

4. 41 cards (publisher and date)--this information replaced the author's by-line, which was dropped off of
the 21 card when it appeared in the author catalog.
When the 21 card is punched, an ampersand is
punched immediately following the title and preceding the by-line. The ampersand is a signal
to the computer to drop all information following
it when this is called for in the programming.

Title Catalog

1. All 21 cards (title cards)--with the author by-lines--
sorted alphabetically.

2. All 22 and 23 cards (title reference cards or title
analytics)--these follow the title card immediately.

Subject Catalog

1. All 61, 71, 81, 91 cards (subject entries)--sorted
alphabetically. Each subject appears only once in
the catalog. Duplicates are not printed out.

2. All 11, 12, 13 cards (subject reference cards).
These follow the subject entry immediately.

3. All 21 cards for titles with subject assigned. These
titles are listed in alphabetic order under the subject entry.

The programming for correcting material was simple
but called for special data code and card code for each correction or deletion to be made:

1. Author correction - data code 11, card code 99,
serial number

2. Title correction - data code 21, card code 99,
serial number

3. By-line correction - data code 31, card code 99,
serial number

4. Call number correction - data code 41, card code 99, serial number

5. Publisher and/or date correction - data code 81, card code 99, serial number

6. Subject corrections require two cards. The first card is punched with the incorrect subject, data code 91, card code 99, serial number. The second card is punched with the corrected subject, data code 92, card code 99, serial number

7. Deletions - coded 2 99 99, serial number. This completely removes all records on the master tape carrying that serial number

Before actual work on the machines could begin, much preparation had to be made. Preliminary operations involved were the reviewing of subject heading lists to improve consistency, to provide punctuation acceptable to the computer, and to develop cross references; scanning of shelf list cards of the Extension collection to select titles to be included in the book catalogs (generally, any title no copy of which had been purchased since 1956 was eliminated, except for titles appearing in standard lists such as Standard Catalog for Public Libraries and Children's Catalog); adapting information on each shelf card to make it fit the desired format; coding and stamping of a serial number on each card (shelf cards were used as the source documents for the keypunching); training library staff members to operate the keypunch and the verifier.

The equipment used to produce these book catalogs included an IBM keypunch and verifier used in the library by library personnel and an IBM 1401 computer in the Data Processing Center. The configuration involved was a central processing unit containing 16,000 positions of core memory, five tape drives, printer, and a card read-punch unit.

The time element is also of interest. Investigation into the possibilities of a book catalog began in the Spring of 1964. Work began immediately on the revision of the subject lists and the selection of titles for inclusion. The first conference with the City Data Processing staff took place in mid-summer. The programming required two months to complete, including extensive program testing and correction. During all of this time, the preparation of

materials was proceeding.   Keypunching began the first of
March 1965 and the children's titles were complete in two
months.   Proofing and correcting required about three additional months.   Keypunching for the catalogs for adult
books began early in August and required another two months.
October was spent on final proofing, printing the multilith
mats, and the final printing and binding.   The computer sort
time for each catalog was approximately one hour each. Print
time (multilith mats) was approximately one and one half
hours for author and title catalogs and two hours for subject
catalogs.   Approximately a year and a half elapsed between
the first plans and the finished product; but it should be
pointed out that neither Data Processing personnel nor library
staff were doing this work only.   It had to be fitted into
schedules that were already full.

        The final cost of the first edition of the adult and
juvenile catalogs was around $7, 000, as originally estimated.
This figure includes data processing costs including programming, printing costs, rental on keypunch and verifier, and
the salaries of two part-time people for keypunching.   The
salaries of the two professional catalogers involved in the
planning and preparation of materials is not included in this
figure since they were already on the payroll and did this
work as part of their regular schedule.   One hundred copies
of the catalogs were printed and they included 10,084 adult
titles and 8,876 juvenile titles.

        It is interesting to note that so far as is known this
was the only book catalog produced locally and as a joint
project of three city departments: Library, Data Processing,
and Print Shop.

        The staff of the Technical Services Division of the
Austin Public Library has found there are problems to be
solved and disadvantages to be overcome.   Two of the chief
problems have been mentioned previously: lack of experience
and difficulty of communication between library and data
processing personnel.   These have been solved.   Another
problem is the time limitation in the Data Processing Center
and the scheduling difficulties when new editions are due.
All city departments are served by the Data Processing
Center and some jobs, such as tax notices and city payroll,
have priority no matter what else is scheduled.   Computer
filing presents a problem since it sorts (files) column by
column within a given field, not word by word or letter by
letter as is common in library practice.   Computer filing

order is the unpunched column first followed by dash, comma,
period, letter, and numeral. This giving of value to punctuation marks was difficult to work with since library filing is
alphabetic without reference to punctuation. Special care has
to be taken in preparing the material for punching to assure
that a form is used that will follow computer sorting rules.
Some reprogramming has been necessary as minor flaws
were detected. For example, reference copies and circulating copies of the same title have given us problems. In
some editions the reference copy prints out and not the circulating copy while at other times the reverse is true. Occasionally both the reference and circulating titles print out,
but print out in duplicate.

The first book catalogs were produced in 1965. Since
that time the Austin Public Library has continued to expand
into a large library system. It now offers service through
ten branches, four bookmobiles, and three stations including
outlets in a hospital and in a housing project for the aged. It
has strengthened its book collection, built new buildings, re-
modeled old ones, added new staff--all to meet requirements
of a growing population. But with all this, it had no effective media for informing patrons of its total resources. The
Central Library card catalog reflected only what was available in the main building; the book catalogs included only the
Extension Division's collection. Service to patrons was
hindered because there was no record of the library's complete holdings without recourse to the Official Catalog in the
Technical Services Division. In the second edition of the
book catalogs, the entire holdings of the library system's
juvenile collection was included, and the card catalog for
juvenile books in Central Library was eliminated. The result
was pleasing. Children found no difficulty in adjusting to the
new form of catalog, and the staff, for the most part, was
agreeably surprised.

Logically the third and final step toward complete conversion to the book catalogs was the inclusion of all books
for adults in the library system, and this is now in the
process of being accomplished. When we passed the halfway mark in this undertaking we felt that card catalogs were
no longer necessary, and removed them, thus relinquishing
much needed floor space for additional stacks and other
necessary equipment.

By the end of 1968 the adult book catalogs were growing cumbersome and a decision had to be made limiting their

size in some way.   Either two volumes for each catalog
would be required for the next edition (with the expectation
that four or five volumes would ultimately be necessary) or
the size of print would have to be reduced.   Reduction of
print size seemed to provide the best answer since the print
would still be legible and the patron would be freed of the
necessity of searching several volumes for needed
information.

         To carry out this change, new printing instructions
had to be devised.   Instead of using multilith mats, the computer was instructed to print out the adult catalogs on un-
ruled 15 lb. weight paper.   These sheets were separated;
information for each page of the catalog was pasted on card-
board; pages were reduced in size by a photographic process;
catalogs were printed, assembled, and bound.

         Special printing instructions to Data Processing were
as follows:

INSTRUCTIONS FOR PRINTING THE ADULT BOOK CATALOGS

1.   Print on 15 lb. weight paper with 8 lines to an inch.
(The finished catalog is printed on 11"x9" paper).

2.   What prints out on computer as one column will be one
half of a page.

3.   Of each two columns, the first one will be printed with
word AUTHOR, TITLE, or SUBJECT at upper right corner
and word PAGE at lower right.   Next column will be printed
with word CATALOG at upper left and appropriate page number at lower left.

4.   Regardless of how 21 card is punched, leave 3 spaces
between column 15 and 16 in printing out call number and
titles in all three catalogs.

5.   Author Catalog--special instructions:

         a. At beginning of each column on each page the
            author's name last printed out in the preceding
            column should be repeated at top of column
            UNLESS there is a change in the author's name.

b. Whenever 22 and 23 cards follow 21 cards which equate with other 21 cards, ALL 22 and 23 cards must print out although the 21 card should print out only once.

c. ALL 22 and 23 cards should be INDENTED 3 spaces in the print-out.

d. A line should be skipped after the last title under each author's name.

6. Subject Catalog--special instructions:

a. At beginning of each column on each page the subject last printed out in the preceding column should be repeated at the top of the column UNLESS there is a change in the subject.

b. A line should be skipped after the last title under each subject.

c. All 11, 12, and 13 cards following a 61 card should be INDENTED 3 spaces in print-out.

7. Title Catalogs--special instructions:

a. Whenever 22 and 23 cards follow 21 cards which equate with other 21 cards, ALL 22 and 23 cards must print out although the 21 card should print out only once.

b. A line should be skipped after each fifth title.

Cost of producing the book catalogs has risen slightly since the publication of the first edition late in 1965. In November 1968 we figured the average annual cost over a three year period was $5,180.00 excluding cost of preparation of material, keypunching, and proofing, all of which is done by Technical Services personnel on regular library time. We also estimated the cost of input per title at less than 1/2¢, again excluding preparation of material, etc. However the cost of the current catalog is higher since data processing costs have gone up and some reprogramming has been necessary. Also the cost of a photographic process to reduce size of print has been added, and the catalogs are now being sent to a commercial firm for hard bindings rather than the

soft covers provided previously by the City Print Shop. However the fewer number of pages in current catalogs and less
time consumed in assembling, etc. have gone far to compensate for these new charges. There are more than three
times as many titles in the current edition, and the cost is
still far under that of commercially produced catalogs.

The Austin Public Library has found that the book
catalog can be an effective show case for its services. It is
convenient to use. There are no catalog drawers to handle
and get out of order. It can be used in comfort by the
patron at desk or table because it is accessible, portable,
and easily handled.

There are certain distinct benefits that both the staff
and patron receive from the use of the book catalog which
the card catalog could not offer. From the standpoint of
library administration it offers the advantages of making
certain the most economical and efficient use of personnel,
and insures that the opening of new branches within short
periods of time poses no problem so far as catalogs are
concerned. It saves staff time by the elimination of reproducing, filing, and withdrawing catalog cards. This saving
in time enables the staff to keep up-to-date inventories,
weeding of out-of-date material, and pulling of books from
the shelves which need mending or rebinding, thus providing
a more attractive, current book collection. It facilitates
the transfer of materials from one collection to another
when necessary (a card catalog doubles the work and cost
involved because of the necessity of pulling, correcting, and
refiling of catalog cards). It improves the efficiency of
operations because with the book catalog revision is easier
and faster; and the original cataloging and processing is
simplified because all books are handled in the same way in
one operation. It provides non-Technical Services Division
agencies with a compact, portable, complete system's holdings list which may be easily used for preparation of book
lists, for book selection, etc. (e. g. , provides an easy way
for the Book Selection Committee to check the holdings in a
subject area to determine if more material is needed or if the
holdings are adequate). It is helpful in answering telephone
and Telex requests; and saves time and work by enabling the
staff member to easily and quickly verify inter-library loan
requests.

The book catalog offers improved service to the public because it displays the entire variety and quantity of books

available by offering access to the entire holdings of the library system. The range of the entries displayed on a page gives at one glance a more complete idea of the contents of the catalog, and it is easier to handle than the drawers of the card catalog. It allows more people to use the catalog at one time because multiple copies of the book catalog are possible whereas multiple drawers of a card catalog are not. It can be carried to convenient work areas for do-it-yourself reference work. In particular, the subject catalog is helpful to patrons because it serves as an instant bibliography. It makes for the maximum use of the book collection because the various sub-divisions of a subject are spread out on the page in such a way that the patron can see at a glance the wide range of material available in a subject area, and it suggests acceptable substitutes many times when a specific title is not available. It is much easier to glance down a page at subject breakdowns than it is to thumb through card after card in a catalog drawer. The subject catalog also offers many see and see also references to help the patron or staff member locate books under various subject headings but in related subject areas. And finally, it uses more up-to-date terminology in its subject headings since more revisions are possible than with a card catalog.

Our book catalog also plays a part in improving interlibrary cooperation since it has proved to be an aid in the development of regional service by offering member libraries full information on materials available from their regional resource center, the Austin Public Library. It is also extremely helpful to the operator of the Telex system.

The chief criticism of book catalogs in general has been the difficulty of keeping them current. To overcome this problem, the Austin Public Library issues three new editions of the adult book catalog each year and one new edition of the juvenile book catalog. In the middle of each month, between editions, a cumulative list of all titles added since the publication of the last edition is available. In addition a duplicate "on order" file is accessible to the staff of the Reference and Circulation Divisions at the Central Library. As books are received, the slip which accompanies each new title to its destination is pulled from the book and filed in the on order file, replacing the on order slip. In this way there is complete up-to-the minute information readily available in the public service areas on all books in the collection or on order. This facilitates the filling of reserves and the requests for new titles.

Any major departure from established routine requires adjustment. The acceptance of the book catalogs by both the staff and the public requires some re-education. Librarians and patrons alike have been used to a card catalog, but it has been proven that children adjust with no difficulty to the use of a printed catalog; and the staff of the Austin Public Library feels that its adult patrons are making the adjustment rapidly, especially since the staff points out the benefits derived from the book catalogs, and does a good selling job on their convenience and usefulness.

Reference

1.   Enoch Pratt Staff Reporter, Dec. 15, 1965.

Sources of information

McCurdy, May Lea.   "The Book Catalog Program of the Austin Public Library: the Librarian's Viewpoint," in Proceedings of the First Texas Conference on Library Mechanization. Texas Library & Historical Commission, 1966, p. 13-16.

McCaslin, O. R. "The Book Catalog Program of the Austin Public Library: the Programmer's Viewpoint," in Proceedings of the First Texas Conference on Library Mechanization. Texas Library & Historical Commission, 1966, p. 17-20.

Chapter X

Applications and Techniques:

School Library

Programming the Library Catalog

by Jessica L. Harris

The author is Assistant Professor, School of
Library Service, Columbia University.   This
article is reprinted by permission from Drexel
Library Quarterly, 5(2):84-91, April 1969.

Programming the library catalog is as difficult to
discuss as to do; we are just beginning to reach the state
of the art where it is possible to tell, with some assurance,
some of the things that should not be done.   In only a few
areas have we gone far enough to be able to say what should
be done.   Broadly interpreted, programming the library catalog is a subject for a book, not for a single paper; narrowly
speaking, the technical operations of writing the computer
programs for a catalog are a relatively minor part of the
problem.   I shall discuss the processes of developing a book
catalog system, getting the data keyed in machine-readable
form, and producing a printed book catalog from the data.

Producing a book catalog on a computer is one of the
more common and sensible first steps for a library to take
in the process of mechanizing its procedures.   Yet, to the
best of our knowledge, the book catalog which Dr. Hines and
I cooperated with the Farmingdale (N. Y.)school system in
producing for their junior high schools is the first school
library book catalog produced on data processing equipment.
A book catalog system was planned and announced for the
Brentwood (N. Y.) schools but seems not to have been completed as yet.   We have received several inquiries from other
school systems showing interest in the potential of a book
catalog at this level.

The first question is why produce a book catalog for
any kind of library in the first place?   It costs money--far
more than whatever is estimated.   Worse, the money it costs
usually shows up more in the budget than the money it saves,

and the added service potential does not show anywhere in the
budget.   It does get out of date.   Unfortunately, despite the
future promise of MARC (that we may be able to buy our
data from the Library of Congress in machine-readable form),
it still means keying the catalog data instead of simply using
printed cards.   And, of course, it is different from the sort
of catalog we librarians are most accustomed to using in the
library.

   The book catalog does have major advantages to offset
these disadvantages.   The whole picture today is different
from what it was not many years ago.   Short-run offset
processes have cut printing costs and time drastically; use
of the computer eliminates or reduces many of the more
repetitious and expensive chores involved in producing a book
catalog, such as interfiling of new entries and multiple keyings
of the same entry for each access point.   It can also take
care of page layout, producing camera-ready copy for the
printer.

   In the school itself, the time of librarians is released
from filing chores; unfortunately, this cost saving does not
appear in the budget.   The catalog can be placed on every
teacher's desk and at several points in the library.   Selective listings can be produced.   It is more compact than the
card catalog.   The printed page makes scanning of several
entries at a time easier.   It also makes the errors inevitable
in any catalog more prominent, more likely to be noticed
and criticized--perhaps because the catalog is more used,
too--and more likely to be corrected.   Increasing centraliza-
tion of school systems makes the use of a book catalog far
more feasible for school libraries since the advantages of
the book catalog lie largely in distribution of multiple copies.
The rate of duplication of titles among school libraries on
the same level is high--though not necessarily so high as
might be supposed.

   All things considered, it is surprising that the bookform catalog has not been more widely used in school libraries.   Some possible reasons for this state of affairs
have been discussed by Dr. Hines.[1]   In the first place, in
too many school districts, a school library supervisory
position either does not exist at all or has little administrative authority.   Then, even in school systems with a real
central library authority, there is a lack of knowledge of how
to go about using the computer in library applications and an
overworked data processing center is unlikely to have the

time to find out. Furthermore, outside firms usually have
no more knowledge of school library problems than of any
other library problems. Still, the time is ripe for school
systems of a reasonable size to experiment with the bookform catalog for their libraries.

The Farmingdale book catalog, in a system with only
three junior high school libraries, is in its second edition
and may be expected to continue.

A little background should be useful here. The
Farmingdale Public School system comprises six elementary
schools with nine libraries and two junior highs with three
libraries, with a full-time librarian in each library, and
one senior high school with three librarians in its library.
There is a central library coordinator's office, headed by
Miss Roberta Everitt, which orders and processes all materials for the libraries. This office sets overall policy for
all the libraries in the system. There was a card catalog
in each school library of that library's holdings and a union
shelflist in the library coordinator's office. The school
system has a full data processing office but no computing
equipment. This office had traditionally been used for the
usual system administration and scheduling work.

In the summer of 1964, Miss Everitt approached Dr.
Frances Henne of the Columbia University School of Library
Service for advice on application of the newer technology in
the Farmingdale School Libraries. Dr. Henne referred Miss
Everitt to Dr. Hines, and the end result was the Farmingdale Junior High School Libraries Catalog. The first edition
of the Farmingdale school library catalog was produced on
the school system's EAM equipment but was designed to be
convertible to computer production later. While the decision
made sense at the time, we have since concluded that it
would have been preferable to produce the catalog on the
computer in the first place. In its original incarnation, the
catalog was produced under a grant from the U.S. Office of
Education, ESEA Title III. The project was to be supervised
chiefly by Miss Everitt and her staff, in consultation with
Dr. Hines and others at Columbia. In an experimental
project, there are always changes; this one was no exception.
Some of the changes will come out in description of the production of the first edition of the catalog.

The elementary school level is ordinarily the most
logical one on which to start a book catalog. There is more

overlap in the collections, fewer titles, and usually more schools and libraries than on the higher levels.   In Farmingdale we started with the junior high because a new one was scheduled to open in the fall of 1966.   We had a good opportunity to avoid making an entire card catalog for the new library.   In addition, the original plan called for the keying to be done before ordering the new bookstock.   Had this been possible, one keying could have served for ordering and catalog production.   Unfortunately, circumstances beyond our control prevented this.   If the new library were to open anywhere near the time when its school did, the books had to be ordered before the punching was begun.

The limitations of EAM equipment naturally imposed severe restrictions on the format of the data for the catalog. Everything had to be in fixed fields.   The final decision was to make the author, title, and subject lists title-a-liners and to include more information in the classed-order list.   Sampling of the existing catalogs showed that enough of author's name and title of the book for adequate identification would fit on a single punched card without too much abbreviation in all but a small percentage of cases.   In addition, the first card contained the class number and an item number within the class (the two together uniquely identifying the book), the year of publication, and location symbols.

A second card, for use only in the classed list, contained further information--a continuation of the title statement, including an illustration statement, if needed; pagination; and reading level.   This card was also intended to provide order information; space was therefore left for price, number of copies, and type of binding.

Given the circumstances--fixed fields, elimination of some information, and the unavailability of keypunchers familiar with library forms for such a relatively small project--it was necessary to transfer the information on the shelflist cards to code sheets.   This work took a great deal of time, and it was here that we learned some of the most important lessons of the whole project.

The quality of the cataloging at Farmingdale is certainly well above average; since central processing has been used for a number of years, it is relatively consistent. Even so, situations kept turning up which seemed to demand editing.   It is very difficult to resist the temptation to correct this or that anomaly since a time when the form of the

catalog is being changed is certainly a convenient one for
doing so. Errors which had caused little or no trouble for
years in the card catalog seemed glaring when we were editing for publication. Also, since we had no idea at the beginning of the magnitude of the editing job we would be undertaking, no real policy decision was made to guide the editing
process.

When keying and other machine operations for the book
catalog began, it rapidly became evident that, even with the
best will in the world, an overloaded school data processing
facility could not hope to process the bulk work involved in
a catalog in a reasonable length of time. When a payroll is
due, the catalog waits! Be that as it may, after the usual
mishaps in any major project, the first edition of the catalog
was published in April 1967. Catalogs of the professional
and audiovisual collections were published a few weeks
earlier. The latter was integrated into the second edition of
the main catalog. Integration of non-book media with the
book listings was one important side benefit we had hoped
to gain in producing the book catalog. Now the person looking for the resources of the library on any subject is made
aware of everything without artificial limitations by medium.

A major part of the work of converting the catalog
was done by the regular personnel at Farmingdale in addition
to their regular duties. Dr. Hines gave consulting assistance;
I was responsible for technical supervision of several phases
and for some editing. Several library school students did a
large part of the coding. The remainder of the coding and
all of the keypunching was done by people hired at
Farmingdale.

When publishing time came around again last fall, we
decided to go directly to the computer. We knew the school's
EDP office could not deal with the new edition. We had experimented with using a service bureau's EAM equipment for
the two smaller catalogs the preceding year and found this
also unsatisfactory. We were fortunate to have access to
the facilities of the Columbia University computer center for
experimental work. Since the Office of Education grant did
not cover a second year, it was necessary to cut all possible
corners to avoid overburdening the library's budget. It is
difficult to persuade administrative officials that a new budget
item is really saving them money because their librarians
are no longer filing cards and services have been increased--
especially in a year when the whole school system's budget
difficulties are even worse than usual.

Since I had some programming experience, I wrote the program for this edition of the catalog. I must make a disclaimer, however; I am by no means a programmer. My research involves use of the computer; problems of information handling are so ill-defined that communicating needs to a programmer is difficult, even if one with knowledge and interest in handling strings of alphabetic characters can be found. Fortunately, there is a high-level programming language available which is oriented to string-handling applications; by using this language, I was able to write and debug a very simple program for the catalog in a few weeks.

The programming is far simpler than I would like it to be. Under the circumstances, it was impossible to design a whole new format for the catalog; there was not even enough time to make some of the minor improvements we would all like to have seen made. As it stands, the program runs single-column pages in a format similar to that produced by the EAM equipment. Numbering, heading, and pasting up (though not measurement) of the columns for a two-column page is done by hand.

Computer running time on the IBM 7094 for the catalog is about 2-1/4 hours, assuming no mishaps. With the inevitable mishaps in this first computer edition, we used about five hours of time. At Columbia's rates, this would be about $700. However, the same program will run--more slowly, of course--on any 1620 with a line printer. Also, much of this time was taken up in card reading. For a variety of reasons, we did not use tape at all, and, as a result, some of the operations were not done as economically as possible. For instance, we did not attempt a computer sort for the various lists. Instead the cards were run through a sorter. For both editions of the catalog, a good deal of editing was done after the print-outs were made. We feel fairly certain that, once the catalog is thoroughly shaken down, this post-editing will not be necessary, but for the moment it is.

A very important issue is the cost of the catalog. It is, of course, quite expensive to make in the first place since an entry must be keyed for each title, and a certain amount of editing is inevitable. Once the initial keying is done, later additions probably cost about the same as printed cards. The other major cost--and this is a recurring one-- is for printing and binding. Printing costs are the ones likely to cause recurring budget problems. In a system

where the book catalog replaces several card catalogs, filing and other costs are probably reduced enough to pay for
printing.   However, the saving in filing is usually represented in the librarians having more time for service, not by a
reduction in the budget.   No matter how carefully future requirements are explained to administrators, it is difficult to
make them realize and accept the fact that the printing item
in the library's budget comes every year, and we find this
to have been typical in other book catalog projects as well,
no matter how carefully the fact that these costs would recur
had been explained beforehand.

       We have not been able to carry out a scientific evalua-
tion of the book catalog.   A grant application is in at the
Office of Education now for this purpose.   We do know some
adjustment has been required, especially on the part of the
adults who use the catalog.

       We have all learned a great deal in the production of
the Farmingdale book catalog.   I'm afraid most of it is what
not to do the next time, however.   The main thing we would
do differently would be to go directly to the computer.   Even
though the catalog was planned from the beginning with an
eventual transition to the computer in mind, the use of EAM
equipment inevitably imposed constraints.   We did without
data we could have had if we had not been held to fixed
fields and two cards per title.   Furthermore, some of the
qualities that make the data suitable for EAM actually cause
programming problems.   One note, however: enough data
appears in the catalog for each entry to fulfill quite adequately its function as a finding list.   One possible exception
is the subject list, which lacks location symbols.   The catalog consists of four lists.   The classed-order list contains
fullest information: author, full title, some illustration information, date, publisher, pagination, reading level, and
location.   The author and title lists contain author, title,
date, and location; the subject list includes author, title,
and date.   The book form makes possible inclusion of some
information not found in most card catalogs; many of the subject headers include a Dewey number or numbers applicable
to the subject; all the class headings give the subject of the
class.

       In the original plan, locations were to be given only
in the classed list; the other lists were to function as indexes to this list.   The subject list is the only one that might
be said to serve this purpose now.   When we decided that

locations should be given directly wherever possible, the card
format was already settled. With the fixed fields, the only
possible place for the location symbols was to substitute them
for the last three characters of the title. Since the book titles
on the subject cards were already shortened by six spaces for
a subject heading number, we could not shorten them more to
provide for location symbols. These subject heading numbers
were another constraint of the use of EAM equipment. To
have punched the entire subject heading for each book would
have made it impossible to put the remainder of the required
information on a single card. It also saved sorting time.

Even if EAM equipment is available in the school
system and a computer is not, the time required on each
machine is more likely to be measured in days than hours
The school system with this kind of time available on its
machinery all at once, and when it is needed, is certainly
suffering from overcapacity. Use of a service bureau, in
our experience, is unlikely to be satisfactory. The job is
not likely to be large enough to inspire the bureau with any
great willingness to work out different methods. Never let
a data processing person tell you librarians are tradition-
bound! We were not even able to persuade the bureau to
change ribbons often enough to produce really good copy for
the printer. Using a computer at a service bureau will, of
course, present problems, too. However, perhaps because
we haven't had occasion to do this as yet, we don't think the
problems would be as bad as the alternatives.

Another necessity for such a major project as putting
a library catalog in machine-readable form and producing a
printed book catalog is adequate and consistent professional
supervision from beginning to end. It is unrealistic to expect an overworked school library staff to be able to oversee
an entire major project (involving a technology with which
the staff members are probably unfamiliar) in addition to
keeping the library's system running from day to day.

The project coordinator should be involved at as early a
stage as possible, and certainly before the system design is
complete. The only extra professional help (aside from consulting aid) on the Farmingdale catalog was based at Columbia,
did not become significantly involved until the work was well
under way, and was full-time only for a few months. With
this kind of arrangement, there are inevitable communication
problems, delays, and misunderstandings. Unforeseeable
problems continually arise; unless a person whose full

energies are devoted to the project is on the scene, these problems often will not be resolved in terms of their place in the total picture.

The presence of a full-time project supervisor on the scene would make it possible to control input more thoroughly. The data processing office at Farmingdale was most cooperative, but it was also overburdened, and its personnel were naturally not always fully aware of the sort of situation that could cause problems. I've always been afraid to ask just how many cards were sorted out by hand and duplicated after many of the non-fiction cards were punched using a drum card that automatically punched an R (for Reference) in column 80.

Having a full-time project supervisor might also have helped in dealing with the editing problem. It really crept up on us. And by editing, I do not mean adjustments of the data for coding purposes. I mean corrections of pre-existing deficiencies or gaps in the cataloging; for example, entering separately all the titles in a series that previously had been treated as a unit. This sort of editing has nothing whatever to do with the requirements of putting the data in machine-readable form. The only relation is that it seems to be natural to fill in these little gaps at a time when the entire catalog is being handled anyway.

If it seems really desirable to edit the catalog information at the same time as the book catalog is being produced, well and good. The important thing is to realize the magnitude of the operation and the preferability of budgeting separately for the editing required. It is not a good idea to burden the book catalog project with unrelated costs: it will look on paper like a very large new expense with very little compensatory reduction in other costs. And speaking of costs, it is vital to make clear to the administration from the beginning that the book catalog will be a continuing item in the budget and will not fully replace any other item. This must be made clear over and over again.

Of course, while you're about it, it's a good idea to make clear that, for this relatively small expense, a number of benefits are being received. Even if it is not possible to integrate ordering procedures into the system immediately, the library's resources become far more available. The teacher with a copy of the book catalog on his desk not only will be able easily to determine the resources of his library

and others in the system but may even be inspired to notify
the library if its resources are inadequate for some planned
mass assignment.   Each student will be able to have a copy
at his desk in library instruction.   The librarians will be
able to know just what is available elsewhere in the system
and won't have to spend their time filing.

All this so far stays within very narrow limits.   Much
more is easily conceivable once the catalog is in machine-
readable form: preparation of specialized bibliographies;
integration of non-book media in the main catalog; inclusion
of other agencies,   such as the local public library as additional locations,   to name just a few.   To go even further,
it seems likely that the machine-readable cataloging information can also be used for circulation control.

The issue of keeping the catalog up to date is one
that seems to arise in all discussions of the book catalog
as a form.   A number of expedients are possible, but in
order to keep a proper balance,   it is necessary to remember
that the card catalog is never completely up to date either.
We had planned to issue monthly or bi-monthly supplements,
but so far have not been able to.   Of course, anyone who
wants to be completely up to date on the library's holdings
can call the library coordinator's office; sooner or later the
catalog will have supplements.   In the meantime, we would
like to feel that the greater availability of the catalog com-
pensates for its not being quite up to date for part of the
year.

Two more cautions.   It is expensive and time-consuming to do so, but the old system should be run in parallel until the new system is actually shaken down and operating; i. e. , in this case, cards should continue to be filed in
the catalogs   or at least prepared for filing, until the day
the book catalog is actually delivered to the library.   A year
is not long enough to produce the first edition of a book catalog, except under the most ideal circumstances.   Even with
the system design work done long before, the Farmingdale
catalog took more than a year.

All this probably sounds discouraging, but it is certainly not intended to be.   It is intended to emphasize that
a book catalog is not a project to be undertaken lightly.   Extremely careful planning and preparation are required--not
least on the part of the people who will be expected to work
with the catalog.   It is not a matter of a year or two: almost

three years of planning went into the Farmingdale catalog
before it was issued.   It has been in existence now for about
a year; we estimate that three or four years from now it
will be thoroughly shaken down and running well.   But it's
worth doing: availability of the system's resources is greatly
increased, and that, after all, is the purpose of the catalog.

Reference

1. Hines, Theodore C., "Computers, Supervisors, Libraries,"
   ALA Bulletin, 62: 153-5, February 1968.

Chapter XI

Applications and Techniques:

Mail Order Library Service

Mail Order Library Service:

A Report on the North Central Regional Library's

Mail Order Book Catalog Experiment

by Mike Lynch

> The author is the Director of the North Central
> Regional Library, Wenatchee, Washington.

Mail Order library service, featuring an illustrated
catalog for home use, is now available to residents in two
of the five counties served by the North Central Regional
Library.

The North Central System with headquarters in
Wenatchee, Washington, serves a population of 125, 000
spread over an area slightly larger than the state of Massachusetts. Library service has traditionally been extended
through 25 branch libraries and three bookmobiles featuring
over 262 individual semimonthly stops throughout the year.

A conscious effort is made to carry out a fair,
flexible, yet consistent program, and as nearly as possible,
to provide equal service to citizens of all ages living within
the area. The challenge is considerable. The legal district
consists of the rural areas of five counties. Twenty-nine
incorporated communities, where all but four branch outlets
are located, contract on a voluntary year-to-year basis.
Though bookmobile service has traditionally been extended
to residents living in areas where access to a branch library
is either inconvenient or impractical, 1966 survey requested
by the Board of Trustees revealed that from 60 to 80 percent of
the total bookmobile circulation was actually to school students during the school year.

Robert Woods, library board member and newspaper
man, first suggested direct mail service as a possible

alternative to existing bookmobile service and an additional
means of reaching a broader audience.   Mr. Woods proposed
that use of direct mail service be encouraged by providing
all residents in a given test area with a newsprint catalog of
selected adult and juvenile titles.

The "Woods Plan" as it was dubbed at the time was
enthusiastically endorsed by the staff and the regional board
of library trustees and was to provide the basis for an LSCA
Research and Planning grant request submitted to the Washington State Library Commission in September 1967.   The
Commission awarded the regional library $67,131 to finance
the 18 month project.

The grant request specified that branch library outlets
were to continue as primary points for public service.   The
Mail Order Program was designed as a supplementary service, analogous to that of the bookmobile in spirit if not in
approach.   Every effort was to be made to reach those who
were not presently using any type of library service.

The experiment consisted of an organizational phase of
six months, to work out the many routines needed to handle
an untried program, and an operational phase of one year,
terminating in June, 1969.

Douglas County, population 15,800, located centrally
in the district, was selected as the area to test the new service.   At the time, the county was served by one branch library located in Waterville, population 1,000; 68 semimonthly
bookmobile stops; and the regional library headquarters in
Wenatchee, which is located across the Columbia River from
the most densely populated area in the county.   Four incorporated communities with a combined population of 2,700
were not contracting for the services of the regional library.

During the operational phase of the Mail Order experiment, public hours were increased at the Waterville branch
library and direct mail service was extended to residents
living in non-contracting communities as well as those resid-
ing within the legal district.   Bookmobile service was withdrawn during the test period.

The results of the one-year experiment have favorably
impressed members of the regional library board, the library
staff, and the users themselves.   Mail Order circulation to
the county's 4800 families was 42,170, a figure 2.21 times
greater than the projected bookmobile circulation for the same
period of time.

The new service appears to have stimulated rather than to have suppressed use of other library services. Circulation at the Waterville branch jumped from 8,108 to 11,272, an increase of 21 percent, and local residents ordered an additional 2,112 books from the Mail Order Catalog. Bridgeport, the county's largest non-contracting community, population 1,085, has signed a contract for branch library service in 1970.

As a result of the experiment, mail order library service has been adopted as an on-going locally supported program by the North Central Regional Library Board of Trustees.

In September 1969 the service was extended to Ferry County, population 3,898, located in the library district's northeast corner. In Ferry County bookmobile and mail order service is offered concurrently. The interrelationship between the two services will be assessed during the coming year.

The Mail Order Book Catalog

The mail order book catalog is the heart of the project. In appearance it resembles a tabloid newspaper. A Douglas County scene is pictured on the cover of the experimental editions.

A brief annotation appears with each title. Book cover illustrations are featured throughout the publication. Titles appear under broad reader interest headings such as "People and Places," "On the Home Front," and "For Reading Aloud to the Very Young." Fiction and non-fiction titles are intermixed at will. Approximately 1/3 of the titles listed are for children.

The catalog was distributed to Douglas County residents by a commercial mailing service on three occasions during the one year experiment. A base edition of 1,500 titles was issued in May, 1968. The identical edition with a supplement insert containing some 300 additional titles was mailed the following November. A second edition featuring all previous titles plus 350 new entries was mailed in April, 1969.

Information on related library services and instructions on how to order books by mail are included in the publication.

Collection and Circulation Procedures

The mail order book collection, developed separately
from the main collection during the experimental phase of
the project, numbered about 21,500 volumes in June, 1969.
Books were purchased in paperback whenever possible and
current holdings are approximately 95 percent soft cover.

Titles were chosen on the basis of popular appeal
and general interest.   Selection was shared by members of
the regional headquarters staff and branch librarians.   From
its inception the collection was intended to represent those
titles, old and new, which would likely appeal to the casual
reader.   Although it is explained to users of the service
that orders need not be limited to titles included in the
catalog, only 218 orders for non-included titles or subject
information were received during the experimental period.

Most titles were purchased in a quantity of ten copies.
A local paperback distributor offered a 20 percent discount on
all trade items and agreed to accept for credit any unused
copies should the mail order experiment fail.

The mail order department, with its collection, occupied 400 square feet when service commenced and currently takes 750 square feet.   The present area provides
work space for the project supervisor, who is charged with
catalog and collection department; a clerical assistant,
responsible for processing orders and maintaining circulation
records; and a part time mailing clerk.   All books in the
collection are shelved on standard library shelving.

Effective management of the book collection is
achieved with a few basic procedures.   A catalog code
number of four digits is assigned each title.   This number
appears as a part of the catalog entry, thus permitting
ordering by number rather than by author-title, as well as
providing a system for shelf arrangement.

Processing is a matter of stamping the catalog number on a wrap-around gummed label attached to the spine,
an ownership stamp, and assignment of a copy number.   A
control card for each title, filed by catalog number, furnishes purchase and inventory information.   A duplicate card
in author arrangement provides cross reference to the
catalog number.

Use of the Kaiser circulation system eliminates the

need for book cards and pockets.   The order card mailed in
by the customer becomes the circulation record.

Orders are packaged in jiffy bags.   An addressed
return mailing label, postage stamps enclosed in small
glassine envelopes, and a new order card are mailed with
each order.   Books may be returned by mail, as most are,
or dropped off at a branch library.

Cost Information

More money was expended for mail order service
during the period of the experiment than would have been
spent on projected bookmobile service, due to high circulation figures and initial capital expenditures.   However, a
study undertaken by the Washington State Library disclosed
a program cost-per-circulation of 73¢ for mail service
compared with a projected bookmobile cost-per-circulation
of $1.03 for the period between June 1, 1968 and January
1, 1969.   Costs were compiled on a program basis for
comparative purposes.   Incorporated in these costs were
staff salaries,   including administrative and staff time for
those employees not directly assigned to the project;
depreciation expense on building, furniture and equipment
computed on a straight line method; and collection depreciation, rather than actual expenditures for materials.   It
should be noted that the data from which bookmobile costs
were projected were not as detailed as desirable.   This is
especially true of the labor costs of supporting staff.

These line budget expenditures were made; staff,
$19,367; collection, $34,878; and operational and capital
outlay expenditure, $13,366.   A total actual dollar amount
of $67,611 was expended during the eighteen-month period.

Operational costs were lower than expected.   Supplies
to mail four books (including return postage) cost an average
of 17¢.   Processing costs were minimal, as book cards and
pockets were not needed.   Paperbacks were processed for
10¢ per volume, hardbacks for 17¢.

Total catalog printing expenditures for the base edition,
supplement and cumulative edition totalled $3,144.   The cost
of reproducing the 40-page second edition of the newsprint
catalog as of October 1, 1969 is estimated at $1,217 for an
initial 25,000 copies and $845 for each additional 25,000
copies, a unit cost of less than 5¢.

Library Use Survey

The Washington State Library, with the assistance of college students briefed by the professional staff of the sociology department of the Wenatchee Valley College, inter-viewed 807 families in Douglas County in April 1969. The random sampling was derived from voter registration records from the 1968 general election. Surveyors were assigned an average of ten interviews to be conducted within the confines of pre-mapped precinct subdivisions. The 807 completed interviews represented 94 percent of those assigned and included 16.34 percent of the county population; 1,660 adults, and 1,107 children were included in the sampling.

Sixty-eight percent of those interviewed reported using one or more services of the North Central Regional Library within the six-month period preceding the survey. Thirty-one percent reported using direct mail service. Ten percent of those interviewed reported that they had not heard of the new mail service or had not received a catalog.

Mail order service was preferred by 80 percent of those who had used both bookmobile and mail service in the random sampling.

A "straw vote" postcard survey, conducted two months following the random sampling, was distributed to 1,448 Douglas County residents who were known to have used both mail order and bookmobile service; 898 responses were re-ceived indicating an 87 percent preference for mail order service. "Convenience" was the most frequent response given in answer to the open-ended question, "Why do you use mail order service?"

Conclusion

Mail Order Library service was adopted as an on-going program of the North Central Regional Library Board when grant funding terminated in June, 1969. The favorable response to the experiment on the part of Douglas County residents prompted the Board to extend the program to Ferry County this September. Ferry County is served by one branch library in the town of Republic and widely scattered bookmobile stops. The bookmobile crosses into Canada and back into the United States in serving the isolated eastern half of the County where residents are lo-cated up to sixty miles from the nearest branch library.

The extension of mail order service on a non-geo-
graphic basis is presently being considered. A joint program
with the public health departments in the five-county library
district is in the planning stage. Under this program, direct
mail service will be extended to home service medicare
patients.

Use of a condensed version of the mail order library
catalog in a branch and bookmobile paperback experiment
is being considered. Selected titles would be placed in key
outlets and an annotated list featuring catalog titles would
be mailed to all residents in a given test area.

In effect, while the Mail Order Library Project has
become an on-going program of the North Central Regional
Library, the experiment continues.

Chapter XII

Catalog Production

Catalog Production

by Hilda Feinberg

The author is Head Librarian, Revlon Research
Center, Inc. , Bronx, New York.

An increasing acceptance of library catalogs in book
form has been generally established in recent years.   In a
1968 survey of 400 libraries selected from a cross-section
of college and university, public, and special libraries in
the United States and Canada, it was found that 8. 8 percent
were actively involved in book catalog production. [1]

A library considering the adoption of a catalog in
book form should be familiar with the various methods available for the production of book catalogs, and the advantages
and disadvantages inherent in each process.

Various methods for producing book catalogs have
been discussed in previous chapters.   Sample book catalog
pages, with descriptions of their production, are provided
in subsequent pages.   Investigations of present practices
indicate a definite trend toward the employment of computers in the preparation of book catalogs.

The system for computerized publishing of such catalogs may be viewed as consisting of the following components:[2]

1.   Input Procedures and Hardware to convert the
catalog data into machine-readable form for manipulation.

2.   Computer Hardware and Software.   The software
programs may include programs that can format the page,
set up columns, strip in running heads, number the pages,
prevent widows, justify margins, hyphenate, correct errors,
and update subsequent editions.

3. Output Hardware includes such machines as computer print chains and photocomposition equipment which convert the computer output tapes to reproduction copy for printing.

Input

The computer will accept the catalog data only in machine-readable form. At the present time, various methods exist for inputting data to machine-readable form. Input may be accomplished with punch cards, paper tape, magnetic tape, on-line terminals, scanner-readable characters read by optical character recognition equipment (OCR), or previously prepared magnetic tape records such as those supplied by the Library of Congress MARC program. Keypunching, paper tape punching, and magnetic tape writing utilize keystroking to encode the information.[3] In addition to offline procedures, on-line terminals may be used for keying data directly into a computer. Data is usually simultaneously typed out, or displayed on a cathode ray tube (CRT).

Keying on a paper tape typewriter is faster than on a keypunch, and offers an advantage in that one of the products of typing is a hard copy. This may be used for proofreading. Correction of errors however, is difficult on paper tape. It is now possible to enter data directly on magnetic tape from a typewriter-like keyboard. Magnetic tapes can be read into a computer at much higher speeds than perforated tape. Additional advantages offered by magnetic tape are the ease of erasing and correcting the tapes, and the fact that it confines its information to a shorter length than punched paper tape. For example, a typical page might be contained in two inches of magnetic tape, compared with 200 inches of paper tape. The magnetic tape is also thinner. When there is no further need for the information on the tape, it can be erased and used over again. At the present time the least expensive and most widely available input device is the card punch.[4]

The input to the computer is the slowest element in the total cycle. It requires about 16 man-hours of keypunch and key verifier time to keep the computer processer occupied for .075 of a second.[5] It is for this reason that interest in optical scanners, or optical character recognition machines has become evident.[6-10] The machine consists of a photoelectric device which scans the document,

recognizes each character, and translates it into machine-
readable language, recording it on punch cards, paper tape,
or magnetic tape. The OCR scanner eliminates keystroking
altogether by automatically scanning and reading printed,
typed, and occasionally special handwritten material. OCR
equipment falls into two classes: readers which can recognize only special fonts; and devices capable of reading
several different fonts. A typewriter equipped with normal
type font can be converted to a rigid optical font. Libraries
may make arrangements with commercial service bureaus
to have typewritten copy scanned and converted to magnetic
tape.[11] The costs for purchase or rental of optical page
readers, paper tape readers, and keyboard equipment have
been compiled by Dolby.[12]

The opinion has been expressed that a direct on-line
terminal connected to the computer is the best, but most expensive means for capturing data, as information can be encoded directly into the computer via a typewriter or visual
display terminals.

> Such on-line preparation of inputs can take ad-
> vantage of the powerful editing capabilities of the
> computer. On-line operation not only permits the
> capture of information while the actual record is
> being prepared, but, in an integrated or 'total'
> library system, such capture begins with the first
> acquisitions record. Erroneous data can be
> 'erased' during initial typing. Changes, additions
> and reorganization of text can be made simply by
> updating the necessary portions of the original in-
> formation in storage. Manual retyping of cor-
> rected draft or final text is eliminated. Informa-
> tion, therefore, can be captured as it is generated,
> eliminating the cost and time of retranscription by
> a keypunch operator.[13]

Computer Hardward and Software

Electronic processing of the catalog data is accomplished with the computer. Its performance is influenced
by the accuracy of the input data as well as the input instructions, as the computer can only follow instructions which
are stored in its electronic memory. Such instructions are
known as the "software." Special book catalog programs usually

involve the normal card-to-tape and edit modules
as well as the various sort and format modules to
set up the individual outputs desired: shelf list,
author catalog, and subject catalog--the title
breakdown usually being combined with the author
or subject catalog.   There may be other programs
such as special cross reference print, special
merge modules to print cumulations, authority list
prints, especially for catalogs which include report
literature where corporate author, contract, and
report number cross reference lists are required. [14]

Output

A review and survey of output printing devices has
been prepared by Sparks, et al. [15] Methods which can be
used to print book catalogs may be summarized as follows: [16]
directly by the computer line printer or terminal in the
form of an original and carbons; by line printer onto offset
masters, and printing from the masters; photoreduction of
line printer copy, printed on an offset press; electrostatic
reproduction directly from paper copy printed by the computer printer (full size or reduced); microfilm copy; electrostatic printed copy produced from microfilm input;
photocomposition; and electronic composition.

Until recently the line printer and photocomposition
were generally employed for printing book catalogs.   A third
generation typesetting system has introduced electronic
composition machines based on electronic character generation, exhibiting exceedingly high speeds as compared to
formerly used composition machines.   Photocomposition
machines employ a tape input to control the exposure of a
film negative, character by character.   Precise positioning
of characters, as well as precise control of spacing between
lines is accomplished.   The earlier photocomposition machines were paper-tape driven, operating at speeds of about
10-40 characters per second.   Faster magnetic tape driven
systems operate at speeds of from 300-500 characters per
second.

An obvious advantage of photocomposition over the
computer line printer is the diversity of print available.
While the cost of creating page masters by means of photocomposition is higher than it is on the computer-printer,
the number of pages required is lower, as photocomposition
offers multiple type fonts and variable width characters,

making it possible to include more entries on a page and
still retain legibility.   It has been estimated that photocomposition printout averages about 60 percent of the
number of pages that result from the computer-printer.   As
a result, the cost of reproducing multiple copies and of
binding is reduced. [17]

Experiences in developing electronic photocomposing
machines have been described in recent publications. [18-22].
With this method of typesetting, characters may be described
as collections of electronic dots that have been projected
onto the face of a cathode ray tube (CRT).   Composition of
letters is accomplished by the placement of dots at exact
positions on an electronic matrix.   Positioning of the placement of dots is directed by a program which stores the
individual characters in a computer memory.   As each letter is required to set copy, it is brought out of the memory
and displayed on a tube where it exposes a film, or sensitized
paper.

Among the benefits to be derived by using electronic
data processing equipment in typographic composition are the
reduction in manual clerical effort and the shortening of
publication time.   CRT systems have the capacity to produce
a page of camera-ready type in a few seconds.   However, a
number of problems have been identified.   These include
restrictive available character sets, poor legibility in some
cases, lags in programming, problems occurring with program languages, lack of standards, and incompatibility with
respect to input and output devices.

The years 1968 and 1969 saw the recognition and
growth of computer output microfilming (COM).   A computer
output microfilmer accepts digital output from the computer,
converts it to analog signals, and prints it on microfilm at
rates from 25,000 to 100,000 characters per second.   It
has been described as a third-generation output device that
overcomes numerous problems created by the impact
printer, and one COM unit is the equivalent of as many as
30 impact printers operating simultaneously. [23, 24]

> The relatively new COM (computer-output-microfilm)
> technology may well provide the solution to the
> problem of producing small editions of book cata-
> logs at acceptable costs... The cost of producing
> the film is considerably less than line printer
> output, and the quality of the print image is some-

what superior to that of the line printer. However, it does not compare with photocomposed copy which is significantly better but several times more costly. [25]

Legibility

The effect of typography on the readability and esthetic quality of the printed page is an area which should not be overlooked in the production of book catalogs.

The Legibility Project of the Research Information Center and Advisory Service on Information Processing, a part of the Information Technology Division, Institute for Applied Technology, National Bureau of Standards (NBS), sponsored jointly by the NBS and the National Science Foundation, has produced a series of legibility reports, including a Reference Handbook. The research is especially directed toward

> those people interested in information processing problems and those areas of information selection and retrieval in which the human acceptability of machine printouts and various displays of document identification, abstracts and text is clearly related to questions of legibility. Closely related are the problems involved in the design of characters and symbols developed for automatic character recognition, and also the development of standards and specifications for printing, including automatic photocomposition techniques... In general, legibility refers to the characteristics of printed, written, or other displayed meaningful symbolic material which determine the speed and accuracy with which the material may be read or identified. [26]

Readability, on the other hand, has been used to "express the integral effect of physical factors which influence ease of reading."[27] Although legibility and beauty are not synonymous, they have been described as "not separable."[28]

Involved in readability and legibility are such factors as style of type face; type form (bold face, italics, all-capitals, etc.); size of type; line length; column length and column arrangement; spacing between individual characters, words and lines; size of margins; indentations; type, quality, surface and color of paper; quality of ink; format used; contrast

with background; and use of visual aids, as well as the
interactions of these different characteristics.[29, 30]

The optimum type face for various types of book
catalogs presents a complex problem.   In general, experience has indicated that styles with clearcut delineation of
characters, with openness, and without unnecessary details
contribute to good legibility.

Boldness may be used when emphasis is desired.
Greek letters, italics and digits (particularly exponents and
subscripts) tend to be less legible than other characters. It
has been recommended that they be as black and as clear
as possible,[31]   and that italics be used only when needed
for contrast or emphasis.

Readers have judged lower case print to be more
legible and more pleasing to the eye than material printed
entirely in capital letters.   Subjective judgments of legibility
have indicated that over 90 percent of subjects favor lower
case.[32]   It has been found that lower case print is read
more rapidly than all-upper case type, and that all-capital
text requires a 35 percent increase in printing surface.[33]
As a device for attracting attention, however, all-upper case
is useful.

Mixed typographical arrangements, or "change of
pace" type forms in comparison with straight lower case
Roman characters may produce possible distraction, or may
offer a more pleasing page in a book catalog.[34]

When size of type has been investigated as an isolated
factor, and evaluated in terms of visability and speed of
reading,   ten point type has appeared to be the most legible
under ordinary reading conditions.   It has been found that
this can be varied from eight to twelve points without
seriously retarding speed of reading.[35]   It has also been
demonstrated that unusually small type sizes as well as
unusually large type sizes are less legible when compared
with ten point type as a standard.

The spatial arrangement of the printed page is critical
in terms of the ease with which a book catalog may be consulted.   Vital are decisions as to optimum space between
individual characters, words, lines, entries, and columns,
as well as marginal space.   It has been determined that a
vertical line between columns does not promote legibility to

the degree that proper inter-columnar space accomplishes. [36]
Reduced visibility of words may result in larger bound volumes where there tends to be considerable curvature of the
lines of print and letter-distortion near the inner margin. Use
of a wider inner margin in large books may be employed to
avoid this defect. [37]

Variations in paper surface, degree of glossiness or
dullness, color, quality and thickness must be considered
in order to obtain the optimum paper for the book catalog.
Some book catalogs employ different colors to differentiate
specific sections of the catalog. Highly colored paper for
pages which must be consulted for extended periods is not
recommended. Color added to white paper decreases the
contrast.

Little is known as to the most legible formats for
book catalogs. A format which is suitable for one class of
users is not necessarily best for all patrons. Needed are
investigations related to general features of organization and
style of presentation. Presence of unnecessary lines,
marks or ornaments should be avoided.

In the following pages, selected sample pages from a
variety of book catalogs are presented. Various techniques
for producing the catalogs are described and illustrated. It
is recognized that methods of production are in a state of
evolution, and that improvements and changes have made
since the appearance of some of the catalogs. Some book
catalogs have undergone minor or major changes in format
or method of production, others have been terminated for
economic reasons, lack of user acceptance, or other considerations, while other book catalogs are still in the planning or production stage.

Problems and user reaction, as well as costs are
analyzed. Some of the advantages and disadvantages inherent
in each method may be outlined:

A.   Photographing of Catalog Cards

The photographic method eliminates proofreading and
page composition. Several drawbacks, however, limit the
usefulness of this procedure for producing book catalogs. In
addition to its bulkiness and the presence of excessive unused
space on the page, this type of catalog cannot be kept up-to-
date except by a process of manual interfiling of new cards,

and repetition of the steps involved in placing the cards on
sheets, and rephotographing. In an effort to decrease bulkiness, catalogs may be printed in reduced size. This procedure may be undesirable in terms of legibility. Large,
bulky catalogs present problems in respect to binding,
handling, and the occupation of excessive space on the
shelves.

An additional disadvantage of the photographic process
is the uneven appearance of the catalog cards on the page.
Generally, the cards have been prepared in a variety of ways
by many persons, using different rules, over a span of time.
The lack of standardization is obvious as one turns the pages
of the book catalog.

B.   Punch cards; Line Printer

While the punch card system is relatively inexpensive
for a library which owns the equipment, obvious disadvantages
are apparent. The most common criticisms have been
directed to the lack of flexibility for composition (italics,
etc.), and to the appearance of the page. Many book catalogs are printed in all upper case characters, a practice
which produces a monotonous, difficult-to-read page. The
punch card is restricted in the number of special characters
it can offer. Neither bold-face nor italics are available.
An excessive number of pages are required because the line
printer does not produce proportionally-spaced characters.

The excessive bulkiness of the catalog makes it unwieldy to handle, and occasionally presents binding problems.

A further disadvantage encountered in this method of
book catalog production is the necessity for handling and
storing large quantities of punch cards.

C.   Sequential Camera

This method offers the advantages of varied type
faces and sizes, resulting in a book catalog with improved
printing quality, a more efficient utilization of space, smaller
size, and improved ease in handling. In the photographic
process, the data can be either reduced or enlarged, offering the possibility of producing juvenile catalogs in an enlarged print.

Drawbacks which limit the usefulness of this method

involve the many manual operations which are required.
Records must be retyped before being photographed. In
order to correct errors, the appropriate cards must be
located, removed, corrected, and then refiled. Additional
manual operations are required to create multiple entries, as
each separate entry for the citation must be typed individually. Other disadvantages include the rigidity of the system,
the difficulty in changing the format of the page, the need
for handling large quantities of cards, the lack of creation
of a machine-readable record, and the limited ability of
the system to use catalog copy produced elsewhere. [38]

D. Computer-based Systems

Many advantages accrue from the use of computer-
based systems for book catalog production. The method
provides an opportunity to create a variety of approaches to
the holdings of the library, increasing the number of access
points to the collection. The facility of the computer to sort
information rapidly into a variety of sequences makes multiple uses of the machine-readable catalog files possible.
Various listings can be produced--by author, subject, title,
type of material, language, chronological, and others. The
machine-readable data may be used for acquisitions, circulation, and information retrieval purposes, as well as for
the preparation of special bibliographies.

Reduction of human effort is accomplished, as computer programs have been used to format pages, set up
columns, strip in running heads, number pages, prevent
widows, justify margins, hyphenate, and correct errors.

Computerization has facilitated the updating of book
catalogs; the periodical issuance of supplements and new
editions is generally scheduled at frequent intervals.

The necessity to modify standard library filing practice
in some cases, in order to operate within machine limitations
and within reasonable cost limits, has been considered to be a
disadvantage by some producers of computerized catalogs.

At the present time, the smaller library may find
that the cost of a computerized catalog exceeds its financial
resources. The cost of mechanization, the lack of equipment, facilities, and trained personnel, and a natural resistance to change, have been responsible for lack of progress
or experimentation in this area in many libraries.

References

1.   LARC Report, 1 (36): 36-1 to 36-3, Dec., 1968.

2.   Markus, John, "State of the Art of Computers in Com-
      mercial Publishing," Amer. Documentation 17:76-
      88, 1966.

3.   Library Automation--Computer Produced Book Catalog.
      N.Y., International Business Machines, Inc., 1969,
      p. 1.

4.   Chapin, Richard E., and Dale, H.P., "Comparative
      Costs for Converting Shelf List Records to Machine
      Readable Form," Journal of Library Automation,
      1:66-74, 1968.

5.   Lannon, E.R., "Optical Character Recognition in the
      U.S. Government," in Advances in Computer Type-
      Setting, Proceedings of the 1966 International Com-
      puter Typesetting Conference. London, The
      Institute of Printing, 1967, p. 48.

6.   Wishner, Ray, "The Role of Paper Tape and Optical
      Scanning Input in Textual Data Processing," in
      Proceedings, 1965 Congress, International Federa-
      tion for Documentation, Vol. II. Washington,
      Spartan Books, 1966, p. 240.

7.   Nadler, M., "The Perspectives for Practical Optical
      Character Recognition," in Advances in Computer
      Typesetting, Proceedings of the 1966 International
      Computer Typesetting Conference, London, The
      Institute of Printing, 1967, p. 36.

8.   Rabinow, Jacob, "Optical Character Recognition Today,"
      in Computer Yearbook and Directory, 1st ed.
      Detroit, Mich., American Data Processing, Inc.,
      1966, p. 75-82.

9.   Dyer, Ralph, et al., Optical Scanning for the Business
      Man. New York, Hobbs, Dorman, 1966.

10.   Wilson, Robert A., Optical Page Reading Devices.
      New York, Reinhold, 1966.

11. Los Angeles County Public Library, An Optical Character Recognition Research and Demonstration Project. California, Los Angeles County Public Library System, 1968.

12. Dolby, J. L., Forsyth, V., and Resnikoff, H. L., An Evaluation of the Utility and Cost of Computerized Library Catalogs. Washington, D. C., U. S. Office of Education, Bureau of Research, 1968, 55-58.

13. Warheit, I. A., "The Computer Produced Book Catalog," Special Libraries, 60: 574, 1969.

14. Ibid., p. 575.

15. Sparks, D. E., et al., "Output Printing for Library Mechanization," in Markuson, Barbara E., Conference on Libraries and Automation, Airlie Foundation, 1963, Libraries and Automation, Proceedings. Washington, D. C., Library of Congress, 1964, p. 155-200.

16. Library Automation--Computer Produced Book Catalog, op. cit., p. 30.

17. Cartwright, Kelly L., "Automated Production of Book Catalogs," in Salmon, Stephen R., ed., Library Automation; A State of the Art Review. Chicago, American Library Association, 1969, p. 77.

18. Morre, J. K., and Cavanaugh, J. F., "A Picture Worth a Thousand Words," Electronics, 40: 113-28, 1967.

19. Corrado, Victor M., "Experience in Development of an Electronic Photocomposer," in Hattery, Lowell H., and Bush, George, Automation and Electronics in Publishing. Washington, D. C., Spartan Books, 1965, 81-90.

20. Bozman, William R., "Computer-Aided Typesetting," in Alt, Franz, L., and Rubinoff, Morris, eds., Advances in Computers, Vol. 7. New York, Academic Press, 1966.

21.   Makris, Constantine, J., "A Special Purpose Com-
         puter for High-Speed Composition," in American
         Federation of Information Processing Societies,
         Conference Proceedings, 1966 Fall Joint Computer
         Conference, San Francisco. Washington, D.C.,
         Spartan Books, 1966, 137-48.

22.   Lanzendorfer, Max J., "Character-Generating Photo-
         typesetters." Part V., Printing Magazine/National
         Lithographer, 91: 68-9, 94, 1967.

23.   Yerkes, Charles P., "Microfilm--A New Dimension for
         Computers," Datamation, 15: 94-7, Dec., 1969.

24.   Avedon, Don M., Computer Output Microfilm, NMA
         Monograph No. 4. Annapolis, Md., National
         Microfilm Association, 1969.

25.   De Gennaro, Richard, "Harvard University's Widener
         Library Shelflist Conversion and Publication
         Program," College and Research Libraries
         31 (5): 324, 1970.

26.   Cornog, D.Y. and Rose, F.C., Legibility of Alpha-
         numeric Characters and Other Symbols. II.   A
         Reference Handbook. National Bureau of Standards
         Miscellaneous Publication 262-2. Washington,
         D.C., Government Printing Office, Feb., 1967,
         p. 2.

27.   Betts, Emmett A., "A Study of Paper as a Factor
         in Type Visibility," The Optometric Weekly, 33:
         229-32, April 9, 1942.

28.   Design for Legibility of Visual Displays. Bendix
         Radio Div., Bendix Aviation Corp., Baltimore,
         Md., Rept. No.   481-1016-97A (AD-230 962),
         Feb. 15, 1959, p. 15.

29.   Tinker, Miles A. and Paterson, Donald G.,
         "Typography and Legibility in Reading." Section 9
         Chapter II, in Handbook of Applied Psychology,
         Vol. 1, ed. by Douglas H. Fryer and Edwin R.
         Henry. N.Y. Rinehart & Co., 1950, p. 55-60.

30.   Tinker, Miles A., Legibility of Print. Iowa State
         University Press, 1963. 329 p.

31.   Vernon, Magdalen, D., "The Problem of the Optimum
      Format for Scientific Journals," Paper No. 11, in
      The Royal Society Scientific Information Conference,
      June 21-July 2, 1948.   London, The Royal Society,
      1948, p. 349-51.

32.   Tinker, Miles A., op. cit. (29).

33.   Ibid.

34.   Tinker, Miles A. and Paterson, Donald G.,
      "Readability of Mixed Type Forms." J. Appl.
      Psychology, 30 (6): 631-37, Dec., 1946.

35.   Young, Katherine D., Legibility of Printed Materials,
      Memo. Rept. No. TSEAA-8-694-1A (ATI-110570).
      Engineering Div., Air Material Command, Wright-
      Patterson Air Force Base, Ohio, June 10, 1946.
      27 p.

36.   Tinker, Miles A., op. cit. (29).

37.   Tinker, Miles A., "Effect of Curved Text Upon
      Readability of Print," J. Appl. Psychology,
      41 (4): 218-21.

38.   Cartwright, Kelly L., op. cit.,(17), 58-59.

Chapter XIII

Sample Book Catalogs
and Their Characteristics

by Hilda Feinberg

Catalog Samples

1. National Union Catalog
2. Morris Library, Southern Illinois University
3. Purdue University Libraries
4. The Library Board of Western Australia
5. The Free Library of Philadelphia
6. The Public Library of Annapolis and Anne Arundel County (Maryland)
7. Enoch Pratt Free Library
8. Minoa, New York, Elementary School Library
9. The Science Press Inc. (Prince George's County Library)
10. University of Rochester Library
11. Greenwich Library (Connecticut)
12. Albany (Georgia) Public Library
13. Austin (Texas) Public Library
14. Farmingdale (N.Y.) Public Schools
15. Blacktown (Australia) Municipal Library
16. School of Medicine, University of New Mexico
17. North Central Regional Library
18. Montgomery County (Maryland) Department of Public Libraries
19. Tarrant County Junior College District Learning Resources Centers
20. Washington University School of Medicine
21. Stanford Undergraduate Library
22. Ontario New Universities Library Project
23. University of California, Santa Cruz
24. NASA Headquarters Library Catalog
25. East Bay Cooperative Library System
26. Los Angeles County Library
27. Oregon State Library
28. Harvard University
29. Baltimore County Public Library
30. Fairfax County Public Library (Virginia)
31. ALESCO Book Catalogs
32. Chester County (Pennsylvania) Library

THE NATIONAL UNION CATALOG PRE-1956 IMPRINTS

Mansell Information /Publishing Limited
3 Bloomsbury Place
London, W1, England

360 North Michigan Ave.
Chicago, Ill. 60601

Characteristics

Format: 3-column

Specifications: An estimated 610 volumes will be published over 10 years.   Each standard 704-page volume will
contain about 21, 000 entries.

Page size: 10-1 /8 x 13 -3 /4 inches
Bound size: 10-1 /4 x 14 x 1-3 /4 inches
Paper: Acid free, permanent /durable specially manufactured to ALA specifications.
Binding: First grade library quality. Cloth pyroxyline
impregnated over 0.11 inch boards. Spine blocked in gold
with cane silk headbands, top and bottom.[1]

Method of Production

Essentially, the procedure involves the following steps:
"The card as edited at Library of Congress is mounted on a
somewhat larger piece of paper which bears a unique serial
number and identifying prefix. The location symbols which
appear on the card are transcribed on to the mount in a
fixed and uniform relationship to the register number. The
mounted card is then 'marked sensed' so as to trigger the
exposure of such copy as is required to be recorded on the
film. This, as the cards pass through the camera, has the
effect of deleting unwanted copy and extraneous white space
and of bringing the entries into a continuous sequence. The
exposed film is processed, 'spotted' and contacted to provide
a print which is read by the editorial staff."[2] After the necessary corrections have been made, pages are made up by cutting and stripping together column lengths of the negative.
These pages are again checked for accuracy and, when approved, are forwarded for platemaking and printing.

"The operation of the Williamson Mark 6 Abstractor,

as the camera is called, is entirely automatic, requiring
only to be loaded and unloaded with 200-foot spools of film
to be kept fed with 600 or so edited cards each working
hour."[3]

Notes

1.   Prospectus for the National Union Catalog Pre-1956
        Imprints, London, Mansell 1967, p. 29.

2.   Ibid., p. 26.

3.   Ibid.

The National Union Catalog Pre-1956 Imprints

Aalbersberg, Gerard

    Seerumtherapie en intubage bij diphtherie. Waarnemingen gedaan in het stedelij ziekenhuis te Rotterdam van 1900-1904. Amsterdam, G.P. Tierie, 1905.
    1 p.l., 110 p. 8°

NA 0005045   DNLM

Aalberse, Bam B
De liefde van Bob en Daphne. 's-Gravenhage, Oistervijk [1955]

NA 0005046   MH

Aalberse, Petrus Josephus Mattheus, 1871–
   Dr. Molens, bijdragen ...
     see under
   Dr. Nolens; bijdragen van P.J.M. Aalberse [et al.]

Aalberse, Petrus Josephus Mattheus, 1871–
   Een onbekende enquête naar de arbeidstoestanden in Nederland (gehouden in het jaar 1841), door Prof. Mr. P.J.M. Aalberse. Leiden: Uitgevers-Vennootschap "Futura" [1919?]. 50 p. fold. tables. 8°.

1. Labor, Netherlands, 1841. 2. Netherlands (Kingdom, 1815–). Binnenlandsche Zaken, Departement   van.

NA 0005048   NN

AALBORG, Niels Michelsen, 1562-1645
   Svundne Tiders Lægekunst og Lægemidler. (København, Lundbeck, 1947)
   (4) p., facsim.: (22) p. facsim. (Medicinalhistoriske Dokumenter til Belysning af Lægevæsenets og Pharmaciens Udvikling i Danmark. 8)

    Original title page reads: Den fierde Bog, som indeholder Medicin oc Lægdom som hvert Menniske altijd haffver hos sig selff mod atskillige Legemts Breck. Kiøbenhaffn, 1633.

    Includes also reproduction of original title page of the complete work, which reads: Medicin; eller, Læge-Boog ... Tryct paa hans egen Bekaastning ... aff Tyge Nielsen, Anno 1633.
    1. Medicine - Early works to 1800
     Title   Series

NA 0005057   DNLM

Aalborg, *Denmark.*
   Beretning om Aalborg kommunes biblioteksvæsen.
   Aalborg.
     v. illus. 23 cm. annual.
     i. Title.

Z824.A1117   51-50691 ‡

NA 0005058   DLC CU

MORRIS LIBRARY
SOUTHERN ILLINOIS UNIVERSITY

Carbondale, Illinois 62901

Characteristics

Page Size: 11 x 14 inches

Format: 21 cards per page (3 columns, 7 cards each column)

Arrangement: The basic set is an author-title catalog; the supplement is a main entry catalog.

Description: ... "Morris Library has a printed book catalog. The purpose is: 1) Required to furnish catalogs for Lovejoy Library, Edwardsville; the library at Alton; and the library at East St. Louis. These are over 100 miles from the Carbondale campus. 2) To prevent needless duplication between campuses of expensive research materials. 3) To facilitate interlibrary borrowing between campuses by producing the book catalog in multiple copies. 4) To make bibliographical information available in various divisional libraries and branches on both campuses. 5) Reduce wear on the central card catalogs (these will not be eliminated) and relieve congestion there. 6) To aid in our function as one of the four reference and research libraries in the state of Illinois."[1]

Method of Production

"The public catalog was edited before filming was started. Filming was at the rate of 35 trays daily or about two and one-half trays per hour. The catalog contained approximately 686,000 cards at that time; page - 11 x 14, on permalife paper, 800 pages front and back, 3 columns, 7 cards each column, 21 cards per page; 39 volumes, 15 copies printed or 585 volumes... Microfilm was one volume per roll so that it would be easy to reproduce a page or section from any volume. The printing was offset which was economically feasible for 15 sets and the volumes were bound class "A" library buckram.

"The only problem was due to seven different colored

cards in the public catalog.   Carbon copies on blue stock were the most difficult to bring out.   Some sharpness was lost in order to get a copy of all cards."[2]

Frequency of Issue

"One supplement in the same format of 5 volumes--14 sets (one of the original sets was lost in a fire), has been produced.   The supplement contains all white cards, so there was no problem in filming.   We plan to issue supplements when enough cards accummulate for 5 volumes.   An extra main entry card is made for each item cataloged."[3]

Costs

Total cost for filming, printing, and binding, $45,513.85.

Notes

1.   Communication from Sidney E. Matthews, Assistant Director of Morris Library, September 11, 1969.

2.   Ibid.

3.   Ibid.

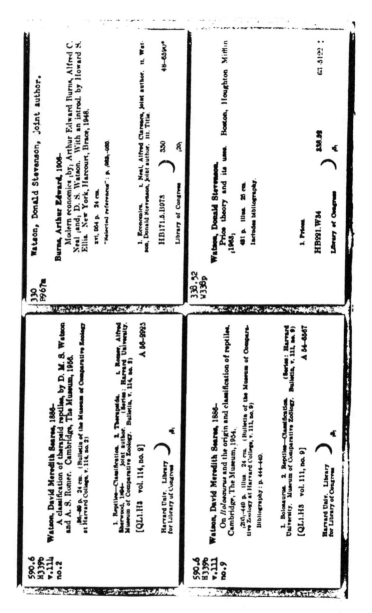

590.6
H339b
v.114
no.2

Watson, David Meredith Searres, 1886–
A classification of therapsid reptiles, by D. M. S. Watson and A. S. Romer. Cambridge, The Museum, 1956.
36–89 p. 24 cm. (Bulletin of the Museum of Comparative Zoology at Harvard College, v. 114, no. 2)

1. Reptiles—Classification. 2. Therapsida. I. Romer, Alfred Sherwood, 1894– joint author. (Series: Harvard University. Museum of Comparative Zoology. Bulletin, v. 114, no. 2)

[QL1.H3   vol. 114, no. 2]   A 56-9925

Harvard Univ. Library
for Library of Congress   [4,

590.6
H339b
v.111
no.9

Watson, David Meredith Searres, 1886–
On *Ichthyosaurus* and the origin and classification of reptiles. Cambridge, The Museum, 1954.
[393]-440 p. illus. 24 cm. (Bulletin of the Museum of Comparative Zoology at Harvard College, v. 111, no. 9)
Bibliography: p. 444–440.

1. Ichthyosaurus. 2. Reptiles—Classification. (Series: Harvard University. Museum of Comparative Zoology. Bulletin, v. 111, no. 9)

[QL1.H3   vol. 111, no. 9]   A 54-8467

Harvard Univ. Library
for Library of Congress   [4,

330
B967m

Watson, Donald Stevenson, joint author.

Burns, Arthur Edward, 1906–
Modern economics [by] Arthur Edward Burns, Alfred C. Neal [and], D. S. Watson. With an introd. by Howard S. Ellis. New York, Harcourt, Brace, 1948.
xvi, 664 p. 24 cm.
"Selected references": p. [663]-653.

1. Economics.   I. Neal, Alfred Clareson, joint author.   II. Watson, Donald Stevenson, joint author.   III. Title.

HB171.5.B973   330

Library of Congress   [20,   48-8560*

338.52
W34p

Watson, Donald Stevenson.
Price theory and its uses. Boston, Houghton Mifflin [1963]
411 p. illus. 25 cm.
Includes bibliography.

1. Prices.

HB991.W34   338.52

Library of Congress   [4,   63-5122 :

PURDUE UNIVERSITY LIBRARIES

Lafayette, Indiana 47907

Book Catalogs Issued

> Goss Library Catalog (History of Engineering)
> Serials Catalog
> Krannert Library Special Collection (Economic History
> Collection)

Goss Library Catalog

A conventionally printed catalog, this book catalog now
consists of two small paperback volumes. The original volume,
published in 1947, contains 218 pages and lists 1,662 titles.
A small supplement published in 1953 includes 671 titles in
60 pages. Both volumes were produced by conventional typeset printing. The original volume includes listings of several
small specialized collections. No supplement is planned at
present.

Serials Catalog

The computer-produced catalog, 1968, contained
30,000 titles and 10,000 cross references, displayed in a
3-column format. In September, 1969, the Catalog consisted of 1,800 pages of serials data. Updating is scheduled
for once in six months. The computer system has the
capability of printing out supplements, but until the catalog
is published in book form rather than in the present printout
form, the whole catalog will be replaced with each updating.
It is available for $30.00 a copy.

A state-wide Indiana Libraries Serials Union Catalog
has been developed which covers serials of 64 libraries, with
46,207 titles, and 65,728 entries.

"The catalog includes all subjects and includes academic, public and special libraries. At the moment it is
in printout form of 2308 pages of 3 column format. The
first issue of this was produced in 1970. An updating will
be done with supplements produced once in 6 months. We
have not yet set a price for it, the data files are not yet
completed, and so we will be adding to it in large quantity

for probably the next six to eight months. "[1]

Krannert Library Special Collection
_____

      This catalog represents a collection that will be
developed more fully as funds are available.   It represents
a small collection in its subject field--the history of economics, and contains a little over 2,600 titles and 223
pages.   The entries are displayed in alphabetic sequence by
author only.   Catalog cards are reproduced by Xerox into
book form.   The catalog will be enlarged as the collection
grows.

Notes

1.   Communication from Donald P. Hammer, Head,
          Libraries Systems Development, May 6, 1970.

1901-

STEINMEN, D. B. *Fifty years of progress in bridge engineering* 55
  pages New York 1929

WELLS, ROSALIE *Covered bridges in America* 135 pages New
  York 1931

FLETCHER, ROBERT *A history of the development of wooden
  bridges* 44 pages New York 1932

FOWLE, F. F. *Early American timber bridges* 8 pages 1937

HYDRAULICS AND HYDRAULIC ENGINEERING

HYDRODYNAMICS, PNEUMATICS

HYDRAULIC MOTORS

Up to 1800

HERO OF ALEXANDRIA *Gli artificiosi, e curiosi moti spiritali* 103
  pages Bologna 1647

———————— *The pneumatics of Hero of Alexandria* 117 pages
  London 1851

CASTELLI, BENEDETTO *Della misura dell' acque correnti* 184
  pages Bologna 1660

BOYLE, ROBERT *Hydrostatical paradoxes* 247 pages Oxford
  1666

Traite des moyens de rendre les rivieres navigables 104 pages
  Amsterdam 1696

MARIOTTE, EDME *Traite du mouvement des eaux* New edition
  414 pages Paris 1718

———————— *The motion of water and other fluids* 290 pages
  London 1718

COTES, ROGER *Hydrostatical and pneumatical lectures* 243 pages
  London 1738

BELIDOR, B. F. DE *Architecture hydraulique* 4 volumes Paris
  1737-53

A Manual of the William Freeman Myrick Goss Library
of the History of Engineering and Associated Collections,
Purdue University Libraries, 1947

MOBIL TRAVEL GUIDE, GREAT LAKES AREA,
GOOD FOOD, LODGING, AND SIGHTSEEING.
   INMB   F 551 M64
   1964,1968

MOBIL TRAVEL GUIDE, MIDDLE ATLANTIC
STATES, GOOD FOOD, LODGING AND
SIGHTSEEING.
   INMB   F 106 M67
   1964,1968

MOBIL TRAVEL GUIDE, NORTHWEST AND
GREAT PLAINS STATES, GOOD FOOD,
LODGING AND SIGHTSEEING.
   INMB   F 597 M6
   1964

MOBIL TRAVEL GUIDE, SOUTH CENTRAL AND
SOUTHWESTERN STATES, GOOD FOOD,
LODGING, AND SIGHTSEEING.
   TITLE VARIES   Call#
Library Location → (INMB) (F 207.3 M6) ←
   1964,1968 ←   holdings

MOBIL TRAVEL GUIDE, SOUTHEAST STATES.
GOOD FOOD, LODGING, SIGHTSEEING.
   INMB   F 207.3 M59
   1968

MOBILIA.
   INLP   749.05 M71
   PURDUE HOLDINGS NOT YET CONVERTED
   INMB
   114-119,126-   1965-

MODEL AIRPLANE NEWS. (DUNELLEN, NEW
JERSY).
   V1 NO 1-6, JL-D 1929 AS MODEL
AIRPLANE NEWS, 2-3, JA-D 1930 JUNIOR
MECHANICS AND MODEL AIRPLANE NEWS, V7
NO 3-V12 NO1, S 1932-MR 1935 UNIVERSAL
MODEL AIRPLANE NEWS.
   INI
   LATEST YEAR ONLY.
   INTI
   LAST FIVE YEARS ONLY.

THE LIBRARY BOARD OF WESTERN AUSTRALIA
CATALOGUE OF BOOKS

3 Francis Street
Perth, Western Australia 6000

Characteristics

Page Size: 8-1/2 x 10-1/2 inches

Format: One column, printed across the page.

Arrangement: The catalog is divided into a book section and a musical scores section.   The 17th edition of the Dewey Decimal scheme of classification is the basis of the arrangement.   The musical scores section, printed on colored paper, is arranged by the system of classification which is used in the British Catalogue of Music.

Description: The catalog lists the non-fiction books in all public libraries in the State, the books and musical scores in the Central Music Library, and all books added to the State Library since 1955, together with some earlier works in the State Library.   It does not include serial publications, nor children's books, and in general, is restricted to books published within the last twenty-five years, and earlier standard works which are still in current use.

The catalog is in three volumes; the last issue contains 2180 pages of schedules and 250 pages of index.   The musical scores section has a separate index of musical performances, forms and instruments, at the end of the section, and musical scores do not appear in the main index.

Method of Production

The compilation is in the hands of one professional cataloger who has other duties, and one full-time typist, who does the clerical work.

"The Catalogue is compiled on 8-1/8 in. Kalamazoo copystrips using an 11 pt. IBM documentary typeface and assembled in binders, Model S 1711, on a page 13 ins. long.   In the photographic reproduction the type is reduced to 8 pt. and the height of the type area to 9-1/4 ins.   The pages are reproduced, printed and bound by a commercial printer. "[1]

Costs

"Precise details of cost have not been calculated. The official reckoning is that the annual cost is less than 1 per cent of the total cost of the service, for which in 1968/69 the budget was A$783,000. Printing is the most expensive factor and for the last issue cost A$5256. If allowance were made for a proportion of salaries and of the cost of equipment (the permanent Kalamazoo equipment represents an outlay of approximately A5000), I should expect a strict accounting to reach a figure a little more than 1 per cent. "[2]

Notes

1.   Communication from C. L. Drake, Chief Cataloguer, July 14, 1969.

2.   Ibid.

733   CLASSICAL SCULPTURE

BLUEMEL, C.   Greek sculptors at work.   1955.   il.   Q733
CARPENTER, R.   Greek sculpture.   1960.   il, bib.   733.3R
CORBETT, P.E.   The sculpture of the Parthenon.   1959.   il, bib.   733
FORMAN, W., von., photographer.   The Parthenon frieze.   [195].   il.   733
MATT, L. von., photographer.   Ancient Roman sculpture.   1960.   il.   Q733.5
NEW YORK.   Metropolitan Museum of Art.   Catalogue of Greek sculptures.   1954.   il.   Q733R

STRONG, D.E.   Roman imperial sculpture.   1961.   il, bib.   733.5R
YALOURIS, N.   Classical Greece: the sculpture of the Parthenon.   1960.   il.   Q733.3

Books

HEAD, M.   Lean out of the window: Eng.   [1961].   KFVDW CM
- - Lone dog: Eng.   [1960].   KFVDW CM
- - More songs of the countryside: no.1,   Fox gloves: Eng.   [1933].   KFVDW CM
- - Slumber song of the Madonna: Eng.   Various eds.   KFVDW CM
- - Twins: Eng.   [1960].   KFVDW CM
HELY-HUTCHINSON, V.   Ruthless rhymes for heartless homes: Eng.   [1945].   KFVDW CM
HOLST, G.   Heart worships: Eng.   [1910].   KFVDW CM
IRELAND, J.   Songs of a wayfarer: cycle: Eng.   [1912].   KFVDW CM
JACOBSON, M., arr.   Swansea town: Eng.   [1958].   KFVDW CM
JAMES, W.G.   Australian bush songs: Eng.   1922.   KFVDW CM
JONES, P.   Men of Eureka: Eng.   [1954].   KFVDW CM

Musical Scores

THE FREE LIBRARY OF PHILADELPHIA
EXTENSION DIVISION

Logan Square
Philadelphia, Pennsylvania 19103

Characteristics

Page Size: 11 x 13-3/4 inches

Format: 3-column

Arrangement: The catalog is issued in two parts,
one for the children's collection and the other for the adult
and young adult collections. All authors, subjects, titles,
etc., are arranged in a single alphabet.

Description: Books are listed under author, and
when appropriate, under subject, title, editor, illustrator,
and translator. Works of fiction are not listed under subject. A book is entered under title when the title is distinctive. If there are several books on the same subject,
these are listed alphabetically by author under the subject.
If there are several books by the same author, these are
listed alphabetically by title under the author's name.

Method of Production

The catalogs are produced using a sequential card
camera (Compos-o-Line) by Data-Matic Systems Co. (P.O.
Box 30, Chestnut St., & Garfield Ave., West Point, Pa.).

"Cumulative supplements are side wire stitched with
wrap-around covers of appropriate weight. Basic issues
are wire stitched also, but covers are of .059-inch thick
binders' boards with a sheet of buckram glued around the
spine of the volume and a paper cover trimmed to board
and glued on to board."[1] (See also Brown, Margaret C., "A
Book Catalog at Work," p. 318).

Frequency of Issue

Cumulative supplements to the basic catalog are issued monthly for adult and young adult catalog, and bimonthly for the children's catalog. Periodically the entire basic
catalog is reissued incorporating all additions and withdrawals of previous months.

Costs[2]

> Total cost of the book catalog for the year
>   1969: $74, 291. 00
> Cost per page, Adult /Young Adult: $ 5, 430
> Cost per page, Children   5, 931
> Cost of 12 issues of A /YA including
>   a 12-volume basic issue of 8862
>   pages and 239, 274 entries: $ 61, 190. 00
>
> Cost of 6 issues of Children's includ-
>   ing a 3-volume basic issue of
>   1837 pages and 49, 599 entries: 13, 101. 00
>
>   Total $ 74, 291. 00

Cost covers cost of binding as well as printing.

Notes

1.   Communication from Margaret C. Brown, Chief,
        Processing Division, March 30, 1970.

2.   Ibid.

325.73
R799c
Rowse, Alfred Leslie, 1903-
    The Cousin Jacks; the Cornish in America.
    Scribner [c1969]
    451p.

322
F945zr
Roy, Emil
    Christopher Fry. With a pref. by Harry
    T. Moore. Southern Illinois University
    Press [c1968]
    179p. (Crosscurrents: modern critiques)

540.1
F318r
    The royal art of alchemy.
Federmann, Reinhard, 1923-
    The royal art of alchemy. Translated
    from the German by Richard H. Weber.
    Chilton Book Co. [c1969]
    264p. illus.

    Translation of Die königliche Kunst.

709.06
R824d
Rubin, William Stanley
    Dada, Surrealism, and their heritage.
    Museum of Modern Art; distributed by New
    York Graphic Society [c1968]
    251p. illus. (part col.)

    Exhibition shown Mar. 27-June 9, 1968, at
    the Museum of Modern Art; July 16-Sept. 8,
    1968, at the Los Angeles County Museum of
    Art; and Oct. 19-Dec. 8, 1968, at the Art
    Institute of Chicago.

343.1
R827g
    RUBY, JACK
Gertz, Elmer, 1906-
    Moment of madness; the people vs. Jack
    Ruby. With a pref. by Jon R. Waltz. Fol-
    lett Pub. Co. [c1968]
    564p.

ANNE ARUNDEL COUNTY PUBLIC LIBRARY - BOOK CATALOG[1]

Characteristics

Size: 9 x 12"

Format: 3-column

Arrangement: Books are entered alphabetically in separate Author, Title, and Subject lists in three volumes. Records are listed in separate Author, Title, and Subject section of the Title volume. There is a separate one volume Children's list arranged alphabetically in separate Author, Title and Subject lists with a record section arranged identically in the same volume.

Description: In the author and subject sections, the entries give authors, titles, editions, publishers, date of publication, and class number. The title section is abbreviated, omitting publisher and date of publication. Items are displayed in alphabetic sequence in the record section. The entries in the author and subject sections are identical. The title entry is abbreviated.

Method of Production

Library furnishes one card containing call number, author's name, book title, edition, publisher, copyright date, and tracings. This information is transferred onto three decks of IBM cards, one sorted alphabetically by author, one alphabetically by title and a third complete subjects alphabetically. These cards are hand-sorted and filed, making the operation much cheaper. Cards from all three decks are counted to determine correct number of lines per column. Page numbers and running heads are added to the decks prior to photography. A portion of the IBM card is then photographed on a high speed sequential camera.

Frequency of Issue

Book catalog is issued in five cumulative supplements with a bound annual for twelve months, and a three volume hard bound issue, author, title and subject, every two years.

Costs

      Five paper supplements and a casebound annual, based
on 5000 new titles are estimated at $15,037.10 for
1969-1970. Five paper supplements, with casebound adult
volumes and one children's volume based on 5000 new titles,
plus complete holdings are estimated at $36,594.55 for
1970-71.

Comments

      With the exception of a few titles, the complete hold-
ings appear in the catalog. Between each supplement the
libraries maintain a "current file" drawer, alphabetically
by author and title, which also includes the titles omitted
from book catalog. For nine libraries, 100 copies are run
for the paper supplements, and casebound annual, 200
copies when complete holdings are done every two years.

> Changes: Locators have been eliminated - too
>   costly in time and staff.
>
>   Spacing between each entry has increased
>   readability 100 percent.
>
>   Bi-Monthly cumulative supplements mean
>   faster service at the branch.

> User Reaction:
> 1.   Staff and public value mobility of book
>   catalog vs stationary card catalog.
>
> 2.   Smaller Branches are no longer restricted
>   by the size of their collection, which was
>   all the card catalog included, but now have
>   access to the total holdings of the
>   system.
>
> 3.   Even the "current file" is of more value,
>   because the new holdings are interfiled
>   each day as new books arrive, not at
>   some future date.
>
> 4.   Public requires no more instruction in
>   use of book catalog than of card catalog.
>
> 5.   The chief complaint, especially of older

persons is that they cannot read the print as well as that on a file card.

6. A number of users class the book catalog as "progress".

Notes

1. Information contributed by Ester K. King, Administrator, March 9, 1970.

MP4 C	CARNIVAL ON THE RHINE. Hanns Steinkopf and the Polydor Brass Band & others. Decca DL 8704
MP3 C	CHARLIE CHRISTIAN WITH THE BENNY GOODMAN SEXTET AND ORCHESTRA. Columbia CS 652
821.17 C	CHAUCER, Geoffrey. The wife of Bath's prologue. The wife of Bath's tale. Read by Dame Peggy Ashcroft. Caedmon TC 1102
Stereo MP3 C	CHAUSSON, Ernest. Symphony in B-flat, Op. 20. Charles Munch, conductor. RCA Victor LSC 2647. With: Franck, Cesar: Le chasseur maudit (The wild huntsman)
MP2➤ C	CHINESE FOLK & ART SONGS. Sung by Wonona W. Chang. Anna Mi Lee, piano. Spoken Arts SA 205
MP7 C	CHRISTMAS IN GERMANY. Capitol T 10095. In German.

Record Section--Authors

MP3 C Stereo MP3 C	CHARLIE CHRISTIAN WITH THE BENNY GOODMAN SEXTET AND ORCHESTRA. LE CHASSEUR MAUDIT. Franck, Cesar. With: Chausson, Ernest. Symphony in B-flat, Op. 20.
MP2➤ C	CHINESE FOLK & ART SONGS..
MP7 C	CHRISTMAS IN GERMANY.
MP7 C	CHRISTMAS IN SWEDEN.
Stereo MP3 M	CLARINET CONCERTO IN A MAJOR K 622. Mozart, Wolfgang A.

Record Section--Titles

SONGS

Stereo MP6 S	SCHUMANN, Robert. "Dichterliebe", Op. 48 & Four songs. Eberhard Wachter, Alfred Brendel, piano. London OS 25330

SONGS, AUSTRALIAN

MP2 S	SONGS OF ABORIGINAL AUSTRALIA AND TORRES STRAIT. Recorded by Geoffrey N. & Alix O'Grady. Folkways FE 4102

➤ **SONGS, CHINESE**

MP2 C	CHINESE FOLK & ART SONGS. Sung by Wonona W. Chang. Anna Mi Lee, piano. Spoken Arts SA 205

SONGS, GERMAN

MP7 A	AUSTRIA REVISITED. Songs in German by the Wiener Sangerknaben. The Vienna Choir Boys. Capitol T 10217.
MP8 G	GERMANY TODAY. Wolfgang Sauer. Capitol T 10032
Stereo MP6 S	SCHUBERT, Franz. "Die Winterreise" D 911. Dietrich Fischer-Dieskau, Gerald Moore, piano. Angel SB 3640

SONGS, MEXICAN

MP6 M	MEXICAN RANCHERAS. Los Centauros and Dora Maria. Capitol T 10102

Record Section--Subjects

921 Cromwell	ASHLEY, Maurice P., ed. Cromwell. Prentice 1969
921 Marl- borough	ASHLEY, Maurice P. Marlborough. London, Duckworth 1956
R 398.469	ASHTON, John. Curious creatures in zoology. Singing Tree 1968 illus
R ➤ 914.203	ASHTON, John. Dawn of the XIXth century in England. Singing Tree 1968 illus
581. 13342	ASIMOV, Isaac. Photosynthesis. Basic Bks 1968 illus
508	ASIMOV, Isaac. Twentieth century discovery. Doubleday 1969

Authors

F	DAVIS. Scanlan, John.
973.47	DAWN LIKE THUNDER. Tucker, Glenn.
Y 610.9	DAWN OF MEDICINE. Silverberg, Robert.
R ➤ 914.203	DAWN OF THE XIXTH CENTURY IN ENGLAND. Ashton, John.
F Sci	DAY BEFORE FOREVER AND THUNDERHEAD. Laumer, Keith.
F	DAY OF THE DOLPHIN. Merle, Robert.
Y Sci	DAY OF THE DRONES. Lightner, A. M.

Titles

GREAT BRITAIN—SOCIAL LIFE AND CUSTOMS—19TH CENTURY

R ➤ 914.203	ASHTON, John. Dawn of the XIXth century in England. Singing Tree 1968 illus
942.08 Quarto	DE VRIES, Leonard. Panorama 1842-1865: the world of the early Victorians. Houghton 1967 illus
914.2	MARGETSON, Stella. Leisure and pleasure in the nineteenth century. Coward 1969 illus

GREECE—ANTIQUITIES

| 913.38 Folio | LIBERMAN, Alexander. Greece, gods and art. Viking 1968 |

GREECE—HISTORY

| 938 | COOK, Robert M. Greeks until Alexander. Praeger 1962 illus |

Subjects

ENOCH PRATT FREE LIBRARY

400 Cathedral Street
Baltimore, Maryland 21201

Characteristics

>Size: 8-1/2 x 11 inches

>Format: 3-column

>Arrangement: Entries follow the dictionary arrange-
ment. Authors, subjects, and titles are included in one
listing. A separate listing is used for musical phonorecords.

>Description: The main entry carries complete
bibliographic information, including author, title, sub-title,
edition, imprint, collation, notes, and tracings. The other
entries are abbreviated. The arrangement of entries and
the bibliographic information included for the Musical
Phonorecords section follow the pattern applied to the book
titles.

>Running heads occur at the top of each page.

Method of Production

>The catalog is produced by photography of sequential
cards and offset duplication.[1]

Frequency of Issue

>Three supplements are issued each year. The total
catalog is reprinted annually. The 1969 cumulation consisted of eight volumes of approximately 700 pages, and contained about 57,000 titles.[2]

Notes

1, 2.   Information contributed by Marian Sanner, Chief of
        Processing, October 10, 1969.

Enoch Pratt
Free Library

LASERS
Melia, Terence Patrick
  An introduction to masers and lasers
[c1967] 162p.
TK7871.3.M37

Laski, Audrey Louise, 1931-
  The Keeper. [c1968]
  I. Title.
FICT.

Laski, Harold Joseph, 1893-1950
  Authority in the modern state.
Archon, 1968 [c1946] 398p. bibl.
"An unaltered and unabridged
[reprint] edition." Contents. -
Authority in the modern state. -
Bonald. - Lamennais. - Royer-
Collard. - Administrative
syndicalism in France. - Note
on the bibliography of Lamennais
(p.[388]-389)
  1. State, The. 2. Sovereignty.
3. Church and state. I. Title.
II. Title: Modern state.
JC327.L35 1946

The last day the dogbushes bloomed
Smith, Lee, 1944-
FICT.

Main Entry

AUTHORITY
Simon, Yves René Marie, 1903-1961
  Freedom and community [c1968] 201p.
JC585.S517

Authority in the modern state
Laski, Harold Joseph, 1893-1950
JC327.L35 1946

AUTHORS, AMERICAN
American Academy of Arts and Letters
  Commemorative tributes of the American
Academy of Arts and Letters, 1905-1941
[1968] c1942] 432p.
AS36.A48A16

AUTHORS, AMERICAN
Karsner, David, 1889-1941
  Sixteen authors to one [1968]
290p.
PS221.K37

An author's guide to business
  publications
Wolf, William B.
XPN4888.B8W6q

AUTHORSHIP
Overton, Grant Martin, 1887-1930
  Why authors go wrong [1968]
212p.
PN145.O 8

Subject Entry.

Baker, Julius
Nielsen, Carl, 1865-1931
  [Concerto, flute]
  Concerto for flute and orchestra
MP.N5C66

Ballad for Americans
Robinson, Earl, 1910-
  [Ballad for Americans]
MP2.U6A42

BALLADS
Brown, Oscar
  Mr. Oscar Brown, Jr. goes to
Washington
XMPJ.B76

BALLADS
*Richard Dyer-Bennet
MP2.AIR5

Musical Phonorecords

MINOA, NEW YORK
ELEMENTARY SCHOOL LIBRARY CATALOG

East Syracuse-Minoa Central School
East Syracuse, New York 1968

"Dedicated to the boys and girls, teachers, and staff of
Minoa Elementary School and to that sacred cow of the library profession, the card catalog--soon may it pass on to
its reward--whose shortcomings inspired this work."[1]

Characteristics

Page Size: 8-1/4 x 11 inches

Format: One column, printed across the page.

Arrangement: Catalog is divided into four sections:
Author List, on yellow pages, and including editors and
compilers; Subject List, on white pages; Title List, on pink
pages, including listing for periodicals; and Phonograph
Record List, on blue pages, divided into author/composer,
subject, and title lists.

Description: The Author Catalog contains the most
complete entries for the books in the library. The author,
title, sub-title, edition, illustrator, publisher, date of publication, pagination, grade level, and Dewey decimal classification numbers are given. The Subject Catalog lists books
alphabetically under subject. Where there are two or more
books on the same subject, they are listed alphabetically
by author. Entries in the Subject and Title catalogs are abbreviated. The Title catalog contains a list of periodicals
which the library is receiving. In the Phonograph Record
Catalog, the records are classified by the Dewey decimal
system. The call number not only indicates the Dewey
classification and author (or composer) initial, but record
speed as well.

Frequency of Issue

The supplement, listing new books and records, is
issued on the first school day of each month. Succeeding
editions of the supplements are cumulated. New annual
editions of the catalog are planned.

Method of Production

The catalog is produced by Sequalog, 7 Prospect Street, Stamford, New York, by means of a sequential camera.

Costs

A catalogue containing about 500 pages and 26,000 inserts for about 8,000 titles, was produced at a cost of about $2,000.00 for the first copy, plus $2.90 for each additional copy.[2]

Comments

"The number of copies printed varies with each edition, depending on anticipated need. We ordered 125 copies of the 1968 edition and have contracted for 200 copies of our next edition, which incorporates the card catalog listings of two other libraries. We may order a few more at about $3.00 per copy. We plan distribution as follows: 1 per classroom, about 30 in each library for general use and instructional purposes, 1 per main school office, 1 for school district office, 1 for superintendent, 1 for each other district school library still using a card catalog, 1 for district resource center, 1 for each local public library, 1 for Syracuse University School of Library Science, 1 for Onondaga Library System, 1 for each librarian, and several for general circulation in schools represented in catalog, 1 for each reading specialist, and 1 for writing in corrections and revisions.

"User reaction appears largely positive among children and adults in this school. Our secondary school librarians are not interested in changing to a book catalog. Our other elementary librarians are studying the matter."[3]

Cards will be discarded when the 1970 book catalog is issued; however, a union shelf list will be maintained. The system is planning for centralized cataloging and processing.

Notes

1. Stott, Keith, Librarian, Minoa Elementary Schools.

2. Communication from Sven Rahmas, Sequalog, May 25, 1969.

3. Communication from Keith Stott, March 25, 1970.

4. The 1970 edition, a union list for three libraries, contains about 46,500 lines, consisting of 9,200 book titles plus 715 phonograph record titles. It runs about 800 pages and costs roughly $6,000 for 200 copies. Additional copies would be $4.00.

Allen, Merritt Parmelee
Johnny Reb; il Ralph Ray. Longmans c1952. 250p il. (g7-9).

Allen, William D.
Africa, Fideler c1964. 160p glos il maps (g4-7)· 960

American Association of School Librarians
Discussion guide for use with Standards for school library programs. ALA c1960. 16p pa. t027.8
Standards for school library programs. ALA c1960. 132p pa. t027.8

Author Catalog

Aesop for children. Aesop. e398.2
Aesop's fables. Aesop. 398.2
Africa. Allen, William D. 960
African wonder tales. Carpenter, Frances. 398.2
After the sun goes down. Blough, Glenn Orlando. e591
Age of reptiles. Shuttlesworth, Dorothy Edwards. 5A8

Title Catalog

AFRICA
Allen, William D. Africa. 960
Carr, Archie. The land and wildlife of Africa. 574.96
Fritz, Jean. The animals of Doctor Schweitzer. 591
Jackson, Kathryn. Homes around the world (p99-107). 301.42
AFRICA—CENTRAL
Caldwell, John C. Let's visit Middle Africa. 967

Subject Catalog

Minoa (New York)
Elementary School
Library Catalog

THE SCIENCE PRESS INCORPORATED[1]

4069 Chain Bridge Road
Fairfax, Virginia, 22030

The Science Press produces two types of book
catalogs:

1. A computer is used in conjunction with high
   speed typesetting.

2. Data is recorded onto I. B. M. cards. After this
   information has been sorted, it is photographed on
   a high speed sequential camera.

Computerized System

The computer system involves four steps. All of the
operations or any part are available from Science Press:

a. Input to the computer. The library may send a
3"x5" main entry card, and the data will be processed for
input into the Honeywell 200 Computer, or the library may
furnish paper tapes to use with the Science Press computer.
If the library uses an IBM typewriter with an OCR font type
segment, main entry cards can be typed for input to the
computer via Optical Scanning.

b. Development of a master file or data bank. From
the data bank are obtained all the entries necessary to create author, title and subject sections.

c. Interfacing, or bringing together of computer output and high speed typesetting equipment. Author, title and
subject listing are photocomposed on a photon 901. The
composition is in upper and lower case, and a choice of
mixing bold face Roman and Italic letters is offered. A
wide range of size is available in either single or multiple
columns.

d. Printing and binding. All data may be printed
out on a local computer, and the print-outs sent to Science
Press for printing and binding. A wide choice of bindings
from plastic spiral to case bound books in various styles is
available.

Should the library have access to either its own or

other computers, programming support is available.

Sequential Card System (Produced for Prince George's County Library, Maryland)

The library submits one card to Science Press containing the call number, author's name, book title, publisher and copyright date, tracings, and in some cases, branches where the book may be found. Science Press transfers this information onto three decks of IBM cards. One deck will contain all titles sorted into alphabetical order by author; another deck will contain the titles sorted by book title; and the third deck will contain subjects in alphabetical order. Page numbers and running heads are added to the decks prior to photography. A portion of the IBM card is photographed at high speeds on the Eastman Kodak Listomatic Camera. The film roll is cut apart into columns and the columns are stripped together to form a page. The film is used for the preparation of offset printing plates. The plates are printed and the volumes are bound.

Comments

It is suggested by Science Press that libraries with 20,000 titles or under in their basic collection, and with yearly purchases of 7,000 titles (not volumes) or less, would discover that the sequential camera method is practical, whereas for larger library collections the computer may be the most practical method.

The Science Press has been producing catalogs for Fairfax County Library and Prince George's County, Maryland, since July, 1964. The titles acquired by the Northern Virginia Community College have been merged with the adult supplements of the Fairfax County Book Catalog. Each book held by the County Library has the branch location listed under the author, title, and subject entries in Roman style type. If a book is owned by the college, the campus location is listed by the use of italic type.

Note

1. Information contributed by Alfred W. Baker, The Science Press, Inc., January 9, 1970.

Prince George's County
Sequential Camera - Produced Sample

AUTHORS

R 020.6 A — ALA MEMBERSHIP DIRECTORY, 1967. Author c1967 R U

970.2 B — AARON, Chester. About us. 1st ed. McGraw-Hill c1967 A B BK G L M R S T

AARON, Daniel, 1912- . Essays on history and literature by Robert H. Brenner, 1917- , ed. R U

818.54 Abbey A — ABBEY, Edward, 1927- . Desert solitaire. 1st ed. McGraw-Hill c1968 BK G R S

608 — ABBOT, Charles G. Great inventions. Smithsonian Inst c1932 R

ABBOTT, Edwin A. Flatland. Dover c1952 C G R S T

371.26 A — ABELS, Cyrilly, ed. 40 best stories from Mademoiselle 1945-1960. Mademoiselle. B BK HH R T

629.4 A — ADAMS, Carsbie C. Careers in astronautics and rocketry. McGraw c1962 A BK C F L R S T U

641.5 A — ADAMS, Charlotte, 1899- . Cooking with style. Doubleday c1967 BK G T

641.5 — ADAMS, Charlotte. SAS world-wide restaurant cookbook. Random c1960 BK L R T

B Sukarno A — ADAMS, Cindy H. My friend the dictator. Bobbs-Merrill c1967 C HH U

W A — ADAMS, Clifton. The most dangerous profession. 1st ed. Doubleday c1967 BK L T U

W — ADAMS, Clifton. A partnership with death. 1st ed. Doubleday c1967 BK D T U

371.26 A — ADAMS, Georgia W. S., 1913- Measurement and evaluation in education, psychology, and guidance. Holt, Rinehart & Winston c1964

131.34 — ADLER, Alfred. Individual psychology. Basic Bks c1956 R T U

959.704 — ADLER, Bill, ed. Letters from Vietnam. 1st ed. Dutton c1967 A B BK C D G HH L MR R S T U

610 A — ADLER, Bill, comp. Prescription: laughter. 1st ed. Harcourt, Brace & World c1968 A B BK G L R T U

817.54 Stevenson YA — ADLER, Bill, ed. The Stevenson wit by Adlai E. Stevenson, 1900-1965. G T U

975.3 A — ADLER, Bill, comp. Washington: a reader. 1st ed. Meredith Pr c1967 BK HH M R S T U

150.195 A — ADLER, Gerhard, 1904- . Studies in analytical psychology. New ed. Putnam 1966 A T U

512.86 A — ADLER, Irving. Groups in the new mathematics. Day c1967 BK R S T U

Science Press, Inc.

UNIVERSITY OF ROCHESTER LIBRARY[1]

Rochester, New York

Characteristics

Page Size: 8-1/4 x 11"

Format: One column printed across the page.

Arrangement: The catalog consists of an author listing and a title listing. As of January, 1966, serials are
covered in a separate list.

Description: The Consolidated Short-title Catalog of
Books of the Science Libraries is designed as a supplement
to the catalogs on cards. As a one-line, short-title, printed
catalog, it is designed as an author-title finding list. All
upper-case characters are used. Each page contains 68
entries.

Each entry consists of author, title, year of publication, Library of Congress classification number, and location. No cross-references are used. As the names of
corporate bodies are usually abbreviated, a list of special
abbreviations is included in each catalog.

Method of Production

The original catalogs were made with the standard
IBM electronic accounting machinery in the University's Data
Processing Center. The Consolidated Catalog was produced
with the University's IBM 7040 computer in the Computing
Center. Programming was performed by a member of the
Computing Center staff.

Frequency of Issue

The catalog is issued every 18 to 24 months.

Costs

About $7.50/vol (includes library office's labor and
print shop costs.)

1. See also: Richmond, Phyllis A., "Book Catalogs as Sup-
    plements to Card Catalogs," and "Note on Updating and
    Searching Computerized Catalogs," pages 214-229.

University of Rochester Library
Science Libraries Consolidated Short-Title Catalog, 1967

UNESCO	REVIEW NATURAL RESOURCES AFRICAN CONTINENT	63 HC0502	5
UNGER LAWRENCE ERNST	EFFECT ANNEALING ON MICROHARDNESS OF BRONZES	36 AS0038.49	1
UNIO INTERNATIONLIS	PROCEEDINGS	64 RC0261	4
	UNION LIST OF SERIALS LIB U.S. + CANADA ED. 3	65 ZAP001	124
U.N.SCI COMM RADIATN	REPORT	58 QH0652	4
U.N.SCI COMM RADIATN	REPORT	62 QH0652	4
U.N.SCI COMM RADIATN	REPORT	64 QH0652	4
U.S.	ADVANCED MAP + AERIAL PHOTOGRAPH READING	41 UG0470	5
U.S.	AERODYNAMIC DESIGN OF AXIAL-FLOW COMPRESSORS	65 TJ0267.5	1
U.S.	AERONAUTICAL + SPACE SERIAL PUBLICATIONS	62 ZTL504	1
U.S.	AIR POLLUTION PUBLICATIONS, 1955-1962	62 ZTD883	1
U.S.	AIR POLLUTION PUBLICATIONS, 1955-1963	64 ZTD883	1
U.S.	AIRCRAFT NOISE + ITS PROBLEMS	62 ZTL574	1
U.S.	ALASKA	38 HC0107.32	5

Author Listing

AERATION + AIR-CONTENT	CLEMENTS FREDERIC E	21 QK0891	4
AERIAL PHOTOGRAPHS + THEIR APPLICATIONS	SMITH HAROLD THEODORE	43 TA0593	5
AERIAL PHOTOGRAPHS IN FIELD GEOLOGY	LATTMAN LAURENCE H	65 QE0033	5
AERO-SPACE APPLIED THERMODYNAMICS MANUAL	SOC AUTOMOTIVE ENGRS	C TL0671	1
AERODYNAMIC COMPONENTS OF AIRCRAFT	DONOVAN ALLEN F	57 TL0573	1
AERODYNAMIC DESIGN OF AXIAL-FLOW COMPRESSORS	U.S.	65 TJ0267.5	1
AERODYNAMIC THEORY	DURAND WILLIAM F	63 TL0570	1
AERODYNAMICS	VON KARMAN THEODORE	54 QA0930	2
AERODYNAMICS FOR ENGINEERING STUDENTS	HOUGHTON EDWARD LEWIS	60 TL0570	1
AERODYNAMICS OF POWERED FLIGHT	CARROLL ROBERT L	60 TL0570	1
AERODYNAMICS OF THE AIRPLANE	MILLIKAN CLARK B	41 TL0570	1
AERODYNAMICS OF TURBINES + COMPRESSORS	HAWTHORNE WILLIAM R	64 TJ0267	1
AERODYNAMICS OF WINGS + BODIES	ASHLEY HOLT	65 TL0570	1

Title Listing

GREENWICH LIBRARY

Greenwich, Connecticut

<u>Title</u>: Fiction in the Greenwich Library

<u>Characteristics</u>

   <u>Page Size</u>: 7 x 10 inches

   <u>Format</u>: One column, printed across the page.

   <u>Arrangement</u>: The catalog consists of two sections,
author and title.

   <u>Description</u>: Entries include author, title, publisher,
and date, when available. The type is all upper case, 8
point Univers Medium and Univers Bold.

   The catalog was prepared in order to list the fiction
holdings of the library by author and by title in alphabetical
order for public use as a finding list.   A separate fiction
card catalog had formerly been maintained by the library
because of the separate location of fiction books.

<u>Method of Production</u>

   "Entries are limited--by the 80 column punched card
input format.   Fixed fields were assigned as follows:

Author	-	25 spaces
Title	-	40 spaces
Publisher	-	11 spaces
Date	-	4 spaces

Date chosen was the most <u>recent</u> date available.

   "Cards were punched and interpreted by the Town of
Greenwich Data Processing Department, proof read and
sorted by the staff of the Catalog Department of the Green-
wich Library, under the direction of Mrs. Maureen Hattasch.
The cards were then converted onto Magnetic Tape and the
Tape used to produce phototypeset pages which were then
reproduced by Offset, bound and delivered to the library.
Sedgwick Printout Systems (NYC) directed this phase of the
work, which was done by Composition Systems of White
Plains and Edwards Brothers. "[1]

Frequency of Issue

"Updating of the catalog is a monthly cumulative
process carried out by utilizing Town of Greenwich equipment to punch up new titles and prepare a printout on an
IBM 360-20 computer. Complete new editions are planned
every two years."[2]

Costs

"Cost for conversion from card to tape, simple programming, printing and binding the initial catalog of 15,000
titles was $4,000 for 100 copies. Copies may be purchased
from the Greenwich Library for $10.00."[3]

Notes

1, 2, 3. Communication from Nolan Lushington, Director,
    September 15, 1969.

Greenwich Libaary

KINGSLEY, MICHAEL	SHADOW OVER ELVERON	RANDOM	1963
KINSLEY, PETER	PIMPERNEL 60	DUTTON	1968
	THREE CHEERS FOR NOTHING	DUTTON	1964
KIPLING, RUDYARD	ACTIONS AND REACTIONS	SCRIBNER	1909
	BEST SHORT STORIES	DOUBLEDAY	1961
	CAPTAINS COURAGEOUS	DOUBLEDAY	1953
	COLLECTED DOG STORIES	DOUBLEDAY	1934
	DEBITS AND CREDITS	DOUBLEDAY	1926
	DIVERSITY OF CREATURES	MACMILLAN	1952
	JUNGLE BOOK	DOUBLEDAY	1932
	KIM	DOUBLEDAY	1905
	LIGHT THAT FAILED	DOUBLEDAY	1936
	MAUGHAM'S CHOICE	DOUBLEDAY	1953
	PUCK OF POOK'S HILL	DOUBLEDAY	1906
	REWARDS AND FAIRIES	DORAN	1928
	SELECTION OF STORIES AND POEMS	DOUBLEDAY	1956
	SOLDIERS THREE	MACMILLAN	1960
	TEEM A TREASURE HUNTER	DOUBLEDAY	1939
	THEY AND THE BRUSHWOOD BOY	DOUBLEDAY	1926
	TRAFFICS AND DISCOVERIES	MACMILLAN	1904
	TWO JUNGLE BOOKS	DOUBLEDAY	1895
KIRK, IRINA	BORN WITH THE DEAD	HOUGHTON	1963

Author Section

Greenwich Library

Title	Author	Publisher	Year
GENTLEMAN'S AGREEMENT	HOBSON, LAURA KEANE Z	SIMON	1947
GENTLEMEN	MARSHALL, EDISON	FARRAR	1956
GENTLEMEN HUSH	WHEELWRIGHT, JERE H	SCRIBNER	1948
GENTLEMEN I ADDRESS YOU	BOYLE, KAY	SMITH	1933
GENTLEMEN IN THE PARLOUR	MAUGHAM, W SOMERSET	AVON	1930
GENTLEMEN IN THEIR SEASON	FIELDING, GABRIEL	MORROW	1966
GENTLEMEN PREFER BLONDES	LOOS, ANITA	LIVERIGHT	1925
GENTLEWOMEN OF EVIL	HAINING, PETER ED	TAPLINGER	1967
GEORDIE	WALKER, DAVID	HOUGHTON	1950
GEORGE ARBUTHNOTT JARRETT	TOMS, BERNARD	HARCOURT	1965
GEORGE WASHINGTON SEPTEMBER SIR	HARWOOD, RONALD	FARRAR	1961
GEORGIA BOY	CALDWELL, ERSKINE	DUELL	1943
GEORGIE WINTHROP	WILSON, SLOAN	HARPER	1963
GERMAN STORIES AND TALES	PICK, ROBERT ED	KNOPF	1954
GERMINAL	ZOLA, EMILE	DUTTON	1964
GESTURE	COOPER, JOHN COBB	HARPER	1948
GET HOME FREE	HOLMES, JOHN CLELLON	DUTTON	1964
GET READY FOR BATTLE	JHABVALA, R PRAWER	NORTON	1963
GETTING STRAIGHT	KOLB, KEN	CHILTON	1967
GHOST AND MRS MUIR	LESLIE, JOSEPHINE A	ZIFF DAVIS	1945

Title Section

ALBANY PUBLIC LIBRARY

2215 Barnsdale Way
Albany, Georgia

Characteristics

Page Size: 8-1/2 x 11 inches

Format: One column printed across the page.

Arrangement: Separate author, title, and subject lists
are printed. Separate catalogs are printed for adult and
juvenile books.

Description: The entries, arranged alphabetically,
contain classification number, author, title, year of publication, and location. Books are classified as to fiction,
biography, juvenile, short stories, reference, western,
mystery, and science fiction. All upper-case computer print-
out is used.

Method of Production

The catalog is printed directly on three-part paper.
Equipment is being changed from an IBM 403 to an IBM 360.
The annual volumes are bound and lettered with a periodical
binding from a regular bindery. The bi-weekly supplements
are bound in the city printing room.

Frequency of Issue

"We print an annual author, title and subject catalog
for adult books and another for juvenile. We then make
cumulative supplements including all new books, since the
last bound catalogs, at two week intervals until our acquisitions money runs out. We then collate, reprint the big
catalog and await a new budget appropriation."[1]

Costs

"We had offered to sell added copies to libraries at
$100 per year for an author catalog only and all cumulative
supplements. I remember that our "out of pocket" cost for
this would be about $60/65. We now furnish old sets to
neighbors as a service, free of charge."[2]

Comments

     "We do not maintain a card catalog. We have heard almost no adverse user reaction and much that was favorable. Our own (outbound) interlibrary loans have increased many times over since we have given old catalogs to our neighbors. We make 9, 12 or 15 (any combination of three) copies of the Catalog."[3]

Notes

1.   Communication from H.W. Todd, Director, Feb. 27, 1970.

2.   Ibid., March 17, 1970.

3.   Ibid., Feb. 27, 1970.

Book Catalogs

ALBANY PUBLIC LIBRARY

ALBANY, GEORGIA

CLASSIFICATION NO.	AUTHOR AND TITLE		CARNEGIE	NORTHWEST	TALLULAH M.	BOOKMOBILE
	AUTHOR SUPPLEMENT AS OF 1/29/70	PAGE 18				
R728	DANIEL, JEAN H EXECUTIVE MANSIONS AND CAPITOLS			1		
651.82	DARBY, EDWIN IT ALL ADDS UP	1968	1			
293	DAVIDSON, HILDA R E PAGAN SCANDINAVIA.	1967		1		
SF	DAVIES, LESLIE P DIMENSION A	1969		1		
636.94	DAVIS, JOSEPH A BEEVER AND COMPANY	1969	1	1		
796.09	DAVIS, MAC 100 GREATEST SPORTS HEROES. 1958		1			

Author Supplement, January 29, 1970

AUSTIN PUBLIC LIBRARY[1]

Austin, Texas

Characteristics

Page Size: 9 x 11 inches

Format: 2-column for adult catalogs; children's catalogs extend across the page.

Arrangement: Separate author, title, and subject catalogs exist for juvenile and adult books.

Description: The catalogs, intended as finding lists, contain one-line entries printed in upper case letters. Entries in the author catalogs, displayed in alphabetic sequence, give author, title, publisher, date of publication, symbols, and classification number. Under each author, works are listed alphabetically by title. The title and subject catalogs omit imprint information. In the subject catalogs works are displayed under subject headings in alphabetic sequence by the first meaningful word in the title.

Method of Production

The book catalog was produced locally as a joint project of three city departments: Library, Data Processing, and Print Shop. The information was punched on IBM cards by library personnel; the program for the computer was prepared by the Data Processing Center; the punched cards were stored on magnetic tape; the stored information was sorted and printed on multilith mats by the computer; and the mats were sent to the City Print Shop where the catalogs were printed and bound. An IBM 1401 computer was employed. (See Bock, Faye, "Book Catalogs in the Austin Public Libraries," pages 331-344).

Frequency of Issue

Three new editions of the adult book catalog, and one new edition of the juvenile catalog are issued each year. At the first of each month, between editions, a cumulative list of all titles added since the publication of the last edition is available.

Costs

The cost of the first edition of the adult and juvenile catalogs was about $7,000. This figure included data processing costs (including programming), printing, rental of keypunch and verifier, and the salaries of two part-time keypunchers. The salaries of two professional catalogers involved in the planning and preparation of materials was not included in this figure, as they were already on the payroll and performed this work as part of their regular schedule. One hundred copies of the catalogs were printed, including 10,084 adult titles and 8,876 juvenile titles.

Comments

The card catalog for juvenile books in the Central Library has been eliminated. The card catalog for adult books in the library system will also be eliminated when all books have been converted to the book catalog.

Note

1. Information and sample pages supplied by David Earl Holt, Director of Libraries.

Austin Public Library
Books for Adults

ADAMS, CLIFTON
"   DOOMSDAY CREEK   DOUBLEDAY 1964
"   MOST DANGEROUS PROFESSION   DOUBLEDAY 1967
"   PARTNERSHIP WITH DEATH   DOUBLEDAY 1967
"   RECKLESS MEN   DOUBLEDAY 1962
"   SHORTY   DOUBLEDAY 1966
"   TRAGGS CHOICE   DOUBLEDAY 1969

ADAMS, DORIS SUTCLIFFE
       POWER OF DARKNESS   WALKER 1967
       PRICE OF BLOOD   SCRIBNER 1962

ADAMS, FRANK DAVIS
       LIFE AND TIMES OF BUCKSHOT SOUTH   DUTTON 1959

ADAMS, GEORGE BURTON
  342.42 AD   CONSTITUTIONAL HISTORY OF ENGLAND   HOLT 1934

ADAMS, HAMPTON
  286.6 AD   WHY I AM A DISCIPLE OF CHRIST   NELSON 1957

ADAMS, HAZARD
  809.1 AD   CONTEXTS OF POETRY   LITTLE 1964
               HORSES OF INSTRUCTION   HARCOURT 1968

Author Catalog

             ADAM   BY D BOLT
             ADAM BEDE   BY G ELIOT
921 P8716H   ADAM CLAYTON POWELL, POLITICS OF RACE   BY N HICKEY
             ADAM IN
808.82 CL   WORLD DRAMA, VOL 1 BY B H CLARK

572.994 SI   ADAM IN OCHRE, ABORIGINAL AUSTRALIA   BY C SIMPSON
330.153 PI   ADAM SMITH, FATHER OF SCIENCE OF ECONOMICS   BY E R PIKE
             ADAM THE CREATOR   BY K CAPEK IN
808.82 MO   DRAMAS OF MODERNISM AND THEIR FORERUNNERS BY M J MOSES
221.93 CO   ADAM TO DANIEL   BY G CORNFELD

973.4 AL   ADAMS AND JEFFERSON   BY J M ALLISON
M   ADAMS CASE   BY M UNDERWOOD
920 AD   ADAMS FAMILY   BY J T ADAMS
             ADAMS OF THE BOUNTY   BY E WILSON
574.52 WA   ADAPTATION   BY B WALLACE

613.7 DA   ADAPTED PHYSICAL EDUCATION   BY A S DANIELS
SS   ADD A DASH OF PITY   BY P USTINOV
618.97 BO   ADD LIFE TO YOUR YEARS   BY E P BOAS
M   ADDERS ON THE HEATH   BY G MITCHELL
301.47686 WA ADDICT   BY D WAKEFIELD

Title Catalog

ADMINISTRATIVE REMEDIES
  328.345 GE   OMBUDSMEN AND OTHERS   BY W GELLHORN
  353 GE   WHEN AMERICANS COMPLAIN   BY W GELLHORN

ADMIRALS
  J R 920 CO   FAMOUS GENERALS AND ADMIRALS   BY R P COFFMAN

ADOBE
  693.22 SO   BUILD WITH ADOBE   BY M SOUTHWICK

ADOLESCENCE
  SEE ALSO   YOUTH.   BOYS
  155.5 WI   ADOLESCENCE AND DISCIPLINE   BY R M WITTENBERG
  155.5 LA   ADOLESCENCE AND YOUTH   BY P H LANDIS
  155.5 BA   ADOLESCENT AGGRESSION   BY A BANDURA
  155.5 HU   ADOLESCENT DEVELOPMENT   BY E B HURLOCK
  301.4315 KO ADOLESCENT GIRL IN CONFLICT   BY G KONOPKA
  155.5 HA   ADOLESCENT PERSONALITY AND BEHAVIOR   BY S R HATHAWAY
  301.431 CO   ADOLESCENT SOCIETY   BY J S COLEMAN
  155.5 ST   ADOLESCENT VIEWS HIMSELF   BY R M STRANG
  155.5 WA   ADOLESCENT YEARS   BY W W WATTENBERG
  155.5 SC   ADOLESCENTS CHALLENGE OF MATURITY   BY A A SCHNEIDERS
  155.5 RE   AMERICAN TEENAGER   BY M H REMMERS
  301.42 LA   ANN LANDERS SAYS TRUTH IS STRANGER   BY A LANDERS
  155.4 ST   CHILDHOOD AND ADOLESCENCE   BY L J STONE
  155.4 MA   CHILDREN AND ADOLESCENTS   BY B R MCCANDLESS
  301.427 FR   CHILDREN AND THEIR PARENTS   BY S S FREMON
  155.5 FR   COMING OF AGE IN AMERICA   BY E Z FRIEDENBERG

Subject Catalog

Austin Public Library, Children's Books

ABORIGINES
  SEE AFRICA - NATIVE RACES. ANTHROPOLOGY. BUSHMEN
  NATIVE RACES. NORTH AMERICA - ANTIQUITIES

ACADIANS
J 976.3 TA   EVANGELINE AND THE ACADIANS BY R TALLANT

ACTING
J 792.028 SC FIRST BOOK OF ACTING BY K SCHUON

ACTORS AND ACTRESSES
J J 921 SI13D ACTRESS SARAH SIDDONS BY L DELATORRE
J J 921 R633K BOYS LIFE OF WILL ROGERS BY H KEITH
J J 920 WA   FAMOUS AMERICAN ACTORS AND ACTRESSES BY F WAGNER

Subject Catalog

J 973 SL   A E C BOOK OF EARLY AMERICANA BY E SLOANE
E G   A E C BUNNY BY W GAG
E G   A E C HUNT BY I GORDON

J   A E C MOLLY BY J RIETVELD
E A   A E C OF CARS AND TRUCKS BY A ALEXANDER
J 636.7 BA A E C OF DOG CARE FOR YOUNG OWNERS BY C BAKER
J 736.9 SA A E C OF ORIGAMI BY C SARASAS
E M   A E C. AN ALPHABET BOOK BY T MATTHIESEN

J J R 540 GA A E CS OF CHEMISTRY BY R A GALLANT
J 540 GA   A E CS OF CHEMISTRY BY R A GALLANT
E D   A FOR THE ARK BY R A DUVOISIN
J 611 CC   A IS FOR ANATOMY BY M COSGROVE
E T   A IS FOR ANNABELLE BY T TUDOR

Title Catalog

USING THE BOOK CATALOG

If you know the title —

> The title catalog is arranged alphabetically by
> the first important word in the title of the
> books. Each title in the children's collection is
> listed with the following information:

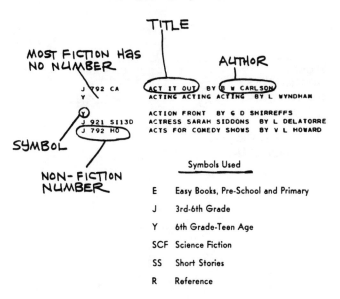

Symbols Used

E — Easy Books, Pre-School and Primary

J — 3rd-6th Grade

Y — 6th Grade-Teen Age

SCF — Science Fiction

SS — Short Stories

R — Reference

Children's **FICTION** Is On The Shelf By Last Name Of Author

Children's **NON-FICTION** Is On The Shelf By Number

USING THE BOOK CATALOG

If you know the title —

> The title catalog is arranged alphabetically by
> the first important word in the title of the
> books. Each title in the adult collection is
> listed with the following information:

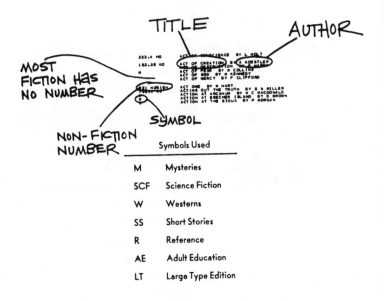

Symbols Used	
M	Mysteries
SCF	Science Fiction
W	Westerns
SS	Short Stories
R	Reference
AE	Adult Education
LT	Large Type Edition

Adult NON-FICTION Books Are Arranged
On The Shelves By Number

Adult FICTION Books Are Arranged On The Shelves
By Last Name Of Author

FARMINGDALE PUBLIC SCHOOLS

Farmingdale, New York 11735

Title: Catalog of the Junior High School Libraries

Characteristics

Page Size: 10 x 13 inches

Format: 2-column, fixed field arrangement. Author, title, and subject lists are "title-a-liners"; classed list contains more information.

Arrangement: The catalog provides separate subject, title, author, and class lists. The class list gives the most complete information about a book, and arranges the books in the same order in which they appear on the shelves (non-fiction according to the Dewey Decimal Classification System; the biographies alphabetically by biographee, and the fiction alphabetically by author).

Description: The catalog consists of Farmingdale's three junior high school library collections. In addition to books, the catalog includes the district's films, housed in the District Audio-Visual Office; filmstrips, slides, and transparencies housed at the Howitt Junior High School; and recordings housed in the respective libraries. The letter and number following each filmstrip title denotes its specific location in the filmstrip cabinet in the Howitt Junior High School AV office.

The classed-order list contains the following information: author, full title, illustration information, date, publisher, pagination, reading level, and location. The author and title lists contains author, title, date, and location; the subject section includes author, title, and date.

Upper case computer printout is used.

Method of Production

Data processing machinery was used to make the first edition of the catalog; the second edition was computer-produced. (See Harris, Jessica, "Programming the Library Catalog," pages 346-356).

Frequency of Issue

Two editions of the catalog were produced.   It has
been discontinued.

Catalog of the Junior High School Libraries,
Farmingdale Public Schools, Jan. 1968

```
HELLMUTH JEROME          WOLF IN THE FAMILY
    IL                            NEW AMER 1964   186P.   J    L
HOGNER DOROTHY           ANIMAL BOOK  AMERICAN MAMMALS
    BY...+ NILS HOGNER  IL          OXFORD   1942   223P.   J    H
HOKE HELEN               FIRST BOOK OF TROPICAL MAMMALS
    ILLUS                         WATTS     1958    62P.  IJ       X
JOHNSON GAYLORD          STORY OF ANIMALS  MAMMALS AROUND THE WORLD
                                  HARVEY    1958   120P.  IJ    HL
LEMMON ROBERT STELL      ALL ABOUT MONKEYS
    IL BY JEAN ZALLINGER  ALLABOUT BOOKS  RANDOM   1958   144P.  IJ    HL
LEMMON ROBERT S          JUNIOR SCIENCE BOOK OF BIG CATS
    ILLUS                         GARRARD   1962    64P.   J       X
LIERS EMIL ERNEST        BEAVERS STORY
    IL BY RAY SHERIN              VIKING    1958   192P.  IJ    H X
```

Class List

```
JUNIOR SCIENCE BOOK OF LIGHT               FERAVOLO  ROCCO V    61   X   535
JUNIOR SCIENCE BOOK OF WATER EXPERIMENTS   FERAVOLO  ROCCO V    65   X   532
JUNIOR SCIENCE BOOK OF HEAT                FERAVOLO  ROCCO V    64   X   536
JUNIOR SCIENCE BOOK OF ELECTRICITY         FERAVOLO  ROCCO V    60   X   537
JUNIOR SCIENCE BOOK OF MAGNETS             FERAVOLO  ROCCO V    60   X   538
JUNIOR SCIENCE BOOK OF RAIN HAIL SLEET +   LARRICK NANCY        61   X   551.5
JUNIOR SCIENCE BOOK OF VOLCANOES           LAJBER PATRICIA      65   X   551
JUNIOR SCIENCE BOOK OF ICEBERGS + GLACIERS LAJBER PATRICIA      61   X   551.4
JUNIOR SCIENCE BOOK OF BIG CATS            LEMMON ROBERT S      62   X   599
JUNIOR SCIENCE BOOK OF BACTERIA            LIETZ GERALD S       64   X   589
```

Title List

```
CATS                                 636.8
    BRONSON WILFRID S      CATS                                       50   636.8
    BEEBE B F              OCELOT                                     66   599
    GALLICO PAUL W         SILENT MIAOW, MANUAL FOR KITTENS STRAYS 64 636.8
    LEMMON ROBERT S        JUNIOR SCIENCE BOOK OF BIG CATS            62   599
    WHITNEY LEON F         COMPLETE BOOK OF CAT CARE                  53   636.8
    ZIM HERBERT SPENCER    BIG CATS                                   55   599

CATS - FICTION
    BELTING NATALIA MAREE  CAT TALES                                  59   398.2
    BAKER MARGARET J       CASTLE AND SIXPENCE                        51   F    B
    COBLENTZ CATHERINE     BLUE CAT OF CASTLE TOWN                    49   F    C
```

Subject List

```
AVF        FILMS

   COL S PG1        ABOUT THE HUMAN BODY
                                             15MN    IJ
   COL S PG1        ADAPTATION OF PLANTS AND ANIMALS
                                             14MN    IJ
   B+W S PG1        ADVENTURES OF BUNNY RABBIT
                                              1 MN   P
   B+W S PG1        AGE OF DISCOVERY - ENG FREN + DUTCH EXPL
                                              1 MN     JS
   B+W S PG1        AGE OF DISCOV - SPANISH + PORTUGESE EXPL
                                              1 MN     JS
   B+W S PG1        AIR ALL AROUND US
                                             11MN    IJ
   B+W S PG2        AIRPLANE TRIP
```

Films

BLACKTOWN MUNICIPAL LIBRARY

Flushcombe Road
Blacktown, NSW, 2148
Australia

Title: Catalogue; Books held in the Library as at March
          1967.

"Blacktown Municipal Library was opened to the public
only in April, 1967.   The Municipal Library serves a rapidly growing population (104,000 in 1965, now estimated at
125,000) and it is because of its present and anticipated
size and the likelihood of having, ultimately, a number of
branch libraries, that I persuaded my Council to settle on
a printed catalogue from the outset, thus avoiding the expense of a changeover later."[1]

Characteristics

Page Size: 9-1/2 x 13 inches

Format: 2-column

Arrangement: The catalog is divided into three
separately-bound sections: Author, title and subject catalogs.
Both junior and adult catalogs are published.

Description: The catalog lists book on hand at the
date of the first opening of the library.   Entries include
author, title, and classification number.   Edition is indicated
if the book is not a first edition.   Books in important series
are listed alphabetically by author under the series title in
the title catalog, as well as in the author catalog, directly
under the author's name.   The subject catalog is arranged
by subject, then alphabetically by author under the subject.
"See" and "See also" references are included.   Upper-case
computer printout is used.   Reference books are not listed
in the catalog.

Method of Production

The catalogs are produced with the aid of a 360-40 computer.   The text of the main catalogs is photoreduced 70 percent, but the supplements are printed directly onto continuous
paper.   "I.B.M. looks after every aspect of production--
we receive the catalogues ready for use."[2]

Frequency of Issue

Three supplements have been issued. A new edition of the main catalog and cumulating supplements are planned.

Costs

A $10,000 was estimated as the cost of a new edition of the main catalog, plus 3 quarterly cumulating supplements, plus 2 extraction lists for 1969, but the catalog was not printed.

Comments

"Another fact worth mentioning is that we receive only 5 copies of Supplements and extraction lists, but our contract with I.B.M. provides for 120 copies of each edition of the Junior volumes (Author, Title and Subject) and 90 of each of the 3 adult volumes. This is to enable us to distribute copies of the catalogues to all local primary schools (Junior catalogue) and high schools (Adult and Junior catalogues), and the Adult catalogue to all Sydney metropolitan libraries, of which there are 29."[3]

Notes

1, 2, 3. Communication from W.A.C. Dalte, Town Clerk, Blacktown Municipal Council, Feb. 13, 1969.

Blacktown Municipal Library
March, 1967

590   DILLON, LAWRENCE S. AND DILLON,
                    ELIZABETH S.
                    PRINCIPLES OF ANIMAL BIOLOGY. MACMILLAN,
                    1965
                    (PORTIONS OF THIS BOOK PREVIOUSLY APPEARED
                    UNDER THE TITLE 'THE SCIENCE OF LIFE').

796.357   DIMAGGIO, JOE
                    BASEBALL FOR EVERYONE: A TREASURY OF BASE-
                    BALL LORE AND INSTRUCTION FOR FANS AND
                    PLAYERS. MCGRAW, 1948

                DIMINNO, NICHOLAS
                    THE GENTLE MARTYRDOM OF BROTHER BERTRAM.

372.5   →   DIMMACK, MAX

Adult Author Catalog

                MODERN ALGEBRA: FIRST COURSE.
512   JOHNSON, RICHARD E. (AND OTHERS)

                A MODERN ANALYTIC GEOMETRY.
516   EDGETT, G.L. (AND OTHERS)

           →   MODERN ART EDUCATION IN THE PRIMARY
                    SCHOOL. 2ND ED.
372.5   DIMMACK, MAX

                MODERN AUSTRALIAN AND NEW ZEALAND TRAINS.
Q385.0994   SHENNEN, FRANK (ED.)

                MODERN AUSTRALIAN PAINTING.
F759.994   FINLEY, DONALD J.

Adult Title Catalog

                ♦   ART - STUDY AND TEACHING

Q707   BERGER, RENE
                    THE LANGUAGE OF ART. THAMES, 1963
Q707   CANADAY, JOHN
                    LOOK, OR THE KEYS TO ART. METHUEN, 1962
372.5   DIMMACK, MAX
           →   MODERN ART EDUCATION IN THE PRIMARY
                    SCHOOL. 2ND ED. MACMILLAN, 1960
707   ORBAN, DESIDERIUS
                    A LAYMAN'S GUIDE TO CREATIVE ART. 2ND ED.
                    EDWARDS, 1960
707   READ, HERBERT
                    ART AND EDUCATION. CHESHIRE, 1964
Q707   SILVA, ANIL DE AND SIMSON, OTTO VON (EDS.)

Adult Subject Catalog

LIBRARY OF THE MEDICAL SCIENCES
SCHOOL OF MEDICINE, UNIVERSITY OF NEW MEXICO

Albuquerque, New Mexico

Characteristics

Size: 6 x 9 inches

Format: 2-column

Arrangement: The book catalog consists of three sections: Section 1, Author and Name Catalog; Section 2, Title Catalog; and Section 3, Subject Catalog.

Description: The Author and Name Catalog, Section 1, is arranged in strict letter-by-letter alphabetical order. The Title Catalog is also alphabetized letter-by-letter. Since each entry in the catalog is a unit entry, it is necessary to look down to the title line of the unit entry to locate the alphabetizing word or words. In case of added title entries, the title is inserted between the author and normal title. Section 3, Subject Catalog, is arranged alphabetically by subject headings, and roughly alphabetically by author within subject headings.

All upper-case letters are used. The 1965 catalog consisted of 676 pages.

Method of Production

The copy for this catalog was produced on the IBM 1401 computer housed in the University of New Mexico Data Processing Center. The library's staff participated in the task of pasting up the sheets preparatory for photo offset production of the catalog by the University of New Mexico printing plant.

Frequency

This 1965 catalog represented the third year's cataloging of books and monographs of the library. It was planned that one additional supplementary catalog would be produced for 1966. A five year cumulation was planned for the following year. Temporary updating of the catalog was planned as a monthly short title book list, and a six month short title catalog. The 1966 edition was prepared, but

never published. As reported by the librarian, "the primary reason for not producing later editions was because we
expected that the file would be placed on an on-line computer
terminal program within a short time. We have, however,
had financial problems that have precluded the operation of
the on-line terminal programs even though they are ready."[1]

Comments:

"The 1966 edition, had it been printed, would have
shown less white space since white space increases the number of pages and thus the cost of printing. The entry would
have looked much like an LC card entry. New programs
were written to produce the 1966 edition. These were for
use on the IBM System 360 Model 40 256K Computer. With
the larger computer we solved the column overflow problem
and largely relieved the filing problem. These two factors
had caused us some problems on the two earlier catalogs and
had necessitated some modification while pasting up for offset photography."[2]

Notes

1. Communication from Robert T. Divett, Librarian,
       September 8, 1969.

2. Ibid.

Library of the Medical Sciences
School of Medicine, The University of New Mexico
Book Catalog, 1965 (Published 1966)

WE /0300/R 74/965   03004

➤ ROTSTEIN, JEROME

SIMPLE SPLINTING. USE OF LIGHT SPLINTS
AND RELATED CONSERVATIVE THERAPY IN
JOINT DISEASES. FOREWORD BY JEROME S.
TOBIS. WITH CHAPTER ON HISTORY OF THE
TREATMENT OF ARTHRITIS. BY LAURA S.
ROTSTEIN. PHOTOGRAPHY BY WARREN COOPER.
PHILADELPHIA, SAUNDERS, 1965.

126 P. ILLUS. 27 CM.

Author Catalog

WE /0300/R 74/965   03004

ROTSTEIN, JEROME

➤ SIMPLE SPLINTING. USE OF LIGHT SPLINTS
AND RELATED CONSERVATIVE THERAPY IN
JOINT DISEASES. FOREWORD BY JEROME S.
TOBIS. WITH CHAPTER ON HISTORY OF THE
TREATMENT OF ARTHRITIS. BY LAURA S.
ROTSTEIN. PHOTOGRAPHY BY WARREN COOPER.
PHILADELPHIA, SAUNDERS, 1965.

126 P. ILLUS. 27 CM.

Title Catalog

ARTHRITIS-HISTORY

WE /0300/R 74/965   03004

➤ ROTSTEIN, JEROME

SIMPLE SPLINTING. USE OF LIGHT SPLINTS
AND RELATED CONSERVATIVE THERAPY IN
JOINT DISEASES. FOREWORD BY JEROME S.
TOBIS. WITH CHAPTER ON HISTORY OF THE
TREATMENT OF ARTHRITIS. BY LAURA S.
ROTSTEIN. PHOTOGRAPHY BY WARREN COOPER.
PHILADELPHIA, SAUNDERS, 1965.

126 P. ILLUS. 27 CM.

ARTHRITIS, JUVENILE RHEUMATOID

WS /0270/G 89/962   02695

GROKOEST, ALBERT W.   1917-

JUVENILE RHEUMATOID ARTHRITIS, BY ALBERT
W. GROKOEST ET AL.
BOSTON, LITTLE, BRUWN, 1962.

120 P. ILLUS. 24 CM.

Subject Catalog

NORTH CENTRAL REGIONAL LIBRARY

310 Douglas Street
Wenatchee, Washington, 98801

Characteristics

  Size: 8-1/2 x 11 inches

  Format: 2 columns

  The catalog is produced by the Washington State
Library.

  "The catalog for the North Central Regional Library
is published every two months, cumulating all titles purchased for that library from April 1967 on. They have, in
addition a base catalog of titles up through 1962, revised
for deletions in 1966, and a supplement from 1963 to March
1967. The volumes have adult and juvenile sections, each
with author, title, and subject divisions. Input is on
punched cards, one set being punched for each title. The
set consists of author cards, title cards and data cards,
with subject heading and "see" reference cards produced
when necessary. Author, title, and subject data elements
are handled as variable length fields. The data base is on
magnetic tape, a separate tape being kept for author, titles,
and subjects. The computer programs were written in 1401
Autocoder, and are presently being run on an IBM 360 Mod.
30.

  "Proper filing sequence is maintained by assignment
of author, title, and subject codes. These are 8-position
numeric codes, updated manually by coding clerks.

  "Printing of the original is done on an IBM 1400-
series printer in single-column format on a 14-inch page.
The pages are pasted to make a double-column sheet and
then photo-reduced to an 8-1/2 x 11 inch Ektolith master
from which the offset printing is done. Fifty copies are
produced on each run, with additional copies for twice-
yearly distribution to schools. We do our printing in-house,
and avoid the delay and expense of binding by using McBee
swing hinge binders for the updated catalog. Permanent
catalogs are bound in 200 pound tag cover stock with cloth
spines.

  "Costs are shown for fiscal year 1968:

The only EDP equipment we have in-house is one 029 keypunch and a number 059 verifier. The necessary manipulation of the punched cards was done for us on an hourly basis at $7.50 an hour. IBM 1401 computer charges were $60.00 an hour, including operator's time.

Costs for key punching, verifying, and correction of the data base averaged $0.515 per title. This consists of a complete set of cards punched for one book (approximately six cards per title). It is high because, unfortunately, the correction routines are mostly manual and are included in this cost.

"All EDP costs are calculated on the number of times an access point is manipulated by the machine. A book will have several access points--one title, one or more in authors, one or more in subject. Depending on when a book is input, the machines will manipulate each entry from one to six times a year. Average cost per entry is $0.042.

"We calculate printing costs differently. These include everything from pasting up the sheets for the photo-reproduction to packaging the volumes for shipping. These are determined by multiplying the number of access points in the catalog times the number of volumes printed (in the case of North Central Regional Library, 50), and dividing this into total expenses. The cost of printing one entry calculated in this manner is an average of $0.012.

N.C.R.L. Production Costs

	UNIT	TOTAL UNITS	COST
Keypunch	title	total titles entered	.515
E.D.P.	access points	access points x runs	.042
Printing	access points	access points x runs x volumes printed	.012

"The Washington State Library also produces a book catalog, on a contract basis, for the Timberland Regional

Library.   Methods of production are quite similar to those
for North Central, except that there is little use made of a
computer.   It is used only to reproduce cards for the title
and subject catalogs.   All the cards are then sorted and
listed on an IBM 407 electric accounting machine.

"The Timberland catalog uses an author card, a
title card, and a collation card, again with subject headings
and "see" references punched when necessary.   As on
NCRL, all entries are variable length.

"The Timberland Library has a published data base
of titles and authors purchased for the library through 1963.
The base catalog for subjects was not produced until 1966,
and includes subject listings for all books purchased through
1966.   There is a published title and author 1964-'66 supplement, and a title, author, and subject supplement for
1967-'68/ We are cumulating the 1969 supplement every
two months and furnish a biweekly list, in title order, of
the books processed between cumulations.   A sample of
the latest catalog is enclosed.

"Costs for the Timberland catalog are a little
different:

T. R. L. Production Costs

	UNIT	TOTAL UNITS	COST
Keypunch	title	total titles	. 850
E. D. P.	access points	access points x runs	. 014
Printing	access points	access points x runs x volumes printed	. 00042

"In the near future we hope to be able to completely
revise our production of these two catalogs.   We plan to
use the MARC distribution service tapes and input only for
those books not entered on MARC.   Numeric coding will be
eliminated.   The experimental catalog which we produced
during the MARC Pilot Project is described in the MARC
Pilot Project: Final Report.   (Library of Congress,
1968). "[1]

Note

1. Communication from Mrs. Jeanette M. Whitcher,
    Systems Analyst, Washington State Library, Olympia,
    November 26, 1969.

North Central Regional Library
Supplement, April 1967-July 1969

CAIDIN, MARTIN.
940.5449 FLYING FORTS.
            MEREDITH, 1968. 516P ILLUS.

➤ CAILLEUX, ANDRE.
    550   ANATOMY OF THE EARTH.
               MCGRAW, 1968. 255P ILLUS. WORLD
               UNIVERSITY LIBRARY

    575   THREE BILLION YEARS OF LIFE.
               STEIN, 1969. 239P ILLUS.

CAILLOU, ALAN   SEE   LYLE-SMYTHE, ALAN.

CAIN, JAMES MALLAHAN.
            CAIN X 3.
            KNOPF, 1969.
            CONTENTS. -POSTMAN ALWAYS RINGS TWICE. -
                   Adult Authors

    ANATOMY OF CAPTIVITY.
       365.45   LAFFIN, JOHN.

➤   ANATOMY OF THE EARTH.
       550   CAILLEUX, ANDRE.

    ANATOMY OF THE SS STATF.
       943.086 INSTITUT FUR ZEITGESCHICHTE, MUNICH.

    ANCIENT CHINA FROM THE BEGINNINGS TO THE
    FMPIRF.
       951   GERNET, JACQUES.

    AND OTHER DIRTY STORIES.
       818.54   KING, LARRY L.
                   Adult Titles

  DWELLINGS
     647   DOWD, MERLE E.
               HOW TO GET MORE FOR YOUR MONEY IN RUNNING
               YOUR HOME.
               PARKER, 1968. 263P ILLUS.

  DWELLINGS - REMODELING
     643.7   DAY, RICHARD.
               REMODELING ROOMS, WALLS, FLOORS, CEILINGS.
               ARCO, 1968. 111P ILLUS.

➤ EARTH
     550   CAILLEUX, ANDRE.
               ANATOMY OF THE EARTH.
               MCGRAW, 1968. 255P ILLUS. WORLD
               UNIVERSITY LIBRARY

     551   PHILLIPS, OWEN M.
               HEART OF THE EARTH.
               FREEMAN, 1968. 236P ILLUS.
                   Adult Subjects

North Central Regional Library
Supplement, April 1967 - July 1969

TAYLOR, SYDNEY.   21470000
    J   PAPA LIKE EVERYONE ELSE. 1966.

TEE-VAN, HELEN D.   21480000
    J599   SMALL MAMMALS ARE WHERE YOU FIND THEM.
                1966.

TERHUNE, ALFRED P.   21510000
    J   BRUCE. 1920.

TERZIAN, KATHRYN.   21547500
    JB--CUR   GLENN CURTISS, PIONEER PILOT. 1966.

➤THOMPSON, ELIZABETH B.   21620000
    J960   AFRICA, PAST AND PRESENT. 1966.

Juvenile Authors

J591.929   ADVENTURES WITH FRESHWATER   00555000
            ANIMALS.   HEADSTROM, BIRGER R.   1964.

J398.2   AESOPS FABLES.   NEW TR. BY V. S.   00565000
            VERNON JONES.   AESOPUS.   1968.

J398.2   AESOPS FABLES.   LARGE TYPE FOR   00570000
            LIMITED VISION.   AESOPUS.

J960   ➤   AFRICA, PAST AND PRESENT.   00575000
            THOMPSON, ELIZABETH B.   1966.

J569   AFTER THE DINOSAURS.   GREENE,   00615000
            CARLA.   1968.

J   AGATON SAX AND THE DIAMOND   00630000
            THIEVES.   FRANZEN, NILS-OLOF.   1967.

Juvenile Titles

AFRICA - FICTION   0004450
    J   PRICE, WILLARD D.   GORILLA ADVENTURE.
            1969.

AFRICA - JUVENILE LITERATURE   0004660
    J960 ➤ THOMPSON, ELIZABETH B.   AFRICA, PAST AND
            PRESENT.   1966.

AFRICA, SUB-SAHARAN   0005350
    J916.703 KIMBLE, GEORGE H.   TROPICAL AFRICA
              TODAY.   1966.

AGASSIZ, LOUIS   0005431
    JB--AGA   PEARE, CATHERINE O.   SCIENTIST OF TWO
              WORLDS--LOUIS AGASSIZ.   1958.

AIR - POLLUTION - U. S.   0007000
    J628.5097 LEWIS, ALFRED.   CLEAN THE AIR.
              1965.

Juvenile Subjects

Timberland Regional Library
Supplement, January-August 1969

GOLDSTON, ROBERT C.
914.672   BARCELONA--THE CIVIC STAGE, A PORTRAIT
          IN URBAN CIVILIZATION.
          MACMILLAN, 1969.   199P   ILLUS.

914.2103 LONDON--THE CIVIC SPIRIT.
          MACMILLAN, 1969.   211P   ILLUS.

973.0974 NEGRO REVOLUTION.
          MACMILLAN, 1968.   247P   ILLUS,

GOLDTHWAITE, EATON K.
          ONCE YOU STOP, YOURE DEAD.
          MORROW, 1968.

Authors

NATURAL HISTORY.
    574.074   HELLMAN, GEOFFREY THEODORE.

BARBARA HUTTON, A CANDID BIOGRAPHY.
    B917.3039 JENNINGS, DEAN SOUTHERN.

BARCELONA--THE CIVIC STAGE, A PORTRAIT
IN URBAN CIVILIZATION.
    914.672   GOLDSTON, ROBERT C.

BARLOWS KINGDOM.
          REDGATE, JOHN.

BARNSTORMERS, FLYING DAREDEVILS OF THE
ROARING TWENTIES.
    797.5409 DWIGGINS, DON.

Titles

BARBECUE COOKERY
    641.578   HARWOOD, PAISLEY.
              GOURMET AT THE GRILL.
              DOUBLEDAY, 1969.   135P

BARCELONA
    914.672   GOLDSTON, ROBERT C.
              BARCELONA--THE CIVIC STAGE, A PORTRAIT
              IN URBAN CIVILIZATION.
              MACMILLAN, 1969.   199P   ILLUS.

BASEBALL
    796.3572 LISS, HOWARD.
              FATHER AND SON BASEBALL BOOK, THE ABCS
              OF COACHING AND PLAYING.
              HARPER, 1969.   144P   ILLUS.

Subjects

MONTGOMERY COUNTY, MARYLAND
DEPARTMENT OF PUBLIC LIBRARIES

6400 Democracy Boulevard
Bethesda, Maryland 20034

Characteristics

Size: 8-1/2 x 11 inches

Format: 2-column

Arrangement: The catalog is issued in three
separate volumes: Subject, Author, and Title.

Description: In the author catalog, items are listed
alphabetically by authors, editors, compilers, joint authors,
and by titles of books for which there is no author. Works
of fiction are designated FICTION, MYSTERY, or SHORT
STORIES. For non-fiction, classification numbers appear
at the right of each entry. In the title catalog, books are
listed alphabetically by the first word of the title. In the
subject catalog, subjects are displayed in alphabetic sequence.
Under subjects, entries are listed alphabetically by author.
Cross references to related subjects are included. Symbols
show location of books at 17 locations. Complete bibliographic information is presented in the author and subject
catalogs; an abbreviated entry is found in the title section.
All upper case letters are used.

It is estimated that there are 69,000 entries in the
adult catalog for monographs, as well as 620 periodicals
and 400 telephone books. The Children's Catalog lists
8,300 titles.[1] A catalog for phonographic recordings is
being prepared. It will list recordings by composer, per-
former, title and subject in a divided catalog form. About
8,000 entries will be included. Supplements will be printed
no oftener than semi-annually with a cumulation of total
holdings about once in eighteen months.

Characteristics Peculiar to Montgomery County's
Computer-Produced Book Catalog:[2]

The advantages of a computer-produced book catalog
are many. The catalog can be reproduced in multiple copies
and cumulated frequently at a relatively low cost. Input
is reduced to a minimum since one small set of punched

cards can be manipulated to produce entries in all catalogs.
Typing and hand filing of catalog cards, both at Central
and in the branches is eliminated. Since thousands of sets
of catalog cards do not need to be typed in the Cataloging
and Preparations Section, many more books can be prepared
and sent out by a relatively small staff. The very obvious
advantage of having a catalog showing <u>every</u> branch's holdings
cannot be overlooked. This would be impossible if card
catalogs were used. In addition, special lists can be produced from information stored on tape--the Children's Services replacement order list is an example of this.

We have made every effort to produce as useful and
logical a catalog as possible. Certain adjustments, however,
have had to be made, and it is hoped that we can point out
some of these to you and help you use the catalog to the
greatest advantage.

<u>FORMAT</u>

Since this is a divided catalog; author, subject, and
title in separated volumes, there are some differences, in
comparison with a card catalog, to be noted.

    1.   <u>Author entry</u>
        In the author catalog, an author's name is
        listed only once, no matter how many of his
        works are shown. His books are listed alpha-
        betically by title under the one name entry.
        This is also true for corporate authors.

    2.   <u>Subject entry</u>
        In the subject catalog, works are listed alpha-
        betically by author and title under the appro-
        priate subject with the author's name repeated
        if he has written more than one book on that
        subject. Full bibliographical information is
        given here as well as in the author catalog.

    3.   <u>Title entry</u>
        a.   The title entry is as brief as possible,
             giving only title and author, e.g. <u>Cream</u>
             <u>Hill</u>, by L. S. Gannett. If the book has
             been entered under a corporate author, the
             title entry has the following form:
             <u>Domestic architecture of England during</u>
             <u>the Tudor period.</u> -- Boston architectural

club (the corporate author). A book
entered under title in the author catalog
shows only the title in the title catalog.

b.   All books with title main entry are listed
in the author catalog as well as in the
title catalog. Each title entry is preceded
by a brief title followed by ... (This is in
the author position and recognized by the
computer as the main entry). e.g.
Dance World ...
Dance world, ed. by J. Willis. Crown
1966-

c.   When there are several titles beginning
with the same word or words, this key
entry is repeated only once, as in an
author. e.g.
Encyclopedia ...
Encyclopaedia Britannica
Encyclopaedia of the arts
Encyclopedia Americana
Encyclopedia of chemical technology
Please note, however, that under En-
cyclopedia ... the various works are filed
alphabetically as spelled.

d.   There are many more title entries in a
divided catalog than a dictionary card
catalog. Titles of all books are listed
in the title catalog except for those titles
beginning with such phrases as: "Collected
works", "Collected poems" (tales,
stories, etc.), "Poems" (tales, stories),
"Selected poems" (works, tales, etc.).
For each one of this type of heading
there is a note which reads as follows:
Collected stories ...
For titles beginning "Collected
stories" see entries under individual
author.

4.   Autobiographies and biographies
Since we have a divided catalog, it was
decided to give a subject heading to the
subject of autobiographies as well as
biographies (this is not usually done in a card

catalog). A title entry is given for all
biographies and autobiographies.

5. Editions

    When we own several editions of a work, all
    editions are listed in the author catalog, but in
    the subject and title catalogs only one edition
    is listed. This is usually the latest edition.
    The entry in subject and title catalogs is fol-
    lowed by a note which reads: "For other edi-
    tions, see author catalog."

6. Punctuation

    Punctuation is limited, in that certain punctua-
    tion marks are not on the computer print drum
    and so cannot be used. These include paren-
    theses, question mark, colon, and semicolon.
    A dash has been substituted for a colon, a com-
    ma for a semi-colon, and dashes or commas
    for parentheses. Since there is nothing to sub-
    stitute for a question mark, such books as
    "Where did you go?" "Out" and Where's Annie?
    are punctuated by a period. (We do have
    quotes!)

7. See references

    There have been many see references for both
    authors and subjects included in the author and
    subject catalogs. However, none will be listed
    in both bound catalog and supplement. Duplica-
    tion is not feasible and would confuse the
    computer when we cumulate the two! In view
    of this, it is necessary to consult bound and
    supplement catalogs when a see reference is
    sought. See also references are also included
    although at this time in not as great a number.
    The composing of see also references is a
    complicated and time-consuming task and we
    have not yet had time to complete it. We
    anticipate that in the next year we shall be able
    to do many more of these.

8. Telephone Directories

    These are listed in author, subject and title
    catalogs in the following manner:

    a.   In the author catalog all are listed under
the heading Telephone directory... and then
arranged alphabetically under the name of
the first place listed on the directory itself.
e. g.

       Telephone directory...

         Abilene, Tex., telephone directory
         Anne Arundel Co., Md., telephone
           directory, including Annapolis,
           Armiger, Bay Ridge (etc.)
         Augusta, Ga., North Augusta, S. C.,
           and Hephzibah, Ga., telephone
           directory
         Augusta-Gardiner area, Me., telephone
           directory

    b.   In the subject catalog, every directory is
listed under the name of appropriate state,
so that all New Jersey telephone directories
may be found under subject heading: NEW
JERSEY - DIRECTORIES - TELEPHONE.
When a directory is for one city, or area,
there is also an entry for the city or area.
e. g. NEWARK, N. J. - DIRECTORIES -
TELEPHONE; ANNE ARUNDEL CO., MD. -
DIRECTORIES - TELEPHONE.

    c.   In the title catalog, telephone directories
are listed alphabetically as the title is
given on the directory itself. There is not
an entry for every small town listed on these
directories, but since all are listed under
the state, we hope they can be found
relatively easily.

9. Periodicals

    Periodicals are listed only in the title and sub-
ject catalogs. Subjects are used for all
periodicals whose subject content is confined to
one or two subjects, such as:

       Education - Periodicals
       Physics - Periodicals

FILING

    Certain adjustments necessitated by the characteristics
of a computer have been necessary.

1. Names beginning with Mac and Mc, which are
   traditionally interfiled in a card catalog, are
   filed in a strictly alphabetical order here, as
   follows:
   >MacArthur
   Macauley
   Mac Fall
   Macy
   Madrid
   Mahoney
   Mann
   Maryland
   Mboya
   Mc Adam
   McWhirter
   Meacham

2. If a name begins with a prefix, such as, Da, De,
   Di, La, Le, Van, etc. the prefex is treated
   as a separate word and will be filed at the beginning of the De's, Da's, La's as the case may
   be, in the following order:

De Costa, Phil	La Bree
Dabbs, James	La Sorte
Daniels	Laas
De Antonio	Lane
De Rochemont	Le Carre'
Dean	Le May
Dewey	Lea
Di Donato	Leary
Diat	Lewin

3. In the author catalog, U.S. is filed as initials at
   the beginning of the U's. However, in the subject catalog, where subject headings are arranged by subject code number we are able to
   control filing, and these U.S. subject headings
   are filed in the traditional manner--as though
   U.S. were spelled out. This is true of other
   names which are filed peculiarly in the author
   catalog.

4. Alphabetizing of titles is done on the basis of the
   first sixteen letters (including spaces) and the
   initial letters of the next four words. This
   usually is sufficient for proper filing but there are
   exceptions as can be seen in the following example:

How to raise and train an afghan
How to raise and train a collie
How to raise and train a Cairn terrier
How to raise and train a chihuahua
How to raise and train a great dane
How to raise and train a German shepherd

This filing limitation also holds true in the author catalog where we have such arrangements as:

U.S. President's Commission
U.S. President's Council
U.S. President's Committee

5. Punctuation is ignored in filing except in the case of hyphens. Here the hyphen is noted by the computer and the hyphenated words are filed as one word. In this way Scott-Giles and Scott-Maxwell properly follow all Scott surnames. However, in the title catalog hyphenated words are treated in the same way as above, so that there are places here where two alphabets can be found as follows:

Twentieth century authors
Twentieth century China
Twentieth century painting
Twentieth Maine
Twentieth-century Britain
Twentieth-century music
Twentieth century plays

We are eliminating these hyphens as quickly as possible.

Since commas are ignored by the computer in filing, another somewhat unnatural filing condition exists, i.e., corporate authors and title entries are interfiled with authors in the author catalog. An example follows:

Ford, Bacon and Davis, Inc.
Ford, Boris
Ford, Corey
Ford motor company
Ford, Norman D
Ford treasury of favorite recipes
Ford, William Ebenezer

6. Dr., Mrs., St., Ft., etc., are filed as spelled, not as if written out.

7. Acronyms are filed as words rather than as
   initials, so that COBOL would file between
   Cobbett and Coca-cola company instead of at
   the beginning of the alphabet.

8. All numerals in titles have been spelled out since
   the computer files numerals before any alpha-
   betics and we file numerals as though spoken.
   This accounts for "Seventeen seventy five, by
   Noel Hume" rather than 1775, by Noel Hume as
   it is shown on the title page of the book.

Some of these filing peculiarities could have been
eliminated with more small programs, perhaps, but sorting
uses more computer time than any other operation and every
exception to general rules requires much additional sorting
time.

Method of Production

The catalog is produced on an NCR 315 computer
from punched card input. The programs were written by
Aries Corporation of McLean, Virginia. "Out Own County
Data Processing Division, using these programs and additional ones they have written, generates and prints the
catalog on 16-1/2 x 13" sheets. These sheets go to our
County Print Shop which makes photographic offset masters
and prints the catalog by the offset process."[3]

Frequency of Issue

Supplements for Adult Catalog are cumulated and issued bi-monthly. A cumulation of total library holdings is
printed annually. These are hard bound. At present, this
is in nine volumes.

Costs

"In reply to your query concerning the cost of producing our book catalog, it is difficult to quote an exact figure,
particularly since some of our costs (such as computer
time, key punch machine rental, and printing) are charged
to other agencies in our county government. It seemed to
me that perhaps the cost per entry would be the most meaningful figure I could give you. Therefore, I have based this
estimate on the following: salaries of one and one-half professional librarians and one keypunch operator; costs of
computer time and printing costs as given me by the county

agencies involved; and supplies used.   As I have calculated, the cost per entry is as follows:

Salaries	$0.98
Computer time	0.08
Printing costs	0.01
Supplies	0.01
Total cost per entry	**$1.08**

"This may seem high, but when we remember the savings achieved in typing of catalog cards, file maintenance in 16 branches, equipment not needed and space saved, we are very pleased."[4]

Comments:

Virtually the total holdings are now listed in book catalog form, and branch libraries are discarding their card catalogs.   User reaction is reported as very good. "Although some of our borrowers may miss a card catalog in the beginning, the obvious advantages, such as our branch location line, the number of catalogs available for use, and the fact that each catalog is a Union list, are appreciated."[5]

Notes

1.   Communication from Martha T. Jett, Chief, Technical Services, March 3, 1970.

2.   Ibid.

3.   Ibid.

4.   Ibid., December 9, 1969.

5.   Ibid.

AUTHOR CATALOG SUPPLEMENT
January – June, 1969

COURTHION, PIERRE
GEORGES ROUAULT. ABRAMS, 1962.
T WO   759.4 R852CO
➤ COURTNEY, WINIFRED F
READER'S ADVISER, A GUIDE TO THE BEST IN LITERATURE.
ED. BY W. F. COURTNEY, 11TH ED., REV. AND ENL.
BOWKER, 1968=. V. 10TH ED., REV. AND ENL. BY M. R.
HOFFMAN, 9TH ED. PUB. UNDER TITLE, READER'S ADVISER
AND BOOKMAN'S MANUAL.
A B C CH D K LF S SH T W WO   R016 R286H11
ALSO CIRCULATING
C
COUSINS, NORMAN
IN PLACE OF FOLLY. HARPER, 1961.
B C K LF T W   172.4 C867I

SUBJECT

BOOKS AND READING
HERE ARE ENTERED WORKS ON THE
SIGNIFICANCE OF BOOKS IN MAN'S LIFE, HIS
ATTITUDE TOWARD, AND INTEREST IN,
READING BOOKS.
BROWN, ERNEST FRANCIS. PAGE TWO, THE BEST OF SPEAKING
OF BOOKS FROM THE NEW YORK TIMES BOOK REVIEW, ED., AND
WITH AN INTROD. BY E. F. BROWN. HOLT, 1968.
B LF S W   820.9 B877P
➤ READER'S ADVISER, A GUIDE TO THE BEST IN LITERATURE.
ED. BY W. F. COURTNEY, 11TH ED., REV. AND ENL.
BOWKER, 1968=. V. 10TH ED., REV. AND ENL. BY M. R.
HOFFMAN, 9TH ED. PUB. UNDER TITLE, READER'S ADVISER
AND BOOKMAN'S MANUAL.
A B C CH D K LF S SH T W WO   R016 R286H11
ALSO CIRCULATING
C
FOR OTHER EDITIONS, SEE AUTHOR CATALOG
ROOS, JEAN CAROLYN. PATTERNS IN READING, AN ANNOTATED
BOOK LIST FOR YOUNG ADULTS. 2D ED. A.L.A., 1961.
C LF S T W   028.5 R781P2
ALSO REFERENCE
B T
SEE ALSO AUTHORS AND READERS.
BIBLIOGRAPHY - BEST BOOKS. BOOK
SELECTION. BOOKS - REVIEWS.
CLASSIFICATION - BOOKS. LIBRARIES.
LITERATURE. PROHIBITED BOOKS.
REFERENCE BOOKS.

TITLE

READER IN LIBRARY ADMINISTRATION, ED. BY P. WASSERMAN
AND M. L. BUNDY
A C S   025.1 W322R
➤ READER'S ADVISER   V.
A B C CH D K LF S SH T W WO   R016 R286H11
ALSO CIRCULATING
C

TARRANT COUNTY JUNIOR COLLEGE DISTRICT
LEARNING RESOURCES CENTERS

Fort Worth, Texas

Characteristics

       Page Size: 9 x 12 inches

       Format: 2-column

       Arrangement: Separate catalogs are issued for authors, titles and subjects.

       Description:[1] The Learning Resources Center on each campus of the Tarrant County Junior College has been designed to provide a variety of materials and services for its students, faculty, and staff. Materials housed in each include books, pamphlets, maps, both current and back-files of periodicals, music scores, microfilms, phonodiscs, audio tapes, motion pictures, film-strips, and other materials. While the L.C. classification scheme is used to arrange the materials on the shelves of each library, periodicals, microfilm, phonodiscs, audio tapes, motion pictures and filmstrips are not classified by the L.C. scheme, but are arranged by title, date, or other means peculiar to the particular medium. All materials indexed in the book catalogs, however, are indexed by author, title, and subject. Periodicals are listed only in the title and subject catalogs. Full entries for all materials are found in all three parts of the catalog (beginning with the February, 1970 edition).

       The catalog entry includes author, title, edition, publisher, date of publication, classification number, and campus location(s).

Method of Production

       "Computer-printed pages are mounted, four to a sheet, and photographically reduced approximately 60 percent on a multilith master for mass production. Pages are collated and bound into volumes by Author, Title, and Subject. This work is done by a commercial printer and costs approximately $10 per finished set (four parts since we are dividing the subject volume into two parts because of its size) for 300 copies."[2]

Frequency of Issue

Once per year until 1969--twice annually since then. Supplements are produced monthly, but are not mass produced. Five copies of the computer printout are bound and placed in the Learning Resource Centers.

Costs

"We have made no meaningful estimate of total costs of the catalogs. Binding costs have run about $10 per copy in 300 lot runs, as noted above."[3]

Comments

"Student and faculty reception of the book catalog has been excellent. Copies are distributed to all faculty members (supplements are not distributed, as noted above) and students have access to catalogs in many locations throughout the Learning Resource Buildings on each campus. The Catalog is a union index to holdings of both (soon to be three campuses. Students say they prefer the book catalog to a card catalog."[4]

Notes

1. Corbin, John B., Director of Automation Services.

2. Communication from J. Paul Vagt, Dean of Learning Resources, March 13, 1970.

3, 4. Ibid.

Tarrant County Junior College
District Learning Resource Centers

*JACKSON, BARBARA WARD
    INDIA AND THE WEST. REV ED. NORTON 1964   ←
    HC435.J23 1964 SOUTH, NORTHEAST

*JACKSON, BARBARA WARD
    INTERPLAY OF EAST AND WEST; POINTS OF CONFLICT AND CO-OPERATION.
    NORTON 1962 (SIR EDWARD BEATTY MEMORIAL LECTURES, SERIES 2)
    CB251.J3 1962 SOUTH, NORTHEAST

*JACKSON, BARBARA WARD
    LOPSIDED WORLD. NORTON 1968 (CHRISTIAN A HERTER LECTURE SERIES, 1965)
    HC59.7.J26 SOUTH

Author Catalog, February 1970

INDIA AND THE WEST.
*JACKSON, BARBARA WARD
    REV ED. NORTON 1964   ←
    HC435.J23 1964 SOUTH, NORTHEAST

INDIA AND WORLD POLITICS, KRISHNA MENON'S VIEW OF THE WORLD.
*BRECHER, MICHAEL
    PRAEGER 1968
    DS448.B64 NORTHEAST

INDIA; A REFERENCE ANNUAL, 1967.
    INDIA MINISTRY OF INFORMATION AND BROADCASTING 1967
    DS405.I64 1967 REFERENCE NORTHEAST

Title Catalog

ECONOMIC DEVELOPMENT
----

*DRUCKER, PETER FERDINAND
    AGE OF DISCONTINUITY, GUIDELINES TO OUR CHANGING SOCIETY. HARPER 1969
    HC59.D69 SOUTH

*HARBISON, FREDERICK HARRIS
    EDUCATION, MANPOWER, AND ECONOMIC GROWTH. MCGRAW 1964
    HD5707.H3 SOUTH, NORTHEAST

*HEILBRONER, ROBERT L
    GREAT ASCENT, THE STRUGGLE FOR ECONOMIC DEVELOPMENT IN OUR TIME.
    HARPER 1963
    HD82.H39 SOUTH, NORTHEAST

*HIRSCHMAN, ALBERT O
    STRATEGY OF ECONOMIC DEVELOPMENT. YALE UNIV PRESS 1958 (YALE STUDIES
    IN ECONOMICS, 10)
    HD82.H49 SOUTH, NORTHEAST

*JACKSON, BARBARA WARD
    INDIA AND THE WEST. REV ED. NORTON 1964   ←
    HC435.J23 1964 SOUTH, NORTHEAST

*JACKSON, BARBARA WARD
    RICH NATIONS AND THE POOR NATIONS. NORTON 1962
    HC60.J28 SOUTH, NORTHEAST

Subject Catalog

LIBRARY
WASHINGTON UNIVERSITY SCHOOL OF MEDICINE

St. Louis, Missouri

Characteristics

Page Size: 8-1/2 x 11 inches

Format: 2-column

Arrangement: The catalog is divided into two parts: subjects on white paper and authors on green paper.

Description: The basic computer-produced Catalog of Books covered the period January 1, 1965 through January 31, 1967. A 1967 and 1968 supplement were subsequently printed. The next catalog planned will be a quinquennial cumulation 1965-1969. Entries consist of author, title, edition, imprint, number of pages, and classification. The catalog is printed from metal plates instead of from multilith mats to give added clarity. Subject headings are overprinted to produce bold-faced typography. The 1967 supplement contained 3,163 subject and 4,184 author entries; 1968, 4,267 subject and 5,107 author entries. All upper-case characters are used. Type is reduced about 45 percent.

Entries in the subject catalog are arranged (1) alphabetically by subject; (2) under each subject by date of publication in inverse chronological order; and (3) alphabetically by main entry under each date.

Method of Production

The catalogs were produced on the 1401 computer. The system was designed to produce acquisitions and fiscal records, new book lists, and book catalogs of nonserial works from a single punched card input, manipulated by the computer under the control of programs written for the task.

200 copies of the first 1965-67 catalog were printed; 500 copies of the second, 1967 catalog. The smaller quantity was decided upon for the third Catalog of Books 1968, as plans for a quinquennial edition which would supercede the previous ones were completed.

An annual Catalog has been supplemented by quarterly lists produced for internal use within the library.   These have been cumulated to form the annual volume.

Costs

1965-67 Catalog

Cost of Machine Time

Updating old tapes (20 Min. on IBM 1401 at $30/hour	$10.00
Edit I (20 min. on IBM 1401 at $30/hour)	10.00
Edit II (20 min. on IBM 1401 at $30/hour)	10.00
Sorting subjects (IBM 360/50, 15 min. at $300/hour).........	75.00
Sorting authors (IBM 360/50, 15 min. at $300/hour..........	75.00
Listing subjects (60 min., IBM 1401 at $20/hour)..........	20.00
Listing authors (60 min., IBM 1401 at $20/hour)..........	20.00
Total Machine time	230.00
Printing and binding costs for 200 copies	1,730.00
Total	$1,960.00

1968 Supplement

Printing and Binding................	$2,050.00
Sorting and listing both author and subject files.....	320.00
Total	$2,370.00

"As you know, these figures are somewhat deceptive. They represent a small portion of our costs of the computer-produced book catalog.   The costs of designing, programming, debugging, and data preparation--all should be taken into consideration and prorated."[2]

The Catalog of Books was available for purchase at
$12. 50 for the 1965-67 volume, and $7. 50 for each annual
cumulation.

Comments:

"A new system has been designed and new programs
written using MARC II format for the IBM 360/50 with upper
and lower case print chain.   The quinquennial Catalog of
Books 1965-1969 will consist of one list with full cataloging
entries arranged in sequential record number order. Author,
subject, and title indexes arranged alphabetically with brief
entries will refer user, by record number, to main list.   In
future years, the main list will not be cumulated.   Instead,
lists of additional cataloging entries in the order they have
been cataloged will be appended.   The indexes, however,
will be cumulated, referring user, by record number, to
quinquennial and appended lists."[3]

Notes

1.   Moore, Evelyn A.; Brodman, Estelle; Cohen, Geraldine
      S., "Mechanization of Library Procedures in the
      Medium-sized Library: III. Acquisitions and Catalog-
      ing." Bull. Med. Lib. Assoc. 53(3), 305-28, July,
      1965; ibid., 54, 259-60, July, 1966.

2.   Communication from Doris Bolef, Deputy Librarian,
      September 17, 1969.

3.   Ibid., March 9, 1970.

(See also: Brodman, Estelle and Bolef, Doris, "Printed
Catalogs; Retrospect and Prospect," p. 248; and Bolef,
Doris, et. al., "Mechanization of Library Procedures in
the Medium-Sized Medical Library," p. 258).

Washington University, School of Medicine
Catalog of Books, 1967

HISTORY OF MEDICINE

1967

SCHOUTEN, JAN. THE ROD AND SERPENT OF ASKLEPIOS. N. Y.,
ELSEVIER, 1967. 260 P.
WZ 334 S376R   1967

STENN, FREDERICK. THE GROWTH OF MEDICINE. SPRINGFIELD,
THOMAS, 1967. 199 P.
WZ 40 S825G   1967

1966

ADELMANN, HOWARD B. MARCELLO MALPIGHI AND THE EVOLUTION
OF EMBRYOLOGY. ITHACA, N. Y., CORNELL UNIV. PRESS,
1966. 5 V.   XXWZ 100 M259A 1966

CLARK, GEORGE NORMAN. A HISTORY OF THE ROYAL COLLEGE OF
PHYSICIANS OF LONDON. OXFORD, CLARENDON PRESS,
1964-1966. 2 V.   WB 1FE5 C593H 1966

FORBES, THOMAS ROGER. THE MIDWIFE AND THE WITCH. NEW
HAVEN, CONN., YALE UNIV. PRESS, 1966. 196 P.
WQ 11 F695M   1966

HENSCHEN, FOLKE. THE HISTORY AND GEOGRAPHY OF DISEASES.
N. Y., DELACORTE PRESS, 1966. 344 P.
WZ 40 H526H   1966

HIRSCH, EDWIN FREDERICK. FRANK BILLINGS, CHICAGO, UNIV.
OF CHICAGO, 1966. 144 P.
WZ 100 B597H   1966

REGIMEN SANITATIS SALERNITANUM. THE SCHOOL OF SALERNUM.
SALERNO, ENTE PROVINCIALE PER IL TURISMO, 1966. 92 P.
WZ 54 R335S   1966

RIST, EDOUARD, 1871-1956. HISTOIRE CRITIQUE DE LA
MEDECINE DANS L'ANTIQUITE. PARIS, LES AMIS D'EDOUARD
RIST, 1966. 276 P.   WZ 40 R597H   1966

1965

Subjects

ADELMANN, HOWARD B. MARCELLO MALPIGHI AND THE EVOLUTION
OF EMBRYOLOGY. ITHACA, N. Y., CORNELL UNIV. PRESS,
1966. 5 V.   XXWZ 100 M259A 1966

ADELSON, JOSEPH. SEE DOUVAN, ELIZABETH....
NURLIB BF 724 C739A 1966

ADLER, FRANCIS HEED. PHYSIOLOGY OF THE EYE. 4TH ED.
CLINICAL APPLICATION. ST. LOUIS, MOSBY, 1965. 889 P.
RES   WW 100 A237P 1965

Authors

STANFORD UNDERGRADUATE LIBRARY
(J. Henry Meyer Memorial Library)

Stanford University Libraries
Stanford, California 94305

Characteristics

Page Size: 8 x 10-3/4 inches

Format: 2-column

Arrangement: The catalog has two principal parts, each in several volumes: The Author-Title Catalog, and the Subject Catalog. In addition, a shelf list, in book form, lists all copies and volumes of books in the library.

Description: The Author-Title Catalog lists books, journals, microfilms, and audio recordings by their authors and any distinctive titles. The Subject Catalog lists these materials under Library of Congress subject headings. In the Stanford system a new unit record was introduced. The first element is the title paragraph. All headings, main or added, are placed directly above it. Title entries are made in hanging indention form. The catalog thus does away with the main entry concept.

Method of Production

The complete operation is performed in house. (See Johnson, Richard D., "A Book Catalog at Stanford," p. 134-174) 75 copies of the 41,000-title (60,000-volume) catalog were issued in 1967.

Costs

See "A Book Catalog at Stanford."

Frequency of Issue

The basic catalog is issued annually. Originally, monthly supplements were proposed, but cost factors and staff time expended led to the adoption of quarterly supplements.

Stanford Undergraduate Library

Hornblow, Arthur
The captive, by Edouard Bourdet. Translated by Arthur Hornblow, Jr. Introd. by J. Brooks Atkinson. Brentano's, 1926. 255 p. PQ2603.O777P72

The triumph of death, by Gabriele d'Annunzio. Translated by Arthur Hornblow. Introd. by Burton Rascoe. Boni and Liveright, 1923. 412 p. PQ4803.Z3T7

Horne, Alistair
The price of glory: Verdun 1916. St. Martin's Press, 1963. 371 p. D545.V3H6

Return to power: a report on the new Germany. Praeger, 1956. 415 p. DD259.4.H65

Horne, C. Silvester
Puritanism and art; an inquiry into a popular fallacy. By Joseph Crouch. Introd. by the Rev. C. Silvester Horne. Cassell, 1910. 381 p. N72.C8

Horned moon; an account of a journey through Pakistan, Kashmir, and Afghanistan. By Ian Stephens. Indiana Univ. Press, 1955. 288 p. DS377.S8

Horner, Harlan Hoyt
Lincoln and Greeley. Univ. of Illinois Press, 1953. 432 p.

Author-Title Catalog, June, 1966

Horowitz, Irving Louis
The idea of war and peace in contemporary philosophy. With an introductory essay by Roy Wood Sellars. Paine-Whitman, 1957. 224 p. JX1952.H72

The new sociology: essays in social science and social theory in honor of C. Wright Mills. Edited by Irving Louis Horowitz. Oxford Univ. Press, 1964. 512 p. H35.H68

Radicalism and the revolt against reason; the social theories of Georges Sorel, with a translation of his essay on The decomposition of Marxism. Humanities Press, 1961. 264 p. HX263.S6H5

Revolution in Brazil; politics and society in a developing nation. E.P. Dutton, 1964. 430 p. F2538.2.H6

Horrabin, J.F.
An atlas of Africa. 2d, rev. ed. F.A. Praeger, 1961. 126 p. G2445.H6

Mathematics for the million, by Lancelot Hogben. Illustrations by J.F. Horrabin. W.W. Norton, 1937. 647 p. QA36.H6

Horrocks, John E.
The psychology of adolescence: behavior and development. 2d ed. Houghton, 1962. 711 p. BF724.H6

Stanford Undergraduate Library

CRUSADES

An Arab-Syrian gentleman and warrior in the period of the crusades; memoirs of Usamah Ibn-Munqidh. Translated from the original manuscript by Philip K. Hitti. Columbia Univ. Press, 1929. 265 p.   DS97.U5

Background to the Crusades, a BBC publication. British Broadcasting Corporation, n.d. 38 p.   D159.B7

The crusades, by Richard A. Newhall. Rev. ed. Holt, Rinehart and Winston, 1964. 136 p.   D158.N4

The Crusades; iron men and saints. By Harold Lamb. Doubleday, Doran, 1930. 368 p.   D157.L3

The Crusades; the story of the Latin Kingdom of Jerusalem. By T-A. Archer and Charles L. Kingsford. G.P. Putnam, 1936. 467 p.   D158.A67

A history of the Crusades, by Steven Runciman. Cambridge, Eng., Univ. Press, 1957. 3 v.   D157.R8

CRYSTAL OPTICS

The microscopical characters of artificial inorganic solid substances: optical properties of artificial minerals. By Alexander Newton Winchell and Horace Winchell. 3d ed. Academic Press, 1964. 439 p.   QE367.W78

Optical crystallography, with particular reference to the use and theory of the polarizing microscope. By Ernest E. Wahlstrom. 3d ed. J. Wiley, 1962. 365 p.   QD941.W28

Practical optical crystallography, by N.H. Hartshorne and A. Stuart. American Elsevier Pub. Co., 1964. 326 p.   QD941.H34

CRYSTALLIZATION

Crystallization; theory and practice. By Andrew Van Hook. Reinhold, 1961. 325 p.   QD548.V3

CRYSTALLOGRAPHY

Crystal orientation manual, by Elizabeth A. Wood. Columbia Univ. Press, 1963. 75 p.   QD905.W58

ONTARIO NEW UNIVERSITIES LIBRARY PROJECT

University of Toronto
Canada

Characteristics

Page Size: 9 x 12 inches

Format: 3-column

Arrangement: The catalog is divided into two sections: an author-title catalog listing, and a subject listing.

Description: The Author-Title catalog contains main entry records, title added entries, name added entries, and series added entries. The main entry record includes full catalog information. "Information used for all secondary entry records however, is more selective, and certain categories of data are displayed in abbreviated form. The secondary entry records, both added entry records for the author-title catalog and subject entry records for the subject catalog contain only the call number, the secondary entry, the main entry, abbreviated title, brief edition statement, date of publication, and paging, as well as location information. The abbreviation of all secondary entry records is performed automatically by the computer."[1] The type font contains upper and lower case characters.

The cataloging and classification conform to the practice followed by the University of Toronto Library Catalogue Department.

Method of Production

The catalog is compiled and printed by computer. Complete bibliographic information is keyed into a master record, which is subsequently manipulated, selected, and reformatted for printout as shelf-list cards, author-title book catalogs, and subject book catalogs. The filing sequence of entries, much of the editing, and abbreviations of records are pre-programmed and automatic. The printing of the catalogs is done on an IBM 1403 model II printer.

Frequency of Issue

"Issue of the book form catalogs follows a cumulative

pattern. Monthly issues containing information added to the master record during the current month are prepared for each of the first two months of each quarter of the year. Quarterly cumulations are produced for the third and ninth month of the year, semi-annual cumulation for the first half of the year, and a total cumulation of the entire information store at the end of the year."

Notes

1. Bregzis, Ritvars, "The Ontario New Universities Library Project--An Automated Bibliographic Data Control System," College & Research Libraries, Nov., 1965, 495-508.

2. Ibid., 503.

Ontario New Universities Library Project
Catalogue 1964-1967

PR 3562. G5 1966

Gilbert, Allan H., 1888-
   On the composition of Paradise lost;
a study of the ordering and insertion of
material. New York, Octagon Books,
1966.
      x, 185 p. facsims.
   Bibliographical footnotes.
   1. Milton, John, 1608-1674. Paradise
   lost I. Title
BROC   ERIN   GLPH   SCAR   TREN

➡   PR 2829. G37

Gilbert, Allan H., 1888-
   The principles and practice of
criticism: Othello, The merry wives,
Hamlet. [Lectures. Edited by Esther
Ellen Jacoby] Detroit, Wayne State
University Press, 1959.
      xviii, 152 p. illus.
   Bibliographical footnotes.
   1. Shakespeare, William, 1564-1616.
   Othello 2. Shakespeare, William,
   1564-1616. Merry wives of Windsor
   3. Shakespeare, William, 1564-1616.

Author-Title

   Shakespeare, William, 1564-1616.
   Merry wives of Windsor

➡   PR 2829. G37

Gilbert, Allan H., 1888-
   The principles and practice of
criticism: Othello, The merry wives,
Hamlet. [Lectures. 1959. xviii, 152
p.
BROC   ERIN   GLPH   SCAR   TREN

                              PR 2826. G7 1962

Green, William, 1926-
   Shakespeare's Merry wives of Windsor.
1962. xiii, 239 p.
BROC   ERIN   GLPH   SCAR   TREN

   Shakespeare, William, 1564-1616.
   Much ado about nothing

                              PR 2828. M84

Mulryne, J.R.
   Shakespeare: Much ado about nothing.
1965. 61 p.
BROC   ERIN   GLPH   SCAR   TREN

Subjects

UNIVERSITY OF CALIFORNIA, SANTA CRUZ
THE UNIVERSITY LIBRARY

Santa Cruz, California 95060

Characteristics

Page Size: Straight computer print-out

Format: 3-column

Arrangement: Separate listings are provided for authors, titles and subjects.

Description: The author catalog, presenting full entries, lists items alphabetically by title under names of authors. The subject catalog lists works alphabetically by author under subject headings. The title catalog consists of titles displayed in alphabetic sequence with abbreviated entries. Upper and lower case characters are used.

Method of Production

The catalog is issued in the form of a straight computer print-out in six copies each. In October, 1969 the subject catalog contained 183,083 entries and filled 7,132 pages (bound into 15 volumes). The author catalog contained 155,124 main and added entries, and filled 9,538 pages (bound into 20 volumes). 20 hours of computer printing time was required. In the title catalog, 3,014 pages were bound into 8 volumes. Eight hours of computer printing time was involved.

Frequency of Issue

A full cumulation is planned each year. The catalog supplement will be a dictionary card catalog.

Costs

"Hard cost figures for our catalog are not yet available. We do know that we can print about 500 pages an hour on an IBM 1403 printer. The cheapest time available for a printer is about $25.00 per hour. We have developed a very detailed cost model for book catalog production. Now we need to insert all the Santa Cruz variables into this model in order to come up with the specific cost for a single catalog production."[1]

Comments

"Currently we are engaged in an effort to increase the efficiency of our programs, correct and maintain the data base, find an economic means of producing more than six copies on a reduced page format, and develop a method for incorporating MARC II data into our data base."[2]

"Users have not reacted, as far as I know, specifically to the book form of the catalog. As one might expect, most of the negative response has stemmed from the catalog not being up-to-date. We have not yet been able to provide a coherent supplement to the yearly printings."[3]

Notes

1. Communication from John F. Knapp, Library Systems Analyst, March 18, 1970.

2. Ibid., August 11, 1969.

3. Ibid., March 18, 1970.

University of California, Santa Cruz

CHICAGO. ART INSTITUTE
      Seurat, paintings and drawings; exhi-
   bition. The Art Institute of Chicago,
   January 16-March 7, 1958. The Museum of
   Modern Art, New York, March 24-May 11,
   1958. Edited by Daniel Catton Rich.
   With an essay on Seurat'sdrawings by
   Robert L. Herbert.
      Chicago. illus.
   ND553.S5C45   92 p.   1958

CHILTON, C.W
      Diogenis Oenoandensis fragmenta;
   edidit C.W. Chilton.
      Lipsiae, in aedibus B.G. Teubneri.
   xviii, 106 p. illus.
      (Bibliotheca scriptorum graecorum et
   romanorum Teubneriana) Includes bibliography
   PA3965.E8 1967   106 p.   1967

CHOU, PEI CHI, 1924-
      Elasticity; tensor, dyadic, and
   engineering approaches by Pei Chi Chou
   and Nicholas J. Pagano.
      Princeton, N.J., Van Nostrand. illus.
      (University series in basic
   engineering) Includes bibliographical
   references
   Sci Lib: QA931.C5   290 p.   1967

CHRISTOPHER, JOHN
      The little people.
      New York, Simon and Schuster.
   PR6053.H7L5   224 p.   1966

CHUNG, JUN-AI, 1865-
      My seventy nine years in Hawaii.
      Hong Kong, Cosmorama Pictorial Publi-
   sher. 430, 128, i.e. 558 p., illus.,
   map.
   CT2918.C5A3   Author Catalog   558 p.   1960

University of California, Santa Cruz

ENGLISH LITERATURE--20TH CENTURY.
--Maugham, William Somerset, 1874-1965. W.
    Somerset Maugham's Introduction to
    modern English and American literature.
    New York, The New Home Library 1943.
    618 p.
    PR1149.M28
--Morley, Christopher Darlington, 1890-.
    The Panorama of modern literature,
    contributed by thirty-one great modern
    writers; with an introduction by Chris-
    topher Morley. Garden City, N.Y., Doub-
    leday, Doran & Co 1934. 555 p.
    PR1149.P3

ENGLISH LITERATURE--20TH CENTURY--HISTORY
AND CRITICISM.
--Fehr, Bernhard, 1876-1938. Die englische
    Literatur des 19. und 20. Jahrhunderts
    mit :iner Einfuhrung in die englische
    Fruhromantik. Berlin-Neubabelsberg,
    Akademische Verlagsgesellschaft, 1923-
    25. 524 p.
    PR461.F4

                    Subject Catalog
Bach the borrower: preface by Basil Lam.
    Carrell, Norman
    ML410.B1C227   3-39p.   1967

Bachelor-of arts, by John Erskine.
    Erskine, John, 1879-
    PS3509.R5B3   331 p.   1934

The background of our war, from lectures
    prepared by the Orientation course, War
    department, ...
    U.S. War dept. Bureau of public rela-
    tions
    D743.U5   279 p.   1942
                    Title Catalog

NASA HEADQUARTERS LIBRARY CATALOG

Characteristics

Page Size: 10-1/2 x 14 inches

Format: The Record of Holdings consists of photographed cards, 21 per page.

Arrangement: The catalog is issued in two parts: Part 1 is a Record of Holdings; Part 2 contains author, title and subject indexes to the holdings (Cumulative Indexes).

Description: Part 1, Record of Holdings, issued in looseleaf form, is a photoreproduction of the main entry catalog cards arranged in alphabetical order. The indexes in Part 2 include book classification number, author, title, editor (if applicable), and date of publication of entries. The author index includes primary and secondary personal authors, corporate authors, and primary editors and compilers. The title index is an alphabetical arrangement. The subject index is based on the Library of Congress Subject Headings. The index entries refer the user to the corresponding items in the book catalog which give complete bibliographical descriptions for each publication.

Method of Production

The catalog was produced by keypunching cataloging data taken from conventional catalog cards. The data were stored on magnetic tape. Alanar Book Processing Center served as contractor.

Frequency of Issue

The catalog was updated by monthly supplements which were added to the back of the original binder. Cumulative quarterly indexes were prepared. The last updating occurred in May, 1966. "The NASA Headquarters Library Catalog was a low-cost experiment in the book catalog concept. In mid-1966, when the original contract terminated, the catalog was discontinued indefinitely in the face of increased costs. The data represented in the Catalog are stored on magnetic tape, and the associated programs are now under study, with others, to create a system for having wider application within NASA."[1]

Note

1. Communication from Alfred C. String, Jr., Head, Head-
   quarters Library, Scientific and Technical Information
   Division, Office of Technology Utilization, National
   Aeronautics and Space Administration, April 17, 1970.

NASA Headquarters Library Catalog
Cumulative Index, Sept. 1965

INFORMATION HANDLING AND SCIENCE INFORMATION 62   •Z699.2.A51
   AMER INST OF BIOLOGICAL SCIENCES.   7U

INFORMATION HANDLING FIRST PRINCIPLES 63   Z699.143
   INFORMATION FOR INDUSTRY, INC.   93A

INFORMATION INDEXING AND SUBJECT CATALOGING 57   Z696.M58
   METCALFE, JOHN WALLACE   230U

INFORMATION NETWORKS, PROCEEDINGS 55   TK5101.S98   14ے

INFORMATION PLEASE ALMANAC. 1947- 47   •AY64.161   93C

Titles

AMER INST OF AERONAUTICS & ASTRONAUTICS   SEE
   AIAA

AMER INST OF BIOLOGICAL SCIENCES.   •Z699.2.A51
   INFORMATION HANDLING AND SCIENCE INFORMATION 62   7U

AMER INST OF CHEMICAL ENGINEERS.   •Z699.5.A512
   CHEMICAL ENGINEERING THESAURUS 61   7W

AMER INST OF CHEMICAL ENGINEERS.   TP185.A51
   PROCESS SYSTEMS ENGINEERING 63   8A

Authors

NASA Headquarters Library Catalog
Cumulative Index, Sept. 1965

PERRY, JAMES WHITNEY   Z699.P46
TOOLS FOR MACHINE LITERATURE SEARCHING SEMANTIC CODE DICTIONARY □ 58   147D

STEVENS, NORMAN D   Z699.S84
COMPARATIVE STUDY OF THREE SYSTEMS OF INFORMATION RETRIEVAL 61   178F

WESTERN RESERVE UNIV   Z695.92.W52
INFORMATION SYSTEMS IN DOCUMENTATION 57   207F

INFORMATION STORAGE AND RETRIEVAL SYSTEMS--BIBL.

AMER INST OF BIOLOGICAL SCIENCES.   *Z699.2.A51
INFORMATION HANDLING AND SCIENCE INFORMATION 62   7U

INFORMATION STORAGE AND RETRIEVAL SYSTEMS--CONGRESSES.

                                                                Z699.I61
INFORMATION RETRIEVAL AND MACHINE TRANSLATION 61   94J

LOS ANGELES. U OF SOUTHERN CAL   Z699.L87
MODERN TRENDS IN DOCUMENTATION 59   117N

TAUBE, MORTIMER   Z699.S98
INFORMATION STORAGE AND RETRIEVAL THEORY, SYSTEMS, AND DEVICES 58   182T

U. S. NATIONAL SCIENCE FOUNDATION.   Z699.5.S3U58
PREPRINTS OF PAPERS FOR THE INTERNATIONAL CONF ON SCIENTIFIC INFO 58   199K

INFORMATION STORAGE AND RETRIEVAL SYSTEMS--MATERIALS.

PURDUE UNIV   *Z5853.M38P98
RETRIEVAL GUIDE TO THERMOPHYSICAL PROPERTIES RESEARCH LITERATURE 60   153G

Subjects

NASA Headquarters Library Catalog
Record of Holdings, Part 1., Sept., 1965

Q 111 .A51

American Foundation for Continuing Education.
Exploring the universe. Edited by Louise B. Young.
New York, McGraw-Hill [1963]

457 p. illus. 20 cm.
Includes bibliography.

1. Science—Collected works. 2. Astronomy. i. Young, Louise B., ed. ii. Title.

Q111.A5   •   508.2   [636]

62—21787 ‡

Library of Congress

HD 9581 .U53 A51

American Gas Association. *Rate Committee.*
Gas rate fundamentals. New York, 1960.

357 p. illus. 24 cm.

1. Gas, Natural—U. S.—Rates. i. Title.

HD9581.U53A7   •   338.476657   [61e5]

60—1786 ‡

Library of Congress

Z 699.2 .A51

American Institute of Biological Sciences. *Biological Sciences Communications Project.*
Information handling and science information : a selected bibliography, 1957–1961. Prepared by the American Institute of Biological Sciences, Biological Sciences Communication Project in cooperation with the American University Center of Technology & Administration. School of Government & Public Administration. Paul C. Janaske, editor. Washington, 1962.

1 v. (unpaged) 28 cm.
"Part ii of the report of the Seminar on Biological Science Communication (June 19–30, 1961) ... Part i ... is entitled, Information and communication in biological science."

(Continued on next card)

62—19910

[10]

Z 699.2 .A51

American Institute of Biological Sciences. *Biological Sciences Communications Project.* Information handling and science information ... 1962. (Card 2)

1. Information storage and retrieval systems—Science—Bibl. 2. Science—Information service—Bibl. i. Janaske, Paul C., ed. ii. Seminar on Biological Science Communication, American University, 1961. iii. Title.

Z699.2.A6   •   016.01078   [10]

62—19910

Library of Congress

EAST BAY COOPERATIVE LIBRARY SYSTEM[1]

(Consisting of the public libraries of: Alameda County,
Alameda City, City of Richmond and Contra Costa County,
Calif. Mailing address: c/o Alameda County Library, 224 W.
Winton Avenue, Hayward, Calif. 94544)

Characteristics

      Page Size: Adult Catalogs/Register, 11" x 14"
                     Juvenile Catalogs/Register, 9-1/2"x12-1/2"

      Format: Catalog Card Register - Adult: 21 cards
                    per page, Children: 12 cards per page

                 Catalogs - 2 column

      Arrangement: Separate adult and juvenile catalog
card registers are issued. Separate adult and juvenile
author, subject and title indexes to the registers are published. Adult supplements to the indexes are issued monthly,
with bi-monthly cumulative editions. Juvenile supplements
are issued periodically.

      Description: Entries in each catalog include (a)
author, (b) title, (c) year of publication, when available,
(d) call number, (e) location symbols, (f) distinctive number
by which a title can be located in the Catalog Card Register.
(Register consists of sheets containing photographic reproductions of catalog cards).

      All upper case typography is used.

      Catalogs are printed on 50 lb., white offset book
paper. Maximum length of any catalog is 375 pages.
Multiple volumes are used for lengths greater than 375 pages.

      The third edition of the adult basic catalog, cumulative
to July, 1969 contains over 50,000 entries and is in six
volumes. The third edition of the juvenile contains over
6,400 entries (one volume).

      Annual indexes are hard bound; interim indexes, paper
bound. Binding of indexes includes fan glueing of pages.

Method of Production

The catalogs are produced by Alanar Book Processing Center, Inc., 1609 Memorial Ave., P.O. Box 921, Williamsport, Pennsylvania (Subsidiary of Bro-Dart Industries, Inc.). The Center's IBM System 360 Computer Department prepares the index data. All printing and binding are done by Alanar's facilities. Arrangement of entries follows a computerized filing code created by Theodore Hines and Jessica L. Harris of Columbia University School of Library Service. Indexes are reproduced from computer print-outs, reduced by 38 percent. Alanar furnishes 155 copies of indexes for all Adult Catalogs, and 145 copies of all Juvenile Catalogs.

Frequency of Issue

New editions of the adult basic catalog are planned annually. Monthly author/title and subject supplements are issued, with cumulations every other month. Juvenile catalog is supplemented as deemed necessary. Catalog card registers are continuously up-dated.

Costs

From March 1966 to January 1, 1970, the costs of three editions of the adult basic catalog and 16 supplements has been $139,873.16. The costs of the three editions of the juvenile catalog, and 8 supplements has been $16,028.61.

Costs of each new edition/supplement are based on $1.40 per new title, $.50 per old title (previously included) and nominal charges for cross references, additions, changes and deletions. Expected annual cost for producing 12 planned adult supplements, adding 12,000 new titles to the basic catalog, is $36,000. Printing of the 4th edition of the adult basic catalog (January 1971) is expected to cost approximately an additional $36,000.

Comments

"The percentage of titles to total collection is difficult to ascertain as the catalog is primarily based on recent acquisitions of four member libraries and the number of duplications in the remaining collection of the individual members is unknown. An estimate would be between 20-33-1/2 percent. Card Catalogs are still available.

"Recently replaced basic catalogs show use. Supplements also indicate use. Few unfavorable comments have been received, but the need for card files and basic catalogs and supplements (possibility of search through three separate sources) is recognized as a patron problem. Also the resistance to change from the traditional card catalogs has required constant use of publicity and educational techniques."[2]

Notes

1. Information contributed by Bruce A. Linsley, Administrative Assistant.

2. Communication from Bruce A. Linsley, March 25, 1970.

Book Catalogs, East Bay Cooperative Library Systems

AUTHOR
1964 – 1967

796.088	MURRAY, JIM BEST OF JIM MURRAY	A C	65	253Q
233	MURRAY, JOHN COURTNEY, ED FREEDOM AND MAN	C	65	1192C
915.4	MURRAY, JOHN COURTNEY HANDBOOK FOR TRAVELLERS IN INDIA, PAKISTAN, BURMA, AND CEYLON	R	65	901M 20TH ED
262.91	MURRAY, JOHN COURTNEY, ED RELIGIOUS LIBERTY AN END AND A BEGINNING	A C R	66	1065B
261.7	MURRAY, JOHN COURTNEY WE HOLD THESE TRUTHS	C R	60	570D
817	MURRAY, KATHRYN /KOHNFELDER/ FAMILY LAUGH LINES	AI C R	66	1027E
B MURRAY	MURRAY, KATHRYN /KOHNFELDER/ MY HUSBAND, ARTHUR MURRAY	A AI C R	60	450G

TITLE

616.63	HANDBOOK FOR THE YOUNG DIABETIC 3RD ED FISCHER, ALFRED E.	A AI C	64	1284J
915.4	HANDBOOK FOR TRAVELLERS IN INDIA, PAKISTAN, BURMA, AND CEYLON 20TH ED MURRAY, JOHN COURTNEY	R	65	901M
668.3	HANDBOOK OF ADHESIVES SKEIST, IRVING, ED	R	62	919D

Book Catalogs, East Bay Cooperative Library Systems

SUBJECT

SOUTH ASIA - CIVILIZATION

915.   FERSH, SEYMOUR H.   R   65   1298A
4034   INDIA AND SOUTH ASIA

SOUTH ASIA - DESCR. AND TRAV. - GUIDE-BOOKS

915.4   MURRAY, JOHN COURTNEY   R   65   901M
          HANDBOOK FOR TRAVELLERS IN INDIA, PAKISTAN, BURMA, AND CEYLON   20TH ED

SUBJECT SUPPLEMENT
July, 1968

COOKERY FOR INSTITUTIONS, ETC.

R   SULLIVAN, LENORE   A C   64   1564N
641.57   QUANTITY RECIPE FILE   6TH ED

COOKERY, FRENCH

Q   RANHOFER, CHARLES   C R   20   1556K
641.5   EPICUREAN

COOKERY /FRUIT/

641.852 PLAGEMANN, CATHERINE   A AI C R 67   1463S
          FINE PRESERVING

COOKERY /GARLIC/

641.   KAUFMAN, WILLIAM IRVING   A C R 67   1431G
8526   I LOVE GARLIC COOKBOOK

LOS ANGELES COUNTY PUBLIC LIBRARY[1]

320 West Temple Street
Los Angeles, California 90053

Characteristics

Page Size: 8-1/2 x 11"

Format: 2-column

Arrangement: Separate catalogs are issued for adult and juvenile titles, and for authors, titles, and subjects. In addition, fiction is listed separately by subjects. There is a separate foreign language catalog.

Description: The entries in the author and subject catalogs include full author, title, sub-title, publisher, year of publication, collation, analytics, series, notes, and classification number. Sub-arrangement under subjects is alphabetical by title. Entries in the subject volumes include annotations. Upper and lower-case typography is used.

Method of Production

The Los Angeles County Public Library catalogs have evolved through three methods of production: the use of IBM tabulating cards, a sequential card camera process, and now a new computerized format. Catalog material is typed at the library in a machine-readable type font on Selectric typewriters. Continuous pin-feed paper is used. Some adaptations had to be made in subject headings such as, changing Roman numerals to Arabic to make them machine-readable. Compucenters, Inc., Santa Barbara, California, performs the optical scanning and computer work. The Sequential card camera catalogs were produced by Econolist. Samples of both catalogs are demonstrated.

Frequency of Issue

The juvenile master volumes of the new computerized catalog were published in February 1969. The adult master volumes were published in March, 1970. Supplements appear bi-monthly. The juvenile supplement comes out one month, and adult supplement appears the next month. A new master set is planned for 1971.

Comments

The entire holdings of over one-quarter million titles will be included in the new master volumes. Number of copies: 412 adult, 354 juvenile.

The title catalog contains title, author and call number only.

Binding

Master volumes are bound in pearl grey pressboard with distinctive color spines for each catalog.

User Reaction

User reaction is good. The Los Angeles County Library has had book catalogs for over fifteen years. Our patrons are accustomed to using them. They are very convenient for staff use, because copies can be carried to work areas. At our system headquarters sets are located in book evaluation and cataloging work areas where they save time consuming trips for catalog checking.

Number of Volumes

Adult Authors	15
Titles	7
Subjects	28
Foreign	1
Fiction Subjects	5
Juvenile Authors	2
Subjects	4
Titles	1
Total	63

The 63 volumes require about six feet of shelf space.

Note

1. Information contributed by William S. Geller, County Librarian and Virginia Ossen, Head Technical Services Librarian. (See also: Becker, Joseph, "Automatic Preparation of Book Catalogs; MacQuarrie, Catherine, Preparation of Book Catalogs," p. 272; MacQuarrie, Catherine, "The Metamorphosis of the Book Catalogs," p. 264).

Los Angeles County Public Library
Sequential Card Camera-Produced Catalogs

BOUDET, JACQUES

720.9   Great works of mankind; a visual history.   Golden Pr.,   1962.
            293 p.   Illus. (part col.) plans.   Oversize.   1-2-3-4-5-6-7-8
            Translation of "Les Grands travaux de l'humanite".
            SEE
945.6   History of Rome and the Romans.

BOUDIER-BAKKER, INA

D   Aan de grote weg.   4. ed.   Querido, 1959.   5
            First published 1939.
D   Aan den overkant.   P. N. Van Kampen & Zoon, 1920.   5
D   Beloofde land.   P. N. Van Kampen & Zoon.   5
D   Eeuwige andere.   Querido, 1959.   5

BOUGHTON, F. E.

655.3   Flexographic printing.   1958.   1-2-3-5-6-7-8-C

BOUISSOUNOUSE, JANINE

92 L637 Julie, the life of Mademoiselle de Lespinasse.   Appleton,
            1962.   2-3-4-5-6-7-8

BOULDING, REGINALD SIDNEY HENRY

621.3848 Radar pocket book.   2d ed., enl. and reset.   Van Nostrand,
            1962.   248 p.   Illus.   1-2-3-4-5-6-7-8-C

BOULTON, MARJORIE

808.2   Anatomy of drama.   Routledge, 1960.   1-2-3-4-5-6-7-8-C

Author Supplement, May 1963

GEOGRAPHY

910   Murphey, Rhoads.   Introduction to geography.   Rand, 1961.

GEOGRAPHY - DICTIONARIES

R910.3   Columbia Lippincott gazetteer of the world.   Columbia Univ.
1962 ed. Pr., 1962.
            Based on the 1905 ed. of "Lippincott's new gazetteer", first
            published in 1885 as "Lippincott's pronouncing gazetteer".
            For other editions, see author catalog.
R910.3   Webster's geographical dictionary; a dictionary of names of
            places, with geographical and historical information and
            pronunciations.   Rev. ed.   Merriam, 1962.   1293 p.
            Illus., maps.
            For other editions, see Author Catalog.

GEOGRAPHY, HISTORICAL - MAPS

R209   Gaustad, Edwin Scott.   Historical atlas of religion in America.
            Harper, 1962.   179 p.   Maps.   Bibliographies.
            Expansion and present numerical strength of the main religious bodies
            of America, with 78 maps and numerous charts and tables.
912   Hammond, C. S., and Company, Inc.   Curtis-Doubleday world
            atlas.   Doubleday, 1962.   Illus., maps.
            Maps of the world's countries, of states, population indexes, historical
            maps, and illustrated section on natural beauties of America.

Subject Supplement, April 1963

Los Angeles County Public Library
Sequential Card Camera-Produced Catalogs

CATS

J636. 8   Shuttlesworth, Dorothy Edwards.   **Story of**
           cats.   Doubleday, 1962.   56 p.   Illus.
           Oversize.
           History of the cat and characteristics of the
           various domestic breeds we know today.
           Grades 5 and up.

CATS - STORIES

EB   Berg, Jean Horton.   **O'Leary's and friends.**
           Follett, 1961.
           An elusive cat helps a new family make friends.
           Grade 2.

EB   Carroll, Ruth Robinson.   **Where's the kitty?**
           Walck, 1962.
           A small boy and a kitten enjoy a day of play and
           fun together.   Preschool.

J   Fleishman, Seymour.   **Where's Kit?**
           A. Whitman, 1962.
           Karen and Tommy's vacation at the beach is full of
           fun and excitement even though they are worried
           about their pet cat that has disappeared.
           Grades 3-4.

Children's Catalog, Supplement, May 1963

NEW YORK - NEW YORK CITY
Adler, Edward.   **Notes from a dark street.   Knopf, 1961.**
    Sketches of life among the very poor in New York City's Lower East Side slums.
Baldwin, James, 1924-   **Another country.   Dial, 1962.**
Dougherty, Richard.   **Commissioner.   Doubleday, 1962.**
    A three-day manhunt brings into focus the personal and professional lives of
    the New York City Police Department.

NEW YORK - NEW YORK CITY - GREENWICH VILLAGE
Atwell, Lester.   **Love is just around the corner.   Simon, 1962.**
    A comic portrait of the artist as a young woman and how she survived the
    days of the Great Depression in New York City, during the 1930s.
Powell, Dawn.   **Golden Spur.   Viking, 1962.**
    Young man from Ohio comes to Greenwich Village in search of his real father.

Fiction Supplement, May 1963

Los Angeles County Public Library
Computer-Produced Catalogs

BOWKER, P. R., COMPANY, FIRM, PUBLISHERS, NEW YORK
   SEE
   American book publishing record.   R015
   Cumulative (In Title Catalog)
   School library supervisors directory   R020.2
   (In Title Catalog)

BOWKER, RICHARD ROGERS
   SEE
   American Library directory (In Title   R020.2
   Catalog)

BOWLES, FRANK HAMILTON
   How to get into college, by F. H.   371.21
   Bowles, and others. 4th ed., new and rev.
   Dutton, 1968. 160 p. Bibliography.
   Other editions available: 1958; 1960; 3d.

BOWMAN, ISAIAH
   (The) Andes of southern Peru;   551.4
   geographical reconnaissance along the
   seventy-third meridian. Greenwood Pr., 1968,
   c1916. 336 p. Illus., fold. maps., diagrs.
   (part fold.) Bibliographical footnotes.
   "The geographic work of the Yale Peruvian
   Expedition of 1911 was essentially a
   reconnaissance of the Peruvian Andes along
   the 73rd meridian."

Author Supplement, August 1969

GEOLOGY--ANDES
   (The) Andes of southern Peru; by Bowman,   551.4
   Isaiah. Greenwood Pr., 1968, c1916. 336 p.
   Illus., fold. maps., diagrs. (part fold.)
   Bibliographical footnotes.
   Geographical reconnaissance along the
   seventy-third meridian.
   Detailed survey of the 200-mile stretch of
   mountain country of Peru between Abancay and
   the Pacific coast. Compiled by the Yale
   Peruvian Expedition of 1911.

GEOLOGY--ASWAN RESERVOIR
   Desert and river in Nubia; by Butzer,   551.48
   Karl Wilhelm. Univ. of Wis. Pr., c1968. 562 p.
   Illus., maps. Bibliography: p. 537-550.
   Geomorphology and prehistoric environments at
   the Aswan Reservoir by K. W. Butzer and Carl
   L. Hansen, with contributions by Egbert G.
   Leigh, Jr., Madeleine Van Campo and Bruce G.
   Gladfelter.

Subject Supplement, August 1969

Los Angeles County Public Library
Computer-Produced Catalogs

CATS--STORIES

Aha and the jewel of mystery. by Boshinski,　　J
Blanche. Parents Magazine Pr., c1968.
Illus. by Shirley Pulido.
　About 4963 years ago Aha, First Cat of Upper
Egypt, made the mistake of falling asleep in a
bag of wheat thus changing his life. Grades
5-7.

(The) cat who loved the sea. by Goldstein,　　EB
Rhoda. Prentice, 1968. 32 p.
Illus. by Len Ebert.
　When no one has time for Hubert, the sea cat,
he takes to the country but is only able to
stay away until autumn. Preschool - Grade 2.

Horatio. by Clymer, Eleanor Lowenton.　　EB
Atheneum, c1968. 63 p. Col. illus.
Drawings by Robert Quackenbush.
　Only when Horatio the cat is adopted by two
kittens does he admit that helping others
brings happiness. Preschool - Grade 3.

(The) little prince and the tiger cat. by　　J
Damjan, Mischa, pseud. McGraw, c1967. (unpaged)
Oversize.
Illus. by Ralph Steadman.
　How the Emperor's cat in long-ago Japan freed
other cats in the realm from the decree that
they must wear collars and leashes.
Kindergarten - Grade 2.

Manhattan is missing. by Hildick, Edmund　　J
Wallace. Doubleday, c1969. 239 p.
Illus. by Jan Palmer.
　Kidnapped cat leads visiting English children
and local genius on a chase through New York
City. Grades 4-6.

Children's Catalog Supplement, July 1969

NEW YORK

O'Shaughnessy's cafe. by Clune, Henry W.n　　Fic
Macmillan, c1969. 473 p.
　The manufacturing and selling of a food
product involves the inhabitants of a small
western town in some hilarious adventures.

NEW YORK--LONG ISLAND

Chewsday; by Greenburg, Dann Stein, c1968.　　Fic
188 p.
A sex novel.
　A parody on how to write and read "a sex
novel".

(The) devil walks on water; by Murray,　　Fic
John F.h Little, c1969. 273 p.
A novel.

Fiction Supplement, August 1969

OREGON STATE LIBRARY

State Library Building
Salem, Oregon 97310

Characteristics

      Page Size: 8-1/2 x 11"

      Format: 2-column

      Arrangement: Separate listings are provided for sub-
jects, titles, and authors.

      Description: Entries in the author and subject cata-
logs include author, title, sub-title, publisher, date of publication, edition, collation, notes, and classification number.
The title section contains abbreviated entries. Photocomposition printout offers a clear upper- and lower-case font,
and boldface headings. (For additional details see Oregon
State Library Press Release, September 11, 1967, following).

Method of Production

      The Master Catalog is produced by Sedgwick Printout
Systems (410 East 62 Street, New York, N.Y. 10021) by
means of computerized photocomposition, using the Photon
Zip 900, a machine which has a font of 264 different characters.[1] (See Press Release following).

Frequency of Issue

      Original plans called for the issuance of three non-
cumulative supplements per year by author-title-subject, with
an annual cumulation to include the fourth quarter input.
Catalogs for 1966 and 1967 were completed, and April and
July quarterlies in 1968. A contract has been entered into
with Professional Library Service (Xerox) for 1970 supplements. Whereas photocomposition is used for the annual,
computer printout serves for supplements.

Comments

      "We have had 300 copies of the quarterly supplements
and 375 copies of the annual published. Those libraries receiving the book catalogs were required to have a librarian
on duty full time.

"The Oregon State Library supplements local library resources of public, academic, school, and special libraries. The schools and public libraries have been most enthusiastic about the book catalogs and have been most distressed with the delays in keeping the supplements updated. Now that they have become accustomed to the catalogs they find it difficult to do without.

"The staff of the State Library has found it convenient to have sets of the book catalog available in a number of different spots in the State Library building so they are not physically bound to the area of the card catalogs. It has expedited the filling of requests to have the request slips returned with classification numbers. The professionsl reference staff would like a great deal more detailed cataloging and cross reference indexing than we are able to "afford" in the book catalog. Adult non-fiction titles included in the book catalog are not added to the card catalog file. "[2]

Notes

1. Loeber, Thomas S. , "OSL Master Book Catalog Distributed in September; or Mohammed and the Catalog." PNLA Quarterly, October, 1967, p. 6.

2. Communication from Eloise Ebert, State Librarian, March 6, 1970.

Press Release

Oregon State Library
Salem, Oregon
September 11, 1967

FOR IMMEDIATE RELEASE

Distribution of Oregon State Library Master Book Catalog announced by Eloise Ebert, State Librarian.

What is it? The Master Book Catalog of the Oregon State Library is a library catalog prepared in book form. It represents over 350 catalog drawers of the Oregon State Library's adult non-fiction holdings (mainly books), 190,000 separate titles in all. It is an author-title-subject catalog. Regular supplements covering new book purchases will be issued quarterly.

Why a book catalog?   Half of Oregon's population, or
one million people, live in towns with a population of less
than 2,500 so a large part of our state is too thinly settled
to provide the tax base required to give good library service.
As a way of offsetting this condition the Master Book Catalog
is being distributed all over the state to public libraries, high
schools, community colleges, universities, etc.   Here everyone who wants to use the resources of the State Library can
see precisely what is available in the fields in which they are
interested.   They can then either order the book directly from
the State Library or if they live within the jurisdiction of a
local library they should order it through that agency.

This is literally taking the-mountain-to-Mohammed via
the Master Catalog.   The Oregon State Library is sending
out the equivalent of about one hundred thousand library catalog drawers or about eighty million carefully written and
organized catalog cards.   Until very recently the technology
needed to make a book catalog of this size was not available.

Significant data:

1.   The Book Catalog represents a reduction of one-
      fortieth the space the same number of entries
      occupies as a card catalog.

2.   Its twenty-five volumes contain eleven thousand
      pages and eighteen million words but is only 1.2
      cubic feet in volume and takes up but twenty-two
      inches of standard library shelf space.

3.   The Oregon State Library is the first state library
      in America to publish a book catalog of a major
      part of its holdings.

The Catalog is Computer Produced

The information on the original catalog cards in the
State Library at Salem was transferred to IBM punch cards.
These IBM cards were then transferred to 50 magnetic com-
puter tapes and the tapes were then run through an ultra-fast
Photon Zip photocomposing machine under the direction of a
computer program.

The Photon machine sets type photographically at
speeds of up to five hundred letters a second on a continuous
film strip.   The film (usually a paper positive) is then

used to make a photo-offset for printing. The entire ninety million characters in the Master Catalog were phototypeset in 165 hours. This method of typesetting is approximately one hundred times faster than the conventional hot metal process. Printing was done by Metropolitan Press in Portland.

Oregon State Library

BLACKBURN, HENRY

q914.41   Breton folk; an artistic tour in Brittany With one hundred and seventy
               illustrations by R. Caldecott. 1880. 200 p.

BLACKBURN, LURA
                              SEE
373   Oak Park, Ill. Oak Park & River Forest High School. Our high school
                   clubs.

BLACKBURN, PHILIP CONKLIN
                              SEE
817   Dodgson, Charles Lutwidge. Logical nonsense.

BLACKBURN, ROWLAND GEORGE

671 qB562 Sheet metal work, for the intermediate examination of the City and
               Guilds of London Institute, by R. G. Blackburn and J. Cassidy. Arnold,
               c1957 -

BLACKBURN, SAMUEL A.

694   Boy activity projects. Manual Arts Press, 1918. 143 p. Illus.
694   Problems in farm woodwork, for agricultural schools, high schools, and
               country schools. 2d ed. Manual Arts Press, c1915. 128 p.

BLACKBURN, THOMAS

811.9   Price of an eye. Morrow, c1961. 170 p.
811   Smell of burning. Morrow, c1962.

BLACKBURN, VERNON
                              SEE
914   Steevens, George Warrington. Glimpses of three nations.

BLACKER, CHARLES PATON

R176.32   Birth control and the state; a plea and a forecast. Dutton, 1926. 87 p.
               (To-day and to-morrow series)
575.6   Eugenics; Galton and after. Harvard Univ. Press, c1952. 349 p. Illus.

BLACKER, IRWIN R.

904   Irregulars, partisans, guerrillas; great stories from Rogers' Rangers to the
               Haganah. Edited and with commentaries by Irwin R. Blacker. Simon,
               c1954. 487 p.
978   Old West in fact. Obolensky, c1962. 446 p.
                              SEE
973.16   Golden conquistadores.
910.8   Hakluyt, Richard. Hakluy's voyages.

BLACKER, J. F.

738   A B C collecting old continental pottery. With over 250 illustrations in
               half-tone and line. Paul, 1913. 315 p. (The A B C series)
738   A B C collecting old English china; giving a short history of the English
               factories, and showing how to apply tests for umarked china before
               1800. Jacobs, n. d. 386 p. Illus.

Master Book Catalog--Authors

Oregon State Library
Master Book Catalog, 1967

BAR ASSOCIATIONS

340.06   **Winters, Glenn R.** Bar association organization and activities; a
              handbook for bar association officers. Foreword by Howard L.
              Barkdull. Published for the Survey of the Legal Profession and the
              Conference of Bar Association Presidents by the American Judicature
              Society, c1954   243 p. Illus.

BAR ASSOCIATIONS - DIRECTORIES

340.6   **American Bar Foundation.** International directory of bar associations
              1964 - Collection.

BAR ASSOCIATIONS - HISTORY

340   **Pound, Roscoe.** Lawyer from antiquity to modern times, with particular
              reference to the development of bar associations in the United States.
              A study prepared for and published by the Survey of the Legal
              Profession under the auspices of American Bar Association. West,
              c1953. 404 p. Port.

BARANOV, ALEKSANDR ANDREEVICH

921 B227c   **Chevigny, Hector.** Lord of Alaska; Baranov and the Russian adventure.
              Viking, 1942. 320 p.

BARBADOS - BIOGRAPHY

929 qH79o   **Hotten, John Camden.** Original lists of persons of quality; emigrants:
              religious exiles: political rebels: serving men sold for a term of years:
              apprentices: children stolen: maidens pressed: and others who went
              from Great Britain to the American plantations 1600 -1700. With their

Subjects

668.5   Cosmetic recipe book, by Goodman, Herman.
668.5   Cosmetics, by Bushby, Robert.
646.7   Cosmetics, by Harry, Ralph Gordon.
646.7   Cosmetics, by Household Finance Corporation.
155.333   Cosmic consciousness, by Bucke, Richard Maurice.
              Cosmic disturbances of the earth's magnetic field and their influence upon
                 radio communication.
                                    IN
qR538.7   Kennelly, Arthur Edwin. Magnetic field and the earth and its
C21m   atmosphere.
811   Cosmic flight and other poems, by Gilbert, Grace Julia.
572.4   Cosmic forces as they were taught in Mu, by Churchward, James.
182.4   Cosmic fragments, by Heraclitus, of Ephesus.
              Cosmic philosophy, Outlines of
                                    SEE
110   Fiske, John. Outlines of cosmic philosophy.
539.7   Cosmic radiation, by Hooper, John Edward.
506 C21p   Cosmic -ray results, by Carnegie Institution of Washington. Dept. of
no.175   Terrestrial Magnetism.
q506 C21p   Cosmic -ray results: Huancayo, Peru, January 1946 - December 1955, by
no.175   Carnegie Institution of Washington. Dept. of Terrestrial Magnetism.
539.7   Cosmic rays, by Cranshaw, T. E.

Titles

HARVARD UNIVERSITY LIBRARY

Cambridge, Massachusetts 02138

Book Catalogs

> Widener Library Shelflists
> Catalog of the Lamont Library (published in 1953)
> Catalogs of the libraries of the Graduate School of
>   Design, the Peabody Museum of Archeology and
>   Ethnology, the Museum of Comparative Zoology,
>   and the Gray Herbarium, have been published by
>   G. K. Hall.
> Countway Library of Medicine and Baker Library of
>   the Graduate School of Business Administration
>   have produced serial lists in book form.[1]
> Catalogue of Hebrew Books (1968)
> Catalogue of Arabic, Persian, and Ottoman Turkish
>   Books (1968)

Widener Library Shelflists

As part of its effort to computerize certain of its
bibliographical records, the Harvard University Library is
converting to machine-readable form portions of the shelflist
and classification schedules of Widener Library, which is
Harvard's central research collection. "After each class
and its corresponding classification schedule have been converted to machine readable form, a three-part catalog of
the holdings in the class is published in the Widener Library
Shelflist Series. The first part contains the classification
schedule and a list of the entries in the class in call number (i.e. classification) sequence with sub-class headings
(derived by program from the machine readable classification
schedule) interspersed throughout the list. The second part
is an alphabetical listing by author and by title and is obtained by a programmed computer sort of the original entries,
and the third part lists each entry again chronologically by
date of publication. Thus, each entry is listed four times.

"The first twenty volumes in the series were produced
by photo-offset from photographically reduced computer
printouts and averaged about seventy entries per single-
column page. Beginning with volume 21, all page copy has
been set in 6-point Times Roman type in double columns by
a computerized photocomposition technique, with approximately 140 entries per page. Volumes are 8-1/2 x 11 inches,

printed on durable paper, and cloth bound. The library is the publisher."[2]

The shelflist entries are generally less complete than the public catalog entries. The shelflists are intended to supplement rather than replace the subject approach of the public catalog.

(For costs and other details see chapter cited in reference 2.)

Notes

1. Communication from Charles W. Husbands, Systems Librarian in the College Library, December 3, 1969.

2. De Gennaro, Richard. "Harvard University's Widener Library Shelflist Conversion and Publication Program." College and Research Libraries 31: 318-31, Sept., 1970 (see p. 175-191).

Widener Library Shelflist 21
Latin American Literature, 1969

SAL 3621.6.100	Gómez Espinosa, Margarita. La bruja; novela. 1a ed. Barcelona, 1958.
SAL 3570.2.1050	Gomez Espinosa, Margarita. Rubén Darío, patriota. Madrid, 1966.
SAL 1619.28.100	Gomez Flores, F. Narraciones y caprichos. Culiacan, 1889-91.
SAL 1422.15	Gomez Flores, F.J. Bocetos literarios. México, 1881.
SAL 1621.5.31	Gomez Haro, E. Tradiciones y leyendas de Puebla. Puebla, 1904.
SAL 1432.5	Gomez Haro, Eduardo. Historia del teatro principal de Puebla. Puebla, 1902.
SAL 5621.1.8	Gómez Jaime, A. Aves viajeras. Bogotá, 192-
SAL 5621.1.5	Gómez Jaime, A. Cantos de gloria. Bogotá, 1924.
SAL 5621.1.3	Gómez Jaime, A. El enigma de la selva. Bogotá, 1911?
SAL 5621.55.21	Gómez Jaime, A. Poesías de Antonio Gomez Restrepo. Bogotá, 1940.
SAL 5827.5	Gomez Jurado, Miguel A. Antologia de poetas de Imbabura. Quito, 1955.
SAL 4419.96.110	Gomez Masia, R. En la trastienda de Temis. Buenos Aires, 1931.
SAL 4419.96.100	Gomez Masia, R. Temistocles en Salamina. Buenos Aires, 1942.
SAL 4455.2.90	Gomez-Montero, Rafael. El alma de harrita se llama Avila. Madrid, 1949.
SAL 5221.3.100	Gomez Morel, A. Mundo adentro montado en un palo de escoba. Santiago de Chile, 1963. 2v.
SAL 1629.68.100	Gómez Palacio, M. A flor de la vida. Mexico, 1921.
SAL 1619.68.120	Gómez Palacio, M. La ambición del diablo; novela. 1a ed. México, 1962.
SAL 1619.68.110	Gómez Palacio, M. Entre riscos y entre ventisqueros. Mexico, 1931.
SAL 5621.54.100	Gómez Picón, Rafael. 45 relatos de un burocrata. Bogotá, 1941.
➡ SAL 5422.10	Gomez R., A. Critica literaria. Bogotá, 1935.

Author and Title Listing

SAL 4409.90.240	Galvez, Manuel. La noche toca a su fin. Buenos Aires, 1935.
SAL 4399.36.805	Gargaro, Alfredo. Notable conferencia acerca de la obra poética del Dr. Marcoa J. Figueroa. n.p., 1935?
SAL 4413.1.16	Ghiraldo, A. Cancionero libertario. 2a ed. Santiago de Chile, 1935.
SAL 4414.48.100	Gil, Martin. Hablando solo. Buenos Aires, 1935.
SAL 317.6.100	Girón Cerna, Carlos. Ixquic. La Habana, 1935?
➡ SAL 5422.10	Gomez R., A. Critica literaria. Bogotá, 1935.
SAL 5620.27.100	González, Fernando. Cartas a Estanislao. 1a ed. Manizales, 1935.
SAL 1620.53.100	Gonzalez, Martin R.A. Sometime, somewhere. N.Y., 1935.
SAL 1621.3.15	Gonzalez Martinez, Enrique. Poemas truncos. Mexico, 1935.
SAL 7220.71.150	Gonzalez Prada, Manuel. Baladas peruanas. Santiago de Chile, 1935.
SAL 10078.10	Griffith, William. Bermuda troubadours. N.Y., 1935.
SAL 4425.41.132	Guiraldes, Ricardo. Don Segundo Sombra. N.Y., 1935.
SAL 4425.41.133	Guiraldes, Ricardo. Don Segundo Sombra. Santiago de Chile, 1935.
SAL 326.86.100	Gutiérrez Soto, H. Cumbre; epopeya. Dolores, Cuba, 1935.
SAL 5420.25	Guzmán, D.R. de. De la novela. Bogotá, 1935.
SAL 4428.1.15	Hernández, José. The gaucho, Martin Fierro. Oxford, 1935.
SAL 2828.75.140	Herrera, Flavio. La tempestad. Guatemala, 1935.
SAL 60.45.5	Herrera, L.P. Antologia hispano-americana. 2a ed. Buenos Aires, 1935.
SAL 476.2.805	Homenaje a Enrique José Varona. La Habana, 1935.
SAL 6033.5.110	Icaza, Jorge. En las calles. Quito, 1935.
SAL 7639.89.33	Ipuche, P.L. Isla Patrulla; romance. Buenos Aires, 1935.
SAL 340.3.120	Iraizoz y de Villar, Antonio. Estampas panameñas. Tampa, 1935.
SAL 3244.2.120	Izaguirre, Carlos. Alturas y abismos. Tegucigalpa, 1935.
SAL 1647.54.120	Jiménez Rueda, Julio. La desventura del conde Kadski. Mexico, 1935.
SAL 9058.100	Krug, G. Letras rio-grandenses. Porto Alegre, 1935.
SAL 7.55	Leavitt, Sturgis Elleno. A bibliography of theses dealing

Chronological Listing

Widener Library Shelflist 21
Latin American Literature, 1969

SAL 5420   Latin American literature in Spanish - Colombia - General history - General works - cont.

SAL 5420.60	Bronx, H. Clasicos colombianos. Medellin, 1949.
SAL 5420.62	La literatura colombiana. Bogotá, 1952.
SAL 5420.63	Amango Ferrer, J. Dos horas de literatura colombiana. Antioquia, 1963.
SAL 5420.64	Nunez Segura. Literatura colombiana. 7a ed. Medellin, 1964.

SAL 5422   Latin American literature in Spanish - Colombia - General history - Special periods

SAL 5422.4	Laverde Amaya, Isidoro. Fisionomías literarias de colombianos. Curazao, 1890.
SAL 5422.4.5	Laverde Amaya, Isidoro. Ojeada histórico-crítica sobre las origenes de la literatura colombiana. Bogotá, 1963.
SAL 5422.10	Gomez R., A. Crítica literaria. Bogotá, 1935.
SAL 5422.15	Vega, F. de. Critica. Bogotá, 1936.
SAL 5422.20	Otero M., G. La literatura colonial de Colombia. La Paz, 1928.
SAL 5422.25	Zapata, Ramón. Lecciones de literatura colombiana. Bogotá, 1941.
SAL 5422.30	Alvarez d'Orsonville, J.M. Colombia literaria, reportajes. Bogotá, 1956-57. 3v.
SAL 5422.31	Maya, Rafael. Los origenes del modernismo en Colombia. Bogotá, 1961.
SAL 5422.35	Camacho Guizado, Eduardo. Estudios sobre literatura colombiana. 1a ed. Bogotá, 1965-

SAL 5423   Latin American literature in Spanish - Colombia - General history - Local

SAL 5423.3.2	Correa, Ramón C. Historia de la literatura boyacense. 2a ed. Tunja, 1950.
SAL 5423.5	Rincon R., S. Historia del arte literario en Boyacá. Tunja, 1939.
SAL 5423.10	Ortega Ricanite, J.V. La gruta simbolica y reminiscencias. Bogotá, 1952.
SAL 5423.15	Mesa, Carlos E. Cuatro escritores antioqueños. Medellín, 1968.

SAL 5426   Latin American literature in Spanish - Colombia - History of special forms - Poetry - Special periods

SAL 5426.15	Moro, L.M. Los contertutias de la gruta simbolica. Bogotá, 1936.
SAL 5426.15.8	Moro, L.M. Los maestros de principios del siglo. Bogotá, 1938.
SAL 5426.20	Caparroso, Carlos Arturo. Dos ciclos de lirismo colombiano. Bogotá, 1961.
SAL 5426.25	Botero, Ebel. Cinco poetas colombianos. Manizales, 1964.

SAL 5428   Latin American literature in Spanish - Colombia - History of special forms - Poetry - Special topics

SAL 5428.2	Pardo Tovar, Andrés. La poesía popular colombiana y sus origenes españoles. Bogotá, 1966.

SAL 5435   Latin American literature in Spanish - Colombia - History of special forms - Fiction - General works

SAL 5435.5	Curcio Altamar, Antonio. Evolución de la novela en Colombia. Bogotá, 1957.

SAL 5436   Latin American literature in Spanish - Colombia - History of special forms - Fiction - Special periods

SAL 5436.2	Bronx, Humberto. Veinte años de novela colombiana. Medellín, 1966.

SAL 5437   Latin American literature in Spanish - Colombia - History of special forms - Fiction - Local

SAL 5437.5	Casa, Enrique Carlos de la. La novela antioqueña. Mexico, 1942.

Classified Listings by Call Number

BALTIMORE COUNTY PUBLIC LIBRARY[1]

Administrative Offices
25 West Chesapeake Avenue
Towson, Maryland 21204

Characteristics

> Page size: 8-1/2 x 11 inches

> Format: 3-column

> Arrangement: The catalog is divided into three sections, Titles, Subjects, and Authors.

> Description: Simplified cataloging is used, as the catalog is intended as a finding list, rather than a bibliographic tool.   Entries in all catalogs include title, author, date of publication, and call number.   Fiction has no call number. Specific designations are used to indicate special collections of fiction and non-fiction, and special types of fiction. The call number appears in the lower right hand corner of the entry; the contractor's access number in the lower left hand corner.   Edition statements are always used.   The only collation item used is the number of volumes in a multi-volume work.   Annotations are not included.   In the author catalog, cross references are used to refer from one form of the author's name to the one established for use, and for the identification of real names.   No cross references are used in the subject catalog.   In the subject section, entries are sub-arranged alphabetically by author.   Holdings are not included in the catalog.

> Running heads appear at the top of the pages.

Method of Production

> The information is stored on magnetic tape from punched cards generated from the source documents.   The catalog, designed and prepared by Documentation, Inc., Bethesda, Maryland (now LEASCO), is a product of a fully computerized system.   Proprietary programs designed for the IBM 360 and Photon computer complex are employed to manipulate the data and to prepare camera ready copy.   200 copies of the adult catalog, and 249 copies of the juvenile catalog are run.

Frequency of Issue

The initial contract specified a basic book catalog of approximately 55,000 titles. Bi-monthly supplements cumulated for one year, with new cumulations for the second year, and a second basic list incorporating the cumulated supplements and the first basic at the end of two years were specified. 110,000 titles are now listed in book catalog form.

Costs

The cost per year for from 8,000 to 10,000 titles entered was estimated at $25,000 to $40,000 depending upon whether there were to be supplements only, or a basic list with supplements. The cost was based on a fixed charge of 90¢ for each title entered on the magnetic tape, plus a charge of $13.00 per page, depending on the number of copies run.

Comments

The reaction to the book catalogs has been favorable. The card catalogs have been removed from all the branches. The book catalog has been placed in all of the county public schools.

Note

1. Information contributed by Paula Kieffer, Coordinator, Technical Services. (See also Kieffer, Paula, "The Baltimore County Public Library Book Catalog," p. 281-292).

Baltimore County Public Library

Author Catalog

A

ABBOTT, ROBERT TUCKER
Seashells of North America 1968
69003861   594.097 A

ABDY, JANE
French poster Cheret to Cappiello 1969
69004494   741.67 A

ABE, KOBO
Friends 1969
69007092
Ruined map 1969
69003862   895.62 A

ABELS, JULES
In the time of silent Cal 1969
69002386   973.915 A

ADLER, BETTY
Man of letters (H L Mencken) 1969
69007837   Ref 012 M

ADLER, BILL
Growing up Jewish 1969
69004498   915.693 A
Letters from Israel 1968
69000218   956.94 A

AFRICAN BIBLIOGRAPHIC CENTER
African affairs for the general reader a selected and
introductory bibliographical guide 1960 1967
69001360   Ref 016.916 A

AGAY, DENES
Joy of Bach 1968
69007094   7864 A
Joy of boogie and blues 1968
69007095   7864 A

AGEE, JAMES
Collected short prose 1968
69001361   810.8 A

Decorating made simple 1964
69003005   747 A

ALEXANDER, R MCNEILL
Animal mechanics 1968
69005693   591.18 A

ALEXANDERSSON, GUNNAR
Geography of manufacturing 1967
69000450   338.476 A

ALFASSY, LEO
Just blues 1968
69007096   7864 A

ALI, TARIQ
New revolutionaries 1969
69005694   323.208 A

ALISKY, MARVIN
Uruguay 1969
69008145   918.95 A

ALLEN, FORREST CLAIRE
Basketball Enl ed 1968
69003006   796.32 A 1968

Title Catalog

A

A B C FOR BOOK-COLLECTORS
Carter, John 1952
69003738   010.3 C

A B C'S OF ANTENNAS
Lytel, Allan Herbert 1966
69001627   621.384 L

A B C'S OF CITIZENS BAND RADIO
Buckwalter, Len 2d ed 1966
69005782   621.384 B

A B C'S OF COMPUTERS
Lytel, Allan Herbert 2d ed 1966
69008342   510.78 L 1966

A B C'S OF ELECTRONICS
Waters, Earl J 1966
69007036   621.381 W

ACRYLIC LANDSCAPE PAINTING
Pellew, John C 1968
69008197   758.1 P

ACT OF CONGRESS
Eidenberg, Eugene 1969
69003755   379.14 E

ACT OF LOVE
Dale, Celia 1969
69002417

ACTION APPROACH
Weinberg, George 1969
69003714   616.858 W

ACTION DRILLING IN WRESTLING
Gianakaris, George 1969
69004784   796.812 G

ACTION GUIDE FOR EXECUTIVE JOB SEEKERS
AND EMPLOYERS
Uris, Auren 1968
(Also published as The executive job market)
69001173   658.3 U

ADA

Annenberg, Maurice 1969
69002549   659.1 A

ADVISE AND OBSTRUCT
Gallagher, Hugh Gregory 1969
69007323   327.73 G

AERIAL HANDBOOK
Briggs, Gilbert Arthur 1964
69001411   621.384 B

AERIAL-MAP VOLUME OF BALTIMORE COUNTY
MARYLAND
Real estate Directories, inc 1969
69006714   Ref 333.33 R

AERODYNAMICS OF POWERED FLIGHT
Carroll, Robert L 1960
64019299   629.132 C

AESTHETIC ADVENTURE
Gaunt, William 1967
69005915   709.03 G 1967

AESTHETIC MOVEMENT
Aslin, Elizabeth 1969
69007845   709.04 A

Baltimore County Public Library

AFRICA--POLITICS--1960-

Porter, Eliot Forever wild 1966
917.4753 P
69005610

ADOLESCENCE
Caplan, Gerald Adolescence psychosocial
perspectives 1969
69001428 **155.5 C**
Caprio, Frank Samuel Parents and teenagers 1968
69002616 **155.5 C**
Garrison, Karl Claudius Psychology of adolescence
6th ed 1965
69005912 **155.5 G**
Ginott, Haim G Between parent and teenager 1969
69002704 **301.4315 G**
Grinder, Robert E Studies in adolescence 1963
69004814 **155.5 G**

McClement, Fred It doesn't matter where you sit 1969
69005024 **614.869 M**
Serling, Robert J Loud and clear 1969
69001085 **629.13 S**

AERONAUTICS--YEARBOOKS
Jane's All the world's airships 1909 1909
69006018 **629.13 J**
Taylor, John William Ransom Aircraft sixtynine 1968
69000404 **629.13 T**

AEROPLANES, MILITARY
Taylor, John William Ransom Combat aircraft of the
world 1969
69007730 **629.133 T**

AFGHAN HOUNDS
Brearley, Joan McDonald This is the Afghan

Subject Catalog

Cross References

Abnormal children *See* EXCEPTIONAL CHILDREN

Abnormal psychology *See* PSYCHOLOGY, PATHOLOGICAL

Accelerators, Electron *See* PARTICLE ACCELERATORS

Accidents, Traffic *See* TRAFFIC ACCIDENTS

Acoustics *See* ARCHITECTURAL ACOUSTICS, HEARING
MUSIC--ACOUSTICS AND PHYSICS, SOUND

Adding Machines *See* CALCULATING MACHINES

Administration *See* MANAGEMENT

Aeroplanes *See* AIRPLANES

African relations *See* PAN AFRICANISM

Army posts *See* MILITARY POSTS

Art and nature *See* NATURE ESTHETICS

Art, Commercial *See* COMMERCIAL ART

Art forgeries *See* FORGERY OF WORKS OF ART

Art, Negro *See* NEGRO ART

Artificial satellites *See* SATELLITES, ARTIFICIAL

Athletes, Negro *See* NEGRO ATHLETES

Atomic nuclei *See* NUCLEAR PHYSICS

Authors, Negro *See* NEGRO AUTHORS

FAIRFAX COUNTY PUBLIC LIBRARY

3915 Chain Bridge Road
Fairfax, Virginia 22030

Characteristics

     Size: 9 x 12 inches

     Format: 3-column

     Arrangement: Separate sections are provided for
Author, Title and Subject entries.

Description; Method of Production

     "Fairfax County Public Library began publishing a
book catalog of adult titles using Varityper composition and
high speed listomatic cameras in 1964. This method of production was used by the printer, Science Press, until January 1969, when the Northern Virginia Community College
and Fairfax County Public Library began a cooperative pilot
project subsidized by Federal Funds (LSCA, Title III),
whereby the holdings of both systems are included in one
computer-photocomposed catalog incorporating both Dewey
Decimal (FCPL) and L.C. (NVCC) Classifications. As far
as could be determined the pilot project was the first combined college-public and D.D.-L.C. catalog.

     "Fairfax County Public Library prepares input on a
Friden Flexowriter, which produces paper tape and a hard
copy. The paper tape is converted by Science Press into
magnetic tape and fed into the computer which is programmed
to arrange the data into a specified format, cross-reference
it and add it to the master file. According to a predetermined
schedule, in this case every other month, the output from the
updated master file is interfaced with an automatic Photon
typesetting machine which prepares the catalog pages. High
speed printing and binding equipment is utilized to produce
the catalog in upper and lower case composition. Supplements
and master are printed in three books, author, title and
subject. Smaller books are stapled, larger issues are Smythe
sewn. The Master issue is Smythe sewn with a hard cover.
Under our present plan, five cumulative supplements and a
hardbound master issue are produced annually. The succeeding issue starts a new accumulation. All current acquisitions
are listed in each supplement. "Backlog" is brought forward

when a new Branch is added to the system or new holdings
are added to a title.   At the current rate of additions and
growth, all titles including "backlog" should be in the data
bank by January 1972.

"Three Hundred and fifty copies of each supplement are
printed and distributed to Fairfax County Public Library
branches, Northern Virginia Community College branches,
all County intermediate and senior high schools, the Virginia
State Library, the University of Virginia, suburban Washington public libraries, Northern Virginia colleges and other
Virginia community colleges."

"Adult Card Catalogs have been removed from all
Branches.   However, Shelf Lists are still maintained.

"User reaction has generally been favorable.   Library
staff and public have gradually been educated to make more
efficient use of the catalog.   Younger patrons have more
readily accepted the change than others.

"Because costs of a book catalog are determined by so
many factors, i.e. format, type style, length of entries,
timing, holdings and addition of new branches, we are including a schedule of charges instead of actual costs.

One-time Costs

Programming	$13,300
Friden Flexowriter	
and stand	4,120
Other equipment	297

Charges per supplement

Personnel - Input for 20 records can be produced per
hour.   Two additional units of time per unit of machine time
is required for corrections, proofing, checking and filing.

Computer Set Up	$ 1,000.
Processing of Records	30.70 per M
Printing and binding	
of pages	13.66 each
	(approximately)"[1]

Note

1.   Communication from William L. Whitesides, Director,
        April 16, 1970.

Fairfax County Library

Wells, Henry Willis 1895-
The realm of literature. Kennikat 1955
PN45.W4   NV   E
Langland, William 1330?-1400? The vision
of Piers Plowman. Greenwood Pr 1968
821 L   H

Wells, Herbert George 1866-1946
Bennett, Arnold 1867-1931 Arnold Bennett
and H. G. Wells Univ of Ill Pr 1960
B Bennett   H T
The croquet player. Viking 1937
Fiction   H   M   D
A modern utopia. Univ of Neb Pr 1967
Reproduced from the 1st ed. published in
1905.
321.07 W   HXTMGDRW C
The outline of history, being a plain history of
life and mankind. Rev. Garden City Bks
1961
909 W 1961   X   DR   PJC E
D21.W4   NV C E
Three novels: The time machine. The war of
the worlds. The island of Doctor Moreau.
Heinemann 1965
Fiction   M D W
The time machine, an invention. Heinemann
1963
SF   HXT D W J
War of the worlds. Pop Lib 1962
SF   HXTMGDRWPJ

Welty, Eudora 1909-
Delta wedding. Harcourt 1946
Fiction   HXTMGDRWPJC
The Ponder heart. Harcourt 1954
Fiction   HXTMGD   E
Selected stories of Eudora Welty: containing
all of A curtain of green and otherstories.
Modern Lib 1943
Fiction   HXTMGDRWPJC E

Wemyss, Francis Courtney 1797-1859
Chronology of the American stage. from 1752
to 1852. Blom 1968
Reprint of 1852 ed.
R792.097 W   H

Wendell, Barrett 1855-1921
The traditions of European literature. from
Homer to Dante. Ungar 1964   2 v
PN610.W4   NV   E

Wendt, Paul Francis 1908-
Real estate investment analysis and taxation.
McGraw 1969
T333.33 W   H   W

Wenger, John Christian 1910-
The Mennonite Church in America. sometimes
called Old Mennonites. Herald Pr 1966
289.7 W   H

Authors

Fairfax County Library

World Council of Peace
Ehrenburg, Il'ia Grigor'evich 1891-1967
   Post-war years, 1945-1954.   World Pub
1967
891.78 E   H TM DRW

   World economics *see* **Commercial policy**
      see **Economic policy**
      see **Geography, Economic**

   World federation *see* **International**
      organization

   World government *see* **International**
      organization

   World history
McNeill, William Hardy 1917-
   A world history.   Oxford Univ Pr 1967
909 M   H   MGDRWP   E
► Wells, Herbert George 1866-1946
   The outline of history   Rev.   Garden City Bks
1961
909 W 1961   X   DR PJC E
D21.W4   *NV C E*

Subjects

   World enough and time.
Warren, Robert Penn 1905-
Fiction   HXTMGDRWPJC E

   The world food problem.
U. S. Panel on the World Food Supply
338.19 U
   v.1-2   H   MGDRWPJ

   The world grows round my door.
Fairchild, David Grandison 1869-1954
917.59 F   H   R

   The world guide to combat planes.
Green, William
623.746 G   H TMGDRWPJC E
R623.746 G   H   G

   World guide to science information and
   documentation services.
United Nations Educational, Scientific and
      Cultural Organization
Q223.U45   *NV   E*

   A world history.
McNeill, William Hardy 1917-
909 M   H **MGDRWP**   E

Titles

ALESCO BOOK CATALOGS

ALESCO (American Library and Educational Service Company) is a book distribution company which selects, prepares, warehouses and distributes books to public and parochial schools in the United States and Canada.

Characteristics

Page Size: 8-1/2 x 11 inches

Format: 2-column

Arrangement: The catalog consists of text pages arranged in Dewey number sequence, and author and title indexes. An order form in tabular style is also printed.

Description: The text page entries include Dewey number, author, title, purchase group, grade level, interest areas (boys, girls, religious), annotation, recommending agencies, biographical identification, and price. The elementary school catalog contains an index showing Author-Title-Page; Title-Author-Page; and Grade Level-Subject-Author-Title-Page. The order form contains Author-Title-Abbreviated Dewey number-Grade-Price.

Method of Production

The catalogs are produced by Rocappi, Inc., Pennsauken, New Jersey. The initial input, entered into the computer via paper tape, is stored on magnetic tape. "When the file is complete and correct the desired entries are extracted and formatted for a sort by a special extraction pass. A sorting field of 86 characters is created for each record type, followed by the entire entry as a trailer, or those portions of the entry which may be desired for a particular application. Since the ALESCO indexes require the addition of the page number on which the entry occurs, only the first record type (which is the text material) is extracted on the first extraction pass. This material, now in the proper sequence for the text setting, is then subjected to a format program which strips the sort field from the variable-length trailer and translates the trailer into the Rocappi typesetting language. Subsequent computer passes perform hyphenation and justification, pagination, and produce an output paper tape for Rocappi's Photon 713 typesetting equipment."[1]

Costs

"The cost of creating the initial file was said to be no greater than the normal cost of typesetting (in hot metal) the equivalent book catalogs. Subsequent typesetting may be as low as 50 percent of that initial cost, and also substantially less than the cost of updating a less flexible hot metal standing galley.... Most significant of all, however, is the fact that the production time cycle is dramatically reduced. The entire catalog can be produced from a corrected tape file in less than two weeks."[2]

Notes

1. LARC Report #14, "Mechanized Procedures of Rocappi Inc., 1968, p. 14-7 to 14-14.

2. Ibid.

ALESCO Book Catalog--Text page

920   COLLECTIVE BIOGRAPHY

920 A   3rd Purchase $3.68
The Army Times
Jr. High
Famous American military leaders of World War II, by the editors of The Army Times. Dodd. 1962

Contents: George Marshall. Ernest King. Douglas MacArthur. Dwight Eisenhower. Chester Nimitz. Curtis LeMay. George Patton. Evans Carlson. Omar Bradley. Henry Arnold. William Halsey. James Doolittle.
A. H. IS. LJ

920 B   3rd Purchase $4.82LB
Bailey, Carolyn S.
Children of the handcrafts; with lithographs by Grace Paull. Viking. 1935

Grades 4-6
Exciting stories about boys and girls who played a part in the development of American crafts. Partial contents: Paul Revere. Duncan Phyfe. Henry Thoreau. Johnny Appleseed. Caroline Pickersgill.
A. BJ. C. IJ. SII. SS

920 B   2nd Purchase $4.61
Bakeless, Katherine
Story-lives of great composers. Rev. 1962. Lippincott. 1953.

Includes scientists of several nations: Copernicus. Galileo. Newton. Herschel. Faraday. Kelvin. Edison. the Curies. Marconi. Burbank. Reed. the Comptons. Fleming. Einstein. Urey. Mark. Fermi. Salk. Tsung Dao Lee. Chen Ning Yang
A. BJ. C. H. IS. J. LJ. PL. PR. SB. V

920 B   2nd Purchase $4.01
Bolton, Sarah
Lives of girls who became famous, illus. by Constance Joan Naar. Crowell. 1949

Jr. High
Among women who achieved fame against great odds were Jane Addams. Louisa May Alcott. Marian Anderson. Elizabeth Barrett Browning. Katherine Cornell. Marie Curie. Amelia Earhart. Julia Ward Howe. Florence Nightingale. and Eleanor Roosevelt.
A. C. H. J. PL

920 B   2nd Purchase $4.01
Bolton, Sarah
Lives of poor boys who became famous, illus. by Constance Joan Naar. Crowell. 1962

Jr. High
Several countries, races and vocations are represented in the lives of these men who overcame all obstacles to become leaders in their fields. Partial contents: Franklin. Mozart. Lincoln. Dickens. Rockefeller. Pius XI. Carver. Ford
A. C. H. J. PL

Author	Title	Page
Coe, Douglas — Marconi, pioneer of radio		149
Coit, Margaret L. — Andrew Jackson		144
Commager, Henry Steele — America's Robert E. Lee		147
Coolidge, Olivia — Winston Churchill, and the story of two world wars		137
Criss, Mildred — Isabella		144
Daniel, Anita — Story of Albert Schweitzer		154
Daniels, Jonathan — Mosby		150
Daugherty, James — Abraham Lincoln		148
Daugherty, James — Daniel Boone		135
Daugherty, James — Poor Richard		141
De Gering, Etta — Wilderness wife		135
Desmond, Alice Curtis — Glamorous Dolly Madison		149
Dewey, Anne Perkins — Robert Goddard		142

Author

Title	Author	Page
Fly went by, McClintock, M		244
Flying aces of World War I, Gurney, G		118
Fog magic, Sauer, J		218
Folding paper puppets, Lewis, S		83
Folding paper toys, Lewis, S		80
Folk plays for puppets you can make, Tichenor, T		88
Follow your nose, Showers, P		65
Fonabio and the lion, Guillot, R		191
Food: America's biggest business, Arnold, P		13
Food for people, Riedman, S		66
Football for young champions, Antonacci, R		91
Football rebels, Scholz, J		218
Footsteps to freedom, Stevens, W		10
For a child, McFarland, W		99

Title

Author	Title	Dewey	Grade	Price
—Information please almanac (4)		317	J&S	$3.25
—Ingalls, L., Getting to know Kenya (4)		916	4-6	$3.73LB
—Inger, N., Katie and Nan (4)		F	4-6	$3.49
—Invart, G., Jenny (4)		f	4-6	$3.68LB
—Invart, G., Susan & Martin (4)		F	4-6	$3.26LB
—Ipcar, D., I love my anteater with an A (4)		F	1-3	$4.14LB
—Ipcar, D., Wild and tame animals (3)		E	1-3	$3.11
—Ireland, N., Picture file in school, college, and public libraries (4)		025	J&S	$6.80
—Irving, R., Energy and power (3)		531	JrH	$4.24LB
—Irving, R., Hurricanes and twisters (2)		551	JrH	$4.44LB
—Irving, R., Rocks and minerals and the stories they tell (3)		552	4-6	$4.44LB
—Irving W., Legend of Sleepy Hollow (4)		F	JrH	$3.04LB
—Irving, W., Rip Van Winkle & The legend of Sleepy Hollow (1)		F	JrH	$4.29LB
—Irwin, K., Romance of chemistry (3)		540	JrH	$4.61LB
—Irwin, K., Romance of weights and measures (3)		389	JrH	$4.61LB

Order Form

CHESTER COUNTY LIBRARY, PENNSYLVANIA
CATALOG OF BOOKS IN THE LIBRARY SYSTEM

235 W. Market Street
West Chester, Pa. 19380

Characteristics

Page Size: 8-1/2 x 11 inches (formerly 8 x 12-1/8)

Format: 3-column

Description: The catalog is divided into three parts:
1) an author (main entry) section giving complete information about the book. Dewey number and locations are given.
(The 1967 catalog included tracings in the main entry section. These have been omitted in later volumes); 2) a title
index, giving the author, the Dewey number, and the location; 3) a subject index, giving author and title in abbreviated form, the Dewey number, and the locations.

Method of Production

The 1967 and 1968 volumes were produced by Rocappi,
Inc. (Division of Lehigh Press, 7000 N. Park Drive, Pennsauken, New Jersey), using the Photon 713 typesetting
machine. The Photon 713 has been replaced by an improved
and faster machine, the Harris-Intertype Fototronic CRT,
which permits the setting of the type at a speed of about 12
pages (3 column, 8-1/2" x 11") per hour.[1] The press run
of each issue has been cut from 200 to 100 copies. (For
additional details see: Seybold, Gertrude B., "Producing a
Book Catalog: The Chester County Library Experience," p.
293-315).

Frequency of Issue

The first book catalog of the Chester County Library
System, issued in 1967, covered the period between January
1, 1964 and March 1967, and included 30,448 entries.[2] A
cumulation of the three annual supplements issued to date will
list in one volume all new titles added in the system from
March, 1967 to November 15, 1969, approximately 27,000
entries.[3]

Costs

"The current cost of the Book Catalog is based on a

new entry charge of 95¢ per entry, which includes input, computer processing and typesetting, printing and binding; for reprocessing the same entries as they are cumulated in successive supplements--the charge is 68¢ per entry."[4]

Notes

1. Communication from John W. Seybold, President, Rocappi, Inc., December 9, 1969.

2, 3, 4. Communication from Elizabeth T. Pope, Head Technical Services Department, Chester County Library, November 17, 1969.

WARBURTON, Clifford
The study book of power. Bodley Head,
1962. 47p il.
Power (Mechanics)
j621 W   CC

WARD, Charles A
Oracles of Nostradamus. Modern Library,
1942. 366p
Notredame. Michael de. 1503-1566
133.32 W   T

WARD, Winifred Louise, 1884-
*Playmaking with children from kinder-
garten through junior high school.* Appleton,
1957. 341p il.
Drama in education
371.33 W   CC

WATERHOUSE, David B
➤ *Harunobu and his age;* the development of
colour printing in Japan. Trustees of the
British Museum, 1964. 326p il.
Color prints. Japanese; Suzuki, Harunobu,
1725?-1770;   British Museum. Dept. of
Oriental Antiquities (1937-   )
761.2 W   CC

WATSON, Jane (Werner) 1915-
Ethiopia, mountain kingdom. Garrard,
1966. 112p il.
Ethiopia
j916.3 W   T

WATSON, Katherine Williams
Tales for telling. Wilson, 1950. 267p
Tales
j398 W   CC

Author Section

Title Index

Subject Index

National Geographic Society, Washington,
D.C.
Greece and Rome. National Geographic Society, 1968. 448p il.
938 N   T

National Geographic Society, Washington,
D.C.
Vanishing peoples of the earth. National
Geographic Society, 1968. 207p il.
572.7 N   P

NELSON, Aaron Gustave, 1911-
Agricultural finance. Iowa State University
Press, 1967. 561p
332.71 N   CC

NELSON, Truman John, 1912-
The torture of mothers. Beacon, 1968. 121p
il.
323.11 N   T

NELSON, Walter Henry
The Berliners. McKay, 1969. 434p
914.3 N   D

Author Section (Main Entry)

Golf rules in pictures, United States Golf
Association. (T) . . . . 796.352 U
Golfmanship, POTTER, S. (CC) . 796.352 P
Good-byes of Magnus Marmalade, ORGEL, D.
(T) . . . . jE
Good deed, BUCK, P. (CC T A D M W) . F
Good life, WALLOP, D. (CC T C P) . . . F
Good night sleep tight book, LITCHFIELD,
A. (CC) . . . . jE
Good night, sweet prince, FOWLER, G. (A)
. . . . B 792.092 B
Good talk, MAY, D. (CC T E) . . . 828.9 M
Good time at your party, FISHER, H. (A)
. . . . 793.2 F
Goodbye, Dove Square, MC NEILL, J. (CC T
C M) . . . . ►
Goodbye look, MACDONALD, R. (CC D) . F

Gordon Craig, CRAIG, E. (CC T) . B 792 C

Great white hope, SACKLER, H. (CC)
. . . . 812.5 S
Greater infortune, HEPPENSTALL, R. (T) . F

Greatest Cardinals of them all, DEVANEY, J.
(T) . . . . jBC 796.357 D
Greatest Catherine, DE LA BEDOYERE, M.
(C) . . . . B 235.2 C
Greatest treason, THOMPSON, L. (T)
. . . . 940.531 T
Greatness to spare, FEHRENBACH, T. (CC
T) . . . . 973.31 F
Greece & the Greeks, HARRINGTON, L. (T)
. . . . j949.5 H
Greece and Rome, National Geographic
►Society, Washington, D.C... (T) . . . 938 N
Greek fairy tales, WILSON, B. (T)
. . . . j398.21 W
Green children, CROSSLEY-HOLLAND, K.
:E

Title Index

Retirement—United States
Bankers Trust Company., *1965 study of indus-
trial retirement plans, including analyses
of complete programs recently adopted or
revised* (CC)   658.32 B
Revere, Paul, 1735-1818
PHELAN, M., *Midnight alarm* (CC T)
jB 973.3 R
Revolutions
GUEVARA, C., *Guerrilla warfare* (T O)
355.4 G
HARRIS, R., *Independence and after* (T)
321 H
LEIDEN, C., *Politics of violence* (CC)
321.09 L
Revolutions—Case studies
LEIDEN, C., *Politics of violence* (CC)
321.09 L
Rhetoric
BOWEN, C., *Biography* (CC T C D E M)
808.025 B
HILDICK, W., *Writing with care* (CC) 808 H
Rhode Island
CARPENTER, A., *Rhode Island* (T) j974.5 C
Rhodes, Cecil John, 1853-1902
CLOETE, S., *Against these three* (C)

ROCKWELL, N., *Norman Rockwell* (C)
B 759.13 R
Rodentia
SILVERSTEIN, A., *Rats and mice* (CC)
j599.32 S
Roethke, Theodore, 1908-1963
SEAGER, A., *Glass house* (CC) B 811.5 R
Rogers, Will, 1879-1935
DAY, D., *Will Rogers* (C) jB 792 R
Romania
*World and its peoples., Yugoslavia, Ruma-
nia, Bulgaria, and Albania* (CC T)
j914.97 W
Romanov, House of
HARCAVE, S., *Years of the golden cockerel*
(T) 947.07 H
Romanticism
LONGYEAR, R., *Nineteenth-century romanti-
cism in music* (T) 780.9 L
Rome (City)—Description
MORTON, H., *Traveller in Rome* (T)
914.5 M
►**Rome—Civilization**
National Geographic Society, Washington,
D.C., *Greece and Rome* (T) 938 N
Rome—History

Subject Index

Chapter XIV

Retrospects and Recommendations

Retrospects and Recommendations

by Theodore C. Hines and Jessica L. Harris

The authors are both on the faculty of the School of Library Service, Columbia University.

The book for which this is the last chapter is the second of two collections on book catalogs edited by Maurice F. Tauber. The first was compiled by Dr. Tauber in collaboration with Robert F. Kingery, and published by Scarecrow Press in 1963. It was both the product of and a basic contribution to the rebirth of the library catalog in book form, then just really getting started as a product of changing technologies.

The much larger size of this second anthology, edited by Dr. Tauber in collaboration with Hilda Feinberg, bears witness to the growth of activity in this field. And, while its predecessor stood very nearly alone as a book about book catalogs, it is now possible, as we can see from the bibliography given here, to cite a respectable number of monographic works directly on the topic.

Insofar as the published literature and this collection of illustrative materials can provide one, the volume is a picture of the state of the art. A collection of individual published articles can never, however, quite constitute such a picture. We all know of projects which have resulted in no articles or reports, with only the catalogs themselves to bear witness to what has been done. If the catalogs themselves were adequately available and listed in Library Literature, this might be accounted a sufficiency--and, in many instances, a virtue. They are often not so listed or so available. Some, we are sure, have probably even escaped Tauber and Feinberg.

We all know, too--and some of the articles collected

here may represent instances of this kind--cases in which
the published literature has been, shall we say, somewhat
optimistic.   In some instances there have been publications
in which the present tense has been used to describe a
project, or even an apparent product, which did not exist
but which the author hoped would come to fruition in the
future.   In some cases, this is the future, and there is no
fruition.

This anthology does, then, give a picture of the state
of the art, but only when the collection is read as a whole,
not as single articles in isolation.   It should be read, too,
as such works should always be read: with insight, a critical
eye, and an inquiring and suitably skeptical mind.

But, as was the intention of the compilers in producing both this volume and its predecessor, the usefulness of
the work is not simply as a tool to find out what has happened and is happening.   As is the case with any good history, its picture of the past is given in order to help to in-
form and to form the future.   Its most valuable role is as
a tool for those creating the book catalogs (and the information science) of tomorrow, to make both better, and to make
both more nearly suited to the needs of individuals and of
society.

How far have we come and where are we going?
Here, as readers, we will try to do what every other reader
of this book must also do, at least for his own area of
interest: to summarize what seem to us to be in the most
important trends and tendencies the book reveals, and to try
to see, in this light, what it is we need to know, and what
might or should happen next.

Our conclusions and comments, and our recommendations for future work in research and development, are not
made to preclude the reader's own, but to stimulate them.

What are our conclusions?   First, on a rather simple
level, it seems clear that photography of cards is out, except as a means of reproducing or closing off existing card
catalogs.   We must hasten to add that this is despite, not
because of , Mansell's ingenious method of minimizing the
space and time required to produce such a list, as shown by
their continuing success in the mammoth task of producing
the National Union Catalog.   Since there are so many plans
(one must add, so oft delayed) for closing off the old to get

on with the computerized new, we must expect the method to
continue to be used for a considerable time to come for reproduction of existing catalogs--but there is no heart or fire
in it any more.

Secondly, it is safe to say, too, that the use of the
card-actuated camera for book catalog production is dead,
however alive and healthy the technique may be for directories and other single-entry-for-each-element listings. These
systems were embraced for a time by a number of libraries
when short-run offset techniques made printed book catalogs
economically feasible, and while the state of the computer art
was such that programming and computer systems required
cumbersome and unwieldy fixed-field layouts, and the only
output available was all-capitals IBM Gothic.

Card-actuated camera book catalog production was (and
is) more costly than computer-based book catalog production.
The amount of information to be keyed, and of repetitive keying, is far greater than for a computer-based catalog, unless
the user is willing to accept restricted formats and very high
manipulation costs. Data manipulation and file maintenance
must either be done manually, or extensive and extraneous
coding must be added.

Computers have become the dominant means for book
catalog production, and are likely to remain so. The development of the state of the art in this area is still so rapid that
the statements we make now may be out of date by the time
this book is published.

A temporary digression. Librarians have only begun
to see clearly what it is that we are publishing book catalogs
for, and how we can best use this kind of tool. Some existing book catalogs have been issued primarily as bibliographies
with possible additional uses as locating devices for interlibrary loan. Others have been produced primarily as finding
lists for particular library or library system collections.
Still others are intended for both purposes. Some, like the
Harvard shelflists, may begin as internal control devices
but turn out to be of superlative value as specialized bibliographies. Our understanding of the uses of book catalogs,
until now at least, seems to lack any theoretical base.

This may account for the general failure so far, in
the overwhelming majority of cases, to attain the levels of
quality of design in our book catalogs which the best of the

book catalogs of the nineteenth century reached. It is small
consolation at best to realize that most of these older book
catalogs were, bibliographically speaking, feeble instruments
indeed. This feebleness of bibliographic quality reflects
their lack, among other things, of the backing of the Library
of Congress for their bibliographic efforts, and is, certainly
understandable.

Much less understandable today is the fact that most
of our book catalogs, the products of our advanced technology,
do not have running heads, or lack "continued" statements
when running heads do appear, or have columns which are
uneven at the bottom, or awkwardly split entries at page or
column feet. These are not exclusive "or's," nor is this
the end of the ways in which many modern book catalogs
show a lack of even the most rudimentary sense of what
constitutes good book design. Much that could be done, even
within the limitations of offset from computer printout, is
not done, and the same kinds of inattention to design also
appear in catalogs produced by the use of graphic arts output devices. It becomes evident on examination that these
failures to design for use are limitations of the thoughtful-
ness of the designers, not of equipment.

Perhaps, while we are beneficiaries of the Library
of Congress' bibliographic expertise, we have simultaneously
made ourselves the victims of its perfection in the development and exploitation of the unit card, conceived and dedicated on the crest of that new wave of library technology
brought in by the invention of the Linotype. The book catalog of today seems all too often the card catalog made book,
with unit entries and quasi-card format, rather than a living creature in its own right.

This brings us to the computer-based catalog. The
computer seems, too often, to be taking the blame unjustly
for lack of skill on the part of systems designers or programmers, or perhaps for librarians' inability to express
what they want, or for both. If librarians do not understand
the purposes for which they produce catalogs, but only the
particular technical means by which they have produced them
in the past, they will be unable to use a knowledge of the
purposes to produce catalogs using a new technology. This
is not to repeat the oft-made statement that librarians must
understand the limitations of the computer, but rather to in-
sist that they must understand its capabilities. If they are
unable to express what they want in these terms it is

understandable that systems people cannot do it for them or,
if they can, will be reluctant to show their greater expertise
to employers who are supposed to be "experts" in library
matters.

There is no need, in short, to suppress punctuation
in entries, or to limit author or title statements to x
characters, or to use code numbers for filing subject headings; there are frequent occasions to depart from Library
of Congress unit card practices in ways which are easier
in computer technology as the old ways were easier for
Linotype technology, without penalizing the reader.   But
many librarians remain less willing to accept these than
they have been to accept the kinds of design barbarities
listed above.

The most successful of the book catalogs chronicled
in the pages of Tauber and Feinberg are (with, as always,
notable exceptions) those of public and special libraries;
catalogs in newspaper-like format, catalogs in microform,
finding lists--in short, departures from reproductions
of LC cards in book form.   We have already mentioned
the Harvard shelflists,   where a simple approach to
dealing with a shelflist which was becoming illegible
produced a notable tool for scholarship. It would be invidious
to set against the successful, but expensive, Stanford catalogs
the names of those illustrious research libraries which have
announced that, announced that, announced that . . . and
where are the promised catalogs?

Perhaps this is a fault of misunderstanding the whole
systems approach.   This approach requires that we consider
the system as a whole, but not that we try to solve all of
its problems simultaneously with innovative use of a not-yet-
fully-comprehended (and rapidly developing) technology.

What emerges from this collection is, it seems to
us, both fulfillment and promise.   The fulfillment is to be
seen in the case of those who have set objectives for their
book catalogs which were limited but geared to the needs of
their clientele.   Fulfilment may be seen in such large services, essentially book catalogs or indexes in nature, as
Index Medicus which, whatever their flaws, comprehend
large, significant, and important universes in such a way
that they can really be used, and take advantage of the ability
to create spin-off lists and to have computer searching
capabilities.

Promise can be seen in a score of ways. It is evident now, and proven, that the technology is available to give us whatever we might reasonably require at a reasonable cost--but we must learn to justify that cost, even though it is in lieu of expenditures made routinely for so long that their justification was no longer required of us. What we reasonably require--but is it reasonable for a library, previously content with the typography of a typewriter keyboard, to demand for local use every accent to be found in Besterman? Promise even of conversion of existing cataloging--when we learn that editing existing catalogs to make them "consistent" may cost more than the actual keying--even though these same inconsistencies have been accepted or ignored in the existing catalogs?

Promise in MARC--MARC premature, MARC postmature, offers real and important promise. Whether MARC is ready or not, are we ready for it? All does not come from Valhalla, or even from LC. And Valhalla helps those who help themselves. The library installations which will be able to use MARC, when it is usable, will be those which have done small projects themselves; which have cataloged, in book form, some special collection which is either very active or relatively static, and published it if it would be useful elsewhere; computerized their accessions lists; or provided SDI on a small scale for local reports; not the libraries which have waited for the job to be done elsewhere and have no librarians who have faced the agony of realizing that lines conceptually end with a space--mostly--and no systems people who have vainly asked a librarian what the maximum number of elements in an illustration statement might be.

We are at the beginning. Both publishing and indexing experience show, on a commercial basis, that the kinds of things we would like to do with book catalogs can be economic and good. Even a few of our book catalogs show it. This volume shows that the tools are in our hands. It is up to us to use them, wisely and with imagination.

We need research--research on applying book catalog techniques to the neglected and largely uncataloged one-sixth of the collections of our research libraries which are in microform; to the technical reports, government documents, and multi-media materials to which our catalogs now provide so little access. We need research on the possibilities of application in all kinds of libraries of the machine-readable

records for our book catalogs to services new to nearly all
but special libraries--SDI, demand bibliographies, special
listings for area studies, a host of similar applications.

It is a bitter note to end with, but, while the authors
show we could do it, will we? Or, content with our niche,
will we stick with our traditional services, leaving the new
services, the life, the action, to some newer agency that
expresses its role as wanting to serve people, rather than
seeing it as "automating" what was done before?

Bibliography

1970

"Book Form Catalogs: a Listing Compiled from Questionnaires Submitted to the Book Catalogs Directory Subcommittee, ALA, 1968." ALA-RTSD Book Catalogs Committee. Library Resources & Technical Services 14 (3): 341-54, Summer, 1970.

De Gennaro, Richard. "Harvard University's Widener Library Shelflist Conversion and Publication Program." College and Research Libraries 31: 318-31, Sept., 1970.

De Gennaro, Richard. "A National Bibliographical Data Base in Machine Readable Form: Progress and Prospects." Library Trends 18: 537-50, April, 1970.

1969

Bolef, Doris, et al. "Mechanization of Library Procedures in the Medium-sized Medical Library. VIII. Suspension of Computer Catalog." Medical Library Association Bulletin 57: 264-66, July, 1969.

"Book Catalogs: the Rand Afrikaans University in Johannesburg." South Africa Library Journal 94: 1408, April 1, 1969.

Cartwright, Kelley L. "Automated Production of Book Catalogs." In: Salmon, Stephen R., Ed., Library Automation; A State of the Art Review. Chicago, American Library Association, 1969, p. 55-78.

Conversion of Retrospective Catalog Records to Machine Readable Form; A Study of a National Bibliographical Service. Prepared by the RECON Working Task Force. Henriette D. Avram, Chairman. Washington, Library of Congress, 1969.

Dolby, James L., Forsyth, V. J., and Resnikoff, H. L. Computerized Library Catalogs: Their Growth, Cost, and Utility. Cambridge, Mass., M. I. T. Press, 1969. 164 p.

"Fiction Book Catalog at the Greenwich Library." CLA News & Views 11: 27, March, 1969.

"First State-wide Regional Book Catalog." ALA Bulletin 63: 1209, Oct., 1969.

Harris, Jessica L. "Programming the Library Catalog." Drexel Library Quarterly 5(2): 84-91, April, 1969.

Hines, Theodore C. "Book Catalogs." In: Kent, Allen and Lancour, Harold, eds., Encyclopedia of Library and Information Science. Vol. 2. New York, Marcel Dekker, 1969.

International Business Machines Corp. Library Automation-- Computer Produced Book Catalog. White Plains, N.Y., IBM, 1969. 41 p.

Jacob, Mary Ellen. "Book Catalogs: Their Function in Integrated Library Systems." Special Libraries 60: 332-39, July, 1969.

Kilgour, Frederick G. "Library Computerization in the United Kingdom." Journal of Library Automation 2: 116-24, Sept., 1969.

Martin, Lowell A. Library Response to Urban Change. Chicago, American Library Association, 1969. Chapter 7, "Technical Services"; Chapter 8, "New Technology and the Chicago Public Library".

Phillips, B. and Roger, G. "Simon Fraser University Computer Produced Map Catalogue." Journal of Library Automation 2: 105-15, Summer, 1969.

Quigg, P.J. "How to Make a Union Catalogue." Catalogue & Index 13: 14-15, January, 1969.

Simonton, Wesley, "Automation of Cataloging Procedures." In: Salmon, Stephen R., ed., Library Automation; a State of the Art Review. Chicago, American Library Association, 1969, p. 44-54.

Warheit, I.A. "The Computer Produced Book Catalog." Special Libraries 60: 573-77, November, 1969.

Whitesides, W.L. "Cooperative Catalog Pilot Project: Fairfax County Public Library and Northern Virginia Community College." DC Libraries 40: 48-50, Summer, 1969.

1968

Anon. "Fairfax County Public Library Converts to Book Catalog." Virginia Librarian 15: 25-27, Fall, 1968.

Anon. "Reference Catalog Computer Produced." Bookmark 27: 242-43, March, 1968.

Barnholdt, B. "Computer-based System for Production of a UDC-classed Library Catalog at the Technological University Library of Denmark." Libri 18 (3-4): 191-96, 1968.

Bock, Joleen. "The Book Catalog--A Junior College View." California School Libraries 39: 132-36, March, 1968.

Brodman, Estelle and Bolef, Doris. "Printed Catalogs: Retrospect and Prospect." Special Libraries 59: 783-88, December 1968.

Chapin, Richard E. and Pretzer, Dale H. "Comparative Costs of Converting Shelf List Records to Machine Readable Form." Journal of Library Automation 1: 66-74, 1968.

De Gennaro, Richard. "Automation in the Harvard College Library." Harvard Library Bulletin 16: 217-36, July 1968.

Dolby, J. L., Forsyth, V., and Resnikoff, H. L. An Evaluation of the Utility and Cost of Computerized Library Catalogs. Washington, D.C., U.S. Dept. Health, Education and Welfare, Office of Education, Bureau of Research, 1968. 203 p.

Evans, L. H. "Cronin and the Revival of the Book-format Catalog." Library Resources & Technical Service 12: 393-94, Fall, 1968.

Gore, D. "Shortcut to Book Catalogs?" Library Journal 93: 1110-13, March, 1968.

Hammer, Donald P. "Problems in the Conversion of Bibliographic Data--A Keypunching Experiment." American Documentation 19: 12-17, 1968.

Henderson, James W. and Rosenthal, Joseph A., eds. Library Catalogs: Their Preservation and Maintenance by

Photographic and Automated Techniques. (M. I. T. Report No. 14.) Cambridge, Mass., M. I. T. Press, 1968. 267 p.

Johnson, Richard D. "A Book Catalog at Stanford." Journal of Library Automation 1: 13-50, March, 1968.

Jollife, John. "The Tactics of Converting a Catalogue to Machine-readable Form." The Journal of Documentation 24: 149-58, Sept., 1968.

Kountz, John C., "Cost Comparison of Computer Versus Manual Catalog Maintenance." Journal of Library Automation 1: 159-77, Sept., 1968.

Library Automation Research & Consulting (LARC). "The Third Conversion of Book Catalogs for the Los Angeles County Library." The LARC Reports 1: Report 2, April, 1968, 2-1 to 2-23.

Library Automation Research & Consulting (LARC). "Mechanized Concepts of Library Catalog Production; A Comparative Study of IBM Procedures Reported on by IBM Technical Publications Department, and a Report Prepared for The Council on Library Resources," by Lawrence F. Buckland. The LARC Reports 1: Report 4, April, 1968, 4-1 to 4-18.

Library Automation Research & Consulting (LARC). "Comparative Approaches to library Book Catalog Production." (From a Study Conducted by Library Automation Research & Consulting, Denver, Colorado.) The LARC Reports 1: Report 7, April, 1968, 7-1 to 7-3.

Library Automation Research & Consulting (LARC). "Book Catalogs for the State Library of Oregon," by Automated Data Services, Los Angeles California. The LARC Reports 1: Report 5, April, 1968, 5-1 to 5-2.

Library Automation-Research & Consulting (LARC). "Sample Pages of Library Book Catalogs." (Compiled by Library Automation Research and Consulting, Denver, Colorado) The LARC Reports 1: Report 9, April, 1968, 9-1 and sample pages.

Library Automation Research & Consulting (LARC). "Introduction to a Feasibility Study on Library Book Catalogs." Prepared for Economy Lithograph Division of Continental

Graphics, Inc., by John Shaw Associates, Graphic Arts Consultants (Based on a Study by Frank S. Patrinostro for The Science Press, Inc.) The LARC Reports 1: Report 8, April, 1968, 8-1 to 8-5.

Library Automation Research & Consulting (LARC). "Phototypeset Output Versus Computer Print-out Output in Book Catalog Production." (Results of the First of a Series of Comparative Cost Studies Being Conducted by Library Automation Research & Consulting.) The LARC Reports, Report 13, April, 1968, 13-1 to 13-13.

Library Automation Research & Consulting (LARC). "Mechanized Procedures of Rocappi, Inc." (Prepared by Rocappi, Inc.). The LARC Reports, Report 14, April, 1968, 14-1 to 14-28.

Library Automation Research & Consulting (LARC). "Mechanized Procedures of the Science Press, Inc." (Prepared by The Science Press, Inc., Ephrata, Pa.) The LARC Reports, Report 15, April, 1968, 15-1 to 15-10.

Library Automation Research & Consulting (LARC). "Automated Library Procedures Used by Professional Library Services," by Catherine MacQuarrie, Xerox Library Consultant. The LARC Reports, Report 18, April, 1968, 18-1 to 18-13.

Library Automation Research & Consulting (LARC). "Automating the Library Operations of the Idaho Nuclear Corporation--Book List and Printed Catalog," by George B. Stultz, Librarian, The Idaho Nuclear Corp., Idaho Falls, Idaho. The LARC Reports, Report 22, Sept., 1968, 21-28-15 to 21-28-47.

Los Angeles County Public Library. An Optical Character Recognition Research and Demonstration Project. Los Angeles, Los Angeles County Public Library System, 1968.

Noda, O. "Film Catalog." Film Lib. Quarterly 1: 55, Summer, 1968.

Prance, C.A. "Book Catalogues." Private Library, 2d Ser., 1: 37-40, Spring, 1968.

Roberts, Justine. "Mechanization of Library Procedures in the Medium-Sized Medical Library: V. Alphabetization of the Book Catalog." Medical Library Association Bulletin, 56: 71-79, January 1968.

Schaeffer, F. H. "Books in the Bibliothèque Nationale: Developments from Rigault to Delisle." Thesis (M. A.), University of Chicago, 1968. 79 p.

Simmons, P. A. "An Analysis of Bibliographic Data Conversion Costs." Library Resources & Technical Services 12: 296-311, 1968.

1967

Avram, Henriette, D., et al. "Fields of Information on Library of Congress Catalog Cards: Analysis of a Random Sample, 1950-64." Library Quarterly 27: 180-92, April, 1967.

Arnot, J. F. "British Museum Catalogue." Australian Library Journal 16: 82-83, April, 1967.

Baltimore County Public Library. "Book Catalog and Card Catalog: A Cost and Service Study." Baltimore, 1967.

Boyd, A. H. "Computer Processing of L. C. Book Numbers." Program, No. 4, Jan. 1967.

Burgess, William E. "Book Catalog vs. Card Catalog." In: Library Automation, or Else? (Papers and Proceedings). March, 1967. Southern California Technical Processes Group. 4 p.

Cartwright, Kelley L., and Shoffner, Ralph M. Catalogs in Book Form; a Research Study of Their Implications for The California State Library and the California Union Catalog, with a Design for Their Implementation. Berkeley, Calif., Institute of Library Research, University of California, 1967, 69 p.

Childers, Thomas; Koeffer, Paula; Leonard, Faye, and Sasaki, Sharon. Book Catalog and Card Catalog; a Cost and Service Study. Towson, Maryland, Baltimore County Public Library, March, 1967.

Cox, Nigel, S.M. and Grose, Michael W., eds. Organization and Handling of Bibliographic Records by Computer. Seminar on Organization and Handling of Bibliographic Records by Computer, University of Newcastle upon Tyne, July, 1967. Hamden, Conn., Archon Books, 1967. 192 p.

Curran, Ann T. and Avram, Henriette D., Data Elements in Bibliographic Records: Final Report of the Special Project on Data Elements for the Subcommittee on Machine Input Records (SC-2) of the Sectional Committee on Library Work and Documentation (Z-39) of the U.S.A. Standards Institute. U.S.A.S.I., May, 1967. (Various paging).

De Gennaro, Richard A. "A Strategy for the Conversion of Research Library Catalog to Machine Readable Form." College & Research Libraries 28: 253-57, July, 1967.

Dunkin, Paul S. "Cataloging and CCS: 1957-1966:" Library Resources & Technical Services 3: 267-88, 1967.

Fussler, H.H. In: Brasenose Conference on the Automation of Libraries, 30 June-3 July, 1966. Proceedings of the Anglo-American Conference on the Mechanization of Library Services, ed. by John Harrison and Peter Laslett. London, Mansell, 1967, p. 82.

Kozumplik, W.A., and Lange, R.T. "Computer-Produced Microfilm Library Catalog." American Documentation 18: 67-80, April, 1967.

Loeber, Thomas S. "O.S.L. (Oregon State Library) Master Book Catalog Distributed in September, or Mohammed and the Catalog." PNLA Quarterly 32 (1): 4-7, October, 1967.

Matthews, F.W. and Oulton, D.L. (Canadian Industries Limited). "A Simplified Computer Produced Book Catalogue." In: American Documentation Institute, Annual Meeting, N.Y., 22-27 Oct., 1967. Proceedings, vol. 4, p. 191-96.

Mooy, A.J. de. "Mammoetcatalogussen (Mammoth Catalogs)." Bibliotheekleven 52: 205-6, June, 1967.

Moshman, A.G. Survey of Readers' Attitudes towards the Printed Book Catalog of a Suburban Library. Thesis (M.S. in L.S.) Catholic University of America, 1967. 64 p.

Newenham, E. A., comp. Bibliography of Printed Catalogues of the Libraries of Southern Africa, 1820-1920. Johannesburg, Public Library, 1967. 165 p.

Nugent, William R., "The Mechanization of the Filing Rules for the Dictionary Catalogs of the Library of Congress." Library Resources and Technical Services 11: 145-66, Spring, 1967.

Palmer, Foster M. "Conversion of Existing Records in Large Libraries, with Special Reference to the Widener Library Shelflist." In: Brasenose Conference on the Automation of Libraries, 30 June-3 July 1966, Proceedings of the Anglo-American Conference on the Mechanization of Library Services, ed. by John Harrison and Peter Laslett. London, Mansell, 1967, p. 57-80.

Pastan, H. M. E. "Book Catalogs and Automation." Maryland Libraries 33: 12-13, Winter, 1967.

Perreault, Jean M. "Approaches to Library Filing by Computer." Indexer 5: 169-87, August, 1967.

Perreault, Jean N. "The Mechanization of the Filing Rules for the Dictionary Catalogs of the Library of Congress." Library Resources & Technical Services 11: 145-66, Spring, 1967.

Richmond, Phyllis A., and Gill, Marcia L. "Dystal Programs for Library Filing." In: American Documentation Institute, Annual Meeting, N.Y. 22-27 Oct., 1967. Proceedings, vol. 4, p. 197-201.

Roloff, H. "Die Renaissance des Bandkataloges." Zentr. Bibl. 81: 267-73, May, 1967.

Smith, F. R. and Jones, S. O. (Douglas Aircraft Co.). "Cards versus Book-Form Printout in a Mechanized Library System." Special Libraries 58(9): 639-43, Nov., 1967.

Sommerlad, M. J. "Development of a Machine-Readable Catalogue at the University of Essex." Program 7: 1-3, Oct., 1967.

Stansfield, P. "The E. D. P. Catalogue." Librarians' Automation Group. (Australia) Nos. 4-5, June-Sept., 1967, pp. 6-17. (Paper delivered to the 14th Biennial

Conference of the Library Association of Australia, on
Heidelberg City Library).

Truelson, Stanley D. "Review of National Library of
Medicine Current Catalog." American Documentation 18:
189-90, 1967.

Truett, Carol A. J. The Book Catalog of the Extension and
Children's Collections of the Austin, Texas Public Library.
Thesis (M. L. S.) Univ. of Texas. Aug., 1967. 78 p.

Tynell, L. "AKN Med SDB: Kring en Nystartad Försöks-
publikation (Union List with Data Processing; About a
Newly Started Experimental Publication)." Biblioteks-
bladet 52(1): 4-9, 1967.

University of Chicago Library.   Memorandum on Automation
Project.   March, 1967.

Vann, Sarah K., comp. "Book Catalogs: Cost Data."
In: Vann, S. K., Southeastern Pennsylvania Processing
Center Feasibility Study, Final Report. Pennsylvania State
Library, 1967, p. 261-78.

Vann, Sarah K. "Book Catalogs: Quo Animo? Members of
the Black Gold Cooperative Library System Reply."
Library Resources & Technical Services 11: 451-60, Fall,
1967.

Weber, David C. "Book Catalog Trends in 1966." Library
Trends 16: 149-64, July, 1967.

Weinstein, Edward and George, Virginia. "Computer-Produced Book Catalogs: Entry Form and Content." Library
Resources and Technical Services 11: 185-91, Spring,
1967.

Weiss, Irvin J. and Wiggins, Emilie V. "Computer-aided
Centralized Cataloging at the National Library of
Medicine." Library Resources & Technical Services 11:
83-96, Winter, 1967.

Wells, A. J. "The British National Bibliography." In:
Brasenose Conference on the Automation of Libraries, 30
June-3 July, 1966. Proceedings of the Anglo-American
Conference on the Mechanization of Library Services, ed.
by John Harrison and Peter Laslett."

1966. London, Mansell, Feb., 1967, p. 24-32.

Zuckerman, Ronald A. "Computerized Book Catalogs and
their Effects on Integrated Library Data Processing:
Research and Progress at the Los Angeles County Public
Library." In: Carroll, Dewey E., ed., Proceedings of
the 1967 Clinic on Library Applications of Data Processing. Urbana, Illinois, University of Illinois, Graduate
School of Library Science, 1967, p. 70-89.

1966

Anon. "Book Catalog for the Tulsa City-County Library
System" Oklahoma Librarian 16: 87, July, 1966.

Anon. "Computer Produced Book Catalog Available from
Documentation Incorporated." Library Journal 91: 1864-
65, Apr. 1, 1966.

Anon. "Libraries with Book Catalogues" [in California].
California Librarian 27: 41-42, January, 1966.

Anon. Möser-Mersky, Gerlinde and Mihaliuk, Melanie.
Osterreichische Akademie der Wissenschaften, Mittel-
alterliche Bibliothekskataloge Osterreichs (Medieval Library
Catalogs of Austria), v. 4. Salzburg, Böhlaus, 1966.
112p.

Bregzis, Ritvars. "The ONULP Bibliographic Control
System; an Evaluation." In: Clinic on Library Applica-
tions of Data Processing. University of Illinois, 3d, 1965.
Proceedings. Edited by Francis B. Jenkins. Champaign,
Ill., Distributed by the Illini Union Bookstore [1966]
p. 112-40.

Cain, Alexander M. and Jolliffe, J.W. A Method of Convert-
ing the General Catalogue of Printed Books to Machine-
Readable Form. London, British Museum PB/Systems,
April, 1966; Revised June, 1966.

Chadwick, Catherine S. "The Book Catalog: New Hope for
Cooperative Programs." Library Resources & Technical
Services 10: 160-63, Spring, 1966.

The Elementary School Library Collection, Phases 1-2-3.
2d ed. Newark, N.J., Bro-Dart Foundation, 1966.

Hastings, E.R. "Solutions in Establishing a New Catalog at the United States Department of Health, Education and Welfare Library." Library Resources and Technical Services 10: 495-98, Fall, 1966.

Hayes, Robert M., Shoffner, Ralph M., and Weber, David C. "The Economics of Book Catalog Production." Library Resources & Technical Services 10: 57-90, Winter, 1966.

Healey, James S. "An Automated Library in New England" [New Bedford, Mass., Public Library]. Wilson Library Bulletin 41: 411-13, 438, December 1966.

Hines, Theodore C., and Harris, Jessica L. Computer Filing of Index, Bibliographic, and Catalog Entries. Newark, N.J., Bro-Dart Foundation, 1966. 126 p.

Kidd, J. "Romantic Appeal of a Catalogue: the Old Guardbook Style Name Catalogue." Library Review 20: 321-24, Spring, 1966.

Kieffer, Paula. "The Baltimore County Public Library Book Catalog." Library Resources & Technical Services 10: 133-41, Spring, 1966.

Koster, Kurt. "The Use of Computers in Compiling National Bibliographies; Illustrated by the Example of the Deutsche Bibliographie." (Paper presented at the 32nd Session of IFLA, Scheveningen, Sept., 1966). Libri 16(4): 269-81, 1966.

Lazorick, Gerald J., Herling, John, and Atkinson, Hugh. Conversion of Shelf List Bibliographic Information to Machine Readable Form and Production of Book Indexes to Shelf List. Buffalo, State University of New York, Technical Information Dissemination Bureau, 1966.

McCaslin, O.R. "The Book Catalog Program of the Austin Public Library: the Programmer's Viewpoint." In: Texas Conference on Library Mechanization, 1st, Austin, 1966. Proceedings. Ed. by John B. Corbin. Austin, Texas Library & Historical Commission, 1966. (Texas. State Library [Austin] Monograph no. 6) p. 17-20. (Available on loan from LOCATE, Library of Congress, Washington, D.C. 20540.)

McCurdy, May Lea.   The Book Catalog Program of the
    Austin Public Library: the Librarian's Viewpoint." In:
    Texas Conference on Library Mechanization, 1st, Austin,
    1966.   Proceedings.   Ed. by John B. Corbin.   Austin,
    Texas Library & Historical Commission, 1966.   (Texas.
    State Library [Austin] Monograph no. 6) p. 13-16. (Avail-
    able on loan from LOCATE, Library of Congress, Wash-
    ington, D.C. 20540).

Moon, Eric.   "RTSD and the Big Wide World."   Library
    Resources & Technical Services 10: 5-12, Winter, 1966.

Moreland, George B.   "An Unsophisticated Approach to Book
    Catalog and Circulation Control." In: Harvey, John, ed.,
    Data Processing in Public and University Libraries.
    Washington, Spartan Books, 1966 (Drexel Information
    Science Series, v. 3) p. 53-63.

Nelson Associates, Inc.   Centralized Processing for the
    Public Libraries of New York State; a Survey Conducted
    for the New York State Library.   In collaboration with
    the Theodore Stein Co., New York, 1966.   34 p. plus
    appendices.

Nugent, William R.   The Mechanization of the Filing Rules
    for the Dictionary Catalogs of the Library of Congress.
    A report prepared for the Council on Library Resources,
    Inc. Maynard, Mass., Inforonics, 1966.   32 p.

Richmond, Phyllis A.   "Note on Updating and Searching
    Computerized Catalogs."   Library Resources & Technical
    Services 10: 155-60, Spring, 1966.

Rift, Leo R.   Production of the Science Library Catalog at
    Bowling Green State University on the IBM 1050 Unit
    Record System.   Bowling Green, Ohio, 1966.   4 p.

Santa Clara Valley Library System.   Implementation of
    BALANCE [Bay Area Libraries Associated Network for
    Cooperative Exchange] Phase I and II, Book Catalog Pro-
    duction. Santa Clara, Calif., 1966.   52 p.

Sharr, F.A.   "Book-type Catalogues for Developing
    Countries."   UNESCO Library Bulletin 20: 24-26, Jan.,
    1966.

Sharr, F.A., et al., "Production of a New Book-type Catalogue in Australia." Library Resources & Technical
Services 10: 143-54, Spring, 1966.

Stanford University. Stanford Undergraduate Library Book
Catalog: Fact Sheet. Stanford, Calif., 1966, 3 p.

Stromberg, Donald H. "Computer Applications to Book
Catalogs and Library Systems." In: Goldhor, Herbert,
ed., Proceedings of the 1966 Clinic on Library Applications of Data Processing. University of Illinois, April,
1966. Urbana, Illinois, 1966. p. 195-210.

Wasserman, Morton N. "Computer-prepared Book Catalog
for Engineering Transparencies." Special Libraries 57:
111-13, Feb., 1966.

                              1965

Beck, A. "Amerikanske Bogkataloger (American Book
Catalogs)." Bogens Verden 47: 583-87, Dec., 1965.

Blackburn, Robert H. "On Producing Catalogues in Book
Form for Five Libraries at Once [Ontario New Universities
Library Project]." In: Canadian Library Association.
Library Automation Projects; a Collection of Papers by
Canadian Librarians. Ottawa, 1965. p. 20-22. (Oc-
casional paper no. 48.)

Bregzis, Ritvars. "The Ontario New Universities Library
Project--an Automated Bibliographic Data Control
System." College & Research Libraries 26: 495-508,
Nov., 1965.

Bry, Ilse and Afflerbach, Lois. "Bibliographical Challenges
in the Age of the Computer." Library Journal 90: 813-18,
Feb. 15, 1965.

Buckland, Lawrence F. The Recording of Library of Congress Bibliographical Data in Machine Form. A Report
Prepared for the Council on Library Resources. Infor-
onics Inc., November, 1964. Council on Library Resources, 1965.

De Gennaro, Richard. "A Computer Produced Shelflist."
College & Research Libraries 26: 311-15, 353, July, 1965.

Drake, C. L.   "Some Book Catalogues in Western Australia."
    Australian Library Journal 14: 121-26, Sept., 1965.

Dunkin, P. S. "1964: Peek into Paradise." Library Re-
    sources & Technical Services 9: 143-48, Spring, 1965.

Ebert, Eloise.   "Book Catalogs for the Oregon State
    Library." P. N. L. A. Quarterly 29: 134-35, Jan., 1965.

Francis, Sir F. C.   "British Museum Catalog." Library
    Association Record 67:60-61, Feb., 1965.

Goldhor, Herbert, ed.   Proceedings of the 1964 Clinic on
    Library Applications of Data Processing,   University of
    Illinois, April, 1964.   Champaign, Ill., Illini Union
    Bookstore, 1965, 117 p.

Harrison, T. L. and Gassert, L. E.   Report of the Survey
    of Data Processing Feasibility for the Prince George's
    County Memorial Library System.   EDP Systems Dev.
    Services, 1965.

Heiliger, Edward M.   "Use of a Computer at Florida
    Atlantic University Library for Mechanized Catalog
    Production."   In: IBM Library Mechanization Symposi-
    um, Endicott, N. Y., 1964.   Proceedings.   White Plains,
    N. Y., International Business Machines Corp., 1965,
    p. 165-186.

International Business Machines Corp. Library Catalog
    Production - 1401 and 870.   Form 20-0093.   White
    Plains, N. Y., IBM Data Processing Division, 1965,
    25 p.

Johnson, Richard D.   "Book Catalog for the Undergraduate
    Library."   In: Stanford University Libraries. Bulletin
    27: 87-88, July 16, 1965.

Jones, Robert C.   "A Book Catalog for Libraries--Prepared
    by Camera and Computer" [The Junior College District
    of St. Louis].   Library Resources & Technical Services
    9: 205-206, Spring, 1965.

Jordan, Casper L.   "A Book Catalog at the System Level."
    Bookmark 24: 139-40, February, 1965.

MacQuarrie, Catherine O. "Library Catalog, a Comparison." Hawaii Library Association Journal 21: 18-24, Aug., 1965.

Maidment, W. R., "Computer Catalogue in Camden." Library World 67: 40, Aug., 1965.

Matta, Seoud Makram. "The Card Catalog in a Large Research Library: Present Condition and Future Possibilities in the New York Public Library." Dissertation (D. L. S.)--Columbia University, New York, 1965. 248 p.

Meakin, A. O. "The Production of a Printed Union Catalogue by Computer." Library Association Record 67: 311-16, Sept., 1965.

Moreland, George B. "Montgomery County Book Catalogue." In: I. B. M. Library Mechanization Symposium, May 25-27, 1964. Endicott, N. Y., I. B. M., 1965, 252 p.

North Carolina Library Association. Technical Proposal for a Book Program for the Public Libraries of North Carolina. Bethesda, Maryland, Documentation, Inc., 1965, 20 p.

Perreault, Jean M. "Computerized Cataloging: the Computerized Catalog at Florida Atlantic University." Library Resources & Technical Services 9: 20-34, Winter, 1965.

Perreault, Jean M. "The Computer and Catalog Filing Rules." Library Resources & Technical Services 9: 325-31, Summer, 1965.

Pizer, Irwin H. "Book Catalogs Versus Card Catalogs." Medical Library Association Bulletin 53: 225-38, Apr., 1965.

Popecki, Joseph T. "A Filing System for the Machine Age." Library Resources & Technical Services 9: 333-37, Summer, 1965.

Robinson, Charles W. "The Book Catalog: Diving In" [Baltimore County Public Library]. Wilson Library Bulletin 40: 262-68, Nov., 1965.

Vavrek, Bernard. "The Book Catalog: One Step Backward." Wilson Library Bulletin 40: 269-70, Nov., 1965.

Weinstein, Edward A., and George, Virginia S. "Notes Toward a Code for Computer-produced Printed Book

Catalogs." Library Resources & Technical Services 9: 319-24, Summer, 1965.

Wilkinson, W. A. "The Computer-produced Book Catalog: An Application of Data Processing at Monsanto's Information Center." In: Goldhor, Herbert, ed., Proceedings of the 1964 Clinic on Library Applications of Data Processing, University of Illinois, April, 1964. Champaign, Illini Union Bookstore, 1965, p. 7-24.

Yale University, Administrative Data Systems. Library Projects Staff. The Kline [Science Library] Book Catalogues; a Progress Report. New Haven, Conn., 1965. 17 p.

1964

Anon. "Catalog Maintenance and List Production." Library Journal 89: 2729-34, July, 1964.

Anon. "Book Catalogs, a Pacific Northwest View [symposium]." PNLA Quarterly 28: 120-33, Jan., 1964.

Becker, Joseph. "Automatic Preparation of Book Catalogs." ALA Bulletin 58: 714-18, Sept., 1964.

Bromberg, Erik I., Dubinski, G. A., and Remington, Donn. "Preparation of a Book Catalog." Special Libraries 55: 611-14, Nov., 1964.

Brown, Margaret C. "A Book Catalog at Work [Free Library of Philadelphia]." Library Resources & Technical Services 8: 349-58, Fall, 1964.

Chicago. University. Graduate Library School. Library Catalogs: Changing Dimensions. 28th Annual Conference, Aug. 5-7, 1963, ed. by Ruth F. Strout. Chicago, Univ. of Chicago Press, 1964. 127 p.

Cline, Catherine. "Procedures for Developing Timberland's Book Catalog." PNLA Quarterly 28: 128-32, 136, Jan., 1964.

Documentation, Inc. Technical Proposal for a Book Catalog Program for the Public Libraries of North Carolina. Bethesda, Md. Documentation, Inc. [n.d.]

Geller, William Spence. "Duplicate Catalogs in Regional
    and Public Library Systems [Los Angeles County Public
    Library system]." Library Quarterly 34: 57-67, Jan.,
    1964.

Hagler, Ronald. "The Place of the Book Catalog in the
    University Library." PNLA Quarterly 28: 125-27, Jan.
    1964.

Hake, Shirley. "Book Catalogs in the Public Library
    System [King County, Wash.]." PNLA Quarterly 28:
    132-33, 136, Jan., 1964.

Harris, Ira. "Reader Services Aspects of Book Catalogs."
    Library Resources & Technical Services 8: 391-98,
    Fall, 1964.

Hayes, Robert M. and Shoffner, Ralph M. The Economics
    of Book Catalog Production; a Study Prepared for Stan-
    ford University Libraries and the Council on Library
    Resources. Sherman Oaks, California. Advanced In-
    formation Systems Division, Hughes Dynamics, 1964.
    110 p.

Henderson, John D. "The Book Catalogs of the Los
    Angeles County Public Library." In: Goldhor, Herbert, ed.,
    Clinic on Library Applications of Data Processing, Universi-
    ty of Illinois, 1st, 1963. Proceedings. Champaign, Ill.
    (Distributed by the Illini Union Bookstore) [1964] p.
    18-32.

International Business Machines Corp. Library Catalog
    Production with the 1050 System. Form E20-0232.
    White Plains, N.Y., IBM Data Processing Division,
    [n.d.].

International Business Machines Corp. Data Processing at
    Albany, Georgia Public Library. Form E20-0281. White
    Plains, N.Y. IBM Data Processing Division, [n.d.].

Johns, Loeta L. "Book Catalogs--A Pacific Northwest
    View." PNLA Quarterly 28: 120-23, Jan., 1964.

Jones, Robert C. "The Compact Book Catalog--by
    Photographic Process [The Junior College District of St.
    Louis]." Library Resources & Technical Services 8:
    366-69, Fall, 1964.

Kennedy, James H., and Boylan, Merle N., IBM 1401
    Computer Produced and Maintained Printed Book Catalogs
    at the Lawrence Radiation Laboratory. Livermore, Uni-
    versity of California, Lawrence Radiation Laboratory,
    1964. 25 p. (UCRL-7555.)

Kilgour, Frederick G. "Development of Computerization of
    Card Catalogs in Medical and Scientific Libraries at
    Yale University." In: IBM Library Mechanization
    Symposium, 1964, p. 187-204.

Kilgour, Frederick G. "Development of Computerization of
    Card Catalogs in Medical and Scientific Libraries." In:
    Goldhor, Herbert, ed. Proceedings of the 1964 Clinic on
    Library Applications of Data Processing, Champaign, Ill.,
    1965, p. 25-35.

Laubach, A. F. "Putting the Catalog of a Small Company
    Library into the KWIC Index; a Pilot Study." Special
    Libraries 55: 619-20, Nov., 1964.

MacQuarrie, Catherine. "The Metamorphosis of the Book
    Catalogs [Los Angeles County Public Library]." Library
    Resources & Technical Services 8: 370-78, Fall, 1964.

Moreland, George B. "Montgomery County Book Catalog."
    Library Resources & Technical Services 8: 379-89, Fall,
    1964.

New Jersey Library Association. Catalogers Sect. Book
    Catalogs for Smaller Libraries. Maurice F. Tauber,
    Panel Chairman. Atlantic City, N.J., 1964, 9 p.

Parker, Ralph H. "Book Catalogs." Library Resources
    & Technical Services 8: 344-48, Fall, 1964.

Perreault, Jean M. "The Computerized Book Catalog at
    Florida Atlantic University." College & Research
    Libraries 25: 185-97, May, 1964.

Pizer, Irwin H. "Another Look at Printed Catalogs."
    Special Libraries 55: 119, Feb., 1964. [letter]

Ranz, Jim. The Printed Book Catalogue in American Li-
    braries: 1723-1900. Chicago, American Library Associa-
    tion, 1964. 144 p. (ACRL Monograph 26).

Richmond, Phyllis A. "Book Catalogs as Supplements to Card Catalogs." Library Resources & Technical Services 8: 359-65, Fall, 1964.

Simonton, Wesley. "The Computerized Catalog: Possible, Feasible, Desirable?" Library Resources & Technical Services 8: 399-407, Fall, 1964.

Sparks, David E., Berul, Lawrence H., and Waite, David P. "Output Printing for Library Mechanization." In: Libraries and Automation: Proceedings of the Conference on Libraries and Automation held at Airlie Foundation... 1963, ed. by Barbara Evans Markuson. Washington, Library of Congress, 1964, p. 155-89.

Stein, Theodore. "Catalog Maintenance and List Production." Library Journal 89: 2729-34, July, 1964.

Weber, David C. "The Changing Character of the Catalog in America." Library Quarterly 34: 20-33, Jan., 1964.

Weinstein, Edward A., and Spry, Joan. "Boeing SLIP: Computer Produced and Maintained Printed Book Catalogs." American Documentation 15: 185-90, July, 1964.

APPENDIX

Book Catalogs Directory

Reprinted from Library Resources & Technical Services
Vol. 14, No. 3, Summer 1970, by permission of the
American Library Association.

Book Form Catalogs: A Listing Compiled from Questionnaires Submitted to the Book Catalogs Directory Subcommittee, ALA, 1968

ALA-RTSD BOOK CATALOGS COMMITTEE

THIS LISTING INCLUDES active book form catalogs of those institutions which returned the 1968 questionnaire of the ALA Book Catalogs Directory Subcommittee in time for the tabulation. The coverage of this listing has been limited to those characteristics of the reported catalogs which can be consistently compared in terms of common definitions. The individual responses to the survey contain also a number of other characteristics, such as the update pattern, reissue cycle, arrangement of the catalogs, and in part some cost aspects. The reporting of these characteristics, however, does not conform to any consistent and uniform pattern of definition, and the data therefore do not lend themselves to a systematic tabulation of these characteristics.

Thus the frequency of issue described in the survey replies covers two partially overlapping aspects: the frequency of issue or reissue of the basic parts of the catalog, and the frequency and pattern of publication of the updating issues. The update pattern is particularly complicated by the ambiguity of the terminology used to describe the various pattern combinations. For instance, a monthly issued catalog may be quite different under the two following patterns. In one case the reissue cumulation is done yearly only, while during the succeeding eleven months individual issues are published containing the additions during the current month. In another case in addition to the annual reissue cumulation (say in December) issues of current monthly additions are published in January and February, April and May, July and August, and October and November. However, in addition to these, to-date cumulations, within that year, are done in March, June, and September, and they include both the current monthly additions as well as the quarterly cumulated records. In both cases there are twelve issues per year. Without further specification of the frequency and specific pattern of cumulation, little can be deduced about the effect of these two issue patterns on serviceability and on production cost.

The arrangement of the book form catalog presented a similar problem. Again the term has been interpreted variously with respect to the

division between Author, Title, and Subject listings, to the internal sequencing patterns within these divisions and even to the intended
clientele. Thus a reply giving the arrangement "by Author, Title and
Subject" does not really provide an unambiguous definition of the physical or logical arrangement of records in the catalog.

A similar problem was revealed by examining the descriptions of the
size of book catalogs expressed in number of volumes. In some instances
this number refers to the volumes of the initial publication, in others it
includes supplementary volumes, and in still others it appears to refer to
the total number of physical units issued.

In general, it appears that the question of update pattern, reissue
and physical and logical arrangement of the catalogs would have to be
surveyed in extended depth if the true nature, serviceability, and cost
implications are considered of sufficient interest to justify the required
additional effort.

The list of book form catalogs gives for each the name and the address of the related institution, the number of titles included in the catalog at the time of survey, the scope (type of library materials covered),
the year of the first issue of the catalog, and the method of production.
The scope and the method of production are designated by abbreviations
according to the definitions given immediately preceding the list.

Note on a Preliminary Review of the Tabulated Returns

RITVARS BREGZIS, *Chairman*
ALA-RTSD Book Catalogs Committee

A preliminary review of the tabulated returns of the ALA Book Catalogs Directory questionnaire indicates a number of tentative general observations. It is of some interest to note that apart from the commercially
available book form catalogs which were not sought to be included in
the survey, the surveyed catalogs are relatively small in extent; only a
few exceed the size of ten volumes. The catalogs range from a few thousand to approximately one hundred thousand bibliographic records covered, with few exceptions exceeding this number. The larger catalogs,
again with exceptions, tend to be produced by some photographic technique. Meaningfully large machine-readable data bases apparently are
still an exception. The catalogs prepared from such a data base are produced mostly by impact printing techniques, often combined with offset
duplication. Application of photocomposition or other photo-electronic
techniques is still rare.

The organization of the catalogs appears to indicate a trend to reflect
the intended service environment. Thus most of the catalogs in public
libraries are arranged divided between the adult and the juvenile clien-

tele. The author, title, and subject listings in these libraries are in most instances separate.

Libraries with educational and research mission tend to divide their catalogs mainly according to the major types of access points: authors, titles, subjects, classification, and report numbers. Combination of two of these in one file is an occasionally used practice, especially among the school and college libraries. Both the Author/Title and Title/Subject combinations are represented. Dictionary arrangement appears to be popular with about one-half of university library catalogs. Median size of these, however, does not extend beyond three volumes.

The most popular reissue cycle for the surveyed catalogs is annual. Update cycle ranges from daily to semiannual, with monthly being the prevalent cycle length. The pattern of updating ranges from daily issues to one semiannual cumulation, to a maximum of three concurrent update cycles ranging from biweekly to quarterly, with annual reissues.

BOOK CATALOGS DIRECTORY

SCOPE

Di	Phonodiscs	Per	Periodicals
Do	Documents	Rep	Reproduction of paintings
Dr	Drawings	Pa	Pamphlets
Fi	Films	Se	Serials
Fs	Filmstrips	Sl	Slides
Gov R	Govt. reports	Trans	Translations
Mc	Microforms	Ta	Phonotapes
Mcd	Microcards	Tr	Transparencies
Mcf	Microfilms	T Pa	Technical papers
Mcfi	Microfiche	T R	Technical reports
Mcp	Microprints	Vt	Videotapes
M	Maps	X	X-ray pictures
Mo	Monographs		

METHOD OF PRODUCTION

C + P	Computer plus printing	P	Photographic
C + PH	Computer plus photo composition	Pa	Abstracting camera
C + MRP	Computer plus micf. reader printer	Pmp	Microfilm + printing
CPr	Direct computer printout	Po	Photo + offset
Fl	Flexowriter	Ps	Sequential card camera
Litho	Lithography	Px	Xerox + printing
		T	Tabulation equipment

A. ACADEMIC AND RESEARCH LIBRARIES

Name and Address of Institution	No. of Titles in Catalog	Scope	Year of First Issue	Method of Production
1. Bowling Green State University Library, Bowling Green, Ohio 43402	20,000	Mo	Planned 1969	Px
2. William T. Boyce Library, 321 East Chapman Avenue, Fullerton, California 92634	59,086	Mo, Fi, Ta, Di, Fs, Mcf, Mcfi	Planned 1970	C + P
3. California State College, Fullerton Library, 800 N. State College Blvd., Fullerton, California 92631	4,635	Se	1968	CPr
4. Case Western Reserve University, School of Library Science, Bibliographic Systems Center, Cleveland, Ohio 44106	1,650	Mo, Se, Mcf	1967	CPr
5. Center for Research Libraries, 5721 Cottage Grove, Chicago, Illinois 60637	75,000	Mo, Se, Mcf, Mcd, Mcp	Planned 1969	Pa
6. Columbia University, Avery Architectural Library, New York, N.Y. 10027		Mo, Se	1895 1958	Po
7. Cuyahoga Community College Library, 626 Huron Road, Cleveland, Ohio 44115	34,000	Mo	1967	CPr
8. Drexel Institute of Technology Libraries, Philadelphia, Pennsylvania 19104	3,000	Per	1959	CPr
9. Eastern New Mexico University Library, Portales, New Mexico 88130	20,000	Mo, Se	1968	C + P
10. El Centro College Library, Main & Lamar Sts., Dallas, Texas 75202	20,000	Mo	1967	C + P
11. Federal City College Media Center, 424 Second Street, N.W., Washington, D.C. 20009	18,000	Mo, Se, Fi, Ta, Di, Fs, Sl, Mc, Tr	Planned 1969	C + PH
12. Fort Steilacoom Community College Learning Center, Tacoma, Washington 98499	1,456	Mo	1967	C + P
13. Harvard Business School, Baker Library, Boston, Massachusetts 02163	2,400	Se	1965	C + P
14. Harvard Law School Library, Langdell Hall, Cambridge, Massachusetts 02138	70,000	Mo, Se	1965	Po

A. ACADEMIC AND RESEARCH LIBRARIES (*Continued*)

Name and Address of Institution	No. of Titles in Catalog	Scope	Year of First Issue	Method of Production
15. Honnold Library for the Claremont Colleges, 9th and Dartmouth, Claremont, California 91711	40,000	Mo, Fi	1966	CPr
16. Illinois Valley Community College, R.R. 1, Oglesby, Illinois 61348	6,950	Mo, Se	1968	C + P
17. Indiana University of Pennsylvania, Rhodes R. Stabley Library, Indiana, Pennsylvania 15701	130,000	Mo, Se, Di, Sl	1966	C + P
18. Lorain County Community College, 1005 North Abbe Road, Elyria, Ohio 44035	30,000	Mo, Se, Fi, Ta, Di, Fs, Sl, Tr, M, Dr	1965	CPr
19. Lynchburg College, Knight Memorial Library, Lynchburg, Virginia 24504	34,320	Mo	1966	Litho
20. The Massachusetts Institute of Technology Libraries, Cambridge, Massachusetts 02139	8,019	Se	1957	C + P
21. National Agricultural Library, U.S. Department of Agriculture, Washington, D.C. 20250		Mo, Se, Mcf, Mcfi, Mcd	1966	C + PH
22. National Library of Medicine, 8600 Rockville Pike, Bethesda, Maryland 20014	45,000	Mo, Se, Fi, Ta, Di, Sl, X, etc.	1966	C + PH
23. Oral Roberts University, 7777 South Lewis, Tulsa, Oklahoma 74105	100,000	Fs, Ta, Di, Mo, Se, Fi, Sl, Vt	1965	CPr
24. The Pennsylvania State University, Milton S. Hershey Medical Center Library, Hershey, Pennsylvania 17033	2,001	Se	1967	C + P
25. Purdue University Libraries Lafayette, Indiana 47907	30,000 / 2,500	Se / Fi	1968 / 1968	CPr / CPr
26. Rio Hondo Junior College Library, 3600 Workmanmill Road, Whittier, California 90608		Mo	1967	C + P
27. St. Louis Junior College District, 7508 Forsyth, St. Louis, Missouri 63105	30,000		1964	C + P
28. San Antonio College, 1001 Howard Street, San Antonio, Texas 78212	44,000	Mo, Mcf, Mcfi	1963	CPr

A. ACADEMIC AND RESEARCH LIBRARIES (*Continued*)

NAME AND ADDRESS OF INSTITUTION	No. of Titles in Catalog	Scope	Year of First Issue	Method of Production
29. SAN DIEGO MEDICAL SOCIETY– UNIVERSITY LIBRARY, 225 West Dickinson St., San Diego, California 92103	4,496	Mo, Se	Planned 1969	C + P
30. SCARBOROUGH AND ERINDALE COLLEGE LIBRARIES, UNIVERSITY OF TORONTO, 175 Bedford Road, Toronto, 180, Ontario, Canada	80,000	Mo, Se	1964 (ONULP)	C + P
31. SOUTHERN ILLINOIS UNIVERSITY, MORRIS LIBRARY, Carbondale, Illinois 62901	700,000	Mo, Se	1965	Pmp
32. SOUTHERN ILLINOIS UNIVERSITY, ELIJAH P. LOVEJOY MEMORIAL LIBRARY, Edwardsville, Illinois 62025	270,000	Mo, Se, Fi	Planned 1970	Pmp
33. STANFORD UNIVERSITY LIBRARIES, J. HENRY MEYER MEMORIAL LIBRARY, Stanford, California 94305	52,119	Mo, Se, Fi, Ta, Di	1966	C + P
34. STATE UNIVERSITY OF NEW YORK AT ALBANY, UNIVERSITY LIBRARY, 1400 Washington Avenue, Albany, New York 12203		Mo	1966	CPr
35. TARRANT COUNTY JUNIOR COLLEGE DISTRICT, Fort Worth, Texas 76101	11,000	Mo, Se, Fi, Ta, Di, Fs, Sl, Vt, Mcf	1967	C + P
36. TEACHERS COLLEGE LIBRARY– ENGLISH AS A SECOND LANGUAGE, 525 W. 120th Street, New York, N.Y. 10027	871	Se, Fi, Ta, Di, Fs, etc.	1965	CPr
37. UNIVERSITY OF CALIFORNIA LIBRARY/BERKELEY, Berkeley, California 94720		Mo, Se, Mcp	1963	Po
38. UNIVERSITY OF CALIFORNIA/ BERKELEY, BANCROFT LIBRARY, Berkeley, California 94720		Mo, Se, Mcp	1964	Po
39. UNIVERSITY OF CALIFORNIA/ BERKELEY, EAST ASIATIC LIBRARY, Berkeley, California 94720		Mo, Se	1968	Po
40. UNIVERSITY OF CALIFORNIA/ LOS ANGELES, UNIVERSITY LIBRARY, Los Angeles, California 90024		Mo, Se, Fi	1963	Po
41. UNIVERSITY OF CALIFORNIA/ SANTA CRUZ, Santa Cruz, California 95060	200,000	Mo, Se	1968	CPr

A. ACADEMIC AND RESEARCH LIBRARIES (*Continued*)

	Name and Address of Institution	No. of Titles in Catalog	Scope	Year of First Issue	Method of Production
42.	University of Cincinnati, Medical Center Libraries, Cincinnati, Ohio 45219	3,600	Mo	Planned 1969	CPr
43.	University of Colorado Libraries, Boulder, Colorado 80302	32,000	Se	1967	C + P
44.	University of Guelph, McLaughlin Library, Guelph, Ontario, Canada	4,000	Se	1968	C + P
45.	University of Illinois at Urbana–Champaign, Urbana, Illinois 61801	46,428	Se	1966	C + P
46.	University of North Carolina at Chapel Hill, Chapel Hill, North Carolina 27514	35,000	Se	1965	C + P
47.	University of Oklahoma Library, Norman, Oklahoma 73069		Mo Se	1960 1968	CPr CPr
48.	University of Pennsylvania, Van Pelt Library, Edgar Fahs Smith Memorial Collection in the History of Chemistry, Philadelphia, Pennsylvania 19104	10,000	Mo, Se, Fs, Sl	1960	Po
49.	University of Rochester, River Campus Science Libraries, River Boulevard, Rochester, New York 14627	17,700	Mo	1965	C + P
50.	University of Vermont, Charles A. Dana Medical Library, Burlington, Vermont 05401	10,000	Mo	1968	C + P
51.	University of Victoria, McPherson Library, Victoria, B.C., Canada		Mo, Se, Di, Mc		CPr
52.	University of Wisconsin–Milwaukee Library, Milwaukee, Wisconsin 53211	9,799 1,000	Se Se (Spec.)	1966 1967	CPr CPr
53.	Virginia Commonwealth University, Tompkins McCaw Library, Medical College of Virginia, MCV Station, Richmond, Virginia 23219		Mo, Se, Mc	1967	C + P
54.	Washington University, School of Medicine Library, 4580 Scott Avenue, St. Louis, Missouri 63110	7,020	Mo	1965	C + P

A. ACADEMIC AND RESEARCH LIBRARIES (*Continued*)

Name and Address of Institution	No. of Titles in Catalog	Scope	Year of First Issue	Method of Production
55. WAYNE STATE UNIVERSITY, 645 Mullett Street, Detroit, Michigan 48226	6,000	Mo, Se	1967	Fl
56. WINONA UNION CATALOGUE (St. Mary's College, Winona State College, College of St. Theresa and Winona Public Library) c/o St. Mary's College, Winona, Minnesota 55987	210,000	Mo, Mcf	Planned 1969	CPr
57. YORK UNIVERSITY LIBRARIES, 4700 Keele Street, Downsview, Toronto, Ontario, Canada	2,000 3,000	Di Mo, Se	Planned 1969 1968	CPr CPr

B. PUBLIC LIBRARIES

Name and Address of Institution	No. of Titles in Catalog	Scope	Year of First Issue	Method of Production
1. ALBANY PUBLIC LIBRARY, 2215 Barnesdale Way, Albany, Georgia 31705	24,000	Mo, Se, Di	1967	T
2. ANNE ARUNDEL COUNTY PUBLIC LIBRARY, Church Circle, Annapolis, Maryland 21401	48,327	Mo, Se, Di	1966	Ps
3. AUSTIN PUBLIC LIBRARY, 401 West 9th Street, Austin, Texas 78767	45,542		1965	C + P
4. BALTIMORE COUNTY PUBLIC LIBRARY, 25 West Chesapeake Avenue, Towson, Maryland 21204	100,000	Mo	1965	C + P
5. BEAVERTON PUBLIC SCHOOLS DISTRICT CURRICULUM MATERIALS CENTER, 303 S.W. Erickson Street, Beaverton, Oregon 97005	10,000	Fi, Ta, Di, Fs, Sl, Tr, etc.	1968	Px
6. BURLINGTON COUNTY LIBRARY, Court House Square, Mt. Holly, New Jersey 08060		Mo, Se	1967	Ps
7. CHESTER COUNTY LIBRARY SYSTEM, 235 West Market Street, West Chester, Pennsylvania 19380	44,840	Mo	1967	C + PH

B. PUBLIC LIBRARIES (*Continued*)

NAME AND ADDRESS OF INSTITUTION	No. of Titles in Catalog	Scope	Year of First Issue	Method of Production
8. CHESTERFIELD COUNTY LIBRARY, Drawer Y, 12140 Harrowgate Road, Chester, Virginia 23831			Planned 1969	C + P
9. CLARK COUNTY LIBRARY DISTRICT, 1131 J East Tropicana, Las Vegas, Nevada 89109	24,000	Mo	Planned 1969	C + P
10. COBB COUNTY PUBLIC LIBRARY SYSTEM, 30 Atlanta Street S.E., Marietta, Georgia 30060	36,000	Mo	1967	C + P
11. EAST BAY COOPERATIVE LIBRARY SYSTEM c/o CONTRA COSTA COUNTY LIBRARY, 1750 Oak Park Boulevard, Pleasant Hill, Calfiornia 94523	38,416	Mo	1966	C + P
12. ENOCH PRATT FREE LIBRARY, 400 Cathedral Street, Baltimore, Maryland 21201	55,439	Mo, Se, Di	1966	Ps
13. FAIRFAX COUNTY PUBLIC LIBRARY, 3915 Chain Bridge Road, Fairfax, Virginia 22030	68,861	Se	1964	Ps (later C + P)
14. FREE LIBRARY OF PHILA-DELPHIA, Logan Square, Philadelphia, Pa. 19103	73,246	Mo, Se, Mcf	1963	Ps
15. GREENWICH PUBLIC LIBRARY, Greenwich, Connecticut 06830	15,000	Mo	Planned 1969	C + P
16. HENRICO COUNTY PUBLIC LIBRARY, Box 3-V, Richmond, Virginia 23207	17,000	Mo	1968	C + P
17. JEFFERSON COUNTY PUBLIC LIBRARY, 1204½ Washington Avenue, Golden, Colorado 80401	55,221	Mo, Se, Di	1967	C + P
18. KENT COUNTY LIBRARY, 726 Fuller N.E., Grand Rapids, Michigan 49503	100,000		1967	Ps
19. KING COUNTY LIBRARY SYSTEM, 1100 E. Union, Seattle, Wash. 98122	100,000	Mo	1951	T
20. LAKE COUNTY PUBLIC LIBRARY, 221 West Ridge Road, Griffith, Indiana 46319	51,000	Mo	1961	T
21. LOS ANGELES COUNTY PUBLIC LIBRARY, 320 West Temple, P.O. Box 111, Los Angeles, California 90053	245,645	Mo, Se	1968	C + P

B. PUBLIC LIBRARIES (*Continued*)

Name and Address of Institution	No. of Titles in Catalog	Scope	Year of First Issue	Method of Production
22. Mid-Hudson Libraries, 103 Market Street, Poughkeepsie, New York 12601	7,000		1965	C
23. Montgomery County, Md. Dept. of Public Libraries, 6400 Democracy Boulevard, Bethesda, Maryland 20034	78,000	Mo, Se, Di	1963	C + P
24. The New York Public Library, The Branch Library System, 8 East 40 St., New York, N.Y. 10016	60,000	Mo, Se	Planned 1970	C + P
25. North Central Regional Library, 310 Douglas Street, Wenatchee, Washington 98801	62,349	Mo	1962	C
26. Oregon State Library, State Library Building, Salem, Oregon 97310		Mo, Se	1965	C + P
27. Pawtucket Public Library, 13 Summer Street, Pawtucket, Rhode Island 02860	75,000	Mo	Planned 1970	C + P
28. Prince George's County Memorial Library, 6532 Adelphi Road, Hyattsville, Maryland 20782	100,000		1964	Ps
29. Reelfoot Regional Library Center, 408 Jackson Street, Martin, Tennessee 38237	18,900		1968	C + P
30. San Diego County Library, 5555 Overland Avenue, San Diego, California 92123	17,000	Mo	1966	C + P
31. San Francisco Public Library, Civic Center, San Francisco, California 94102	6,630	Se	1968	C + PH
32. Shiloh Regional Library Center, 227 West Baltimore, Jackson, Tennessee 38301	16,000	Mo, Di, Rep	1965	C + P
33. Tennessee Regional State Catalog, Public Libraries Division, Nashville, Tennessee 37202	50,000		Planned 1969	C + P
34. Timberland Library Demonstration, Mrs. L.M. Morrison, Director, 7th and Franklin, Olympia, Washington 98501	120,000	Mo, Se	1964	C + P
35. Vancouver Island Regional Library, 10 Strickland Street, Nanaimo, British Columbia, Canada	77,000	Mo, Se	1967	C + P

B. PUBLIC LIBRARIES (*Continued*)

NAME AND ADDRESS OF INSTITUTION	No. of Titles in Catalog	Scope	Year of First Issue	Method of Production
36. VENTURA COUNTY AND CITY LIBRARY (AND BLACK GOLD COOP. LIBRARY SYSTEM LIBRARIES) P.O. Box 771, Ventura, California 93001	53,000	Mo		C + P

C. SCHOOL LIBRARIES

NAME AND ADDRESS OF INSTITUTION	No. of Titles in Catalog	Scope	Year of First Issue	Method of Production
1. CORONA DEL MAR HIGH SCHOOL LIBRARY, 2101 Eastbluff Drive, Newport Beach, California 92677	322	Ta, Di, Fs, Sl	Planned 1969	C + P
2. *WALNUT HIGH SCHOOL, 400 North Pierre Road, Walnut, California 91789	5,367		1968	C + Px
3. *WILSON HIGH SCHOOL, 16455 Wedgewood Drive, Hacienda Heights, California 91745	7,319		1967	C + Px
4. *WORKMAN HIGH SCHOOL, 16303 Temple Avenue, City of Industry, California 91744	7,319	Di, Mcf	1967	C + Px

* Union catalog for 3 school collections

D. SPECIAL LIBRARIES

NAME AND ADDRESS OF INSTITUTION	No. of Titles in Catalog	Scope	Year of First Issue	Method of Production
1. AIR CANADA LIBRARY, 38th floor, 1 Place Ville Marie, Montreal 113, Que., Canada	8,500	Mo	1966	C + P
2. AIRFORCE CAMBRIDGE RESEARCH LABORATORIES, DEPT. OF THE AIR FORCE, Laurence G. Hanscom Field, Bedford, Massachusetts 01730	35,000 5,700	Mo Se	Under development	

D. SPECIAL LIBRARIES (*Continued*)

Name and Address of Institution	No. of Titles in Catalog	Scope	Year of First Issue	Method of Production
3. American Numismatic Association Library, 818 North Cascade Avenue, P.O. Box 2366, Colorado Springs, Colorado 80901	2,500	Mo		Litho
4. Ampex Corporation Technical Library, 401 Broadway, Redwood City, California 94063	4,100	Mo, Se, Do	1965	CPr
5. Argonne National Laboratory, 9700 South Cass Avenue, Argonne, Illinois 60439		Mo, Se, Do, Mcf, Mcfi		CPr
6. Armstrong Cork Company– Technical Information Services, 2500 Columbia Avenue, Lancaster, Pennsylvania 17604	6,000	Mo	1968	Ps
7. Bendix Corporation Research Laboratories, 20800 10½ Mile Road, Southfield, Michigan 48076	2,000	T Pa	1965	T
8. The Boeing Company, Aerospace Technical Library, P.O. Box 3999, Seattle, Washington 98124	80,000	Mo, Se	1964	C + Px
9. Bonneville Power Administration Library, 1002 Holladay Street, P.O. Box 3621, Portland, Oregon 97208				C + P
10. Computer Sciences Corporation, 650 N. Sepulveda Boulevard, El Segundo, California 90245	725	Mo, Se		CPr
11. Du Pont of Canada Limited, Economist's Office Library, Box 660, Montreal 101, Que., Canada	8,400	Pa	1967	CPr
12. Eastman Kodak Company, Research Library, Research Laboratories, Kodak Park Division, Rochester, N.Y. 14650 (Filmstrips – not printed book cat.)	10,000	Mo, Fi, Mcfi	1966	C + MRP
13. Goddard Space Flight Center, Glenn Dale Road, Greenbelt, Maryland 20771	12,000	Mo	1966	CPr
14. IBM Development Laboratory Library, Highway 52 & N W 37th Street, Rochester, Minnesota 55901	6,000	Mo, Do		CPr

D. SPECIAL LIBRARIES (Continued)

Name and Address of Institution	No. of Titles in Catalog	Scope	Year of First Issue	Method of Production
15. IBM–SDD LIBRARY (Holdings of 7 IBM Libraries) Monterey & Cottle Roads, San Jose, California 95114	11,700	Mo, Se	1962	CPr
16. IMPERIAL OIL LTD., TECHNICAL INFO. SERVICE REGIONAL LIBRARY (Union Catalogue for 3 libraries) 500 6th Avenue S.W., Calgary, Alberta, Canada	21,864	Mo, Se, Fi, Ta, Di, Fs, Sl, M	1964	CPr
17. JET PROPULSION LABORATORY LIBRARY, 4800 Oak Grove Drive, Pasadena, California 91103	10,000	Do	1964	CPr
18. McDONNELL DOUGLAS CORPORATION LIBRARIES, Box 516, St. Louis, Missouri 63166	100,000	T R	1967	C + P
19. MARTIN–MARIETTA CORP. RESEARCH LIBRARY, P.O. Box 179, Denver, Colorado 80201	35,000	Mo, Gov R	1962	Po
20. MASSACHUSETTS HORTICULTURAL SOCIETY, 300 Massachusetts Avenue, Boston, Massachusetts 02115	31,000	Mo, Se, Pa	1962	Po
21. MAYO CLINIC LIBRARY, Rochester, Minnesota 55901		Mo, Se, Fi, Ta, Fs	Planned 1970	C + P
22. MELLONICS SYSTEMS DEVELOPMENT TECHNICAL LIBRARY, 1001 W. Maude Avenue, Sunnyvale, California 94086	10,000	Mo, Se, Mcf	1967	CPr
23. THE METROPOLITAN MUSEUM OF ART, THOMAS J. WATSON LIBRARY, Fifth Avenue & 82nd Street, New York, N.Y. 10028		Mo, Se	1960	Po
24. MONSANTO COMPANY INFORMATION CENTER, 800 N. Lindbergh Boulevard, St. Louis, Missouri 63166	15,964	Mo	1961	C + P
25. NATIONAL CENTER FOR ATMOSPHERIC RESEARCH, MESA LIBRARY, Boulder, Colorado 80302	27,800	Mo, Se	1964	CPr
26. NORTH AMERICAN ROCKWELL CORP., SPACE DIVISION TECHNICAL INFORMATION CENTER, 12214 Lakewood Boulevard, Downey, California 90241 (Mail Code AJ01)	35,000	Fi + Se (Abstract sources)	1964	C + P

D. SPECIAL LIBRARIES (*Continued*)

Name and Address of Institution	No. of Titles in Catalog	Scope	Year of First Issue	Method of Production
27. NRTS Technical Library, Idaho Nuclear Corporation, P.O. Box 1945, Idaho Falls, Idaho 83401	13,000	Mo	1968	C + P
28. Oak Ridge National Laboratory Libraries, P.O. Box X, Oak Ridge, Tennessee 37830	15,000	Mo	1966	CPr
29. Ontario Hydro, 620 University Avenue, Toronto 2, Ontario, Canada	3,700	Mo	1967	C + P
30. Patchogue Medford Public Schools Curriculum Materials Center, 241 South Ocean Avenue, Patchogue, New Jersey 11772	10,000	Mo, Se, Fi, Ta, Di, Fs, Rep	1967	C + P
31. Project Urbandoc, 9 East 40th Street, New York, N.Y. 10016		Mo, Se, Do	1968	C + P
32. Pulp & Paper Research Institute of Canada, 570 St. John's Road, Pointe Claire, Que., Canada	4,800	Mo, Se	1964	T
33. Sandia Laboratories, Library Division, P.O. Box 969, Livermore, California 94550	72,000	Mo, Se, Gov R	1963	CPr
34. Stanford Research Institute, Menlo Park, California 94025	51,900	T R	1963	C + P
35. United Aircraft Corp. Research Library, Silver Lane, East Hartford, Connecticut 06108	18,000	Mo, Se	1963	CPr
36. U.S. Naval Weapons Laboratory, Technical Library, Box 374, Dahlgren, Utah 22448	10,000	Mo	1966	CPr
37. U.S. Army Libraries, Japan, U.S. Army Garrison Command, Japan, APO San Francisco, California 96343	18,000	Mo	1964	Px

INDEX

This index was produced on the computer from human-generated entries using programs written by Dr. Theodore C. Hines and Dr. Jessica L. Harris, Columbia University. The programs are part of an experimental set written for research in unit operations in information handling and for student use at Columbia University School of Library Service. The design used provides great flexibility, especially in formatting. As with all the programs in the set, there was no limit on field length, and coding was limited to the sort that would be used in normal typing.

As these programs are still highly experimental, comments on the format and other features of the index would be most welcome.

Grateful acknowledgments are due to Grolier, Inc. and Bro-Dart Industries, who partially supported the development of the program, and to the Columbia University Computer Center and its Director, Dr. Kenneth King, for their wholehearted support. The authors would like to express their gratitude to Drs. Hines and Harris for their assistance in computerizing the index.

M. F. T. and H. F.

INDEX